The Transformation of American Politics

Princeton Studies in American Politics: Historical, International, and Comparative Perspectives

Ira Katznelson, Martin Shefter, and Theda Skocpol, eds.

A list of titles in this series appears at the back of the book

The Transformation of American Politics

Activist Government and the Rise of Conservatism

Edited by

Paul Pierson

and

Theda Skocpol

PRINCETON UNIVERSITY PRESS

PRINCETON AND OXFORD

Library of Congress Cataloging-in-Publication Data

The transformation of American politics : activist government
and the rise of conservatism / edited by Paul Pierson and
Theda Skocpol.
p. cm. — (Princeton studies in American politics)
Includes bibliographical references and index.
ISBN-13: 978-0-691-12257-1 (hardcover : alk. paper)
ISBN-10: 0-691-12257-1 (hardcover : alk. paper)
ISBN-13: 978-0-691-12258-8 (pbk. : alk. paper)
ISBN-10: 0-691-12258-X (pbk. : alk. paper)
1. Federal government—United States. 2. Politics, Practical—
United States. 3. Political participation—United States.
4. Pressure groups—United States 5. Conservatism—
United States. 6. United States—Politics and government—
20th century. 7. United States—Politics and government—
2001- I. Pierson, Paul. II. Skocpol, Theda.
JK421.T82 2007
320.973—dc22
2006103334

British Library Cataloging-in-Publication Data is available

This book has been composed in Sabon

Printed on acid-free paper. ∞

press.princeton.edu

Printed in the United States of America

2   4   6   8   10   9   7   5   3   1

CONTENTS

FIGURES

TABLES

CONTRIBUTORS

ANDREA LOUISE CAMPBELL is Hayes Career Development Associate Professor of Political Science at MIT, where she studies American politics, political participation, public opinion, and political inequality. Her publications include *How Policies Make Citizens: Senior Political Activism and the American Welfare State* (Princeton University Press) and articles in the *American Political Science Review, Political Behavior, Studies in American Political Development,* and *Comparative Political Studies.*

JACOB S. HACKER is Professor of Political Science at Yale University. He is author or coauthor of numerous articles and chapters, as well as four books, including, most recently, *The Great Risk Shift: The Assault on American Jobs, Families, Health Care, and Retirement—and How You Can Fight Back* (Oxford University Press) and (with Paul Pierson) *Off Center: The Republican Revolution and the Erosion of American Democracy* (Yale University Press).

NOLAN MCCARTY is Professor and Associate Dean at the Woodrow Wilson School of Public and International Affairs of Princeton University. He received his Ph.D. from Carnegie Mellon University and has taught previously at the University of Southern California and Columbia University. His primary areas of interest include U.S. politics, democratic political institutions, and political game theory. He has recently completed two book manuscripts, *Political Game Theory* (with Adam Meirowitz) and *Polarized America: The Dance of Political Ideology and Economic Inequality.* Recent publications include "Bureaucratic Capacity, Delegation, and Political Reform" (2004 with John Huber) in the *American Political Science Review,* "The Appointments Dilemma" (2004) in the *American Journal of Political Science,* "The Hunt for Party Discipline" (2001 with Keith Poole and Howard Rosenthal) in the *American Political Science Review,* and "The Politics of Blame: Bargaining before an Audience" (2000 with Timothy Groseclose) in the *American Journal of Political Science.* McCarty is the founding co-editor-in-chief of the *Quarterly Journal of Political Science.* He is the recipient of the Robert Eckles Swain National Fellowship from the Hoover Institution and was a fellow at the Center for Advanced Study in the Behavioral Sciences for the 2004–5 academic year.

SUZANNE METTLER is Distinguished Professor of Political Science in the Maxwell School of Citizenship and Public Affairs at Syracuse University. She is the author of *Dividing Citizens: Gender and Federalism in New Deal Public Policy,* which won the Kammerer Award of the American Political Science Association for the best book on U.S. national policy published in 1998, and *Soldiers to Citizens: The G.I. Bill and the Making of the Greatest Generation.*

PAUL PIERSON is Professor of Political Science at the University of California, Berkeley, where he holds the Avice Saint Chair of Public Policy. He has written extensively on American and comparative politics. Recent works include *Politics in Time: History, Institutions, and Social Analysis* and (with Jacob Hacker), *Off-Center: The Republican Revoluton and the Erosion of American Democracy.*

THEDA SKOCPOL is Victor S. Thomas Professor of Government and Sociology at Harvard University. She is the author of numerous books, including *Protecting Soldiers and Mothers: The Political Origins of Social Policy in the United States* and *Diminished Democracy: From Membership to Management in American Civic Life.*

MARK A. SMITH is Associate Professor of Political Science and Adjunct Professor of Communication at the University of Washington, where he teaches courses on public opinion, interest groups, American political culture, and religion in American politics. He is the author of *The Right Talk: How Conservatives Transformed the Great Society into the Economic Society* (Princeton University Press). Smith's first book, *American Business and Political Power: Public Opinion, Elections, and Democracy* (University of Chicago Press), won the Leon Epstein Award from the Political Organizations and Parties section of the American Political Science Association.

STEVEN M. TELES is a Fellow at the Center for the Study of American Politics at Yale University and has held previous positions at Brandeis, Hamilton, Holy Cross, the University of London, Boston University, Harvard, and Princeton. He is the author of *Parallel Paths: The Evolution of the Conservative Legal Movement* (Princeton University Press) and *Whose Welfare? AFDC and Elite Politics* (University Press of Kansas), as well as articles and book chapters on pension privatization, affirmative action and social mobility in Britain, the logic of policy analysis, federalism, and U.S.-China relations.

JULIAN E. ZELIZER is Professor of History at Boston University. A frequent commentator in the national media, Zelizer is the author of *On Capitol Hill: The Struggle to Reform Congress and Its Consequences, 1948–2000* (Cambridge University Press) and *Taxing America: Wilbur D. Mills, Congress, and the State, 1945–1975* (Cambridge University Press), which was awarded the 2000 Ellis Hawley Prize and the 1998 D. B. Hardeman Prize. He is the editor of *The Reader's Companion to the American Congress* (Houghton Mifflin), *New Directions in Policy History* (Penn State Press), and the co-editor of *The Democratic Experiment: New Directions in American Political History* (Princeton University Press). The History News Network named Zelizer as one of the "Top Young Historians" in the country.

Introduction

Chapter One

American Politics in the Long Run

PAUL PIERSON AND THEDA SKOCPOL

OVER THE PAST HALF CENTURY, government and politics in the United States have been transformed—so much so that a Rip van Winkle who fell asleep in 1957 and awoke in 2007 would hardly feel it was the same polity. Even as America has achieved a new if troubled hegemony in international relations, at home the national government has become directly and indirectly active in an unprecedentedly broad array of realms. Matters that were once the exclusive purview of state and local governments and private actors are now shaped in Washington. Political parties and voluntary institutions have also been reorganized, and citizen attachments to politics have shifted in dramatic ways. Amid all of this, partisan and ideological balances have been upended. In the 1960s and early 1970s, liberals and Democrats briefly held sway, prompting federal activism on behalf of citizen rights and economic regulation. Subsequently, conservatives successfully mobilized people and ideas to counter liberal practices and limit—or, more often, refocus and redirect—activist government.

This book aims to probe these profound domestic political changes and their consequences. By taking a long-term perspective, we make visible large-scale transformations that too often disappear in narrower short-term studies of American politics. In doing so, we depart from those who believe that everything changed in domestic politics following September 11, 2001. The tragic, unanticipated attacks of that day certainly had important partisan effects—initially strengthening the presidency of George W. Bush and enhancing the sway of conservative Republicans. For a time, these events tipped what had been a closely balanced electorate toward the right. In specific policy areas, such as civil liberties and intelligence gathering, reactions to 9/11 spurred new departures. Nevertheless, in many areas of domestic politics, the main effect of 9/11 was to speed up and reinforce political tendencies long underway. Playing out over several decades, not just in a few months or years, several intertwined transformations have remade politics and governance in our time. Current political realities must be situated in the broader context of these gradual but profound changes.

To start with the greatest change of the contemporary era—notwithstanding Bill Clinton's famous assertion to the contrary—a persistent "era of big government" commenced in the 1960s. This transformation involved significant expansions in the scope and scale of federal government activity, comparable in importance to earlier expansions in the era of the New Deal and World War II. Social spending grew significantly. In many realms, standards of social provision were nationalized. The scope of the regulatory state increased dramatically in areas such as consumer, environmental, and worker protection. A "rights revolution" pursued by Congress, the federal bureaucracy, and the courts led to a greatly broadened set of entitlements for particular categories of citizens, such as minorities, women, and the disabled (Skrentny 2002). Here again, authority shifted to Washington, as matters that had once been resolved in diverse ways (for good or ill) at the local or state level became subject to more uniform national practice. Finally, a "hidden welfare state" of subsidies provided through the tax code became an increasingly important if still largely subterranean instrument of government activism (Howard 1997).

After the early 1980s, federal government expansion was slowed, even rolled back in some areas. Yet the activist state remains a central new fact of modern American politics (cf. McKinnon 2005). It is central in two respects. First, much contemporary political conflict focuses precisely on the role of the activist state. Second, the rise of government activism has created a fundamentally new landscape for political action in the United States, spurring changes in the media, Congress, electoral politics, and interest groups.

A second major transformation in our time has been the emergence of a powerful—and, in some ways, radical—conservative movement. Conservative elites mobilized in large part to counter new forms of federal activism. They confronted liberal policies that had become embedded not just in government but also in a range of surrounding institutions, from the media to the educational system. Even when spearheaded by liberals, institutional reforms and reorganizations in Congress and the rest of the polity ended up opening new opportunities for groups inside and beyond government aiming to advance conservative agendas. Over several decades, social and economic conservatives in and around the Republican Party have made steady headway. Conservatives have channeled popular participation for social causes, linking newly energized associations and networks to partisan politics. They have dominated agendas of public debate over the economy. Despite important limits on what they have so far achieved in public policy, conservatives have been able to trim and shift taxes and federal regulations, preclude major new social policy initiatives, and limit increases in direct, highly visible social expenditures for working-age Americans.

Our investigations of these ongoing political conflicts have convinced us that these two profound changes in American politics—the rise of the activist state and the resurgence of conservatism—cannot be fully understood absent consideration of a third: the redefinition of modes of citizen participation. As the scope of government expanded and new technologies of communication emerged, shifts occurred in the structure of key organizations that linked citizens and the state. Party competition spread to the South. In an era of money-driven campaigns and partisan discord, political parties restructured themselves and differentially targeted various subgroups of citizens (Schier 2000). Disparities of electoral participation have grown, as the old participate more than the young, and the economically privileged and highly educated have increased their advantage over the middle strata and the poor (Campbell 2003; Freeman 2004). The character of voluntary organizations changed as well. Activist federal courts, bureaucrats, and congressional staffers offered new access to lawyers and experts, spurring the professionalization of associations and a turn away from attempts to mobilize active memberships. This shift occurred sooner and more thoroughly on the liberal side of the spectrum, while conservatives perceived different political challenges and opportunities from the 1960s to the 1980s and engaged in more citizen mobilization, at least for a time. Meanwhile, federal subsidies encouraged state and local governments to contract with nonprofit agencies to deliver social services—and this, in turn, spurred the proliferation of professionally managed nonprofits, which have displaced membership entities in many local communities (Berry and Arons 2003, chap. 1; Crenson and Ginsberg 2002).

In many ways, contemporary American politics reflects the ongoing collision, carried out through these new forms of participation, between the rise of the activist state and the emergence of an invigorated conservatism. Conservatives have certainly not destroyed or fundamentally rolled back big, activist government. They have, however, circumscribed and redirected it, upending many of the assumptions made by liberals, who were briefly hegemonic back in the 1960s. Conservatives, moreover, have regularly proved more adept than liberals at using the new institutional and organizational levers available to politically active groups. As we learn throughout this book about changes in civic organizations, political parties, congressional rules, and electoral processes, we will see that these changes have often advantaged conservatives. Partisans have shaped transformations in the organizations and institutions of American politics, but the effects have not always been as the originally influential intended. Repeatedly over the past half century, liberals and Democrats spearheaded organizational, institutional, and policy changes that have ended up helping conservatives and Republicans in surprising ways.

STUDYING POLITICAL TRANSFORMATIONS

Describing and exploring the intertwined transformations that have re-made the face of American governance and politics in our time necessitated that our contributors depart from the styles of analysis prevalent in much academic research. Scholars have produced thousands of books and articles on this or that aspect of contemporary politics. Much of this scholarship, however, is biased toward the short term, examines circumscribed arenas of politics in isolation from one another, and tends to abstract away from the substance of political battles and trends. By focusing instead on long-term, large-scale changes in the U.S. polity—and by considering the relations among goal-directed movements, changing institutions, and substantively redirected policymaking—we endeavor to overcome such biases.

Beyond Short-Term Slices

Consider, to start, what is lost through a preoccupation with short-term processes. All too often, studies of American politics examine only immediate cause-and-effect relationships—such as the impact of quarterly shifts in economic growth percentages on presidential approval ratings, or the effect of a specific election on partisan margins in Congress. Important as such immediate links may be, to focus on them may distract us from structural tendencies and emerging processes (Pierson 2004; Pierson and Skocpol 2002). Some important political developments happen only gradually, yet are profoundly important for shaping and reshaping the terrain on which immediate shifts occur. Tracing institutional, ideological, and organizational patterns over long stretches of time allows us to avoid being mesmerized by event-driven zigs and zags.

Contributors to this volume illustrate the value of tracing long-term transformations and teasing out the (often unexpected) consequences of sustained trends or earlier institutional changes. Nolan McCarty, for example, demonstrates why, over the long run, heightened partisan polarization in U.S. politics has led via legislative stasis to de facto conservative results in a number of important areas of domestic social policy. Andrea Campbell traces sea changes in political parties, electoral mobilization, and voter blocs, not just from one election to the next, but over the course of decades. Her analysis brings structural and strategic changes into view, sharpening our sense of how Democrats and Republicans have shifted their operations and their alignments since the middle of the twentieth century. And Julian Zelizer shows how institutional reforms in Congress, originally spearheaded by liberals in the 1970s, eventually created levers that could be more effectively used by aggressive conservatives—first to undermine moderate Republican and liberal Democratic leadership in Congress and then to consolidate partisan discipline under the leadership of conservative Republicans.

Equally important, long-term analysis allows scholars to trace the efforts of goal-driven political actors engaged in learning, adaptation, and organization building. To take seriously the rise of a new ideological tendency or social movement, for example, is to examine interconnected sets of actors pursuing meaningful goals over time. Inevitably, these are stories of the long haul; they are not stories well captured by "snapshots" of each moment or round of politics in isolation. In this volume, Steven Teles argues that the strategic attempts of conservatives to undo or modify entrenched liberal policies and institutional projects must be understood as deliberate, long-term efforts playing out across a range of institutional domains. Forward-looking actors—organizationally situated and interconnected groups with the willingness and capacity to take a very long view—proceeded through practices of trial-and-error. In both Teles' and Hacker and Pierson's analyses, the rise of conservatism emerges as a set of important but largely subterranean processes moving through several decades of what might otherwise seem disconnected activities.

Of course, that actors sometimes take the long view does not mean they always get things right. On the contrary, in a complex, interdependent, and rapidly shifting world they will often get things wrong. To look at long-term transformations is to take seriously the possibility that important elements of political life will be unintended or unanticipated by powerful actors—and to treat this obvious truth as an integral element of social inquiry rather than just an inconvenient complication. Time and again, we find that political interventions have unexpected results—what was thought to be trivial turns out to be important, and what was expected to produce one effect turns out to do something altogether different.

A final advantage of long-term analyses is that they allow scholars to highlight not just how politics makes policies but also how policies, once enacted, can change further political struggles. As contemporary theorizing and research about "policy feedbacks" shows, policies can influence elite and mass understandings of political issues and possibilities; policies can change governmental capacities to propose and implement subsequent policy changes; and policies can influence the identity and goals of organized groups that get involved in subsequent rounds of policymaking (Mettler and Soss 2004; Pierson 1993; Skocpol 1992). Ideas about policy feedbacks are deployed by contributors to this volume to help make sense of contemporary political transformations. The advantages of tracing policy feedbacks over the long term are especially visible in the chapters by Suzanne Mettler, Theda Skocpol, and Jacob Hacker and Paul Pierson.

The Stuff of Politics

Beyond the preoccupation with the short term, another unfortunate bias that pervades much current research on U.S. politics—including studies that do attempt to track changes over considerable periods of time—is excessive abstraction from the substance of political conflicts. For example, analysts may study trends in legislative "productivity" by counting the number of major laws Congress passed each year, treating each of them as analytically equivalent (cf. Howell et al. 2000; Mayhew 1991). Or analysts may count broad types of issues that appear in the media or congressional hearings in different periods (cf. Baumgartner and Jones 1993; Talbert and Potoski 2002) without considering the partisan or ideological content of the various topics tallied. Hoping to achieve generalizations about the American political system by assembling large data sets susceptible to quantitative description or statistical analysis, scholars look for repeated instances countable as "the same thing."

Although the search for generalization and efforts to build large data sets are admirable, proceeding at such a high level of abstraction comes at a price. Much of the meaning of politics is lost when the actual content and partisan valence of political struggles is squeezed out of the analysis. Politicians, interest groups, and social movements are, after all, contending about the direction of policies. They typically care intensely about the precise content of government activity (or inactivity). The accumulation of successes and failures in such substantive struggles can add up to fundamental shifts in what government undertakes, and the capacities of political coalitions to shape agendas and command public support. Studies that rest content with counting sheer volumes of legislation or mentions of a broad type of issue in the media may illuminate some issues, yet miss other equally or more important aspects of political change.

Contributors to this volume adopt two strategies to bring the content of politics front and center. Some authors examine ongoing struggles about the direction and structure of particular types of public policies, using this as a way to trace larger shifts in the American polity. Concentration on substantive policy lineages helps analysts to stay focused on "where the action is"—even as the locus of that action shifts. Most scholarship on American politics focuses on a specific site or mode of political activity, but the analysis should not stop when the venue shifts. Struggles over policy directions proceed not just in Congress but also in the media, the electoral system, and interest-group struggles—at a given point in time different venues may be most important. Jacob Hacker and Paul Pierson, for example, examine the shifting politics of tax cuts, dissecting legislative processes, interest-group maneuvers, and battles in primary elections. And Suzanne Mettler traces the shifting political effects of social policies during an era in which visible social expenditures have been displaced in many areas by less-visible tax credits and loan subsidies. How has this shift affected citizens' understandings of the role of government in their lives and their proclivities for civic engagement?

In addition to following policy lineages with careful attention to the content and substantive political impact, contributors to this volume place a high priority on understanding the developing activities of political organizations and looser social movements. Because political groupings care about affecting the substance of government activity and the character of ongoing political life, they are often flexible about adapting their strategies and tactics to changing challenges and opportunities that arise in various venues. Tracking these adaptations is an excellent way to identify and understand broader shifts in the political environment. Theda Skocpol's analysis of the increasingly elite-oriented character of American civic organizations, Steve Teles' explorations of the evolving strategies of conservatives in various institutional domains, and Mark Smith's dissection of the growing success of conservative organizations in shaping debates about American economic performance all employ this core strategy. By examining goal-oriented political actors maneuvering in changing contexts, contributors to this volume shed considerable light on aspects of the political process that are important but poorly grasped by more static and abstract attempts to study American politics.

LOOKING AHEAD

Although every chapter in this book helps us to understand government expansion, policy shifts, and the rise of contemporary conservativism—and each chapter makes connections to the ideas and arguments of other chapters—the contributions are grouped into three major parts, dealing in turn with macroscopic reorganizations of the state and political organizations; the rise of contemporary conservatism; and the political roots and effects of public policy trends. To give a sense of what is to come, we can preview the issues taken up in each part and its constituent chapters.

The Shifting Political Landscape

Taking a bird's-eye view of developments over half a century, part I focuses on the changing structure of the U.S. macro polity. Paul Pierson, Theda Skocpol, and Andrea Campbell probe the rise of the activist state and accompanying reorganizations in the universe of interest groups and voluntary associations and in the electoral system and party politics.

To set the stage for the book as a whole, Paul Pierson's chapter on "The Rise and Reconfiguration of Activist Government" brings together evidence on how national government activities expanded in the United States from the 1960s into the 1980s and assesses the ways in which modalities as well as levels of government action shifted over time. The expanding scope of government activities, surges in legislation, trends in government employment, and shifting patterns of regulation and national and subnational expenditures—are all explored, as the late twentieth-century rise in government activism is put in broader historical perspective as a critical episode in U.S. state building.

The expansion of federal activity, Pierson documents, was rapid, large, and broad-based. Whether one looks at spending, social regulation, the entrenchment of social rights, or the deployment of tax subsidies, government activism grew. In some cases, this transformation entailed federal and state activity growing in tandem. In others, such as the "rights revolution," it represented a clear transfer of political authority from localities to Washington. Either way, this marked shift in the character of the national state had lasting effects on political conflict and political organization, as both supporters and opponents of the activist state scrambled to adapt to new opportunities and constraints.

Indeed, changes in the scope and modalities of federal government activities have affected—and, in turn, have been affected by—changes in U.S. interest groups and voluntary associations. In "Government Activism and the Reorganization of American Civic Democracy," Theda Skocpol shows that between the 1960s and the 1990s, the balance of nationally visible groups shifted away from business representation and popularly rooted membership associations and toward professionally managed organizations advocating an unprecedentedly wide variety of public causes. During the same period, blue-collar trade unions also declined, and nonprofit institutions proliferated. "Rights revolutions" and the expansion of higher education helped to spur civic reorganization, yet new degrees and kinds of federal government activism were also critical, because they affected group identities, interest stakes, and organizing resources and offered new venues of access to professional staffers and nonprofit social service providers.

Civic changes were politically uneven, however. They occurred sooner and more pervasively on the liberal side of the spectrum. Conservatives—who felt marginalized during the 1965–80 period—continued or reinvented many cross-class, popularly rooted associations in and around the edges of an increasingly populist and conservative Republican Party, especially by tapping into evangelical church networks. In addition to exploring the roots of uneven civic transformations, this chapter also suggests some of the most important consequences of contemporary civic shifts for inequalities in democratic participation, partisan polarization, and public policymaking.

Paralleling Skocpol's examination of the reorganization of U.S. civic life, Andrea Campbell examines "Parties, Electoral Participation, and Shifting Voting Blocs" since the 1960s. A series of technological, institutional, legal, and cultural changes have reshaped the role and placement of the major parties in the U.S. electoral system. Parties were once broad-based mobilizers of the public, providing the manpower to run labor-intensive political campaigns and appealing to voters with emotional and social ties. From the 1960s, however, advances in communications and reforms of the nomination system led to the rise of candidate-centered elections; and the political parties reconfigured themselves as providers of services to candidates. As parties lost their grass-roots ties to voters and increasingly targeted high-turnout-prone and more affluent citizens, electoral politics functioned to exacerbate political inequality.

And the two parties have fared differently. The Republican Party more quickly and adroitly adapted and expanded its organizational and fund-raising capacities. What is more, the Democrats became associated with a variety of "new politics" groups, ceding populist arguments to the Republicans, who came to be seen as defenders of the middle class. As a result, Democrats lost ground among many pivotal electoral groups, including white men, southerners, Catholics, and evangelical Protestants. In perhaps the most vivid expression of the ascendance of an energized conservative movement in American politics, the Republican Party after 2000 controlled the presidency, both chambers of Congress, and a majority of governorships and state legislatures—a complete reversal of the circumstances of 1964.

Conservatives on the Rise

Part II focuses especially on the long-term activities of conservative elites, tracing their goal-directed maneuvers across various arenas of U.S. politics. As Julian Zelizer, Mark Smith, and Steven Teles reveal, each in his own way, inside and beyond the institutions of government, conservative elites have made remarkable headway in recent decades.

In "Seizing Power: Conservatives and Congress since the 1970s," Julian Zelizer probes the unintended consequences of institutional shifts in the U.S. Congress. Through a series of rules changes and reorganizations in the larger polity in the 1960s and 1970s, Congress moved from an era of committee dominance to an era of multiplying subcommittees, greater openness of operations, and possibilities for more disciplined party leadership. Sponsored by liberals, who were then predominant, shifts in rules and norms were intended to strengthen Congress's operations and reputation and promote liberal policy agendas. Yet something different happened. Institutional reforms in Congress ended up facilitating partisanship and scandal warfare, opening the way for mavericks and advocates of special or minority causes to attack congressional leaders.

Both liberal Democratic leaders and moderate Republican leaders found their sway in Congress challenged. As conservative movements gathered steam in the 1980s and 1990s, a new generation of Republican politicians proved surprisingly adept at using the new legislative rules and practices to their partisan and ideological advantage. Focusing on the House of Representatives in particular, the history presented in Zelizer's chapter also reveals ways in which congressional conservatives have had relatively limited success at curtailing the growth of the U.S. state. Congressional history since the 1960s has been defined by the tension between the political achievements of congressional conservatives and their policy shortfalls—namely, the endurance of a large, pervasive federal government in an era when the center of gravity in congressional and national politics moved to the right.

Like Zelizer's chapter, Mark Smith's "Economic Insecurity, Party Reputations, and the Republican Ascendance" analyzes the efforts of each party to adapt to changing circumstances. Smith focuses on the rise of economic insecurity following the end of the long post-war boom. Since the early 1970s economic issues have grown in significance for the American electorate, and Smith explores some of the crucial political results of this key development. He identifies a striking puzzle, noting that the GOP has gained a sizable and durable advantage in economic reputation among the electorate over the past thirty years, even though evidence suggests that economic performance has been weaker under Republican presidents.

Smith argues that Republicans have developed and sustained a more effective economic message. This effectiveness stems in part from the greater clarity and consistency of GOP demands for lower taxes and less regulation, and in part from the stronger organizational networks that supported and disseminated the Republican message. It also reflects Reagan's successful repositioning of the party to place greater priority on tax cuts, which in turn gradually led Democrats to emphasize the less effective message of deficit reduction.

The final chapter in part II, Steven Teles' exploration of "Conservative Mobilization against Entrenched Liberalism" offers yet another perspective on the rise of conservative elites and movements in our time. By the late 1970s, conservatives were surging in electoral politics, but wholly outgunned in institutional and policy realms beyond electoral politics. They faced old and new liberal ideals and practices that were thoroughly entrenched at the intersection of the modern administrative state and surrounding institutions—for example, in social policy, in the media, and in the educational system, including universities. As they moved toward electoral power, conservatives remained weakest in institutions that are substantially self-reproducing and immune to easy change by elected officeholders. Teles analyzes and compares the strategies developed by conservatives situated in foundations and think tanks to counter and chip away at liberal norms and practices entrenched in the realms of Social Security and the law. In each arena, initial conservative strategies failed. But learning and innovation followed defeat, as conservatives fashioned new approaches that were less reactive and emphasized positive conservative alternatives, parallel institutions, greater populism, and attempts to appeal broadly to the public. While conservatives have made headway in each realm, these nonelectoral projects have also intersected in important ways with conservative activities in the Republican Party.

Policy and Politics in the New American Polity

Building on all that we have learned about major structural and ideological tendencies in the first two parts, part III traces policy lineages and legislative trends. The goal is not simply to tell policy stories for their own sake but to show how broader shifts in U.S. politics have reshaped what government does and the consequences of policies for citizen welfare and political participation. Suzanne Mettler and Nolan McCarty examine the political roots and consequences of trends of social policymaking over recent decades, while Jacob Hacker and Paul Pierson examine another, equally critical aspect of public policy—the taxation decisions through which government decides how much revenue to raise, from whom, and with what likely consequences for future political battles.

In her chapter on the "Transformed Welfare State and the Redistribution of Political Voice," Suzanne Mettler grapples with a paradox: American government spends more than ever on social programs, but citizens are less engaged in politics than in the past and many support an antigovernment political agenda. She explores how the design of different policies and changes in their value and coverage over time may be themselves contributing to such outcomes. Changes in the American welfare state, Mettler suggests, have set in motion processes that are, slowly but surely, transforming the linkages between citizens and government.

During the mid-twentieth century, the U.S. federal government developed social programs and labor regulations that promoted economic security and educational opportunity across broad segments of the population. Some evidence suggests that such programs also helped to generate the active civic engagement of the post-war era. By helping to expand the scope of the active citizenry, broad and generous policies facilitated a more democratic polity, in which political leaders had incentives to be responsive to average Americans. Since the 1970s, however, social programs have faced grave challenges, and some have fared better than others—with distinct social policy fates bearing consequences for the civic engagement of their beneficiaries. Elderly citizens have benefited from a virtuous circle of policies that generate political involvement, responsiveness from policymakers, and mobilization efforts by party officials to further encourage their electoral participation. By contrast, lower- and middle-class nonelderly and nondisabled citizens, even in the midst of rising employment insecurity and financial stress, rely on programs that have been shrinking in value and coverage. In response, they appear to be withdrawing from the electorate to varying degrees in accordance with the severity of retrenchment in the part of the social safety net on which they most rely.

At the same time, tax expenditures offer increasingly generous benefits to the affluent, with the effect of exacerbating their already strong advantage in the exercise of political voice; the associated realm of privately provided social provision compounds this pattern. This growing sector of social policies, in obscuring government's role, threatens to undermine citizens' support for more redistributive forms of social provision. In sum, these gradual shifts in the welfare state make the political voices of ordinary Americans less audible, while amplifying those of the well-to-do. Such dynamics help illuminate why, in turn, government has become increasingly responsive to the concerns of the wealthy and less attuned to the needs of average citizens.

Working with a theory of what it takes to overcome "veto points" and institutional gridlock in the divided-powers system of the U.S. federal government, Nolan McCarty explores "The Policy Effects of Political Polarization." The divide between Democratic and Republican members of Congress has widened greatly over the past twenty-five years, reaching levels of partisan conflict not witnessed since the 1920s. After briefly summarizing arguments about the causes of this polarization, McCarty explores the consequences for public policymaking and politics. Polarization has made it harder to build legislative coalitions, leading to policy "gridlock," he argues. Congress finds it harder to legislate, and the effectiveness of laws it does pass may be undermined by awkward concessions that have to be made to assemble majorities. Polarization has also fundamentally altered the balance of power among national institutions at the expense of Congress, encouraging executives and judges to act unilaterally without legislative consent.

McCarty considers the contents of legislation in an era of polarization, not just the sheer amount of legislative activity. He looks closely at the course of minimum-wage and social welfare legislation over recent decades. Using these cases, he shows that partisan polarization may not be ideologically neutral in its legislative effects. Polarization has hampered the capacity of conservatives to pass laws, hamstringing their efforts to reconfigure policy. When polarization leads to gridlock, it can sometimes have de facto conservative consequences—especially when it stalls repeated action on social policies that require constant updating to hold their value or maintain their effectiveness in a changing society and economy.

Another kind of conservative tendency in policy development is highlighted in the chapter by Jacob Hacker and Paul Pierson on "Tax Politics and the Struggle over Activist Government." The story here is not one of legislative gridlock but of a remarkable growth in radical-conservative capacity to legislate significant cuts in taxes entailing major redistributions in the federal tax burden. Taxation represents the lifeblood of the modern activist state, and conservatives have found it a much more attractive political target than the major social programs that represent the core achievements of modern liberalism. Looking closely at contrasts between the Reagan era of the 1980s and the more recent George W. Bush era of conservative tax policymaking, Hacker and Pierson examine the evolution of taxes as a political issue—in the electorate, among key interest groups, and within the Republican Party establishment. This provides central insights about the developing character of the contemporary conservative movement—especially its shift toward more elite-centered strategies of political mobilization. The analysis also focuses on the development of policy itself, concentrating less on the particularities of each episode of policy change and more on what the broad trends in outcomes suggest about the transformed character of the American polity. Progress has been limited and halting, but over the long haul conservatives have had some success in shifting tax structures in ways that undercut the capacities of the activist state.

In the conclusion to this volume, we consider further what the long-term analyses presented here tell us about the current state and future prospects of American politics. Continued battles about the scope and financing of activist domestic government in the United States are a sure thing—but the contours of many of these conflicts are established by the long-term development of both the combatants and the terrain on which they struggle. The policy feedbacks and reorganizations of electoral, civic, and governmental institutions highlighted in this volume will continue to shape the inclinations and capacities of the conservatives and liberals, Republicans and Democrats. What political actors want to do—and, above all, what they can do—depends very much on prior public policies, the institutional shape of the terrain on which they operate, and on how

PART ONE
The Shifting Political Landscape

Chapter Two

The Rise and Reconfiguration
of Activist Government

PAUL PIERSON

BETWEEN 1960 AND 1980 THE AMERICAN STATE underwent a great transformation. This was no constitutional revolution. On the contrary, despite the political and social upheavals of the 1960s and early 1970s, the formal rules of American governance were quite stable. But this formal stability belied a fundamental institutional shift. In two decades, the domestic role of the American national state underwent a stunning expansion, ushering in a profound set of changes in American politics (Melnick 2005).

For students of comparative politics (Evans, Reuschemeyer, and Skocpol 1985; Lange and Rueschemeyer 2005) and American political history (Skowronek 1982), it is conventional to talk about "state building." For good reason, such transformative episodes are seen as defining developments in the life of a society. But students of contemporary American politics, perhaps averse to thinking of the world we inhabit in such sweeping historical terms, remain only vaguely aware that the American polity has just witnessed something similar. Moreover, the vast political and social implications of this remarkable transformation remain surprisingly underappreciated.

Many chapters in this volume investigate the political consequences of the rise of the activist state in depth. The central goal of this chapter is to document the broad shape of the policy transformation that took place. Detailing the scope and timing of the overall movement toward an activist state, as well as highlighting some of the broad patterns within it, not only documents just how much changed. Many of the chapters in this volume confirm E. E. Schattschneider's (1935) old suggestion that "new policies create new politics." If so, then getting a sense of the contours of this new policy activism is an essential part of understanding the broader transformation of the American polity. This great transformation of the American state generated new political opportunity structures, as liberal groups were eager to seize the reins of this expanded policy apparatus, while conservatives saw it as a springboard for counter-mobilization.

The typical approach to studying government activity would be to focus on particular substantive areas of public policy (e.g., civil rights, health care, or the environment). By necessity, most studies of government activism concentrate on one or a few such areas (Hacker 2002; Melnick 1994; Skrentny 2002). Here, by contrast, I investigate this process of modern state building by examining in turn the development of four central but quite distinct instruments of political authority: spending, regulation, social rights, and tax subsidies. Governments intervene in society through expenditures, either on particular projects or through transfers to individuals of the kind usually described by the term "the welfare state." In addition, there is rule making: in the "regulatory state," this consists of a set of legal requirements that dictate or proscribe behavior for individuals and organizations. Government has also come to recognize and enforce an expanding set of individual rights, some of which protect individuals from discrimination, while others impose positive obligations on public authorities or private organizations. Finally, less well understood but increasingly important, there is the "tax subsidy state." Governments create incentives and subsidize particular groups and practices through features of the tax code—a practice that is in many ways analogous to government spending but has quite distinctive economic, social, and political roots and consequences (Hacker 2002; Howard 1997).

By examining the transformation of each of these four key instruments over an extended period of time we get a richer sense of the broad transformation in the federal government's activities as a whole. Moreover, as we shall see, patterns of transformation in the timing and scope of each instrument are actually quite distinctive. These differences matter, because deploying each type of instrument not only involves distinct governmental capacities. Typically, each type of expansion emerges from somewhat different political configurations. In turn, each creates particular opportunity structures for political action. Understanding these variations thus offers a point of entry for exploring broader shifts in the American political environment.

THE GREAT TRANSFORMATION

In the period after World War II, government activity grew rapidly throughout the advanced industrial world (Steurle and Kawai 1996). The causes of this expansion are beyond the scope of this chapter, but the cross-national uniformity of the broad trend suggests that demands resulting from rising affluence and increasing social and economic complexity played a central role. Protestations of exceptionalism not withstanding, the United States was a full and vigorous participant in this cross-national exercise in state building. In analyses that focus on levels of welfare state spending, the United States is conventionally viewed as a "laggard." It would be more accurate, however, to say that it traveled a unique path, marked by *comparatively* limited increases in public spending, early and aggressive use of regulation (Vogel 2003), extensive deployment of rights-based policies (Melnick 1994), and the development of an unusual public-private welfare state partially grounded in the tax code (Howard 1997; Hacker 2002).

The Growth of Public Spending in the United States

The easiest, and certainly most obvious, place to start an examination of state expansion is with spending. Governments tax (and borrow). With these revenues, they spend. When we speak casually about the size of government, we most often think of what the government spends on services and transfer payments, and of the taxes that are required (in the long run, at least) to pay for them. Many of the key components of the modern activist state—from the provision of public education, pensions, and health care to many forms of agricultural support—rely on government spending. Indeed, the "welfare state" (traditionally defined by government expenditures) and the "activist state" are often seen as nearly synonyms. Budgets, it is sometimes suggested, lay bare the contours of government activism. As the German Socialist Rudolf Goldscheid put it almost a century ago, "the budget is the skeleton of the state stripped of all misleading ideologies" (cited in Bell 1976, 221).

Goldscheid's insistence that we look at what political authorities do, rather than what they say, is admirable. Yet his specific advice is quite misguided. As we shall see, one has to look well beyond spending to get a true sense of the scope and distribution of government activism. Still, spending clearly is a key part of the larger "skeleton of the state." And it remains the most straightforward place to begin an exploration of the rise of the activist state. The broad picture is clear, and the trends can be seen in figure 2.1. The direction of change is unsurprising, but the magnitude of the change is nonetheless striking. Beginning in 1954, federal nondefense spending begins to grow as a share of GDP.[1] Over the following two decades, that share almost *triples*—from 5.7 percent in 1955 to 15.7 percent in 1975. It is worth emphasizing that much of this period was one of historically unprecedented economic growth. Even if the public sector had simply maintained its share of GDP, the rapid growth of the economic pie would have allowed the federal government to do much more. In fact, however, even as the economy as a whole was expanding very rapidly, federal domestic spending was increasing far more rapidly still. After

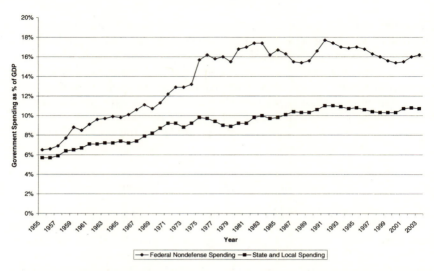

Figure 2.1 Federal Nondefense, State and Local Government Spending as Percentage of GDP, 1955–2003

1975, spending reaches a somewhat uneven plateau, sustained for the quarter century that followed.

Although our focus is on the federal government, it is important to recognize that this transformation of domestic expenditure extended to states and localities. As figure 2.1 indicates, growth was slower but nonetheless dramatic. Between 1955 and 1975, state and local government expenditures from their own resources increased from 5.7 percent of GDP to 9.8 percent of GDP. In addition, a considerable share of the rapidly expanding federal expenditures flowed through the states. As a share of GDP, federal grants more than quadrupled during the same period (0.6 percent of GDP to 2.6 percent). This striking development provides one indication of the growing extent to which state and local activism reflects governmental initiatives in Washington that were channeled through local officials.

Big-ticket and familiar expansions of federal activity were behind much of this remarkable spending growth. Medicare, Medicaid, Disability Insurance, Supplemental Security Income (SSI), Food Stamps, Head Start, and federal aid to education were among the new programs initiated during this period. Already existing programs often underwent stunning enlargements. Here the most notable case is Social Security, where a series of benefit and eligibility reforms produced, by 1974, what the longtime dean of social insurance advocates Robert Ball (1988) termed "our new Social Security system." Because the boom in spending is often associated with Lyndon Baines Johnson, the post-Goldwater Democratic Congresses, and the "Great Society" initiatives, it is worth noting that the expansion extends well beyond Johnson's tenure in both directions. The rapid rise in spending was underway well before LBJ took office. And domestic spending increases as a share of GDP were more rapid under Richard Nixon than they had been under LBJ.

Striking as the transformation was, the raw numbers presented here understate the scale of the change in federal spending. During this period the federal government undertook not only new expenditures but, in creating Medicaid and Medicare and greatly expanding Social Security, huge *promises* of additional spending far into the future (Cordes 1996). What came to be defined as "mandatory" or, more colloquially, "entitlement" spending refers to those programs where statutes *require* expenditures for those meeting defined eligibility criteria. From a long-term perspective, the growth of mandatory spending during this key period of state building is significant. The crucial point is that legislators during this expansionist phase not only spent a lot of money; they also made explicit promises to spend a lot more money in the future. In economists' parlance, they created *unfunded liabilities* stretching ahead for decades. For these promises, they could take political credit. It would fall to their successors to reap the political whirlwinds provoked by their efforts to pay the bills.

The Rise of the Regulatory State

Spending is the most obvious and visible component of government activism, but it remains just a part of the story. No less important is the second major instrument of the activist state, *regulation*. States produce vast systems of rules—a characteristic that has become increasingly prominent in the modern era of dense and complex social interactions. Governments mandate some behaviors, prohibit others, and dictate the ways in which individuals and organizations must act if they undertake certain tasks.

Regulatory activity takes many forms and has long been a central component of political authority. Much of what is sometimes called "old" regulation focused on commercial activity and was typically organized around particular economic sectors in areas such as communications, transportation, and energy. Though often justified to preserve competition and reasonable pricing in areas containing elements of natural monopoly, such systems often in practice created large barriers to entry and benefited existing firms. Yet the potential scope of regulation extends far beyond such activities. Indeed, many of the tasks that can be tackled with government spending can also be addressed with regulation—witness President Clinton's attempt to create universal health care by deploying instruments that were overwhelmingly regulatory in nature. The contemporary European Union, which has extremely limited access to revenues, has built a powerful policy apparatus almost exclusively through regulatory instruments (Majone 1997).

Indeed, there is no doubt that in the United States a vast expansion of regulations was at the heart of the rise of the activist state. In contrast to spending, however, providing an accurate description of this transformation presents a considerable challenge. It is easy to track expenditures over time. It is quite a different thing to measure the scope of regulatory activity systematically. How "big" is a rule? A useful indicator of a rule's significance would be not how much is spent on producing it but what it costs to comply with it. Economists have recently made efforts in this direction, but the results are controversial. Typical estimates seem to be based on ideologically grounded, and highly suspect, assumptions. Moreover, even dubious estimates are available only for a limited range of initiatives for limited periods of time, and thus provide little leverage for an effort to document long-run changes in regulatory activity.

Using a variety of observations, however, it is possible to produce a convincing picture of long-term trends. To begin with, one can look at statutory change. In a remarkably short period of time—concentrated in the half dozen years stretching from 1969 to 1974, the federal government undertook a vastly expanded set of regulatory responsibilities. Traditional economic regulation of particular sectors (the "old regulation") remained largely unchanged. The policy revolution occurred in areas commonly termed "social" regulation, such as consumer protection, workplace health and safety, and the environment (Vogel 1989; Melnick 2003). Landmark laws included the Traffic Safety Act of 1966, the Clean Air Act of 1970, the Occupational Safety and Health Act of 1970, the Clean Water Act of 1972, and the Consumer Product Safety Act of 1972. As David Vogel (2003) has argued, the expansion of the American regulatory state fits poorly with our traditional depiction of the United States as a laggard. In regulatory matters, it was the United States that was most often the "hare," while the traditionally statist European countries played the part of the "tortoises."

A more comprehensive overview of this shift can be derived from David Mayhew's (1991) data set of major legislative enactments over the past half century. Based on both evidence about attention paid to new laws at the time of passage and experts' retrospective judgments, Mayhew has identified 330 "major" laws passed between 1947 and 2002. Figure 2.2 includes those bills whose central features were regulatory or deregulatory. The pattern is striking. Between 1947 and 1964, the federal government adopted only seven major regulatory laws. In the quarter century after 1977, it adopted eleven (while also passing a number of deregulatory initiatives). It was the intervening thirteen years, from 1965 to 1977, that witnessed a vast expansion and reconfiguration of the modern regulatory

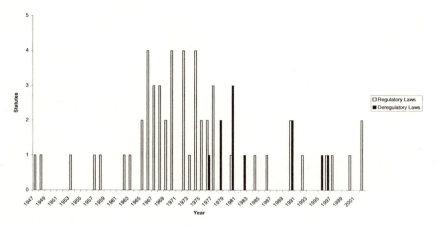

Figure 2.2 Regulatory and Deregulatory Laws, 1947–2002

state. In this relatively brief period, the federal government adopted *thirty-four* major regulatory laws—almost exactly double the total legislative production of the other four decades combined.

Figures about legislative productivity provide a useful, but somewhat indirect, indication of changing regulatory *activity*. The Mayhew data tell us what was enacted at a particular moment. The ongoing flow of regulatory activities over time proves much harder to pin down. Two imperfect but nonetheless revealing measures confirm the scale of expansion.[2] The first, presented in figure 2.3, provides data on federal *spending* on regulatory activities since 1960.[3] The pattern here is similar to that for regulatory statutory change, if somewhat less abrupt—real spending rises rapidly in the late 1960s and early 1970s. After 1975 growth slows and actually dips during Reagan's first term, before beginning to increase again.

Probably not surprisingly, changes in federal regulatory *employment* reveal a similar story. Here, unfortunately, we have data only since 1970. Figure 2.4 provides the overall trends. The data confirm that expansion is heavily concentrated in the "new" social regulation rather than the "old" economic regulation. In most areas of social regulation, there is a striking jump in federal staffing levels during the 1970s. In areas related to consumer protection, federal employment almost triples in a decade but has changed almost not at all in the twenty-five years since. In the case of workplace safety, federal employment more than triples in the 1970s but has fallen by about a third since then. Employment related to environmental protection almost *quadrupled* in the 1970s. It increased by about 50 percent more between 1980 and 2004.

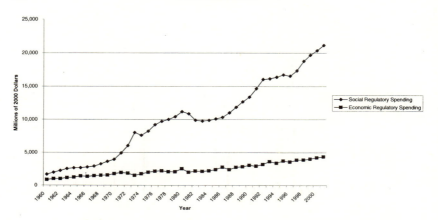

Figure 2.3 Social and Economic Regulatory Spending (in millions of 2000 dollars), 1960–2001

Of course, neither employment nor spending levels adequately measure the extent of regulatory activity. There is no reason to assume that a particular increment of federal spending or federal employment translates in any simple way into an increment of regulatory action. This is especially the case if regulatory policies are designed, as they often are, to externalize costs onto private actors or state and local governments. As Melnick (2005) puts it, the regulatory revolution involved a shift "from tax-and-spend to mandate-and-sue." If so, then unchanging staffing or spending levels may accompany significant changes in regulatory activity.

We must acknowledge the many problems that hinder attempts to get a broad sense of regulatory activity. These obstacles would be more of a concern, however, were it not for the fact that all the available evidence points so strongly in the same direction. Here, as clearly as anywhere else, we can see the broad macrohistorical phenomenon that motivates this chapter. In a relatively short period of time, the United States witnessed a huge expansion of the federal government's regulatory reach. The contours of a new American state were built, with the potential to alter fundamentally a wide range of social and political relationships.

The Rights Revolution

All three branches of the federal government, acting together and separately, produced a major expansion of politically guaranteed social rights during the same period. Of course, the actions stemming from the civil rights movement itself, ranging from the Supreme Court's *Brown v. Board of Education* to the Civil Rights Act of 1964 and the Voting Rights Act

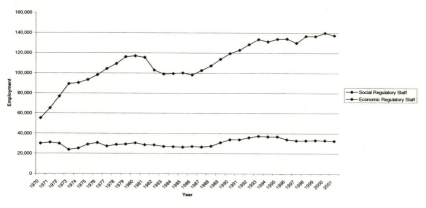

Figure 2.4 Federal Regulatory Staffing, 1970–2001

of 1965, were among the most important and prominent. But both Court and Congress went on to extend rights against discrimination more broadly, as well as to expand the range of rights (most famously, in the Court's *Roe v. Wade* decision, granting abortion constitutionally protected status based on the right to privacy).

Between 1964 and 1978, Congress passed sweeping rights-based legislation in what Robert Kagan (2001, 47) describes as "a truly extraordinary surge of activity." The success of the civil rights movement helped to induce a radical shift in context that made all branches of the federal government more open to rights-based claims (Melnick 1994; Skrentny 2003). Traditional obstacles in Congress broke down, as the power of southern committee chairs who had opposed such initiatives declined. Advocacy groups seized on, and emulated, the organizing tactics of the civil rights movement. At the same time, they were able to advance their goals by arguing that their analogous situation warranted a similar response. In many cases, federal officials acted pro-actively to provide that response—launching administrative or legislative initiatives even without significant lobbying from social groups (Skrentny 2003).

The result of these new circumstances was a rapid diffusion of similar policies, which in aggregate came to be dubbed "the rights revolution." Beyond the Civil Rights and Voting Rights acts, landmark rights-expanding legislation included the 1968 Fair Housing Law, title IX of the Education Amendments of 1972, the Education for All Handicapped Children Act of 1975, the Age Discrimination Act of 1975, and the Pregnancy Discrimination Act of 1978. Figure 2.5 draws on Mayhew's list of major legislation to indicate the pattern of enacting rights-oriented statutes. The "bulge" here is slightly less pronounced than in the case of regulatory initiatives, but it is striking nonetheless: eleven of nineteen

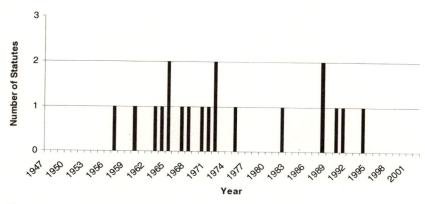

Figure 2.5 Civil Rights Legislation, 1947–2002

rights-oriented statutes are enacted between 1964 and 1976. And, again, this striking expansion does not include extensions of rights that took place through court or administrative action during the same period. Data collected by Charles Epp (1998, 28) indicate that the share of the Supreme Court's agenda devoted to civil rights and civil liberties rose from just 9 percent in its 1933 term to *65 percent* in the 1971 term. This transformation was more gradual, with the share rising steadily from the New Deal onward, but roughly half the increase comes after 1960.

The growth of nationally enforced rights was clearly a central part of the broader transformation in the role of the state reviewed in this chapter. Some might argue that it does not constitute an instance of an expanding "activist state." In many cases, the upshot of legislation or court decisions was to *roll back* government activism at the state or local level, restricting or prohibiting actions that infringed on individual rights. Epp provides a compact summary of how rights initiatives constrained the exercise of public authority:

As late as 1950 state laws relegated most black schoolchildren to separate, poorly funded schools and discriminated against African Americans in public accommodations. State laws also prohibited the sale and use of birth control devices and most states prohibited abortions except in limited circumstances. State police authorities could, by law, use nonphysical coercion in extracting confessions or incriminating information from criminal defendants, and defendants could, by law, be prosecuted, convicted, and sentenced to prison for serious crimes even if they lacked an attorney. In many states, authorities acting without court authorization could search a person's home and seize anything they deemed to be evidence. By 1975 none of those things remained legal; all were banned by the Supreme Court as violations of fundamental constitutional rights. (Epp 1998, 26)

What is clear is that the rights revolution was a fundamental part of the nationalization of political authority and policy in the United States. Decisions that previously had been treated as state and local matters, allowing for considerable variation in policy structures across jurisdictions, were now subject to much greater uniformity. The structure of that uniformity was to be determined by national political authorities—whether courts, legislators, administrators, or some combination of the three. The nationalization of authority related to sensitive issues of race, gender, education, crime and punishment, and religion represented a fundamental change in the American polity, greatly expanding the relative place of the federal government in domestic life.

The Tax Subsidy State

The fourth principal instrument of the activist state is *tax expenditures*. The inclusion of this category in a catalogue of state activity is less familiar and warrants a bit of explanation. Thanks to recent work by political scientists, we now know that the United States has become a hospitable context for a particular form of government activism. Over the past few decades, the federal government has come to operate a vast, largely hidden array of policies that subsidize private activities through the tax code (Howard 1997; Hacker 2002). Among the most expensive of these are the mortgage interest deduction, the deduction for employer provided health care benefits, and the deductibility of private pension contributions.

These tax subsidy arrangements are both huge in scale and highly distinctive in their social and political consequences. Most economists agree that these subsidies are analytically equivalent to budgetary outlays. The difference is that the government, rather than writing a check to a particular individual, simply indicates through favorable tax provisions that the individual in question can write a smaller check to the government. As recent research attests, however, this analytic equivalence between spending and tax subsidies coincides with vast differences in the distribution of benefits each provides—with tax subsidies typically much more heavily weighted toward the affluent. Moreover, the political dynamics surrounding the use of each instrument are very different. Tax subsidy politics is typically low profile, draws support from the center-right of the political spectrum, and relies heavily on the political strength of a range of powerful private-sector intermediaries (e.g., the housing industry in the case of the mortgage interest deduction).

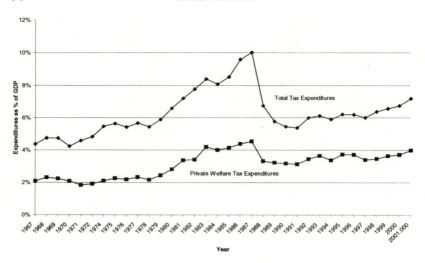

Figure 2.6 Tax Expenditures and Private Welfare Expenditures as Percentage of GDP, 1967–2001

Many of the largest of these tax subsidies were enacted well before World War II, typically with little debate. At a time when the federal income tax was modest, exemptions from the tax were of limited interest—as late as 1940 income taxes raised less than 1 percent of GDP, compared with 9 percent forty years later. That these provisions constituted a distinctive and potentially powerful form of government activism was little understood and rarely discussed. Over time, however, the "tax subsidy state" has also undergone a profound transformation. Figure 2.6 provides aggregate data on tax expenditures as a percentage of GDP from 1967 to 2001.[4] As with on-budget spending, the picture is one of tremendous expansion. As a share of GDP, tax expenditures increase from a bit under 4.4 percent of GDP in 1967 to just over 10 percent twenty years later. The level then falls sharply (as a result of the 1986 Tax Reform Act), before beginning a renewed rise. Breaking out the components of the tax subsidy state to distinguish economic provisions (mostly for business) from social ones (the "hidden welfare state") makes it clear that the latter accounts for much of the expansion that took place beginning in the late 1970s.

Three broad streams fed this enormous expansion of the tax state. First, income taxes increased, mostly through "bracket creep," as inflation and real income growth pushed people into higher tax brackets. As individuals' tax rates rose, so did the value of any exemptions they were able to claim from taxes. Because the great bulk of the income tax's growth preceded 1967, however, this shift can account for relatively little of the post-1967 increase in the scope of tax subsidies. A greatly increased demand for many of the eligible subsidies has been the second source of expansion (Hacker 2002, 2004). Homeownership rose. So did the use of employer-based health care and private pensions. Moreover, housing and health care experienced rising real prices, which also translated into higher tax deductions. The combined effect of these demand-side trends was rapidly increasing real tax expenditures in these areas. This is an excellent example of what Jacob Hacker (2004) has recently termed "policy drift." Because of the way program structures interact with changing social contexts over time, certain policies can come to operate in fundamentally new ways and on dramatically different scales—even in the absence of specific new legislation.

But it isn't all about drift. The third component of growing tax expenditures has been intentional: the creation of new subsidies and the expansion of eligibility conditions for existing ones. If the idea that tax expenditures offered a distinctive instrument of government activism was once novel, this has not been the case for some time. Increasingly, policymakers, especially conservative ones, have seen tax subsidies as a potentially preferable alternative to government spending. It is thus not surprising that the growth of tax expenditures differs in timing from the other expansions charted in this chapter.

An Exercise in Modern State Building

Whichever instrument one examines, the broad story is the same. After 1960 there was a very sharp expansion in the domestic policy role of the national government. If Robert Ball could speak, in 1974, of a "new Social Security system," one could just as easily have put the point more broadly. By then, one could see a new national state in the United States. This new state had far greater spending capacity, regulatory reach, responsibility for a range of social rights, and ability to structure incentives through the tax code than the national state that preceded it.

Beyond this fundamental shift, a number of interesting patterns emerge from comparing the three realms of expanding state activism. Perhaps most illuminating are subtle but important differences in timing. Given the compression of the overall transformation, the differences are not enormous. Nonetheless, there is an evident sequence. The onset of spending increases comes first. It is well underway by the time LBJ becomes president. The growth in spending is also the first part of the overall expansion to lose steam. The main phase of growth for the regulatory state and the expansion of social rights comes next. As we have noted, it is here that the expansion appears most dramatic and rapid. Finally, the expansion of the tax state comes last. Most of the rise in tax expenditures occurs after the other two expansions have begun to taper off.

With respect to spending and regulation, Melnick (2003), among others, suggests that there is nothing accidental about this sequencing. Regulatory activity imposes costs less directly on voters. The price of environmental protection, for instance, appears invisibly in the cost of consumer products. As the political capacity to finance spending begins to approach limits, regulatory instruments become increasingly attractive options.

When one compares the timing of change in the usage of spending and tax subsidy instruments, an equally striking relationship emerges. The growth of the "tax subsidy state" takes off in the late 1970s—just when the expansion of the "spending state" largely stops. In one sense, this is not surprising. The two instruments are almost inevitably in a form of competition. The analogy between tax expenditures and on-budget spending noted earlier becomes apparent when one considers their implications for the federal budget. Like "regular" spending, tax expenditure growth can be financed in only three ways: through higher taxes on less favored groups and activities, cuts in public spending, or increases in the deficit. Given any established levels for revenues and deficits, more tax expenditures can only come at the expense of on-budget spending.

There are strong reasons to suspect that the reasons for this relationship are grounded not just in accounting logic but in politics. As Howard (1997) and Hacker (2002) have emphasized, the political supports for tax subsidies are often profoundly different from the coalitions that typically advance government spending. Employer interests and right-of-center legislators loom considerably larger in advancing these initiatives. Of course, both these sets of actors were becoming stronger in American politics in the late 1970s and 1980s (Vogel 1989). Thus the growing role of tax expenditures may point not only to the exhaustion of one (largely spending-based) coalition. It suggests the gradual emergence of a new one, with its own style of government activism, favoring distinctive policy instruments (Pierson 2001). This observation highlights a claim explored in the second part of this chapter. Particular policy structures create distinct opportunity structures, with implications for both patterns of group mobilization and for the connections between citizens and the state.

One final observation about the long-term policy trends is warranted. The focus of this chapter is on the rise of the activist state. But the volume's broader concerns, especially with the rise of a more powerful and militant conservatism, raise the issue of what has happened to structures of government activism since 1980.

Imagine two broad alternative histories for the activist state. The first is a "rise and decline" story. In this version, a wave of conservatism washes away the previous triumphs of liberal activism. The second version is a "ratchet" story. Here, the expansion of government activism largely stops, but conservatives are unable to turn back the clock. The new, more activist state remains intact, and activism is sustained at a new plateau. This is a topic that must be approached with caution (Hacker 2004). Nonetheless, despite their crudeness, the data presented here are suggestive. Broadly, at least through 2000, they seem more compatible with the plateau story. Breaking the information down into smaller bits would yield some "rise and decline" stories, like the fate of Aid to Families with Dependent Children (AFDC). Of course, it would also have to include some substantial later expansions, like the Earned Income Tax Credit (Howard 1997), the Americans with Disabilities Act (Burke 2002), an extensive new regulatory regime for tobacco (Derthick 2005), new instruments of corporate oversight, and, of course, parts of the large new state apparatus associated with Homeland Security. A convincing rise and decline story would need to be based either on the type of long-term trends in policy drift described by Hacker (2004), or on suggestions that a long-term erosion of the activist state remains underway but, like termites working on a foundation, remains invisible at the surface.

THE ACTIVIST STATE AND NEW OPPORTUNITY STRUCTURES

The major round of state building that occurred in the 1960s and 1970s had tremendous political implications. Indeed, throughout this volume the exploration of these implications takes center stage. In this chapter I wish to highlight just a few of the most important dynamics triggered by the remarkable growth of the American national state.

Political scientists have become increasingly cognizant of the need to see public policy choices as highly consequential for political life (Weir and Skocpol 1985; Pierson 1993, 2006; Huber and Stephens 2001; Campbell 2003). The state's impact on citizens comes mostly through its policies, although this impact may be so masked or indirect that most citizens are only dimly aware of the state's role. Public policies are now recognized to have powerful effects on what citizens want, how they organize, what strategies of political action they employ, and what resources they can bring to bear on the political process (Esping-Andersen 1990; Hacker 2002; Mettler 2002).

In the very long run, moreover, public policies can have a strong influence on the composition of the polity itself. To employ an ecological metaphor, public policy regimes help to constitute environmental niches that allow some actors and activities to flourish while others wither. Small firms, for example, in many ways operate in a much more favorable policy environment in the United States than they do in, say, Sweden (Huber and Stephens 2001). As a result, over the long run, we would expect the

population of small businesses operating in these different environments
to diverge—as indeed they have.

As Steve Teles observes in his contribution to this volume, conventional
arguments about policy effects have stressed their capacity to entrench
certain political arrangements. New policies, such as those associated
with the rise of the activist state, create new opportunity structures.
Strongly supportive constituencies grow up around these programs. These
constituencies include both the ultimate beneficiaries of programs and
those intermediate groups that participate in providing the benefits. Other
actors, perhaps initially less supportive, may gradually adapt to the new
policy arrangements. As more and more elements in society come to recognize the new policies as durable, they make various individual- and
group-level investments based on that recognition. These investments in
turn help to further consolidate the new arrangements. Additional entrenchment can be produced by specific features of policies, such as the
"rolling intergenerational contract" dynamic created by Social Security's
"pay-as-you-go" financing.

As other chapters explore in detail, there is considerable evidence that
the expansion of the activist state generated many of the political repercussions associated with entrenchment. Consider group formation. Public
policies may provide the foundation for particular patterns of collective
mobilization. Policies can create major incentives to organize, and to organize in particular ways. They can also confer substantial resources on
particular types of groups, including direct and indirect financial subsidies, as well as organizational infrastructure and crucial information that
private actors can "piggyback" on in their efforts to generate collective
action (Moe 1980). These can be especially important in addressing the
high start-up costs and coordination problems that create formidable initial obstacles to successful collective action (Marwell and Oliver 1993).

Skocpol's chapter, in particular, documents the contribution of heightened government activism to organizational formation. The "advocacy
explosion" that many see as such a central part of contemporary American politics largely follows, rather than precedes, the expansion of the
activist state. Moreover, the dominant organizational forms and strategic
repertoires of these groups were customized to fit the opportunity structure of government activism. This customization partly reflects the vision
of thoughtful entrepreneurs. But it emerges at least as much from group
adaptation on the fly, as well as from differential survival rates among
those groups which happened to be capable of exploiting the opportunities available.

As has been well established, the rise of the activist state also fostered
the growth of strong constituencies among beneficiaries. Nowhere has
this been more evident than in the major expansion of entitlement spend-

ing associated with Social Security and Medicare (Campbell 2003). As Suzanne Mettler's chapter shows, however, the same case can be made more broadly. Where government programs provide substantial, tangible benefits, they will often generate consistent supporters as well.

At least in the short to medium run, the new policies associated with government activism generated supportive politics. Yet with the transformation of the American state came other political repercussions, less direct, less immediate, and less well understood. An overarching term for much of this less direct fallout from heightened activism is backlash. The expansion of the activist state not only created its own support structure. Through a variety of pathways, it also created many of the conditions for political challenges to its prominence in the decades to follow.

Recent research by political sociologists has emphasized how new institutional arrangements, which necessarily produce exclusion as well as inclusion, can galvanize major counter-mobilizations. Institutions, as Marc Schneiberg and Elisabeth Clemens (2006, 218) write in a recent summary, "generate grievance (through political exclusion). . . . Actors who are aggrieved but not co-opted are an important source of pressure for institutional change." Some groups facing unfavorable circumstances may concede, accepting the new institutional status quo and trying to do the best they can within it. Others, however, may turn oppositional. As Clemens and James Cook (1999, 452) put it, "Denied the social benefits of current institutional configurations, marginal groups have fewer costs associated with deviating from those configurations." This backlash dynamic is evident in Teles' analysis of conservative mobilization, where the emergence of energetic opposition is in large part triggered by the rise of activist government. Hacker and Pierson explore a similar process with respect to the crucial issue of taxation. Rebuffed in their direct efforts to challenge popular public spending programs, conservatives eventually identified tax cuts as the centerpiece for efforts to challenge the nagging durability of government activism.

No other aspects of the transformed American state generated grievances as intensively as the rights revolution. A range of profoundly contentious issues, many containing a strong moral component and raising fundamental matters of identity, became national issues. Abortion, sexuality, education, crime and punishment, the relationship between church and state, and many similarly charged matters became subject to authoritative action in Washington. The character of these issues made compromise difficult, and created incentives for polarizing forms of mobilization (Fiorina et al. 2005). Few would look back with nostalgia at the practices tolerated in many localities prior to the rights revolution. Nonetheless, in retrospect the role of that more decentralized federalism in muting the intensity of "nonmaterial" political conflict is evident.

The transformation of the American state not only triggered a counter-mobilization. It established important contours that both shaped the nature of that counter-mobilization and the strategies that successful elements of the conservative movement came to adopt. Policies, with the apparatus of supportive groups and beneficiaries, along with adaptations of other social actors, created constraints that conservatives needed to circumvent. As Teles details, efforts to undermine the strongly entrenched position of Social Security required that its powerful roots in the new American polity be recognized and taken into account.

At the same time, however, specific patterns of policy intervention also create specific opportunities for counter-mobilization. In Teles' case, Social Security not only produces sources of entrenchment through the creation of committed constituencies and a formidable transition problem. It also operates a "trust fund" system of finance that opens space for a discourse of looming "bankruptcy"—a feature that provides a crucial opportunity for reframing discussions about radical reform of the retirement system.

The opportunities created by the activist state for successful counter-mobilization have been equally evident in the rising role of the tax subsidy state. Although themselves a form of activism, these tax subsidies are in fact the anti-government form of government spending. As Mettler's chapter explores, these subsides for private activity can lead upper-middle-class voters to see the private sector (e.g., homeownership, mutual funds) rather than government (e.g., Social Security) as the guarantor of protection against life's economic hazards (Hacker 2002). For Republicans seeking to curb and redirect the activist state, tax expenditures possessed multiple virtues. They redirected fiscal resources to upper-income constituencies, they diminished the revenue stream available to government for other initiatives, and they did both these things in the form of tax "cuts" or breaks that were rarely perceived as instances of government largesse.

Finally, the rise of activism contributed to the mobilization of backlash in an indirect, long-term manner that has been poorly understood. As noted in the first part of this chapter, a large component of the growth in spending during the wave of government expansion took the form of long-term promises embodied in new or greatly enhanced entitlement programs. Since the early 1970s, the government has witnessed the gradual maturation of these commitments. Growth in public expenditure since then has occurred largely among entitlement programs, along with rising interest payments. Higher interest payments reflected the deficits of the 1980s, themselves a result of a failure to finance these maturing commitments adequately.

The result is that since as early as 1980 politicians have operated largely as the bill collectors for previous promises (Pierson 2001). In the expansionist phase, politicians could make attractive policy promises while deferring most of the costs. Now, the bill has come due, and politicians must pay it, without getting much in the way of credit for the programs enacted by their predecessors. It is not an enviable position. Politicians must run faster and faster just to stand still. Indeed, legislated changes (i.e., explicit policy choices) in entitlements over the past twenty years have almost always been in the direction of retrenchment rather than expansion. Not surprisingly, this unending climate of austerity both weakens popular enthusiasm for social programs and can be utilized to foster more general resentment against government activity.

All of these dynamics underscore the central point of this analysis: no account of contemporary American politics can succeed without grappling with the reality of the new, activist American state. A little more than a generation ago, the United States began a fairly rapid transition toward a markedly expanded federal role. That transition occurred across diverse instruments. While it was part of a broad cross-national trend, it exhibited patterns that were uniquely American. This remarkable exercise in state building contributed in fundamental ways to a remaking of the American polity. It fostered the growth of an unprecedented range of support structures for government action. Paradoxically, and over a longer time frame, it also fueled the rising hostility and growing influence of its greatest detractors.

NOTES

I thank the contributors to this volume, as well as Daniel Carpenter and Kay Schlozman, for very helpful comments on an earlier draft. For valuable research assistance I am grateful to Alison Gash, Alison Post, and Daniel Schlozman.

1. In this chapter, spending and tax expenditures are generally measured as a share of GDP. In a country experiencing dramatic economic and population growth over the period in question, GDP share provides the most appropriate measure of the scope of governmental activity. I make an exception in treating expenditures on regulatory activity, for reasons outlined in note 3.

2. In addition to estimating compliance costs, an approach rejected for reasons mentioned previously, an alternative aggregate measure sometimes employed is pages published in the *Federal Register*. Close examination suggests that this indicator is deeply flawed. Much that is published in the *Federal Register* has little to do with regulation, and agencies vary widely in their views about what (and at what length) they should publish there. For what it is worth, the picture emerging from these figures would be similar. Pages published in the *Federal Register tripled* between 1970 and 1975. Trends are uneven thereafter, rising in the late 1970s,

falling during Reagan's two terms, and then rising again after 1988. By 2000 the level is about 25 percent higher than the level established in 1975.

3. The justification for using real spending levels rather than spending as a percentage of GDP is that this is likely to come closest to capturing actual levels of regulatory output. Although more resources are required to regulate larger populations and economies, there are likely to be considerable economies of scale in regulatory activity. It is worth emphasizing that this choice has major consequences for the analysis of trends. As a share of GDP, regulatory expenditures rise significantly in the late 1960s and early 1970s, but they decline thereafter, and by the 1990s they are actually significantly *lower* than they were at the beginning of the 1960s.

4. Unfortunately, earlier data are not available. This in itself is a reflection of the fact that the need to treat tax expenditures as a form of government activism was recognized only late in the day.

Chapter Three

Government Activism and the Reorganization of American Civic Democracy

THEDA SKOCPOL

AMERICANS HAVE LONG EXCELLED as organizers and joiners of voluntary associations that shape, supplement, and respond to the activities of government. Voluntary activity, even more than electoral participation, has been seen as a special proclivity of U.S. democracy. In the 1890s James Bryce (1895, 278) observed that "associations are created, extended, and worked in the United States more . . . effectively than in any other country." This echoed earlier observations by Alexis de Tocqueville (1969 [1835–40]) and foreshadowed later arguments and findings by scholars working in the mid-twentieth century (such as Almond and Verba 1963; Hausknecht 1962; and Schlesinger 1944).

The late twentieth century, however, witnessed a momentous reorganization of U.S. civic activity and institutions. Americans launched more civic entities than ever before but channeled much less civic energy into shared participatory endeavors. Between the mid-1960s and the 1990s, an expanding universe of nationally visible voluntary organizations shifted away from business associations and popularly rooted membership federations and toward professionally managed groups, often without members, that have pursued an unprecedentedly wide variety of public causes.

Formerly marginalized minorities have gained new organized voice in America's reorganized civic life, and popular causes such as environmentalism have gained ground despite business opposition. In these senses, recent civic changes have been democratizing. But recent civic changes have weakened democracy as well. While privileged Americans continue to join membership groups—especially professional associations—blue-collar unions and long-standing membership federations involving ordinary citizens have dwindled. Professionally managed "public-interest" advocacy groups seek monetary contributions, not active members, and on balance tend to promote causes of special concern to well-to-do and highly educated Americans.

Recent civic transformations in the United States have a paradoxical relationship to activist government. Late twentieth-century expansions in the scope and regulatory reach of the federal government played a strong role in triggering and channeling the reorganization of civic voluntarism. Between 1965 and the 1980s, a new political opportunity structure was created that favored professionally managed advocacy groups and non-profit institutions, many of which pursued liberal causes without engaging in popular mobilization. In contrast, conservatives opposed to many of the new federal interventions continued to build widespread voluntary membership federations and join their fortunes to a rightward-tilting Republican Party opposed to government activism for redistributive purposes. Indeed, recently thriving cross-class voluntary federations are disproportionately on the conservative side of the social and political spectrum, giving contemporary American conservatism strong populist roots. Ironically, therefore, although civic reorganization was originally spurred by activist government, the new U.S. voluntary group universe helps to tilt agendas of public discussion and legislation away from government measures that might broaden popular access to opportunity and security.

To explore the nature, causes, and political consequences of recent civic transformations, this chapter draws on my own research about voluntary associations and social policymaking (see Skocpol 2000, 2003) and includes empirical findings from many other scholars. Given my proclivities as a historical-institutionalist, I highlight what we can learn by focusing on the changing universe of voluntary and interest-group *organizations* as such (for related discussions, see Hayes 1986; Loomis and Cigler 1998). Organizations concentrate resources, voice, and clout in democratic politics—so we should care as much about the organizational as we do the individual level of politics. We should also explore interactions between organized voluntary entities and the changing institutions and policies of government. Social movements and voluntary groups influence politics and government, to be sure—yet the opposite is also true. Access to politics and partnerships with government spur group formation and influence changing forms of voluntary organization.

A Great Civic Transformation

The momentous civic reorganizations that unfolded from the 1960s to the 1990s can only be understood against the backdrop of the classic American civil society that reached a kind of apogee after World War II.

Civil Society in the Mid-Twentieth Century

Mid-twentieth-century American civil society took on different aspects, depending on whether one *counted organizations* or considered the *rela-*

tive membership size of different types of groups. In terms of sheer numbers of groups, business associations predominated. Groups representing businesses or businesspeople constituted about half of all nationally visible voluntary associations in 1950 and more than 40 percent in 1960 (Fox 1952; Skocpol 2003, 146–47, table 4.2). Yet if we examine voluntary groups with large individual memberships, we see another side of midcentury civic life. Pioneering cross-national survey research by Gabriel Almond and Sidney Verba (1963, chap. 11) documented that mid-twentieth-century Americans were unusually likely to join and hold office in membership associations. And compared to Britons and Germans (the other two advanced-industrial citizenries surveyed by Almond and Verba), Americans concentrated their participation in distinct types of groups. Americans were especially likely to claim participation in church-related associations, civic-political groups, and fraternal groups—and were also significantly involved in cooperative and military veterans' associations (Almond and Verba 1963, 302, table 2). Putting it another way, as late as the early 1960s, Americans were avid participants in "fellowship associations"—groups emphasizing and expressing solidarity among fellow citizens, or among "brothers" or "sisters" who see themselves as joined in shared moral undertakings. In 1955 more than two dozen very large membership federations enrolled between 1 percent and 12 percent of American adults apiece.[1] Rooted in dense networks of state and local chapters that gave them a presence in communities across the nation, major fraternal groups, religious groups, civic associations, and veterans' associations predominated among very large membership associations (apart from the AFL-CIO).[2]

Most of the business associations that were so numerous in the 1950s and early 1960s grew up over the course of the twentieth century; and the same was true of professional associations, also numerous by midcentury. But massive, popularly rooted fellowship federations had much deeper historical roots. They started to proliferate in the fledgling United States between the Revolution and the Civil War and then experienced explosive growth in the late nineteenth century (Gamm and Putnam 1999; Skocpol, Ganz, and Munson 2000). Particular voluntary federations rose and fell over time, yet as the United States industrialized from the mid-nineteenth to the mid-twentieth century—an epoch during which business and professional groups and labor unions grew in this country as they did in other industrializing nations—fellowship federations remained a strong presence. In addition to the Civil War, World Wars I and II promoted the growth of fellowship federations, which worked closely with the federal government to mobilize Americans for wars (Skocpol et al. 2002).

Although classic U.S. fellowship associations may seem to have been apolitical, in fact they were often involved in public affairs. Half to two-thirds of the twenty largest membership associations of the 1950s were directly involved in legislative campaigns or public crusades of one sort or another (Skocpol 2003, 26–28, table 2.1). This is perhaps obvious for the AFL-CIO and the American Farm Bureau Federation. But, beyond these, the PTA and the General Federation of Women's Clubs were active in a variety of legislative campaigns having to do with educational and family issues. The Fraternal Order of Eagles championed Social Security and other federal social programs (Davis 1948). And the American Legion drafted and lobbied for the G.I. Bill of 1944 (M. Bennett 1996; Skocpol 1997). Because most very large membership associations were federations that paralleled the local-state-national structure of U.S. governing institutions, they were able to marshal public pressure and influence legislatures across many states and U.S. congressional districts. In eras where political messages between elected representatives and their local constituencies often flowed through organizational venues (see Hansen 1991), membership federations had considerable influence with elected representatives across multiple localities and both major political parties.

Contemporary Civic Reorganizations

If business associations and popularly rooted membership federations held sway in U.S. civil society as of the mid-twentieth century, sudden and remarkable changes occurred thereafter. Three intertwined transformations remade the American civic universe between the 1960s and the 1990s.

First, while business groups continued to proliferate in absolute terms, they lost proportional ground in the universe of nationally visible voluntary associations. The total number of U.S. national associations expanded from about 6,000 in 1960 to reach a new plateau of about 23,000 in 1990 and after. Yet, as this expansion happened, the share of business associations shrank from 42 to 17.5 percent, while those devoted to addressing issues in the realms of "social welfare" and "public affairs" burgeoned from 6 to 17 percent of all nationally visible associations (Skocpol 2003, 146–47, table 4.2).[3] Expanding categories included citizens', or public-interest, associations—that is, nonprofit organizations that aim to further value-laden understandings of the public good: for instance, environmental groups, anti-poverty groups, pro-choice and pro-life groups, family values groups, and associations dealing with the rights of women, racial and ethnic minorities, and other vulnerable categories of Americans (Baumgartner and Jones 1993, 181; Berry 1977, 1999; Walker 1991).

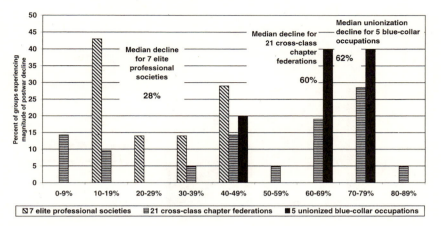

Figure 3.1 Post-war Membership Decline for Cross-Class Chapter Federations, Blue-Collar Unions, and Elite Professional Societies. *Source:* Putnam 2000, 82, for unions; 438–39, for larger cross-class associations. Additional data on elite professional societies supplied personally by Robert Putnam.

Second, previously hefty blue-collar trade unions and fellowship federations went into sharp decline. This fact has been empirically documented both in my own research (Skocpol 2003) and in the research of Robert Putnam. As Putnam (2000) has argued, all kinds of membership associations experienced a considerable drop from the 1960s on. Tellingly, however, as figure 3.1 shows, the declines after World War II have been greatest for blue-collar trade unions and chapter-based voluntary federations, especially once-vibrant women's associations and fraternal groups. Nationally prominent elite professional societies have experienced much less membership decline than have most popularly rooted membership associations. Overall, educated Americans have increased their involvements with professional membership groups—including smaller, more specialized organizations, which have proliferated in recent times (Brint 1994, 4; Skocpol 2003, 217, fig. 5.10).

The third and final contemporary transformation involves shifts in the *structures* of voluntary groups and institutions. Although thousands of new, nationally visible groups were created between the 1960s and the 1990s, many recently proliferating organizations—such as public-interest law groups, think tanks, foundations, and political action committees— are not membership groups at all (Ricci 1993; Rich and Weaver 1998; Conway and Green 1995, 1998). These are professionally run organizations that deploy money and ideas to influence public affairs. Other recently proliferating groups are staff-centered associations that recruit masses of individual adherents through the mail. With a few exceptions—

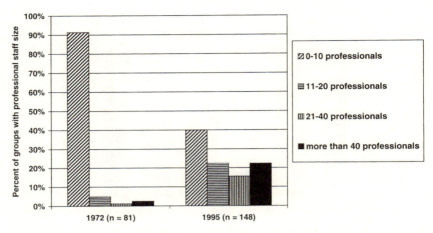

Figure 3.2 Organizational Staffing of U.S. Public Interest Associations, 1972 and 1995. *Source:* Shaiko 1999, 12.

such as the 35-million-member AARP—most contemporary mailing-list groups have followings in the tens of thousands to hundreds of thousands, not millions.[4]

Recently proliferating associations have other telling features. Even when they claim substantial numbers of adherents, most recently founded associations lack chapters—or else they have very sparse networks of sub-national affiliates (Berry 1977; Putnam 2000, 51, using data from Walker 1991). In addition, many recently founded or recently growing groups are heavily invested in professional staffing. This trend is well documented for environmental groups (Baumgartner and Jones 1993, 187). And data from the best across-the-board study of public-interest associations, presented in figure 3.2, shows expanded professional staffing between 1972 and 1995.

Over the past four decades, in sum, American associational life has become more pluralistic and less business-focused—yet it has shifted away from popularly rooted, chapter-based membership federations and toward professionally managed organizations, many with no members or chapters at all.

Tellingly, partial counter-trends to the predominant cast of late twentieth-century civic reorganization have occurred on the conservative side of U.S. civil society. To be sure, professionally managed think tanks, public-interest law firms, political action committees, foundations, and advocacy groups have proliferated across the partisan spectrum. But even as American conservatives have created their share of such organizations, they have done more than liberals to renew and expand massively large, popularly rooted voluntary federations. In the realm of institutionalized religion as such, evangelical Protestant churches, often conservatively oriented, have flourished in recent decades, while mainline Protestant churches have lost ground (Wuthnow 1999). Conservative voluntary associations—distinct from evangelical churches, though often socially connected to them—have also prospered of late. Geographically extensive voluntary membership federations that have exceeded the mark of enrolling 1 percent or more of U.S. adults as members include the rightward-leaning National Right to Life Committee (NRLC), the Christian Coalition, and the National Rifle Association (NRA). All three have professionally managed national centers that recruit millions of mailing-list members; in addition, their national centers are linked to networks of state affiliates and local chapters or clubs where members can meet and get involved as volunteers. Since the 1970s, the only unabashedly liberal chapter-based membership federation to experience comparable massive growth is the National Education Association, a teachers' union.

WHY DID CIVIC REORGANIZATION HAPPEN?

Analysts often presume that societal changes spark social movements and innovations in voluntary organization—which, in turn, produce changes in government activity. This scenario has some relevance to explaining the great civic reorganizations of the late twentieth century. For example, as Americans with college or postgraduate degrees went from 7.7 percent of people age twenty-five and older in 1960 to 25.2 percent by 1999 (National Center for Educational Statistics 2001, 17), such higher-educated citizens developed new racial and gender attitudes and provided new sorts of leaders and adherents for public-interest movements such as environmentalism.

Yet the civic impact of educational expansion and other gradual societal changes (such as those stressed by Putnam 2000) occurred in a context of political upheaval and enhanced governmental activism. Nationally muscular from the 1960s, "rights revolutions" discredited old civic forms and brought new kinds of organizations to the fore. Coterminously, the U.S. federal government greatly expanded and reorganized its social interventions, creating a new "political opportunity structure" for voluntary groups and interest organizations. New modes of ongoing access to government favored the proliferation of professionally run advocacy groups and nonprofit institutions. And as these changes occurred in society and politics, new technologies and models of association building made it easier for professionals engaged with government to create and run associations without interactive, dues-paying members.

Rights Revolutions and Civic Transformation

The modern movement for African American civil rights that peaked in the mid-1960s was one of the pivotal moments in U.S. political history (McAdam 1982; Morris 1984). Battering down the walls of legal racial segregation and political exclusion, this movement transformed societal attitudes and spurred landmark national laws—the Civil Rights Act of 1964 and the Voting Rights Act of 1965 first and foremost. Additional rights movements soon followed (Skrentny 2002). Not surprisingly, the rights revolutions helped to spark the reorganization of American civic life.

Because most traditional U.S. fellowship federations were racially exclusive and gender-segregated, changing attitudes and practices about race and gender hit them like a tornado. Showing the results of attitude shifts that accelerated during and after the rights revolutions, a representative sample of Americans told sociologist Robert Wuthnow in a 1997 survey (1998, 243, n. 51) about the kinds of associations they would be "very unlikely" to join. Ninety percent said that they would not join groups "with a history of racial discrimination," and a clear majority (58 percent) also said that they would be very unlikely to join an association that "accepts only men or women." As segregationist racial ideas waned, many traditional membership federations were understandably delegitimated in the eyes of younger people and found it hard to recruit new members. Likewise, traditional associations were undercut by the rise of feminism, the entry of more and more women into the paid labor force, and the proliferation of female-led families. Women were no longer available as helpmates for exclusively male groups; and changes in work and family life hurt membership groups that needed to coordinate people's availability for recurrent meetings (Costa and Kahn 2003; Crawford and Levitt 1999).

The civil rights struggle and other rights revolutions also raised questions about the forms of organization favored by old-line chapter federations. Across much of U.S. civic history, membership associations trumpeted constitutions paralleling that of the U.S. government and celebrated representative modes of decision making. But such structures traditionally embodied compromises between the racially segregationist South and the rest of the nation. Movements aiming to enhance the rights of minorities and to promote value changes were naturally skeptical of existing majoritarian practices and federated organizational arrangements, which proved obdurate when first faced with demands for racial and gender equality.

Instead of the old majoritarian, federated ways of doing things, the new rights movements depended initially on activist cadres and, later, on professionals—types of leaders who could readily get out in front of laggard majorities. Old-line membership federations such as African American churches, the National Association for the Advancement of Colored

People, and the General Federation of Women's Clubs played visible roles in the rights revolutions of the mid-1950s to the mid-1970s. But even in an era of popular protests, the key roles were often played by newly launched vanguard organizations, such as the Southern Christian Leadership Conference (SCLC), founded in 1957; the Student Nonviolent Coordinating Committee (SNCC), founded in 1960; the National Organization for Women (NOW), founded in 1966; the Women's Equity Action League (WEAL), founded in 1968; and the National Abortion and Reproductive Rights Action League (now called NARAL Pro-Choice America), created in 1973 as a reorientation of an earlier group. SCLC began as a coordinating group of activist African American ministers, and SNCC was a coordinating group of student civil rights activists. In due course, NOW developed chapters and a modest-sized national membership, and WEAL and NARAL eventually developed modest-sized mailing-list memberships. Yet these and other women's rights organizations started out as "leadership and not membership based" (Gelb and Palley 1982, 15). Activists devoted to organizing protests and lobbying the federal government were the key founders and association builders.

Indeed, the strongest influence of rights struggles on civic organizing arguably occurred via the intervening impact of new federal legislation and regulations. As sociologist John Skrentny (2002, 142) argues, the "mass mobilization of the black civil rights movement"—in which activists worked with popularly rooted membership groups, especially the black churches of the South—"helped create agencies for civil rights that obviated any similar need" for other categories of people. "A nonparticipatory minority-rights politics became possible, where self-appointed leaders could pressure and have impact." Skrentny's argument and data can be put together with data that sociologist Debra Minkoff (1995) has gathered from the *Encyclopedia of Associations* on the emergence of hundreds of new rights associations speaking for African Americans, other ethnic minorities, and feminist women. As figures 3.3 and 3.4 show, most of the proliferation of new rights associations occurred *after* the Civil Rights Act of 1964 and the establishment during the next few years of federal agencies to enforce affirmative action regulations. New groups were organized around the identities labeled and legitimated by government; and most of the newly created groups were advocacy oriented, just as Skrentny's argument would lead us to expect.

A New Political Opportunity Structure

This brings us to a key point. Not just in the rights arena, but more broadly, government activism of broader scope and greater intensity spurred the formation and professionalization of voluntary groups.

Number of groups

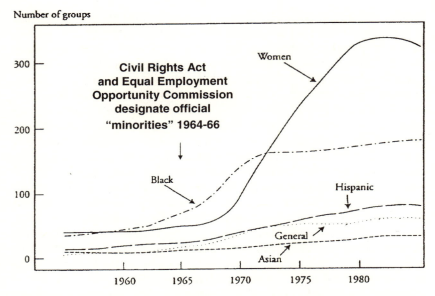

Figure 3.3 Women's and Racial-Ethnic Groups, by Constituency, 1955–85.
Sources: Minkoff 1995, 62; Skrentny 2002, chap. 4.

A sudden "bulge" of important federal legislative enactments started
in the late 1950s and peaked in the 1960s and early 1970s (Howell et al.
2000; Mayhew 1991, chap. 4). This constituted what political scientist
Hugh Heclo (1978, 89) has aptly called a new "age of improvement," in
which the federal government aimed to influence new realms of American
social and economic life (see also Talbert and Potoski 2002). As figure
3.5 suggests, the emergence of thousands of new nationally focused associations followed slightly after heightened federal legislative activism (for
further argument and evidence, see Baumgartner, Leech, and Mahoney
2003). Tellingly, the same basic dynamic occurred across many specific
policy areas, ranging from environmental policy to health care and expanded benefits and new services for older Americans. In each area, innovative federal measures tended to precede the bulk of voluntary group
proliferation. And detailed research has repeatedly shown how expanded
and reorganized federal legislative and administrative measures from the
1960s to the 1980s encouraged new associations to form and afforded
them ongoing access to public policy formation (for documentation in
various policy areas, see Baumgartner and Jones 1993, chap. 9; Baumgartner and Mahoney 2004; Baumgartner, Leech, and Mahoney 2003;
Campbell 2003; Costain 1992; Imig 1996; Peterson 1993; Pratt 1976;
Pratt 1993, chap. 9; Van Tassel and Meyer 1992).

Number of groups

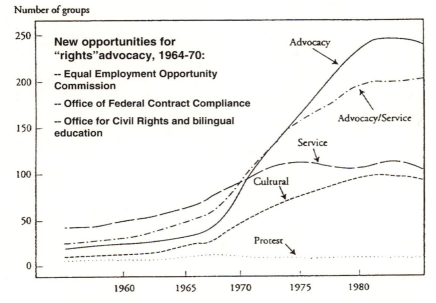

New opportunities for
"rights"advocacy, 1964-70:

-- Equal Employment Opportunity
Commission

-- Office of Federal Contract Compliance

-- Office for Civil Rights and bilingual
education

Advocacy

Advocacy/Service

Service

Cultural

Protest

Figure 3.4 Women's and Racial-Ethnic Groups, by Strategy, 1955–85. *Sources:* Minkoff 1995, 62; Skrentny 2002, chap. 4.

After liberal-leaning rights and public-interest associations emerged in large numbers in the 1960s and 1970s, business associations and conservative public-interest groups proliferated during the 1980s (Berry 1997, chap. 2). This should not surprise us, because new government interventions not only help to define new values, social identities, and economic interests; they also change the stakes for groups on all sides of every issue, encouraging organization and counter-organization to influence further government policymaking. The arrival of the conservative Republican Reagan administration in the 1980s obviously afforded new openings for groups hoping to temper or roll back earlier liberal initiatives. What is more, for interests across the partisan spectrum, federal tax rules prompted the development of clusters of cooperating associations—as 501(c)(3) groups engaged in research and public education, sister 501(c)(4) groups lobbied government, and affiliated political action committees raised money for elections (Conway and Green 1998; Paget 1990).

Late twentieth-century changes in the structures and activities of the federal government encouraged not just the sheer proliferation of groups but also the professionalization of associational leadership. This happened in several ways.

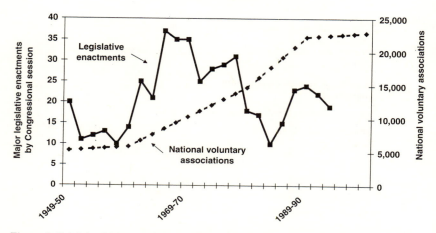

Figure 3.5. Major U.S. Legislative Enactments and the Growth of National Voluntary Associations, 1949–99. *Sources: Encyclopedia of Associations* data with intermediate values interpolated, from Skocpol 2003, 147; legislative enactments from Howell et al. 2000, "A" plus "B" enactments.

One inducement to add professionals to group staffs is perhaps obvious. From the 1960s, the federal courts showed a new willingness to entertain class action suits, and they became intensely involved in adjudicating issues arising from legislation on federal rights, the environment, and social regulation (Melnick 1994). Fighting federal lawsuits became an important way to influence social policymaking—and this naturally encouraged the proliferation of public-interest law firms and stimulated many other advocacy groups to add lawyers to their staffs.

The professionalization of Congress likewise proceeded apace from the 1960s through the 1980s. During this period, congressional representatives were increasingly likely to be college graduates; and thousands of new employees staffed the offices of individual members, providing expert assistance to congressional committees and subcommittees, which grew in number after reorganizations in the early 1970s (Baumgartner and Jones 1993; Ornstein, Mann, and Malbin 2000). Many of these new congressional employees were professionals, persons with the skills and expertise needed to help representatives cope with the intensive and specialized legislative environment.

Similar changes occurred in the federal bureaucracy. National government employment did *not* increase very much—even after the mid-1960s, it increased at a much less spectacular rate than federal spending and regulations did. But the "upper and upper-middle levels of officialdom" did expand, while "employees in the field and in Washington" who performed "routine chores" became relatively less numerous (Heclo 1978, 99). Federal agencies added technical and supervisory personnel to oversee new regulations and implement programs with assistance from private groups as well as state and local officials.

Not surprisingly, the proliferation of national associations closely tracked the expansion of congressional staff and the reorganization of federal employment.[5] After all, there were now more decision makers to contact about policy concerns, new levers to pull in Washington, D.C. Groups with any interest in the expanding realms of federal policy had plenty of places to make their concerns known. Above all, there were opportunities for professionals in associations to contact fellow professionals in government, people with similar policy interests, or perhaps former college classmates.

In this new policymaking environment, old and new associations added professionals to their D.C. offices—people who could do policy research, monitor legislation in Congress, and interact with officials as new laws were administratively defined and implemented (see figure 3.2). "Issue networks" with lots of interacting experts formed in every aspect of federal policymaking—and advocacy group professionals were avid participants (Heclo 1978; see also Beer 1978 on the "technocratic takeover"). Environmental policymaking is an excellent case in point. Enacted in 1969, the National Environmental Policy Act (NEPA) mandated the preparation of "environmental impact statements" by government agencies. This created an incentive for environmental associations to hire policy experts who could influence such statements. After NEPA, as figure 3.6 shows, the staffs of associations grew at an even faster rate than the—also rapidly rising—number of environmental groups.

During the "age of improvement," finally, the federal government engaged in administration "by remote control" (Heclo 1978, 92) in a fashion that greatly encouraged the growth of state and local government and the professionalization of nonprofit agencies. Instead of expanding the federal bureaucracy to administer new programs directly, the new laws of the 1960s and after typically used regulations and subsidies to induce nonfederal actors to pursue desired goals. Federal supervisors hired private contractors or consultants; federal agencies channeled moneys to governors or mayors. In turn, either the federal government or state and local governments often designated private nonprofit agencies to run new social programs established by the War on Poverty, the Great Society, and Nixon-era social legislation. The 1967 amendments to the Social Security Act, for example, included hefty inducements for state governments to contract out social programs to nonprofit agencies (Berry and Arons 2003, chap. 1; Crenson and Ginsberg 2002, 219–26; S. Smith and Lipsky 1993). In response to the new opportunities, thousands of nonprofit social

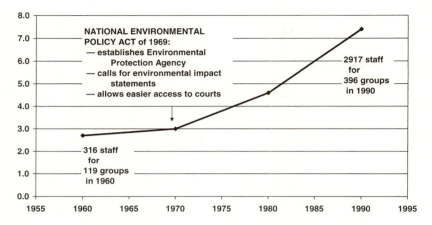

Figure 3.6. Ratio of Staff Members to Groups in the U.S. Environmental Movement, 1960–90. *Source:* Baumgartner and Jones 1993, 37–38, 69, 186–88.

agencies were created, while older service associations expanded their activities, especially activities administered by service professionals.

Many unanticipated civic effects followed from the indirect administration of expanded federal and state programs in late twentieth-century America. Local chapters of old-line voluntary membership federations became less engaged in the provision of social services through mutual aid or voluntary community efforts. Meanwhile, proliferating professionally run nonprofits expanded their staffs—and aimed to recruit civically active politicians, businesspeople, and public figures to their supervisory boards. It is not incidental, I would suggest, that from the mid-1960s on, prestigious forms of civic activity in localities across the United States became less a matter of joining and leading a membership association and more a matter of either working with or serving on the board of a nonprofit service agency. Social service employees, occasional volunteers for local agencies, and members of the boards of service agencies—these are the kinds of people we usually consider the preeminent civic activists today.[6]

New Technologies and Models of Association Building

New technologies and models of association building constitute a final set of factors propelling civic reorganization in the late twentieth century. Obviously, the current vogue for professionalized, staff-led civic associations has been shaped by changes parallel to those affecting political parties since the 1950s—an era during which (as Andrea Campbell details in her chapter in this volume) decentralized party organizations have largely been displaced by a coterie of professional fund raisers, pollsters, and media managers (see Aldrich 1995, part 3; Mayhew 1986; Schier 2000, chap. 2).

Like old-line politicians who relied on state and local party networks to pull as many eligible voters to the polls as possible, the organizers of old-line U.S. voluntary federations took it for granted that the best way to gain national influence was to recruit mass memberships and spread a network of chapters. There were good reasons why this model came to be taken for granted in classic civic America from the mid-nineteenth century to the 1960s. After the start-up phase, the budgets of voluntary federations usually depended heavily on membership dues. Supporters had to be continuously recruited through person-to-person contacts. And if leverage over government was desired, a voluntary federation had to be able to influence legislators, citizens, and newspapers across many legislative districts. For these reasons, classic civic organizers with national ambitions moved quickly to recruit activists and members in every state and across as many towns and cities as possible. Organizers traveled around the country, convened face-to-face meetings, and recruited and encouraged intermediate leaders who could carry on the work of member recruitment and retention. "Interact or die" was the watchword for classic American association builders.

Today, nationally ambitious civic entrepreneurs proceed in quite different ways. When Marian Wright Edelman got the inspiration to found the Children's Defense Fund, she turned to private foundations for funding and then recruited an expert staff of researchers and lobbyists (Edelman 1987; Walls 1993, 279). Ever since the Ford Foundation launched the trend in the late 1950s, foundation grants have been especially important to the funding of U.S. public-interest associations, encouraging their professionalization and allowing many of them to avoid reliance on membership dues.[7] Liberal foundations moved first, but in the past two decades conservative foundations have been major players as well. The late Jack Walker (1991, chap. 5) surveyed hundreds of associations with headquarters in Washington, D.C., and found that foundation grants were especially important for the founding and maintenance of recently established public-interest (citizens') groups.

Alternatively, contemporary advocacy groups can use patron support to get started and then turn to computerized direct-mail solicitations to develop continuing support from individual adherents (Berry 1997; Bosso 1995; Godwin 1992; Godwin and Mitchell 1984; Johnson 1998). This technique has been effectively used by groups across the spectrum, from Common Cause (McFarland 1984) and big environmental groups, to the Concord Coalition and Mothers against Drunk Driving, to many right-wing advocacy associations. Civic entrepreneurs need generous seed grants to start direct-mail solicitation, because appropriate lists must be purchased and hundreds of thousands of letters repeatedly mailed. And staff expertise is equally necessary, because mailings must be honed and deployed again and again. The Internet is modifying these realities, but only modestly.

Ready access to national media outlets is an additional circumstance allowing advocacy associations to forgo recurrent contacts among leaders and members. Rather than coming up through small media markets, elite television, newspaper, and magazine reporters today are often recruited directly from universities and operate from the start out of major metropolitan centers (Fallows 1996). In punditry hubs like Boston, New York, Los Angeles, and Washington, D.C., reporters, politicians, and advocacy spokespersons participate in endless talk shows; and print reporters are always on the phone to advocates as well as politicians. National media outlets want to stage debates among dramatically polarized sets of spokespersons; and advocacy associations need to keep their causes and accomplishments visible. By dramatizing causes through the national media, advocates can enhance their legitimacy and keep contributions flowing from patrons or direct-mail adherents.

The very model of civic effectiveness has, in short, been upended since the 1960s. With some exceptions, civic organizers no longer proceed by constructing vast federations and recruiting interactive citizen members. When a new cause appears, activists open a national office and manage association building as well as national projects from the center. Contemporary organization-building techniques encourage public-interest groups—just like trade and professional associations—to concentrate their efforts in efficiently managed headquarters located close to the federal government and the national media. Even a group aiming to speak for large numbers of Americans does not necessarily need "members" in any meaningful sense of the word.

Opportunities for Conservative Populists

New technologies and modes of civic organization have been used across the board in recent American civic life, as conservatives and liberals alike have developed professionally run lobbying and media strategies and deployed computerized lists to target potential supporters. Yet the stress I have placed on shifting political opportunities can help us to understand why conservatives also sought to adapt traditional forms of voluntary federation building to the new political circumstances of the late twentieth century.

During the late 1960s and the 1970s, when professional advocacy for group rights or public-interest causes was taking hold as a prestigious associational model, conservatives often felt excluded from the "liberal Washington establishment." Even when Ronald Reagan held office during the 1980s as a president openly friendly toward social as well as economic conservatives, the U.S. Congress and the federal courts continued to be sites of considerable Democratic Party strength, and professionally dominated American institutions with links into politics—such as the media, the universities, and secular nonprofits—were viewed by conservatives as bastions of "liberal hegemony." Part of the response to this, of course, took the form of conservative and business efforts to organize and fund new (or newly active) professionally run advocacy groups, think tanks, and foundations. But during the decades when conservatives felt "on the outs" in key centers of national power, opportunities also opened for them to engage in popular mobilizations, working within and across states and localities, and linking subnational to national undertakings.

Across many states and localities, especially in the South, Midwest, and inner West, evangelical Protestantism was flourishing, creating institutional settings and social networks that could be used to get *interconnected sets* of ordinary people involved in voluntary movements. Local struggles often occurred around what would be taught in the public schools, as new emphases on sex education, alternative life-styles, and criticism of aspects of the U.S. past aroused the ire of many social conservatives. U.S. federal government initiatives—often sponsored by Democrats—provided a steady staccato of highly charged interventions in traditional social arrangements that made it easier for conservative organizers to draw people into political movements that linked local community activism to state, national, and party politics. Not only were southern white conservatives riled by civil rights legislation and associated federal regulatory interventions; social conservatives across regions and from many walks of life were negatively aroused by federal court decisions—such as the *Roe v. Wade* decision legalizing abortion in 1974–or put off by new federal laws and regulations affecting education, gender relations, family life, and gun ownership. By the 1990s and early 2000s, hot-button issues such as homosexual rights were also added to the mix. Indeed, just before the pivotal 2004 presidential election, the Massachusetts Supreme Judicial Court ruled that its state's constitution mandated full marriage rights for homosexuals, thus propelling a change viewed as highly threatening by Protestant and Catholic social conservatives toward the forefront of state and national politics.

Amid repeated instances of judicial and regulatory activism sparking social controversy, organizers in the anti-abortion, Christian right, and anti—gun control movements have found it possible—and strategically enticing—to *synthesize* new methods of professional advocacy and fund raising with updated versions of traditional movement building through membership federations networked across many congressional districts. Starting in the 1970s, the National Rifle Association (NRA) was transformed from a historically long-standing network of sporting clubs into a widespread membership federation led by an opulently funded professional staff devoted to agitating and lobbying on behalf of the rights of gun owners (K. Patterson 1998). As it has built professional clout and a mailing-list membership of more than 4 million, the NRA has continued to nurture affiliated state associations and local clubs—and link members and volunteers to local, state, and national policy campaigns. The National Right to Life Committee and other associations—such as the half-million-strong Concerned Women for America—similarly mobilized in a combination of old and updated ways to further pro-life causes in local, state, and national politics (Granberg and Denny 1981; McCarthy 1987). Founded in 1989 following the failed presidential bid of Jerry Falwell, the Christian Coalition furthered and focused efforts already underway to draw millions of conservative Protestants into electoral politics (Guth et al. 1995). In state after state, well-trained local Christian right activists moved into Republican Party venues and either took over or exerted substantial plurality pressure to influence party nominations and platform positions.

Overall, conservative voluntarism in the contemporary United States has revitalized traditions of community-rooted cross-class voluntarism that, prior to the 1970s, were embodied either in blue-collar trade unions or in U.S. voluntary membership federations that were not openly partisan. Both churches and conservative membership federations have come to be connected to electoral and party politics in an explicitly partisan, rightward-leaning way. Organizers created or reoriented populist organizational networks in and around the Republican Party—even as trade unions were losing ground in the national labor force, and as "public-interest" liberals turned away from grass-roots membership mobilization.[8]

CIVIC TRANSFORMATION AND AMERICAN DEMOCRACY

What difference has the reorganization of U.S. civic life made? Looking back over half a century, we can see that contemporary civic reorganizations have had a complex and somewhat paradoxical relationship to shifts in citizen participation and partisan political struggles over the role of government in economic and social life. Democratizing developments have certainly occurred, but civic participation and agendas of public discussion have arguably tilted toward the privileged and away from support for strong government interventions to spread security and opportunity.

Dwindling Avenues of Civic Participation

The racial and gender exclusivity of traditional kinds of membership federations was shattered by the "rights revolutions" of the 1960s and 1970s. Formerly racist and gender-segregated associations were bypassed and mostly went into decline—surely a democratizing development in U.S. civic life. What is more, traditional agendas of public debate were greatly broadened as nonprofit associations, including many "public-interest" citizen associations, proliferated numerically at the relative expense of business and trade associations. Especially in the 1970s and the 1980s, Americans organized more nationally visible associations than ever before, and new groups championed public-interest causes and the rights of the formerly excluded.

But if we consider U.S. democracy in its entirety and bring issues of power and social leverage to the fore, then our conclusions cannot be purely optimistic. Too many valuable aspects of the old civic America are not being reproduced or reinvented in the new civic world largely run by elite trustees and professional staffers. As long-standing popularly rooted unions and fellowship federations have faded while professionally run public-interest associations—along with business and professional groups—have proliferated, avenues for citizen participation have become more constricted. We can see this by contrasting the modi operandi and class appeal of these two types of associations.

Scholars studying political participation have established that a combination of resources, motivation, and mobilization explains variations in who participates, how, and at what levels (see Burns, Schlozman, and Verba 2001; Rosenstone and Hansen 1993; Verba and Nie 1972; Verba, Schlozman, and Brady 1995). Individuals from privileged families have advantages of income and education and also tend to be regularly contacted by civic organizers or election campaigners. What is more, people in managerial and professional careers are likely to gain skills at work that can be transferred to public activities. Nevertheless, such socioeconomic disparities can be partially counteracted if popularly rooted political parties, unions, churches, and associations mobilize and motivate average citizens and spread skills that facilitate participation.

Along with unions and farm groups, traditional U.S. fellowship federations were organizational mechanisms for widely distributing civic skills and motivation. Countless churches and voluntary groups of all sizes needed volunteer leaders. Indeed, the largest, nation-spanning voluntary federations could have as many as 15,000 to 17,000 local chapters, each of which needed twelve to eighteen officers and committee leaders each year. Considering just the twenty largest voluntary federations in 1955, my research group estimates that some 3 to 5 percent of the adult population served in leadership roles in that year. Additional recruits were needed each year thereafter, as members moved through ladders of positions and into "past officer" status. And hundreds of smaller federations also needed regular rounds of volunteer leaders.

As they cycled millions of Americans through official responsibilities, classic voluntary federations taught people how to run meetings, handle moneys, keep records, and participate in group discussions. So many officers and activists were required that there were plenty of opportunities for men and women from blue-collar and lower-level white-collar occupations (Rae 2003, chap. 5). Local activists, furthermore, got on leadership ladders that could lead to responsibilities at district, state, and national levels. Some who moved up were ordinary citizens, and even those who were from more elite backgrounds and occupations had to interact with a cross section of fellow citizens to prove their worthiness for higher associational offices.

Not only did popularly rooted unions, farmers' groups, and cross-class federations spread civic skills widely in the population; they also conveyed politically relevant knowledge and motivation. Many membership organizations were directly involved in electoral or legislative campaigns. But even associations that largely stayed out of politics conveyed knowledge and motivation that could be transferred to other endeavors. The constitutions of voluntary federations taught people about parliamentary rules of discussion; about legislative, judicial, and executive functions; about elections or other forms of representative governance; and about the relationship between taxation and collective services. All traditional voluntary associations reinforced ideals of good citizenship, stressing that members in good standing should understand and obey laws, volunteer for military service, engage in public discussions—and, above all, vote. Alan Gerber and Don Green (2000) show that people are more likely to turn out to vote in response to face-to-face appeals, and America's traditional popular associations routinely provided such appeals.

Contrast the workings of traditional, popularly rooted associations with today's professionally run associations that deemphasize active membership. Because patron grants and computerized mass mailings generate money more readily than modest dues repeatedly collected from millions of members, and because paid experts are more highly valued than volunteer leaders for the public functions of today's public-interest groups, the leaders of these groups have little incentive to engage in mass mobilization and no need to share leadership and organizational control with state and local chapters. Why hold membership meetings or invest in building a dense network of chapters if peer networks are not critical to recruitment or resource mobilization? Professional managers have a greater need to pay attention to foundations and wealthy patrons. And they must cultivate access to government professionals in order to be able to claim to their public audiences that they have an impact on public policymaking.

In the case of mailing-list organizations, most adherents are seen as consumers who send money to buy a certain brand of public-interest representation. Repeat adherents, meanwhile, are viewed as potential big donors (Bosso 2003; Jordan and Maloney 1997). Only a tiny fraction of recipients respond to mass mailings, and of those who do send money a first time, only a fraction renew their contributions in later years. Huge and well-targeted mailings can recruit enough of a changing mass of adherents to help keep the professional organization going—especially if respondents can later be winnowed to find substantial repeat donors, people who contribute much more money than nominal "dues."

Indeed, the focus on donors is critical to understanding the socioeconomic moorings of many public-interest associations. Professional advocacy organizations have become more and more money-hungry operations. This tendency interacts with the increasing inequalities in wealth and income in the United States since the 1970s (Danziger and Gottschalk 1995; Mishel, Bernstein, and Boushey 2003). To be sure, rising economic inequalities did not in any simple way *cause* civic reorganization. But the new socioeconomic disparities reinforce the tendency of professionally led associations to orient their appeals toward potential wealthy contributors. Economically privileged supporters are the constituents many associations and nonprofit institutions seek today.

Another important difference between traditional fellowship federations and contemporary public-interest associations is worth underlining. In the past, ordinary Americans joined voluntary membership federations not only because of their political clout—that did matter to many people—but also in search of sociability, recreation, cultural expression, and social assistance. Recruitment occurred through peer networks, and people usually had a mix of reasons for joining. Men and women could be drawn in, initially, for nonpolitical reasons yet later end up learning about public issues or picking up skills or contacts that could be relevant to legislative campaigns or electoral politics or community projects. People could also be drawn in locally yet end up participating in statewide or national campaigns.

But today's public-interest associations are much more specialized and explicitly devoted to particular causes—like saving the environment, or fighting for affirmative action, or opposing high taxes, or promoting "good government." People have to know what they think and have some interest in national politics and the particular issue *before* they send a check. Today's advocacy groups, in short, are not very likely to entice masses of Americans indirectly into democratic politics.

For the reasons just discussed, adherents of contemporary public-interest associations are heavily skewed toward the highly educated upper-middle class. Of course, well-educated and economically privileged Americans have always been differentially engaged in voluntary associations. But there used to be many federations seeking huge numbers of members; and in a country with thin strata of higher-educated and wealthy people, mass associations could thrive only by reaching deeply into the population. Nowadays, we live in a country where the top quarter of the population holds college degrees, because higher education expanded enormously in the late twentieth century (Mare 1995). In consequence, groups seeking mailing-list followings in the tens of thousands to the hundreds of thousands can focus recruitment on the higher-educated—aiming to attract the very Americans who are most likely to know in advance that they care about public issues. These are the people who appreciate the mass mailings that public-interest groups send out. And because higher-educated Americans have experienced sharply rising incomes in recent decades, they are also the folks who can afford to write big checks.

Available evidence on the membership size and characteristics of professionally run public-interest associations is congruent with this interpretation. In 1980 Americans with college degrees constituted 10.7 percent of the national electorate, and those with postgraduate education constituted another 5.5 percent—adding up to 16.2 of the national electorate at that time. Around then, data were collected on the membership sizes and characteristics of a number of public-interest advocacy groups, including Common Cause, the good-government association; NARAL; and five major environmental associations. As figure 3.7 shows, in six cases out of seven, associational memberships in the tens of thousands to hundreds of thousands were highly skewed toward Americans with college or postgraduate degrees. Of all the groups included in figure 3.7, only the largest group, the National Wildlife Federation, had significant chunks of its membership in the "high school graduate or less" and "some college" categories. At the time, this association placed relatively little emphasis on policy appeals to members, and it offered social incentives through a relatively dense nationwide network of state and local chapters. It was also the only major environmental association that relied heavily on material "selective" benefits to attract members. The others stressed policy representation, although the Sierra Club also offered opportunities for social activities to some of its members through a modest-sized network of chapters (Shaiko 1999, chap. 5).

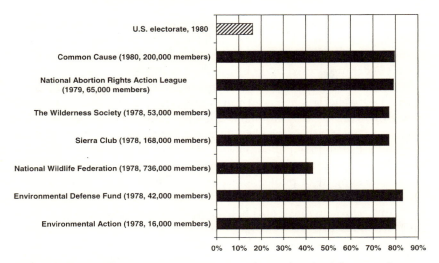

Figure 3.7. College and Postgraduate Members of U.S. Advocacy Groups. *Sources:* Rothenberg 1992, 8–11, 32; Mitchell, McCarthy, and Pearce 1979; Shaiko 1999, 42, 124–25.

Partisanship, Civic Change, and Public Agendas

During an epoch in which partisanship has deepened in electoral politics and the halls of Congress, voluntary associations in America have increasingly sorted themselves along partisan lines—and taken divergent stances on public issues. In the mid-twentieth-century United States, large, cross-class voluntary federations tended to be nonpartisan, so as to appeal to both Democrats and Republicans and cross the divide among whites in the North and the segregationist South. Since the 1970s, however, professionally managed advocacy groups have often identified with either liberal or conservative causes (Berry 1999; Fiorina 1999; Paget 1990; Skerry 1997). And the small numbers of persistent or newly expanded large-scale voluntary membership federations have also sorted themselves along partisan lines; unions have remained on the left, while anti-abortion, pro-gun, and Christian right voluntary federations have flourished on the right.

Ironically, the social-network bases from which conservatives have built vast membership federations tend to be relatively egalitarian compared to the upper-middle-class constituencies disproportionately attracted to liberal mailing-list associations. Church membership is the most socioeconomically equal form of associational involvement (Verba, Schlozman, and Brady 1995, 518–21), and many working-class and lower-middle-class men participate in hunting groups and rifle clubs. Even though hard data are lacking, we can be reasonably certain that Christian right associations and the National Rifle Association include people from a range of occupational strata—just as many traditional, cross-class membership federations used to do before the 1960s.

But if participation in contemporary conservative membership federations is relatively class-balanced and in some respects reminiscent of traditional forms of U.S. associational life, it is also the case that contemporary American conservatives are ideologically strongly opposed to high taxation and redistributive public policies. There is, in short, no correlation today between associations with relatively participatory forms of organization and support of public policies that might seem to further greater socioeconomic equality via progressive taxation or redistributive social programs. Through much of U.S. history, there may have been a stronger correlation, because from the mid-nineteenth through the mid-twentieth century so many popular membership federations championed generous and inclusive public social-expenditure programs, ranging from public schools and social programs for mothers and children and programs for farmers and farm families to the G.I. Bill and Medicare and Social Security (for specifics, see Skocpol 2000, chap. 2). Like traditional federations, contemporary conservative membership federations are mobilizing masses of Americans across class lines to participate actively in community affairs and politics. Yet they are doing so in opposition to public social-welfare programs, on behalf of pro-business agendas, and on behalf of conceptions of community that stress private action and local autonomy.

Meanwhile, today's liberal and middle-of-the-road associations of varying structures and constituencies have a mixed stance toward public policy for redistributive purposes.

In the United States as well as in other advanced-industrial democracies, trade unions expand electoral participation and champion strong and redistributive public social programs (Radcliff and Davis 2000). Most trade unions are aligned with the Democratic Party, just as most Christian right groups are aligned with the Republicans, so we can see that still-existing mass-membership associations are sharply split in their stances toward public policy. But, of course, U.S. trade-union membership—especially in blue-collar private industries—has declined sharply across recent decades (Putnam 2000, 81, fig. 14), weakening this source of widespread popular support for redistributive government. Indeed, with the exception of the service workers, the strongest unions today are organizations of white-collar public employees. Their support for a strong public sector may be intense, but it does not reach as deeply into the ranks of non-college-educated American workers as unions once did.

Do professional advocacy groups take the place of unions and other popularly rooted organizations when it comes to supporting inclusive social programs? With or without mailing-list memberships, some contemporary professional advocacy organizations—such as the Children's Defense Fund—speak unequivocally for programs on behalf of the poor and the racially disadvantaged. And existing public programs for the elderly of all social strata are strongly championed by the AARP and other elder advocacy associations (Campbell 2003; Pratt 1976, 1993). Professionally run groups without mass memberships can take any kind of public policy stance that they can persuade institutional or individual patrons to support with a continuing flow of contributions. And vast mailing-list groups like the AARP can use public policy advocacy to help recruit both individual adherents and institutional patrons. Although I know of no data base that classifies all recently created professional advocacy groups along partisan or public policy dimensions, I think it is safe to guess that only a very small fraction are consistently liberal, or unequivocally champion the needs of the less privileged (a study of groups with a formal presence in Washington, D.C., supports this assertion; see Schlozman, Burch, and Lampert 2004). There is no necessary relationship between organizational structure and resource base, on the one hand, and the purposes for which advocacy organizations agitate, on the other. But there probably is an elective affinity between the increasing professionalization of American voluntary associations and the tilt of public agendas toward causes of interest to the middle class and the wealthy—whether those causes are labeled "conservative" or "liberal." Environmentalism, family values, good government, group rights, and lower taxes—these are the sorts of causes pushed by thousands of professional advocacy groups, as well as by foundations, think tanks, and PACs.

Perhaps the most intriguing evidence on the issue effects of recent civic changes appears in Jeffrey Berry's 1999 book *The New Liberalism.* As Berry's longitudinal research shows, professionally run public-interest groups, many of them championing "new liberal" causes, have increasingly made quality-of-life causes such as environmentalism more visible; and they have often prevailed after going head-to-head with business interests in legislative battles. But Berry also offers some more discouraging data. Recent gains by citizens' associations have crowded out advocacy by unions and other groups speaking for the interests and values of blue-collar Americans. Furthermore, Berry (1999, 57) shows that liberal-leaning citizen advocacy groups have become *less* likely over time to ally with traditional liberal groups on behalf of redistributive social programs. "Liberal citizen groups," he says, "have concentrated on issues that appeal to their middle-class supporters. . . . [A]s the new left grew and grew, the old left was . . . increasingly isolated."[9]

All in all, the reorganization of American civic life since the 1960s has gone hand in hand with a shift of public agendas away from a strong role for government in promoting socioeconomic redistribution. Not only are the largest recently expanding membership federations likely to be conservative in orientation; most of the thousands of recently proliferating professional advocacy groups are at best neutral on issues of socioeconomic redistribution. Many of the new organized voices heard in contemporary American public life may not be oriented to narrowly conceived business interests; thus public discussions have become more wide-ranging, even raucous. But most newly active advocacy associations are speaking for the quality-of-life and economic concerns of well-educated and relatively economically privileged Americans. And if advocacy groups call on government to act, they usually have in mind regulations or court orders or subsidies that are likely to adjust or reinforce rather than mitigate existing class disparities.

Conclusion

Through much of U.S. history, from the mid-nineteenth century through the 1960s, many visible and influential voluntary membership associations took the form of cross-class, chapter-based federations focused on concerns of fellowship and citizenship. Unlike many other industrializing democracies, the United States as late as the era following World War II retained large numbers of cross-class associations, even as the nation also had moderately strong trade unions and associations representing the interests of business people, professionals, and farmers. Traditional membership federations, moreover, paralleled and imitated the arrangements of the U.S. federal government. Bodies existed at the local, state, and national level, taking pride in their "constitutions" with executive, representative, and judicial arrangements just like American government. Members paid taxes called "dues" and elected leaders and representatives. Participants learned the routines of American democracy, and their federations could influence government at all levels.

Culturally and institutionally, in short, much of U.S. associational life existed in close symbiosis with U.S. representative government. It was no coincidence that voluntary associations often championed broad, inclusive, and generous social programs to be enacted and implemented by state and national governments working in close partnership with voluntary membership federations. Government undertakings, such as public education, military veterans' benefits, and Social Security, were not seen as strictly partisan causes, and they were actively championed by popularly rooted voluntary federations that attracted citizens across partisan lines.

But amid the great civic reorganizations of our time, the close links between broadly inclusive security and opportunity programs and popularly rooted membership associations have attenuated. No longer are there large numbers of popularly rooted membership federations, and many of those which still flourish are overtly partisan and in most cases opposed to domestically interventionist government. The enhanced U.S. federal government activism of the 1960s and 1970s often took the form of judicial or regulatory interventions. Ironically, innovative federal interventions into economic and social life initially opened many new advocacy opportunities for liberals. Yet they also provoked powerful counter-actions by conservatives, who proved unusually adept at melding new forms of professional advocacy with populist mobilization against judicial and regulatory initiatives seen as threatening to traditional social practices.

Outside the conservative right, meanwhile, professionally run associations without popular or cross-class followings have become much more the rule these days—and they tend not to espouse redistributive causes or encourage active membership participation. Apart perhaps from conservative evangelical Protestants, most Americans no longer have opportunities to learn the norms and routines of democratic citizenship through active involvement in voluntary associations. And most professional leaders of advocacy groups or nonprofit institutions regard their constituencies as consumers or as clients, rather than as fellow members. Even when professionally run advocacy associations champion public-interest causes or call upon government to take action, they usually call for regulatory adjustments. And the routines of their associational life no longer reinforce norms and practices of representative democratic governance.

The deracination and rightward partisan tilt of civic life in contemporary America is likely to prove highly consequential for the future of democracy and public policy. Inclusive, opportunity-enhancing governance has historically been crucial in the United States, acting as a buffer to the inequalities generated and regenerated by the market. Widespread, active citizenship has been a wellspring of government programs promoting equality and opportunity the United States, thus helping to temper and channel the workings of the market economy. To the degree, therefore, that recent civic reorganizations have loosened long-standing links among popular civic influence, representative democracy, and government involvement in broadly focused social provision, those reorganizations may open the door to the attenuation of shared citizenship and equal opportunity in America's future.

Notes

Although considerably modified and expanded, this chapter draws upon my 2003 presidential address to the American Political Science Association, which was published in the March 2004 issue of *Perspectives on Politics*. For suggested improvements, I am grateful to discussant Kay Lehman Schlozman and other participants in the 4 December 2004, conference on which this volume is based.

1. For a list, see Skocpol 2003, 130–31, table 4.1. The 1 percent of adults threshold refers to men or women alone, for groups that (in practice or formally) consisted only of one gender.

2. Smaller nationwide membership federations also flourished in the immediate post–World War II era—including elite service clubs such as Rotary and the Soroptimists (Charles 1993); civic associations such as the League of Women Voters (L. Young 1989); and dozens of fellowship and cooperative federations with memberships restricted to African Americans or to particular ethnic groups.

3. A recent study (Schlozman, Burch, and Lampert 2004) examining groups with official lobbying representation in Washington, D.C., shows a greater preponderance of business interests than do studies based on counting all nationally visible associations. This study does not examine the period between 1960 and 1980, however; and it counts individual corporations as well as business associations with representation in Washington, D.C. It does seem fair to conclude from this study that business interests have in recent decades remained overwhelmingly preponderant among groups and institutions with formal representation through offices or lawyers operating in Washington, D.C., even though public-interest advocacy groups have also gained ground.

4. When very small groups are factored in, this means that median or mean membership sizes have dropped sharply. A study (D. Smith 1992) of all nonprofit associations listed in the *Encyclopedia of Associations* found a median membership size of about 10,000 in 1962, whereas by 1988 the median membership size was only 1,000, with about half of the 1988 groups reporting no members at all. Examining only associations in the *Encyclopedia* that claimed members, Putnam (2000) found a drop from an average membership of 111,000 in 1956 to an average of 13,000 in 1998. In addition, I looked (Skocpol 1999, 480) more closely at data on "social welfare" and "public-interest" associations founded between 1960 and 1989, groups that survived to be listed in the 1998 *Encyclopedia of Associations*. These groups had time to build memberships if they were trying to do so, yet only tiny fractions had more than 100,000 members, while more than 70 percent either had none or fewer than 1,000 members (in some instances, "memberships" under 1,000 may refer to other organizations, not individuals).

5. Compare the trend in associational proliferation displayed in figure 3.5 to the trends of growth in congressional personal staff and committee staff documented in Ornstein, Mann, and Malbin 2000 (combining the totals given on pp. 131 and 135). For the second half of the twentieth century, the correlation (r) between the increase in national associations and the growth of congressional staff members is 0.94.

6. This generalization may not hold for areas of the United States where churches are the preeminent community institutions. However, if current proponents of expanded public subsidies for "faith-based" social services have their way, an unanticipated effect may be the spread of professionalism into the religious sector as well, displacing the centrality of membership-based fellowship.

7. For overviews of the activities of U.S. foundations, see Kiger 2000; Dowie 2001; Foundation Center 2002. On the extent and effects of foundation funding of associations, see Berry 1977; Gelb and Palley 1982; Jenkins 1998; Jenkins and Halcli 1999.

8. In very recent times, and especially since 2000, nonconservatives have begun to feel excluded from centers of power. Thus it is perhaps not surprising that we see new experiments with federated community organization and popular mobilization in, for example, the labor movement and the environmental movement.

9. A similar conclusion emerges from a study by sociologists Craig Jenkins and Abigail Halcli (1999, 230, 240) of the up to 1 percent of all private foundation grants that channel resources to "previously unorganized or politically excluded" groups. Social movement philanthropy swelled from 21 grants totaling just over a quarter of a million current dollars in 1960 to 3,418 grants channeling more than 88 million current dollars in aid to various causes in 1990. Nevertheless, as the volume of gifts increased, the overall philanthropic effort shifted away from programs intended to further minority rights and economic justice and toward more middle-class causes such as environmentalism, consumer rights, peace and world order, and women's rights.

Chapter Four

Parties, Electoral Participation, and Shifting Voting Blocs

ANDREA LOUISE CAMPBELL

SINCE THE 1960s THE ROLE of the political parties in American politics has fundamentally changed. A series of technological, institutional, legal, and cultural shifts diminished their once central function as the organizers and inclusive mobilizers of American elections. They ceded control over nominations and were pushed aside by new candidate-centered campaigns. Technological advances allowed candidates to speak directly to the people, and the parties lost their monopoly on electoral contestation in the United States.

Faced with this new reality, the parties reconfigured themselves as fund raisers and as providers of services to candidates. In many ways they have performed admirably in their new roles, raising ever greater amounts of money and recruiting and aiding growing legions of candidates. However, the new environment confronting the parties has resulted in two outcomes, one harmful to democratic participation and the other harmful to the Democratic Party.

First, the political parties are now less broad-based mobilizers of American voters than targeted fund raisers and activators of select slices of the electorate (Schier 2000). As campaigns have become more capital-intensive, there is an increased incentive—and increased ability—to target those most likely to vote and to give money. Indeed, over time there is an increasing relationship between party mobilization and voting rates across groups as the parties have honed their strategies, mobilizing the active and abandoning the quiescent. In an earlier era the parties helped enfranchise millions of the disadvantaged, including immigrants, minorities, and workers. Now patterns of party mobilization reinforce rather than combat underlying patterns of political inequality, undermining participatory democracy in the United States.

The second characteristic of this new era is its asymmetric effect: the Republican Party has better adapted to this changed environment. The Democratic Party has lost the enormous advantage in party identification it enjoyed between the 1930s and 1960s, lost partisan control of the

House and Senate, and lost seven of the last ten presidential elections. That the Republican Party is on the rise both within Washington and among the electorate is due partly to serendipity and partly to conscious organizational and strategic choice (aided by Democratic missteps). It helps to be the party of the right in an increasingly center-right country, the party of the affluent in an increasingly money-dominated campaign system, and the party of conservatism in an era of population growth in right-leaning regions. In addition, the party has managed, despite actual performance, to build a reputation as the better steward of the economy (Smith in this volume). But the Republican Party has also benefited from gifted politicians who brought new groups into the Republican fold and from talented party officials who understood far earlier than their Democratic counterparts the potential for direct-mail fund raising, the strengthening of national party committees, and the building of a political farm team even in seemingly noncompetitive states and congressional districts. History tells us that the electoral appeal and strength of each party waxes and wanes over time. Indeed, within the Republican coalition there are significant divisions that may grow over time; at some point, the movement's expansion will reach its natural limit among the electorate. Since the 1960s, however, political conditions and the party's own strategic choices have favored the GOP.

This chapter uses historical and survey data to explore changing patterns of party mobilization, turnout, and partisan identification among the major groups in American politics. It traces the ascent of Republican and conservative forces among American parties and voters and disses which of the cultural, institutional, and structural features that currently favor the Republican Party are ephemeral and which are likely to be more enduring.

TRANSFORMATION OF THE POLITICAL PARTIES

In an earlier era, parties were central to American elections, engaging in broad mobilization efforts. Before advances in mass communications in the 1960s and 1970s, campaigns were labor-intensive affairs, and political parties—from their emergence in modern form in the 1830s to 1960—were uniquely poised to supply both workers and voters (Aldrich 1995). Political machines were active in many areas, most famously in large eastern cities, but also in the Midwest and Great Lakes regions and in the West. These machines could deliver workers and voters in exchange for patronage jobs and other material benefits. Their appeal was social and emotional as well. Political messages were communicated through personal contact; the ward leader or other party functionary making the political appeal was personally known, lived in one's neighborhood, and provided a turkey on Thanksgiving or perhaps a job for one's cousin. This form of mobilization was broad-based, reaching down to lower-income workers, immigrants, and other "common-man" groups, especially in urban areas. The old-fashioned parties were highly effective in eliciting strong party ties and delivering votes.

Since the machine era, American political parties have fundamentally transformed. Change began in the Progressive Era of the early twentieth century with the introduction of voter registration and official, rather than party, ballots. Nonpartisan elections were adopted for municipal offices in some parts of the country. These reforms were successful in reducing patronage in the West, but party machines remained strong through the 1950s in the Northeast and Midwest (Reichley 1992). Nor were New Deal programs fatal to all machines; some party organizations flourished as new resources were pumped into their areas.

The real end of the machines came in the 1950s and especially the 1960s. Even more so than during the New Deal, the machines' welfare functions were overtaken by government programs, and the patronage system was undermined as cities and states professionalized their work forces. With the end of patronage, party leaders were no longer able to provide workers and funds for politicians, and they lost their leverage. Furthermore, with reduced immigration and rising education and income levels, fewer citizens were in need of the machines' services. The migration of blacks to the North in the post-war era also introduced racial tensions into the city machines (Erie 1988). In addition to these forces undermining the machines was the rise of new groups more adept at dealing with the rising activist state; as government activity shifted from distributive policies to increased regulation, specialized interest groups with technical expertise were advantaged over the "more generalist negotiating talents of party leaders" (Silbey 2002, 12).

Moreover, technological change made candidate-centered elections possible. Before, when election campaigns were not only party-dominated but also labor-intensive, the parties, through their strong grass-roots organizations, supplied the manpower. Candidate-centered campaigns are, by contrast, technology-intensive. Advances in mass communications and other technologies facilitated the polling, advertising, fund raising, and travel necessary for the modern candidate (Aldrich 1995, 272). Television made possible direct communication with voters; no longer would candidates have to rely on party workers to be their face to the public.

Political scientist John Aldrich (1995) identifies 1960 as the end of the mass party era. Aided by family wealth, John F. Kennedy built his own campaign organization separate from the Democratic Party. Much as contemporary candidates do, he utilized public opinion polls to discover what issues would sway key electoral groups (L. Jacobs 1993). Even more significantly, he ran in primary elections to prove he was an electable candidate. Direct primaries had been introduced during the Progressive Era, but most expressed presidential preference only—they did not necessarily choose delegates or instruct them how to vote at the national party conventions. Kennedy used primary victories to show that a Catholic could win in Protestant states like West Virginia and thus became the first candidate to "win nomination who *needed* victories in presidential primaries" (Aldrich 1995, 270).

Thus by 1960 technological advances made it possible for candidates to run as individuals, separate from the party organization. Kennedy's strategy demonstrated the important role primaries could potentially play in candidate selection. Then the parties themselves instituted a series of reforms that fundamentally changed their role, ending their power over nomination and turning it over to primary electorates. These reforms were instigated by the Democratic Party in response to an electoral crisis. Ironically, the reforms ultimately proved more harmful to them than to the Republicans.

Reform was prompted by the Democrats' 1968 electoral debacle. President Lyndon B. Johnson, mired in the increasingly unpopular Vietnam War, decided not to run for reelection. Vice President Hubert Humphrey joined the race as the establishment candidate. Wishing to avoid contests with the anti-war candidates, Senator Eugene McCarthy and later Senator Robert F. Kennedy, Humphrey intentionally announced his candidacy after the primary filing deadlines had passed. Thus McCarthy and Kennedy won all fifteen Democratic primaries between them. Humphrey, however, achieved the nomination, which was still controlled by party elites and which could be secured through "behind-the-scenes coalition building" (Aldrich 1995, 255). Particularly in light of his subsequent defeat in the general election, this nomination process was viewed as fundamentally flawed and undemocratic.

After the election, the Democratic Party established the McGovern-Fraser Committee, which sponsored a series of reforms intended to open up the nomination system and encourage more participation from rank-and-file Democrats. In particular new rules intended to make the process more "open, timely, and representative" were adopted. Delegates could no longer be selected by party committees, which were dominated by party leaders, but only by participatory convention or caucus or by primary election. Most states adopted primaries, which were less expensive, simpler logistically, and likely to elicit higher turnout than the convention or caucus alternative. Because of state rule changes to conform to these Democratic reforms, the Republican Party went to a primary system as well. Thus control over party nominations was handed from party elites to primary electorates, and the way to win the nomination altered from courting party leaders to campaigning directly to the public (Bartels 1988). These changes barred anyone from ever again gaining the nomination the way Humphrey had and solidified the contemporary era of the candidate-centered election (Aldrich 1995).

How did parties react to the new reality, that they had lost control over nominations and that candidates could run independently? They reconfigured themselves as providers of services to candidates. A second wave of reform created this strategic opportunity for the political parties: campaign finance regulation. The excesses of fat-cat donations to the Nixon campaign of 1972 prompted the 1974 Federal Election Campaign Act. Along with the act's subsequent amendments and the *Buckley v. Valeo* Supreme Court decision, these reforms limited the size of campaign contributions from individuals and political action committees (PACs). Before, individuals could give unlimited amounts of money to campaigns—literally millions of dollars. The new regulations limited contributions to $1,000 per candidate per election for individuals and $5,000 for PACs.

The cumulative result of these technical, institutional, and legal changes was that candidates were running as individuals; had to mount expensive, media-driven campaigns; and had to do so by raising money in small increments. They needed help. A legion of campaign consultants emerged, from "knowledge" firms that manage data bases of the electorate, to "money" firms that assist with fund-raising, to "media" firms that create advertising materials and devise strategy (Schier 2000, 96-97). But hiring such firms is expensive in itself and represents a bar for many would-be candidates. And so the parties, having lost control over nominations, reinvented themselves as providers of such services to candidates (Aldrich 1995).

On the one hand, the political parties have excelled in their new role. The parties have been able to raise enormous amounts of money and, unlike individual and PAC donors, disburse it in a timely manner, enhancing electoral competition (Aldrich 1995, 273). They provide a marvelous array of polling, media, and policy services to candidates, many of whom cannot otherwise afford them. They also sponsor workshops for prospective candidates, increasing the pool of challengers. The particulars of campaign finance law have resulted in the rejuvenation of state and local parties; national party committees raise more money than they are allowed to spend themselves, and so they send hundreds of millions of dollars to their counterparts at lower levels of the federal system (Bibby 2002).

On the other hand, these technological, institutional, and legal changes have fundamentally altered the nature of political mobilization in the United States, with profound consequences for democratic politics, political inequality, and the prospects for the two major parties. The reimagined parties, despite their enormous bank accounts, have largely lost their grass-roots ties. To the average voter, the face of the major political parties is no longer a ward boss but a computer-generated mass mail letter asking for a donation. While the parties "mobilize" more voters than ever before—44 percent of National Election Study respondents said a political party contacted them during the election season in 2004 compared to 17 percent in 1956–the nature of the contact is fundamentally different. Voters have lost their emotional and social ties to the parties. The political party is yet another professionally run organization like those Theda Skocpol details in this volume—effective fund raisers that do succeed in contacting millions but which no longer forge a personal bond with citizens.[1]

This means two things: first, the political parties now share the same upward socioeconomic tilt in their audience that other fund-raising organizations do. Far from being the broad-based mobilizers of the past, who reached out to rich and poor alike, the political parties now focus their energies on those who can make a donation and who are predisposed to vote. This exacerbates participatory inequality in the United States (Rosenstone and Hansen 1993; Schier 2000). Second, the transfer of nominating control from party bosses to primary electorates increases the power of organized interests within the party coalitions. These organized interests and the party activists who dominate primary electorates are often more interested in ideological purity than in pragmatic compromise. These often "extreme positions" have "further eroded the attachments of many voters to either major party" (Reichley 1992, 317).

IMPLICATIONS FOR THE DEMOCRATIC AND REPUBLICAN PARTIES

These changes have not affected the parties equally: the Republican Party has fared far better, with an increasing share of partisans within the public, continued success at the presidential level, and, after decades of frustration at the hands of Democratic congressional majorities, control of both the House and Senate since 1994. Republican success was not a foregone conclusion. Indeed in 1964, when Democrat Lyndon B. Johnson won a landslide victory in the presidential election and secured enormous margins in the House and Senate, it would have been difficult to imagine the Republican ascendance achieved by 2004. Both parties were subject to "movement politics" starting in the 1960s—the hard right in the Republican Party with Goldwater's nomination in 1964, a liberal version of movement politics arising in the Democratic Party in 1968 (Reichley 1992). Special-interest groups became more dominant after the McGovern-Fraser reforms reduced the roles of party regulars in both parties. The

Republican Party, however, was less harmed by these developments than the Democratic (Ranney 1975; Polsby 1983) and, moreover, strengthened its national party committees and more quickly and adroitly refashioned itself as a provider of services to candidates. Thus, while the Republican Party experienced its ups (1980) and downs (1964, 1992) at the presidential level, it was well poised to take advantage of partisan realignment in the South and to capitalize on early Clinton administration problems to take over Congress in 1994 for the first time in more than forty years. This section explores how strategic choices and missteps by the political parties, as well as larger demographic, geographic, and cultural changes have reshaped the American political landscape from the Great Society to the triumph of an energized conservative movement forty years later.

The Story of the Democrats

Rather than usher in a long period of Democratic dominance of either presidential elections or the American electoral system more generally, the McGovern-Fraser reforms made the party hostage to special-interest groups that were proliferating at the same time. The party also began championing minority rights and abandoned the rhetoric of the "common man." These positions on social issues alienated many of the party's traditional adherents and were exacerbated by the Democrats' failure to convey a consistent message on economic policy (Smith in this volume). Moreover, the Democrats failed to develop a broad-based direct-mail campaign, and so were more beholden to large donors. The Republican Party avoided similar pitfalls, and over time electoral advantage across many societal groups has accrued to the GOP.

The McGovern-Fraser and subsequent reforms were dominated by ideological purists, or "amateur Democrats" (Wilson 1962), who opposed the old machine bosses and who championed liberal causes and descriptive representation among convention delegates. Indeed, for the 1972 election season, there were explicit quotas for convention delegates to ensure the presence of underrepresented groups such as youth, women, and blacks. George McGovern then ran for president under these rules— the very rules he helped craft. He won the nomination but like Humphrey four years earlier lost to Republican Richard Nixon. Democratic tinkering with the nomination process continued, with a new commission suggesting new rules after almost every quadrennial election through 1988.

The overall effect of these rule changes has been problematic for the Democrats. The task of presidential candidates in both parties shifted from appealing to party leaders who controlled slates of delegates to campaigning publicly to win favor among primary voters and participants in the remaining caucuses. These primaries and caucuses were dominated by ideologues and special-interest activists. During the 1960s, the number of interest groups of all sorts expanded dramatically, and these groups took charge of articulating issues, mobilizing voters, and financing campaigns, as well as many other party functions (Silbey 2002). However, while both parties increasingly became "networks of issue activists" (Bibby 2002, 44), the kind of special interests that were ascendant in the Democratic Party were off-putting to many rank-and-file supporters. For example, the "imposition of affirmative action requirements in the Democratic party helped give rise to special-interest caucuses, representing, among others, feminists, blacks, Hispanics, liberal activists, and homosexuals" (Reichley 1992, 345). The results were twofold: the nomination of candidates better suited to pleasing the party activists than to securing broad support in general elections, and the defection of key groups, like white men. As political scientists Jeffrey Berry and Deborah Schildkraut have written, "No one decided that the party would be the party of . . . liberal causes at the expensive of middle-class voters. The Democrats became the party of these causes because it was effectively lobbied" (quoted in Bibby 2002, 44).

These changes can be traced in the party's platforms and in the rhetorical statements of prominent leaders. The language of Democratic Party platforms changed from a rhetoric of "majority rule" to one of "minority rights" (Gerring 1998). From the Populist Era of the 1890s until the 1960s, class-based rhetoric dominated, referring to the "common man" whose advance was impaired by a privileged elite minority that undemocratically controlled industry and government. By the 1960s, however, Democratic rhetoric no longer set "the common people" against a privileged minority but instead "unintentionally" implied that the poor were a separate class of people set apart and different from the "middle class" (Gerring 1998). The opposing minority then became not business and government elites against all workers (poor and middle class alike), but the poor and minority groups against the middle class.

There were two fatal problems with this shift in rhetoric. First, the party abandoned the "class appeal of Populism" and championed instead civil rights and anti-poverty policies that benefited only a small portion of the population, excluding the broader middle class. Turning from representing all workers against a privileged elite, the Democratic Party became the home of a multitude of new groups, each asserting its "own civil, political, and economic rights" (Gerring 1998, 253). Many of these groups had interests far from those of white blue-collar voters, paving the way for Republicans to appeal to these "Reagan Democrats" (Edsall and Edsall 1992).

Second, the Democratic Party shied away from criticizing capital, as it had in the earlier, more radically Populist Era. Indeed, Democratic presidential candidates embraced capitalism and the post-war spread of wealth, and even took pains to distance themselves from labor, which suffered from being associated not with workers but with organized labor (Gerring 1998). At the same time, the party failed to articulate coherent economic policies (Smith in this volume), further losing support among the middle class, union households, and a host of other groups that on objective economic grounds should be Democratic identifiers.

These trends were exacerbated by the failure to develop the party organization. The Democrats were slower than the Republicans to reconfigure their party in light of the new candidate-centered elections that emerged in the 1960s. It was only after the Democrats' huge defeat in 1980–losing the presidency, control of the Senate, and half the party's margin in the House—that entrepreneurs within the party urged outright imitation of the Republicans' party-building and campaign service programs (Herrnson 2002). Charles Manatt became chairman of the Democratic National Committee in 1981 and launched a direct-mail campaign. The Democratic Senatorial Campaign Committee (DSCC) and Democratic Congressional Campaign Committee (DCCC) started catching up with their Republican counterparts; in 1979–80, the Republican committees outspent the Democrats' by a margin of 4.6 to 1; eight years later their advantage was down to 2.1 to 1 (U.S. Bureau of the Census 2001, 254).

To this day, however, the Republicans have the advantage in raising hard money, having a much broader base of partisans who can make $1,000 (now $2,000) campaign contributions (although the Democrats narrowed the gap substantially in 2004). Democrats by contrast are more dependent on a small number of very large donors. Hard-money contribution limits have caused the Democrats to find outlets for their large donors. First they gave "soft money," an outlet opened up by a court decision in the 1990s that allowed the national party committees to raise donations and to spend outside the Federal Election Campaign Act limits; the partisan gap in soft-money receipts between 1992 and 2002 was quite narrow. After the Bipartisan Campaign Reform Act of 2002 banned soft money, large donors gave to 527 organizations—groups codified by the Internal Revenue Service rather than the Federal Election Commission and which can therefore raise and spend unlimited amounts. In the 2004 cycle, these advocacy groups spent on all races $550 million—or about 10 percent more than Democratic and Republican soft money receipts in 2002. Among the presidential-oriented 527s, Democratic groups outspent Republican supporters by three to one (Janofsky 2004).

Some critics believe that the Democrats have lost their ability to mobilize on economic issues because they decline to criticize capital, dependent as they are on large donors. It may not be possible to prove causality in that regard, but certainly the Democrats ceded their rhetorical advantage to the Republicans, allowing them to appeal to the middle class with a populism of the right that extended to both social and economic issues. The rhetorical disadvantage is compounded by the Democrats' failure to develop their party organizations as early and completely as the Republicans.

The Story of the Republicans

In contrast to the Democratic Party, there was considerably less turmoil in the Republican Party concerning the nomination process. Many of the changes implemented by the Democrats inevitably affected the Republicans also, as states changed their laws. But while the Republican Party chooses its convention delegates through primaries as well, this new system proved less problematic for the party, both because its electorate is more homogeneous than the Democrats' and because they implemented rules—like a unit rule whereby the Republican candidate who gets the plurality of votes in a primary state gets all of the state's delegates at the convention—that allow the party to coalesce quickly around a leading candidate.

The Republicans also more quickly reconfigured their national party organizations in light of the new realities of the presidential nomination system. As with the Democrats, the impetus was a political crisis—in this case, Watergate. Not only did President Nixon resign in disgrace, but also Republican candidates at the congressional, gubernatorial, and state legislative levels were trounced. The GOP lost 49 House seats in 1974 and by 1977 controlled only 12 governorships and 4 state legislatures (Herrnson 2002). Battling back from this nadir in the party's fortunes, a new cast of leaders—William Brock at the Republican National Committee (RNC), Representative Guy Vander Jagt (R-MI) at the National Republican Congressional Committee (NRCC), and Senator Bob Packwood (R-OR) at the National Republican Senatorial Committee (NRSC)—built up the national committees both as fund-raising entities and as providers of services to Republican candidates.

Brock's most important decision was to invest in a vast new direct-mail fund-raising campaign. Aided by the party's favorable demographics—Republican identifiers have on average higher incomes and greater education levels than Democratic identifiers—the fund-raising campaign was an enormous success (Herrnson 2002). By 1980 the RNC helped pay the salary of all fifty Republican state chairmen, gave financial support to more than 4,000 state legislative candidates, and sponsored campaign seminars attended by more than 10,000 prospective candidates (Reichley 1992, 355). The NRCC and NRSC pursued similar courses.

Thus with their deep pockets, the national Republican committees were able to fund state parties long before the Democrats followed suit (Bibby

2002), and in the 1990s made almost twice as much in contributions and coordinated expenditures to congressional campaigns (Herrnson 2002).

The Republicans' strategic and monetary advantages came to a head in the election of 1994. For years, the GOP had been recruiting candidates to run for noncompetitive seats, many in the South. This strengthened the state and local party organizations and the candidate pool so that the party could seize the opportunity represented by the 1994 election. A series of Clinton administration scandals and policy failures soured the public's view of government, benefiting the "anti-government" party. Moreover, with good candidates waiting in the wings, backed by an energized NRCC and united by the "Contract with America," the Republican Party was able to capitalize on the political opportunity (Green 1996).

Not only has the Republican Party bested the Democrats in fund raising and party organization. Ideologically the party has ridden the conservative movement to great electoral success and largely avoided the infighting between groups that has plagued the Democrats. Despite the potential for conflict—under the current Republican umbrella there are economic conservatives who want less government involvement and social conservatives who want more, for example—the Republicans thus far have been better able to maintain cohesiveness. One reason is that for all the variety within the Republican Party, Democrats have even greater variation in issue preferences (Mayer 1996). Another reason, according to linguist George Lakoff (2002), is that Republican groups are united under a "strict father" world view that gives rise both to antipathy toward government and to resistance to abortion, feminism, homosexuality and other phenomena that violate this model.

Finally, there is the Republican's embrace of a kind of populism of the right, a rhetoric encompassing both social and economic issues with appeal for a broad and increasing swath of the American electorate. Beginning as early as the 1920s, Republican platforms and leader statements extolled the virtues of the work ethic and of freedom from government (Gerring 1998). The work ethic has been used as a "bludgeon" against the poor and against government bureaucrats, two groups associated with the Democrats. Small business is upheld as a constituency "victimized by government," and the Democrats' plans for everything from affirmative action to universal health care are criticized as "big government" programs undermining the small business owner and the hardworking but embattled middle class. As John Gerring notes, there is an emphasis on volunteerism, the community, private effort, and especially the family. In the 1980s and 1990s this "home-and-hearth" rhetoric was expanded with the extolling of social issues, which benefited the Republicans among southerners and newly political groups like the Christian right.

Moreover, while many commentators attribute Republican electoral success mainly to social and cultural issues (e.g., Frank 2004), the party has long been viewed by voters as the superior handler of the economy as well.[2] As political scientists John Petrocik (1996; Petrocik, Benoit, and Hansen 2003–4) and Mark Smith (in this volume) have shown, Republicans have "owned" the issue of economic stewardship in recent decades. This has proved advantageous for the GOP in several regards. First, with rising economic uncertainty, the economy has increased as an issue concern among the public since the early 1970s, presumably helping the party seen as the issue owner (Smith in this volume). Second, presidential candidates of both parties tend to discuss Republican-owned issues like taxes and spending more than Democratic-owned issues like the welfare state. This occurs perhaps because "most of the problems that presidential candidates are expected to address turn out to be Republican issues" (Petrocik, Benoit, and Hansen 2003–4, 623). Third, the Republican message on the economy, centering on job creation, has been more consistent and appealing than that of Democrats. Indeed, the Democrats' most coherent economic message has been deficit reduction, a policy for which the links to economic prosperity are unclear to many Americans and which is less politically attractive than the Republican mainstays of tax cuts and deregulation (Smith in this volume). The Republican issue advantage on the economy is highly ironic in light of Larry Bartels's finding that in the post-war era the economy has performed better on average under Democratic presidents (lower unemployment, higher GDP growth, same inflation rate). However, Republican presidents have produced higher growth in presidential election years. This successful finessing of the political business cycle may have shifted "the partisan balance of the presidential electorate by three or four percentage points over the entire post-war period" (Bartels 2004, 22).

The Republicans' co-optation of social and economic populism is evidenced by comparing an electoral map of the 1896 election with that of 2000 or 2004: the "red" states that Bush captured are almost precisely the states that Democrat William Jennings Bryan captured in his Populist campaign. Blue becomes red as the Republicans have become the party of the middle class and the small farmer, businessman, and the like. Precisely which groups have abandoned the Democrats and flocked to the Republicans is the subject of the next section.

THE CHANGING AMERICAN ELECTORATE

Both parties have had to reconfigure themselves in an era of money-driven, candidate-centered elections. The electoral success of the Republican Party is a testimony to the GOP's greater ability to survive and even flourish under these changed circumstances. Here we examine the parties' appeals to the dominant groups in American politics and see how the parties' differing reactions to shifting institutional and cultural circumstances play out in their changing electoral coalitions.

The figures reported here are from the National Election Studies (NES), biennial surveys conducted by the University of Michigan since 1952. The focus is on party identification rather than vote choice, although groups' presidential vote choices are considered. Vote choice is more volatile election to election while trends in party identification show the long-term secular movements more relevant to the discussion here. Party identification is the most important factor in vote choice (Green, Palmquist, and Schickler 2002); indeed, it has become a more important predictor of vote choice over time (Bartels 2000). And because it tends to be passed on between generations, party identification is a more durable indicator of the parties' changing fortunes among the electorate.

A large literature in political science concerns realignment—whether a significant and enduring change in the pattern of party identification among the public has taken place. The classic literature agrees on at least three canonical realignments: 1860, when the Republicans replaced the Whigs, who split over slavery; 1896, when the Populists merged with the Democrats, radicalizing that party and ushering in a 30-year era of Republican dominance of national politics; and 1932, when Franklin Delano Roosevelt forged a new coalition behind the Democratic Party that endured at least into the 1960s (Burnham 1970; Key 1955, 1964; Sundquist 1983; but see Mayhew 2002 for a critique).

More controversial is defining what has happened subsequently. Since the 1960s, there have been significant shifts in mass partisanship, but scholars differ in their characterizations. Some authors say that rather than a sudden realignment in the classic sense, there has been a slow resorting—an "issue evolution"—between the parties on the issue of race, beginning with Truman's desegregation of the armed forces in 1948 and culminating in the passage of the Civil Rights and Voting Rights acts by a Democratic-dominated Congress in 1964 and 1965 (Carmines and Stimson 1989). Others say a significant and sustained fall in Democratic partisanship took place between 1980 and 1984 with Ronald Reagan's election (Meffert, Norpoth, and Ruhil 2001). Yet others argue that the 1994 change in party control of Congress marked the culmination of a secular realignment that began in 1980 (Abramowitz and Saunders 1998). Regardless of differences as to whether a classic realignment took place, whether it was a sudden or gradual change, or when exactly it occurred, all of these scholars agree on two things: that something monumental has happened with party identification since the 1960s, and that the advantage—however defined—has redounded to the Republican Party.

The NES party identification questions reveal which respondents are strong or weak partisans and which are independents who lean to one party or true independents. I include independents who lean to one of the parties as party identifiers because research shows that such leaners' turnout and vote choice behavior is at least as partisan as that of weak identifiers (Keith et al. 1992). Doing so gives a view of partisanship that more closely reflects vote choice and party strategy. However, it also disguises the fact that if one considers all independents as a separate group—which they are legally, even if that is not reflected in their electoral behavior—then the precipitous declines in Democratic identification and rise in Republican identification that I describe are actually a decline in Democratic identification, a rise in the number of Independents, and stasis in Republican identification (although an increase for several key groups). In either case, Democrats have lost vote share while Republicans have gained. Table 4.1 lists both measures of party identification for the demographic groups discussed.

The other factor explored is party mobilization—which individuals and groups the parties contacted during the election season. This too comes from self-reports in the NES. Whether one is mobilized to political activity is a major factor in participation (Verba, Schlozman, and Brady 1995). Those contacted by a political party during the election season are more likely to try to persuade others, to work for a party or candidate, to make a campaign donation, and, most important for the discussion here, to vote (Rosenstone and Hansen 1993, 170–73; Wielhouwer and Lockerbie 1994).

In recent years the parties have mobilized record proportions of Americans. From 1956, when the NES first included the party contact item, through 1972, party mobilization rates rose, from 17 percent to 29 percent. After 1972, however, the mobilization rate dropped again, to 20 percent by 1992. Since 1992 party mobilization has soared, to levels far exceeding the previous peaks. The increase can probably be attributed to the vast amounts of money the two major parties have raised since 1992. Figure 4.1 plots the overall mobilization rate and total hard- and soft-money receipts raised by the Democratic and Republican parties from 1976, when Federal Election Commission records begin, to 2004. Between 1976 and 1992, the two major parties raised increasing amounts of money but mobilized fewer voters. After 1992, however, fund raising soared, as did the proportion of the electorate mobilized. Clearly, enough was raised to allow the parties to contact voters in addition to running ads and performing other party activities. The large increase in mobilization after 1992 coincides with the explosion of soft money, although in

TABLE 4.1

TABLE 4.1
Party Identification of Demographic Groups, 1952 versus 2004, by Two Measures

	Year	Leaners as Partisans			Leaners as Independents		
		Democrats + Leaners	Pure Independents	Republicans + Leaners	Democrats	Pure Independents + Leaners	Republicans
All respondents	1952	59	6	35	49	23	28
	2004	50	10	41	32	39	29
Men	1952	59	7	34	48	26	26
	2004	45	10	44	27	43	30
Women	1952	58	5	37	49	21	30
	2004	54	9	37	37	35	28
White Catholics	1960	73	9	19	63	21	17
	1996	53	8	39	41	34	25
White Evangelical Protestants	1960	60	8	32	53	24	23
	1996	40	7	54	28	33	40
White Mainline Protestants	1960	39	9	52	35	21	44
	1996	40	8	52	28	32	40
Blacks	1952	76	4	20	64	21	16
	2004	81	12	7	61	37	2
Nonsouthern white women	1952	50	6	44	42	23	36
	2004	49	8	44	32	35	33
Nonsouthern white men	1952	52	9	40	39	30	32
	2004	41	11	49	19	48	33
Southern white women	1952	81	2	17	75	11	14
	2004	36	8	57	28	26	46
Southern white men	1952	88	2	10	80	13	7
	2004	34	8	58	20	38	43
Low income	1952	63	6	30	55	21	25
	2004	58	12	30	38	43	19
Medium income	1952	63	5	32	54	22	24
	2004	48	8	44	29	42	29
High income	1952	56	6	38	43	27	30
	2004	47	5	48	28	35	37
Married white women	1952	57	4	39	49	21	31
	2004	45	5	50	312	30	38
Unmarried white women	1952	41	10	49	36	22	42
	2004	51	14	35	32	41	27
Married white men	1952	58	7	35	47	26	28
	2004	33	11	56	18	40	42
Unmarried white men	1952	60	10	30	51	26	24
	2004	49	8	43	23	53	24
Age < 35	1952	62	6	32	52	27	21
	2004	57	9	35	32	45	23
Age 65+	1952	52	6	42	46	20	35
	2004	51	11	38	39	33	25
Union members	1952	67	5	29	55	23	22
	2004	59	11	30	40	37	23

Source: National Election Study Cumulative File and 2004 Study.
Note: Comparable denominational measures available for 1960–96 only.

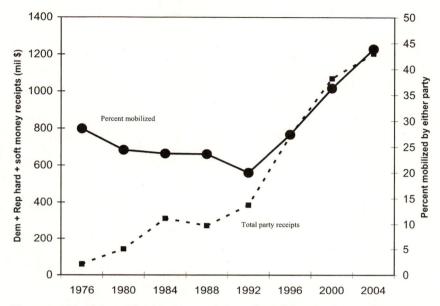

Figure 4.1. Total Party Fund Raising and Overall Mobilization Rate, 1976–2004. *Source:* National Election Study Cumulative File and 2004 Study; Herrnson 2002; and Federal Election Commission 2004.

2004 the parties raised more than ever—$1.2 billion—despite the ban on soft money after the 2002 election.

That party mobilization is increasing might warm the hearts of democratic theorists, suggesting that the parties are reaching out to more and more voters. Indeed, studies show that mobilization has its greatest effects on those ordinarily less likely to vote, like the poor, the less educated, and racial and ethnic minorities (Rosenstone and Hansen 1993, 173). However, those groups are not the targets of mobilization. The political parties, like other "rational prospectors," mobilize those most likely to say yes (Brady, Schlozman, and Verba 1999). Existing patterns of mobilization exacerbate rather than alleviate inequalities in participation.

The positive association between mobilization and voting, found for individuals (Brady, Schlozman, and Verba 1999; Huckfeldt and Sprague 1992), is also seen among politically relevant groups in society. Indeed, over time there is an increasing relationship between mobilization and voting by demographic group. Figure 4.2 shows the rate at which different groups were mobilized and voted in 1956 and 2004. In 1956 group mobilization rates did not vary much. Except for mainline Protestants, only 10 to 20 percent of all group members—a narrow band—said they were contacted by a political party. Also, there was no relationship between

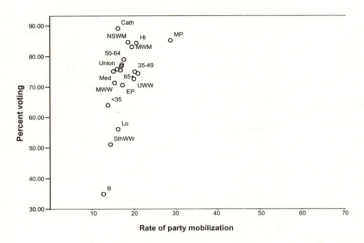

Voting and Mobilization Rates, 1956

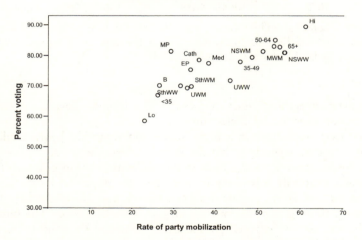

Voting and Mobilization Rates, 2004

Figure 4.2. Voting and Mobilization Rates, 1956 and 2004. *Source:* National Election Study Cumulative File and 2004 Study. Key: Cath = white Catholics; EP = white Evangelical Protestants; MP = white mainline Protestants; B = blacks; NSWW = nonsouthern white women; NSWM = nonsouthern white men; SthWW = southern white women; SthWM = southern white men; Lo = bottom one-third income percentile; Med = middle one-third income percentile; Hi = highest one-third income percentile; MWW = married white women; UWW = unmarried white women; MWM = married white men; UWM = unmarried white men; < 35 = under 35 years old; 35–49 = 35–49 years old; 50–64 = 50–64 years old; 65+ = age 65 and over; Union = union household.

mobilization and voting rates—both high- and low-participation groups were mobilized in the same proportions. By 2004 there is pronounced change. There is both a much greater range of contacting and a strong relationship between party contact and turnout, the result of decades of iterative cycling between mobilization and voting. As the parties have had greater resources and information about voters, they have increasingly mobilized high-turnout groups like the affluent and swing groups like the elderly and white women, while abandoning low turnout groups such as the poor and the young and groups that lean heavily to one party, like blacks.[3] The pattern of 2004 is the culmination of their savvier, more honed strategies. The remainder of this section explores patterns of partisan identification and party targeting by income, age, union status, gender, race, marital status, religion, and region.

Increasing Importance of Affluent Voters

Nowhere are the incentives to mobilize high-turnout (and deep-pocketed) citizens more evident than across income groups. For all the talk of the United States being a "classless" society, a glance at figure 4.3 shows that party identification is structured by class, at least as measured by income. Since these data were first recorded in the 1950s, Democratic identification has been greatest among the bottom third of the income range while Republican identification has been greatest among the top third (these figures are for nonseniors only). In party identification, the parties are mirror images of each other (see also Bartels 2005; Stonecash 2000).

When it comes to mobilization, however, the parties are identical: both the Republicans and the Democrats are most likely to contact top income earners (figure 4.4). Indeed, the rate at which the Democratic Party reaches out to high-income voters doubled from 1980 to 2000, and nearly doubled again in 2004. Democrats may have historically been the party of the little guy, but it is the big guys who get mobilized, because they are more likely to make campaign contributions and to vote. Political scientists Robert Huckfeldt and John Sprague discovered a similar pattern with their network study of mobilization in South Bend, Indiana. They found that the Democratic Party tended to contact the most upscale voters because the criterion for contacting citizens in the general election was voting in the primary, which is structured by income. As in figures 4.3 and 4.4, the "aggregate structure of contacting" was only "weakly related to the social structure underlying party support" (Huckfeldt and Sprague 1992, 78). Thus one difficulty for the Democrats is that their strongest partisans by income are the least attractive electorally. Moreover, the Republican Party seems interested in making inroads into the Democrats'

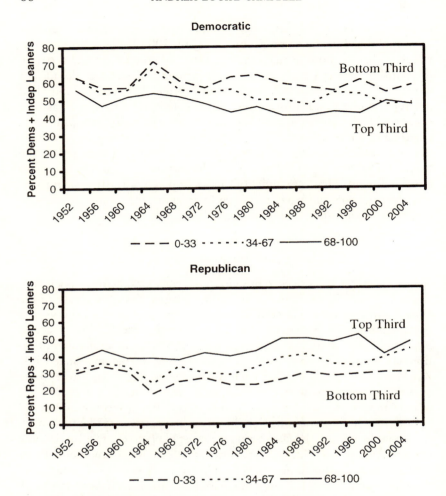

Figure 4.3. Party Identification by Income, among Nonseniors. *Source:* National Election Study Cumulative File and 2004 Study.

traditional class constituency: since 1992, Republican mobilization of low-income voters has increased.

Active Seniors and Absent Youth

While many politically relevant characteristics like race, gender, income, and so on cut across age groups, age remains an important political variable. Campaigns try to mobilize on the basis of age, and commentators often write about the "youth vote" or the "senior bloc."

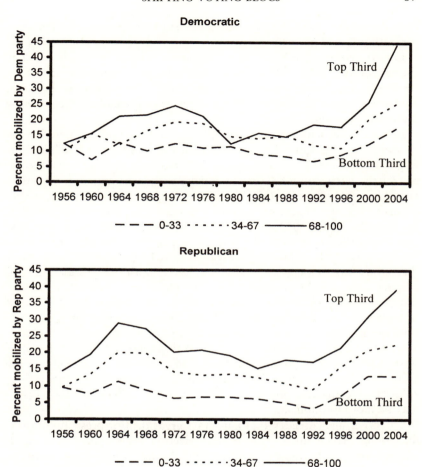

Figure 4.4. Mobilization by Income, among Nonseniors. *Source:* National Election Study Cumulative File and 2004 Study.

In the case of senior citizens, this emphasis on age has an empirical basis. Americans aged sixty-five and older do share some common interests, not because of their age per se, but because Social Security and Medicare, the two largest social welfare programs in the United States, are conferred on the basis of age. These programs forge for this otherwise disparate group a political identity as a program clientele. This provides the basis for mobilization efforts by interest groups and political parties (Campbell 2003). Senior citizens not only have this political identity but also participate in politics at high rates; they vote and make campaign contributions at higher rates than younger citizens. In recent years they have constituted between 25 and 30 percent of voters and contributors for both political parties.

Indeed, senior citizens are the age group most likely to be mobilized by the parties. In 2004 the Democratic Party contacted 41 percent of seniors, the Republican Party 40 percent. In both cases, this is four times the senior contacting rate of the 1950s. For no other age group has party contacting increased as much.

Furthermore, senior citizens are a key group for both parties. The senior population is quite diverse, with wide ranges of income. While some might assume that seniors would be a Democratic-leaning constituency, in fact the party cannot claim the loyalty of a large majority of seniors either because of its historical championing of senior entitlement programs or because of seniors' current dependence on those programs. It is the case that senior citizens socialized to politics during the Depression and World War II are more likely to have Democratic Party identification. And since the mid- to late 1970s, seniors have been modestly more likely than nonseniors to cast Democratic votes at both the presidential and congressional level (Campbell 2003, 71). However, while seniors constituted 26 percent of Clinton's votes in 1996, they constituted 23 percent of Dole's votes (Campbell 2003, 72). In 2000 they voted for George W. Bush at the same rate as other groups, except for those thirty-five to forty-nine, who were more supportive. In 2004 they were less likely to vote for Bush than thirty-five- to sixty-four-year-olds; however, the strength of the GOP vote among sixty- to sixty-four-year-olds suggests that future elderly cohorts—socialized to politics under Eisenhower rather than Roosevelt—may be more Republican.

The other age category that garners a great deal of press attention is the young. Much ink is spilled each election cycle speculating about whether the youth vote can be mobilized. So far no campaign seems to have succeeded. From the modern peak of turnout in 1960, the voting rate of citizens under thirty-five has fallen the most of any age group (from 72 to 58 percent[4] between 1960 and 2000; in contrast, the turnout rate of thirty-five- to forty-nine-year-olds only fell 6 points and turnout for voters fifty and older actually rose). The turnout gap by age is even larger in midterm elections, when just over one-quarter of the under-thirty-five group votes. Youth is also the age group least likely to make campaign contributions, decreasing from 11 percent in 1960 to less than 3 percent in 2000 (while seniors went from 3 percent to more than 14 percent during the same period).

As is the case with senior citizens, young voters are not a monolithic bloc, and the Republican Party seems to recognize this. Democratic mobilization of young voters peaked during the 1960s and early 1970s; since 1980 the rate has been fairly flat, around 10 percent. In most years Democrats contact more young citizens than do Republicans, but in 1996 and 2000, Republicans overtook the Democrats. This is fertile territory for Republicans, as about one-third of young people in recent years identify as Republicans, just slightly lower than among other age groups. However, in 2004 the Democrats reawakened to the youth potential, nearly doubling their mobilization efforts. Youth turnout shot up nine points, and they were the age group most supportive of John Kerry.

Union Households: Still Democratic, but Declining

Unions have long been stalwarts of the Democratic coalition. Union households have retained their Democratic Party identification—60 percent in 1956, 59 percent in 2004–and remain more likely than other households to vote for Democratic presidential candidates. However, the Democrats' margin in union presidential voting has declined over time. In 1956 for example, union households were 17 percent more likely to vote Democrat than Republican; even in 1980, union households were 16 percent more likely to vote Democrat. But by 2000, that margin dropped to 11 points. Of even greater consequence for the long-term fate of the Democratic coalition, union households are declining as a share of the electorate—from one in four as late as 1980, to one in six in 2000.[5]

In 2004 union households represented a ray of hope for the Democrats, much like youth voters. They were 18 points more likely to vote Democratic than Republican, and they increased their share of the electorate over 2000, to one in five. However, while John Kerry won 64 percent of union households' two-party presidential vote in 2004, 2 percent more than Al Gore in 2000, he still won less than Bill Clinton's shares of 68 and 75 percent in 1992 and 1996. And although union households are usually more likely to be contacted by the Democratic Party, the Republicans are catching up. Between 1956 and 2000, the rate of mobilization of non-union households by Republicans doubled, but the mobilization of union households tripled.

Increased Sorting by Gender, Race, and Marital Status

One notable trend of the post-war era has been the increasing electoral importance of women. At one time women were dismissed politically, because they were less likely to vote than men and were thought simply to mirror their husbands when they did. Now, however, women vote at virtually the same rate as men and are just as likely to be mobilized by the political parties. While the turnout gap by gender was 10 to 12 points in the 1950s, and men more likely to be contacted by the parties, women have caught up in both regards.

Despite these similarities in turnout and mobilization, there are major differences in party identification by gender. Between 1964 and 2004, the Democrats lost 16 percent of men, but only 8 percent of women. The Republican Party gained 14 percent of men but only 6 percent of women. In 1964 the Democratic advantage in party identification among men was 61 to 30 percent. In 2004 it had fallen to 45 to 44. In 1964 women too were overwhelmingly identified with the Democratic Party, 62 to 31 percent. But in contrast to men, women were still identifying with the Democratic Party 54 to 37 in 2004. Back in 1956, women were about 6 percent more likely than men to vote Republican for president; by 2004, they were 7 percent less likely to do so.

Political commentators often speak of the "gender gap" and do so in terms suggesting that women are the group that has changed. In fact, the gender gap is caused primarily by the movement of men—especially white men—away from the Democratic Party. For example, in 2004 the same percentage of white women identified with the Democratic Party as did so in 1956–47 percent. But the percentage of white Democratic men dropped from 54 to 39 percent. At the same time, the percentage of white men identifying with the Republican Party climbed from 36 to 51 percent.

Furthermore, the very high percentage of black women identifying with the Democratic Party also increases the overall magnitude of gender differences. With the realignment of the parties around race—a process that began in the 1940s and reached a head in the 1960s—black citizens flocked to the Democratic Party, with identification rates more than 80 percent and Democratic voting more than 90 percent in recent decades. Black women have tended to be even more Democratic than black men.

Not only does race structure the gender gap. So does marital status. Since the 1950s, married white women have become more Republican while their unmarried counterparts (never married, divorced, and widowed) have become more Democratic. By 2004 married white women were Republican by 5 points—50 to 45 percent—while unmarried white women identified with the Democratic Party by a 16-point margin. Indeed, in 2004 married white women were more Republican than white men overall. Married white men also have become significantly more Republican over time, unmarried white men more modestly so.

The increased partisan sorting of gender, race, and marital status groups is due in part to the parties' differential policy stands. Blacks and whites have quite distinct issue opinions (Dawson 1994, 183; Kinder and Sanders 1996), which are reflected in the large gap in party identification by race. Opinion differences by gender are much more muted (Sapiro 2003), and the parties have tried not to polarize on most women's issues outside abortion, given women's crucial place in both parties' coalitions (Sanbonmatsu 2002; but see Wolbrecht 2000).[6] However, the parties have had increasingly distinctive profiles on social issues and the role of government, and men's turn from the Democratic Party is driven largely by the fact that their more conservative attitudes toward social welfare issues began to conform more closely with their party identification starting in the late 1960s (Kaufmann and Petrocik 1999).

Republican Gains across Religious Groups

Some of the most notable shifts in party identification take place along religious lines. The data I examine here are for whites. While the percentage of mainline Protestants who say they are Democrats and Republicans was the same in 1996 as it had been in 1960 (with some mild ups and downs in the intervening period), Democratic Party identification among both Catholics and evangelical Protestants has plummeted, to the benefit of the Republican Party (figure 4.5).[7] The percentage of Catholics identifying as Democrats dropped from 73 percent in 1960 to 53 percent in 1996. There was a 20-point drop among evangelical Protestants as well, from 60 percent to 40 percent. At the same time the percentage of Catholic Republicans increased from 19 to 39 percent and the percentage of evangelical Republicans increased from 32 to 54 percent.

While much of the Republican Party's increase in party identification over time is due to shifts within these two groups, it is only recently that the party stepped up efforts to mobilize them. The Republican mobilization rate of evangelicals was flat to decreasing before ramping up dramatically beginning in 1988, making them the religious group now most likely (by a small margin) to be mobilized by the Republican Party (figure 4.6). Similarly, the mobilization rate of Catholics declined over much of this period, even as Catholics were flocking to the party; only since 1992 has the party significantly increased its mobilization of Catholics.

The Democratic Party has fallen off in the mobilization of mainline Protestants, even though that is the one religious group whose Democratic identification has not decreased significantly. Democratic mobilization of evangelical Protestants is up about 5 percent over 1960 levels, compared to an increase of 12 percent for the Republicans. The mobilization of Catholics too decreased after 1972, although it increased somewhat in 1996.

That evangelical Protestants are increasingly attracted to the Republican Party is a great boost to the party's electoral prospects. Early in the twentieth century, evangelical Protestants rejected politics, both because such worldly pursuits were discouraged by church leaders and because of their "distaste for a larger society that ridiculed their fights against alcohol and evolutionism" (Layman 2001, 10). By the late 1970s and 1980s, however, conservative Christians were encouraged by groups like the Moral

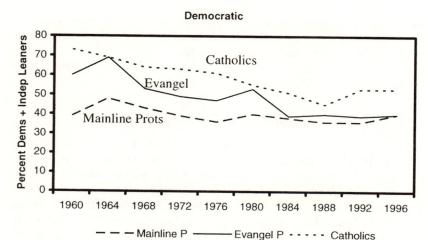

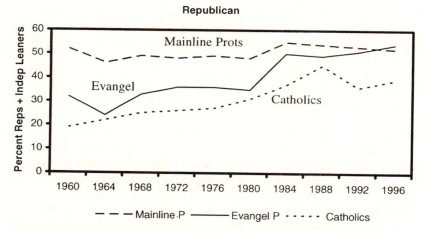

Figure 4.5. Party Identification by Religion, among Whites. *Source:* National Election Study Cumulative File. *Note:* Time series with comparable denominational measures available 1960–96 only.

Majority and later the Christian Coalition and Focus on the Family to engage in political battles over cultural issues. They were spurred by a cumulative series of catalysts—Supreme Court rulings barring school prayer (early 1960s) and permitting abortion (1973), increasing claims of gay rights (late 1970s), and, perhaps most important, a 1978 attempt by the Internal Revenue Service to revoke the tax-exempt status of Christian schools (Stonecash 2000). Ronald Reagan, although not a very religious man himself, appealed to these voters with conservative stances on abor-

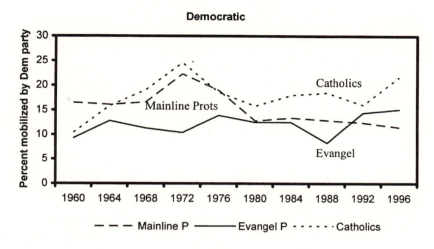

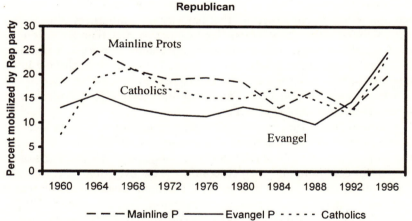

Figure 4.6. Mobilization by Religion, among Whites. *Source:* National Election Study Cumulative File. *Note:* Time series with comparable denominational measures available 1960–96 only.

tion and other issues. They were even more energized by the candidacy of George W. Bush, a born-again Christian, giving him 78 percent of their votes in 2004 according to the national exit poll.[8]

What makes the religious right such a powerful force in American politics, and such an advantage for the Republican Party, which secures most of the group's votes, is not so much its growing numbers—according to the NES, evangelical Protestants constituted 22 percent of all voters in 1960 and 26 percent in 1996–but rather the nature of the church as a mobilizing institution. Despite recent efforts to engage in local-level mobilization (see Bergan et al. 2005), political parties are no longer the proto-typical grass-roots entity—churches are. Moreover, churches are more effective than unions in this regard. There are more church attenders than there are union members; the nature of membership is more intensive; and churches reach down to lower socioeconomic levels (Verba, Schlozman, and Brady 1995, 386–87). Thus the conservative Christian churches are more of a political boon for the party that attracts most of their votes—the Republicans—than are the declining unions for the Democratic Party.

The Rise of a Republican South

Perhaps the most prominent feature of post-war American politics has been the realignment of the political parties around race and the ensuing realignment of southern voters. And once again, the Republican Party is the main beneficiary. For nearly a century after the Civil War and the humiliation of Reconstruction, the majority of southerners were Democrats—conservative Democrats, but Democrats nonetheless, as long as the Republican Party, with whom they might share conservative positions on other issues, remained the party of racial liberalism. Beginning in the late 1940s, however, the parties began to realign around the issue of race (Carmines and Stimson 1989; Black and Black 2002), breaking apart the Democrats' New Deal coalition.

Southern Democrats had been very strong supporters of New Deal legislation in the 1930s—the South as a region received far more in benefits than it paid in taxes. But southerners were uncomfortable members of the New Deal coalition, and their discomfort grew over time. Ideologically, they upheld states' rights and preferred limited government, fearing in particular federal efforts to reduce segregation (Black and Black 1987).

Franklin Delano Roosevelt understood that civil rights could prove explosive for the Democrats, and he succeeded in keeping them off the table. By 1948, however, Truman could no longer ignore the growing presence of blacks in northern cities to whom he had to appeal electorally. He called for a number of civil rights measures such as anti-lynching and anti–poll tax legislation and the establishment of a Civil Rights Commission. Outraged southern Democrats bolted the party, running an alternative candidate, Strom Thurmond, for president on the Dixiecrat ticket (Black and Black 1992). Thurmond won four southern states, and Republican Dewey won most of the Northeast and New York and Pennsylvania, which were still homes to Main Street Republicanism, and a few other states. Truman managed to eke out a narrow victory.

Despite this evidence that race was a divisive issue for the Democrats, the Republicans during the 1950s continued their earlier strong commit-

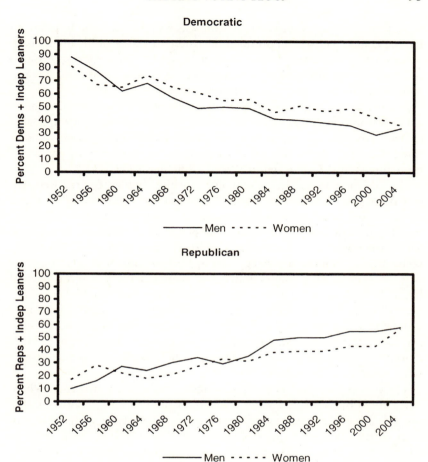

Figure 4.7. Party Identification among Southern Whites. *Source:* National Election Study Cumulative File and 2004 Study.

ment to civil rights (Carmines and Stimson 1989). However, a decline in southern Democratic identification took place even between 1952 and 1960 (figure 4.7).

During the 1960s, party realignment around race was more pronounced—the Democrats became the party of racial liberalism and southern voters moved to the Republican Party. The 1960 Democratic plank was strongly supportive of civil rights, although Kennedy like FDR trod carefully in this area. After Kennedy was assassinated in November 1963, however, Johnson made the passage of the Civil Rights Act of 1964 a memorial to the dead president (Carmines and Stimson 1989). At the same time, the conservative movement was rising within the Republican Party, personified by 1964 presidential candidate Barry Goldwater. A conservative Republican in the new Western mode, he appealed to voters who resented the intrusion of big government, especially the federal government, into their personal and economic lives (Reichley 1992).

Goldwater was not a racist himself, but he objected to federal desegregation efforts on principled conservative grounds. This stance appealed to many southerners, and he won five states—Mississippi, Alabama, Louisiana, Georgia, and South Carolina—where "the Republican party had been almost nonexistent before 1960" (Reichley 1992, 331).

Outside these states, Johnson won a crushing victory. But the Republican Party has had the last laugh. By embracing a philosophy of racial conservatism, small government, and later, conservatism on social issues, the Republican Party has dominated presidential elections ever since. Seeing the potential in Goldwater's regional victories in 1964, Nixon implemented a "Southern strategy" to appeal to conservative Democrats who on many issues might find the Republican Party a more natural home. Indeed, in 1972, Nixon captured 80 percent of the southern presidential vote. Reagan further appealed to southerners and added new groups to those who had supported Goldwater: the religious right and pro-life Catholics (Reichley 1992). Southerners voted Republican by large margins in 1980 and overwhelmingly in 1984, as did evangelical Protestants and many Catholics.

The precipitous shift in party identification among southerners—here represented by the eleven states of the old Confederacy—is shown in figure 4.7. The percentage of southern white men identifying with the Democratic Party has fallen from 88 percent in 1952, to 57 percent in 1968, to 41 percent in 1984, and just 34 percent in 2004. George W. Bush won 71 percent of the southern male vote in 2000. There has been a significant decline of Democratic identification among southern women as well, from 81 to 36 percent between 1952 and 2004, and they gave Bush 65 percent of their votes in 2000 and 70 percent in 2004.[9]

This is the most profound change in American politics. Combined with the population shift—the 11 secession states had 128 electoral college votes in 1950 and 147 in 2000—these changing patterns of party identification and voting have fundamentally altered the political map, to the great advantage of the Republican Party. In both 2000 and 2004 George W. Bush won the now Solid South plus the border states. In 2004 these accounted for 179 of the 270 electoral college votes needed for victory. And in 1994 when the Republicans took control of both the House and Senate for the first time in four decades, the leadership in both chambers was almost exclusively Southern.

Figure 4.8 summarizes the trends in the party identification and mobilization rates of these politically important groups. The vertical axis shows Republican identification divided by Democratic identification for each group; hence groups falling above one are more Republican and those falling below are more Democratic. The horizontal axis shows the rate of Republican mobilization of each group divided by the Democratic mobilization rate; groups falling to the right of one are more likely to be mobilized by the Republican Party and those to the left of one are more likely to be mobilized by the Democrats.

In 1956 all groups except unmarried and nonsouthern white women and mainline Protestants were more likely to be Democratic than Republican, and most groups were more likely to be mobilized by the Democratic Party. In 2000 the picture was completely different. Only blacks and union households were more likely to be mobilized by the Democratic Party. And a host of groups, including some of the largest among the electorate, were more likely to be Republican: southern white men, married white men, unmarried white men, evangelical Protestants, and mainline Protestants. Several others, including married, southern, and nonsouthern white women, high- and medium-income voters, and thirty-five- to forty-nine-year-olds, were close to the line. The formidable advantage in party identification that the Democratic Party enjoyed from the New Deal of the 1930s through the Great Society of the 1960s has largely disappeared. And the Republican Party is out-mobilizing nearly every group in American society, especially southerners and evangelical and mainline Protestants.

Conclusion

Since the 1960s American politics has become more unequal, and patterns of party identification and vote choice more Republican. Both of these trends have their origins in the changing roles of the political parties in the American electoral system. Once broad mobilizers of the public, the parties now face incentives to target high-turnout and affluent groups, and ignore low-turnout groups, which widens the participatory gaps even further. At the same time the Republican Party more effectively adapted to the new era, becoming a formidable fund-raising operation and recruiter and servicer of candidates at all levels of office and in nearly every region of the country.

The Republican Party is now advantaged in mass politics in multiple ways. Partly this is the serendipity of being a party of the right, of affluent groups, and of strong adherents. There are more self-described conservatives than liberals in the United States, and so as party identification has

PID and Mobilization Ratios, 1956

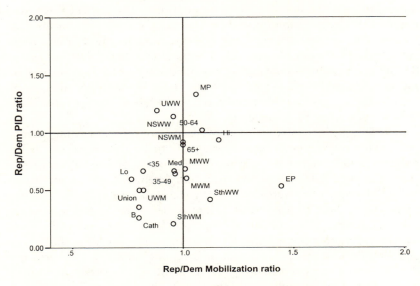

PID and Mobilization Ratios, 2000

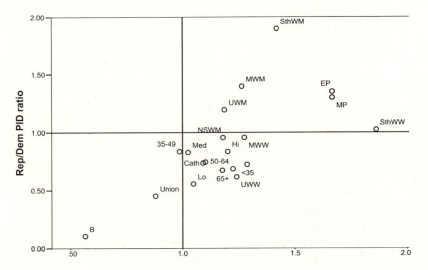

Figure 4.8. Party Identification versus Mobilization Ratios, 1956 and 2000. *Source:* National Election Study Cumulative File. Key: See figure 4.2.

become more closely aligned with ideology over time—as more conservatives regard themselves as Republicans and more liberals as Democrats (largely because of southern realignment, when cross-pressured conservatives finally left the Democratic Party for the Republican)—the Republican Party benefits. The array of interest groups affiliated with the GOP is more homogeneous (Flanigan and Zingale 1998) and happens to include some of the most effective mobilizing agents, like churches. Many conservative groups, like the National Rifle Association and National Right to Life Committee, have combined professional advocacy with a local chapter structure that facilitates grass-roots mobilization (Skocpol in this volume). Other associated groups tend to be affluent—like small-business owners and many professionals and managers—providing an excellent source of campaign funds. In part because of their higher socioeconomic status, Republican identifiers are more likely to vote than Democrats, undermining the Democrats' remaining small partisan advantage (Conway 2000, 167).

Moreover, Republican electoral success is beginning to feed itself, much as Democratic success reinforced itself for much of the mid-twentieth century. During the 1970s, there appeared to be a "dealignment," with new entrants declining to admit any partisan ties and the number of registered independents rising (Wattenberg 1998). The number of independents has now leveled off, and some categories of young people—especially southerners, men, and the affluent—are more Republican than were their parents (Abramowitz and Saunders 1998). One influence seems to be socialization to politics in a post-Reagan world. Another appears to be an embrace of the party in power in Congress—the GOP, from 1994 to 2006.

That much of the American public is on the conservative side of social and cultural issues is also to the Republican advantage (Edsall and Edsall 1992). However, the Republican Party is ascendant not merely because cultural forces favor the party of the right. The GOP also made many wise strategic and institutional choices. It chose to contest elections on social issues. It chose to champion a populism of the right and to define Democratic presidential candidates from Michael Dukakis to John Kerry as elite liberals out of touch with mainstream Americans. It chose to plow money early on into direct mail. It chose to strengthen state party organizations, particularly in the South. It chose to develop a farm team in the hinterland and so became able to capitalize on Democrats' missteps. And despite the fact that economic growth has on average been lower during Republican administrations, the GOP has sustained issue ownership over the economy and prosperity.

However, all hope is not lost for the Democratic Party. Young people—the cohort of the future—were less likely to vote for Bush in 2004 than any other age group. The Democrats showed considerable fund-raising

PID and Mobilization Ratios, 2004

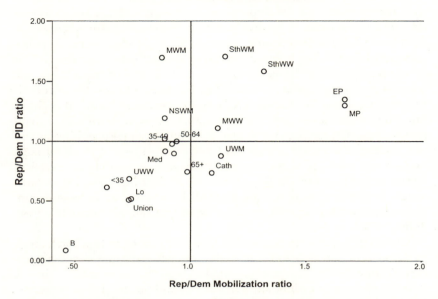

Figure 4.9. Party Identification versus Mobilization Ratios, 2004. *Source:* 2004 National Election Study. Key: See figure 4.2.

prowess in 2004. The DNC raised slightly more than the RNC (although the Republican national committees all together raised more than their Democratic counterparts; see FEC 2004). Democratic-supporting 527 organizations raised more than Republican-leaning ones, especially early in the election season. Howard Dean's campaign showed the potential for the Internet as a fund-raising and organizational device, and his group is now recruiting candidates for office much as Newt Gingrich's did in the early 1990s. The Democrats out-mobilized the Republicans on more groups than in 2000, although these were primarily low-turnout or small groups like low-income voters, youth, blacks, and unmarried white women (figure 4.9).

Perhaps the greatest hope for the Democrats is that Republican margins are not large. In the 2004 election, the Democrats gained ground in governorships, winning six to the Republicans' five. Democrats also advanced modestly at the state legislative level, reducing the Republican advantage in partisan control of legislatures from 21 to 17 (with 11 states with split control) to 20 to 19, with 10 split.[10] The GOP margins in the popular presidential vote and particularly in House and Senate seats in the 2000 through 2004 elections are quite narrow in historical comparison. It is possible that the crises in health insurance and pensions or unease with the Iraq War could lead some voters back to the Democratic Party. There are signs of discord within the Republican Party, with libertarians upset by some domestic anti-terrorism measures and fiscal conservatives by the budget deficits. And of course political parties have long used their time in the wilderness to regroup and come roaring back (Klinkner 1994).

However, the Republican Party now has a structural advantage. Partisan advantage tends to feed upon itself. This occurs in the mass public, where partisanship is often inherited between generations. And this occurs at the elite level, where having control of state legislatures means control over congressional redistricting, and where holding seats at lower levels of government means a steady supply of quality candidates for higher seats. At the congressional level, the Democrats rode such a positive spiral for forty years of partisan control. Whether Republicans, with their much smaller margins, can match that achievement remains to be seen. The coming decades will tell us a great deal about the relative influence of short-term factors like the issues of the day versus long-term factors like redistricting on the electoral and partisan balance between the parties.

In sum, when the role of the parties changed in American politics, the Republican Party far more adeptly and presciently adjusted to the new institutional terrain and is now reaping the benefits. That the present balance will not endure forever does not diminish what is perhaps the greatest contemporary accomplishment of the ascendant conservative movement: the completely transformed map of American politics.

NOTES

I thank Stephen Bird, Barry Burden, Paul Pierson, Theda Skocpol, the participants at the Transformation of an American Polity conference (Harvard University, Cambridge, Mass., 3–4 December 2004), and the anonymous reviewers for their comments on an earlier draft.

1. The efficacy of contemporary mobilization efforts by the parties is disputed. In 2004 voter turnout increased significantly over 2000, from 54.2 percent of eligible voters to 60.3 percent. The parties and their allied groups placed an unusually great emphasis on grass-roots mobilization in 2004. Political scientists estimate, however, that those mobilization efforts accounted for only one-third of the increased turnout (Bergan et al. 2005). Most of the increase was due to the perceived importance of the contest among voters.

2. For critiques of the Frank "culture wars" thesis, see Fiorina et al. 2005 and Ansolabehere, Rodden, and Snyder 2005.

3. On the political and policy marginalization of groups like blacks that are "electorally captured" by one of the parties, see Frymer 1999.

4. These are self-reported turnout rates from the National Election Studies, which are inflated, as many people lie and say they voted when they did not. However, they are still useful in examining change over time and intergroup differences in turnout.

5. See Skocpol in this volume, on the decline in blue-collar trade unions.

6. The parties do have distinctive stances on abortion, and in fact there has been a realignment around the issue. In the early 1970s, Republican members of the public were more pro-choice than Democrats. But Republican members of Congress were already voting in a more pro-life direction than were Democrats, and these differences sharpened after the *Roe v. Wade* decision in 1973 (Adams 1997); now the Republican platform stance on abortion is an extremely conservative one shared by only 10–15 percent of the public. Partly in response to these elite cues, the public has realigned on abortion as well, with Democrats becoming more pro-choice. On other issues, however, like women's labor force participation and entry into politics, the parties have tried to moderate their stances. Economic circumstances mean that many Democratic *and* Republican women must work outside the home, leaving many members of the public "ambivalent" about women's roles (Sanbonmatsu 2002, 182). Neither party has an incentive to antagonize such a large and important political group.

7. Comparable denominational categories are available only for the 1960–96 period.

8. www.cnn.com/election/2004/pages/results/states/US/P/00/epolls.0.html.

9. It is not clear why southern men's Democratic Party identification increased slightly from 29 to 34 percent between 2000 and 2004, or why Bush's vote share fell from 71 to 60 percent. The trends in party identification and vote choice for southern women remain in a pro-Republican direction between 2000 and 2004.

10. http://www.ncsl.org/programs/press/2004/pr041103a.htm.

PART TWO
Conservatives on the Rise

Chapter Five

Seizing Power

CONSERVATIVES AND CONGRESS SINCE THE 1970s

JULIAN E. ZELIZER

THE SCENE SEEMED AS IF someone writing a parody about the American Congress scripted it. In the summer of 2003, the House Ways and Means Committee was debating legislation dealing with pensions and retirement savings. The committee started by reading the language of the bill. Suddenly, committee chairman Bill Thomas (R-CA) introduced a ninety-page substitute measure that had only been released around midnight the previous evening. When New York Democrat Charles Rangel protested that the minority had not been given any opportunity to review the language of the substitute, Thomas ignored him. Condemning what they saw as another attempt by the GOP to use the power of the majority to force legislation down the throats of their opposition, Democrats stormed out of the committee room and into an adjacent library to map out a strategy. Before leaving, Democrats required a full reading of the bill to delay action. A furious Chairman Thomas instructed his staff and the U.S. Capitol Police to round up the Democrats so that the committee could complete its work; Rangel refused to return. Back in the committee room, Thomas dispensed with reading the bill, leading the lone-remaining Democrat, Pete Stark (CA), to protest in vitriolic rhetoric. When Republican Scott McInnis (R-CO) yelled at Stark to shut his mouth, the Californian responded by challenging McInnis to force him to be quiet. In the heat of the moment, Stark called his Republican counterpart a "fruitcake." After the story broke in the media, Republicans said that Democrats were blowing the incident out of proportion and exaggerating events for political effect. "Only one [police officer] walked in, and then walked out, on each of three occasions. For that, [Democrats] want to call us Nazis," complained a Republican aide (Cohen 2003).

While those Americans who noticed this incident were deeply troubled by these events, it was especially disappointing to older liberal Democrats who had struggled in the 1960s and 1970s to bring an end to the committee-era Congress. Although they intended to create an institution that was more progressive, their reforms backfired. The pension confrontation was just one among many stories that revealed how legislators associated with the conservative movement thrived in a congressional process that liberals had helped to create. This chapter examines what went wrong.

During the 1970s, Congress underwent sweeping institutional reforms that closed down an era in legislative history when the chairmen of autonomous committees in the House and Senate dictated the pace of events while operating behind closed doors (for examples of the extensive political science literature on congressional reform in the 1970s, see Shepsle 1989; Polsby 2004; and Sinclair 1989). In addition to electoral changes that resulted in more homogeneous party caucuses, the 1970s congressional reforms had been driven by a liberal coalition of interest groups, legislators, and activists who believed that institutional reform was essential if they wanted to expand the American state into new policy domains and to defend recent gains from retrenchment (Zelizer 2004). While political scientists have focused on the transformation of the committee system, equally important were changes in the media coverage of Congress, campaign finance, and ethics rules. The congressional reforms, broadly defined, of the 1970s fostered decentralization and centralization simultaneously with the hope of creating an institution where strong parties thrived but where it was difficult for legislative leaders to gain the autonomy that committee chairs enjoyed in the previous era.

To the disappointment of liberals, the institutional reforms that were intended to protect the American state created opportunity structures for politicians with a very different policy agenda. During the 1980s, legislators associated with the conservative movement proved adept at working within the new institutional structures of national politics (for discussions of the conservative movement, see McGirr 2001; Perlstein 2001; Schoenwald 2001; Hodgson 1996; Dionne 1991; Nash 1976). Like southern Democrats in the earlier part of the twentieth century, conservative Republicans were highly cognizant that institutions mattered. Conservative Republicans devoted considerable effort to learning how to master the decentralizing processes created by the reforms when they were still a minority (in the 1970s and 1980s) and the centralizing processes when they were a majority (after 1994). Focusing on the House of Representatives, the history presented in this chapter also reveals how congressional conservatives experienced more limited success at curtailing the American state. The tension between the political success of conservatives and their policy failures, namely the endurance of the state in an era when national politics moved to the right, has defined congressional history since the 1960s.

How Congress Was Reformed in the 1970s

The American Congress was a very different place after the 1970s than it was between the 1920s and 1960s. As a result of a reform coalition, electoral transformations in the South and West, as well as changes in institutions external to Congress, the House and Senate moved out of the committee era and into the contemporary era. These institutional changes were extremely important because they changed the fundamental character of legislative politics.

The Committee Era, 1920s–1960s

During the committee era, the chairmen of standing committees held enormous power in both chambers and party caucuses were weak. Committee chairs were shielded from significant pressure because they were selected through seniority, which meant that legislators gained positions of power by remaining in office long enough to reach the highest point in the queue rather than by displaying loyalty to any set of policies or individuals (Hinckley 1971; Polsby, Gallaher, and Rundquist 1969, 787–807; Patterson 1967). Professional norms discouraged mavericks or freshmen from taking action, and there were rarely floor challenges to committee legislation (S. Smith 1989). Even in the Senate, where each individual had the right to filibuster, committee chairs were dominant (Sinclair 1989, 25–28; Matthews 1960). Most deliberations took place behind closed doors. The Board of Education was one of the most famous landmarks of the period, a daily meeting where Speaker Sam Rayburn (D-TX) met, drank, and deliberated with top members of his party to determine how Democrats should act on major issues. The committee system existed in a particular institutional environment, one where the composition of districts favored rural constituents, campaigns revolved around a secretive process that favored concentrated, large contributions, and the print media generally refrained from aggressive investigative reporting.

Politically, southern Democrats were very powerful in the committee era. Southerners enjoyed a large portion of the major chairmanships and relied on a voting alliance with Republicans when legislation that they opposed made it to the floor. Known as "the conservative coalition," southern Democrats and Republicans presented a formidable challenge to liberal presidents and legislators between the 1940s and 1960s on such issues as civil rights legislation and the extension of federal protection for organized labor (Katznelson, Geiger, and Kryder 1993, 283–302; Plotke 1996, 226–61, 350–51; Key 1949, 314–82). Southern conservatives used the pillars of the committee process, such as the House Rules Committee and the House on Un-American Activities Committee, as an institutional base from which to protect themselves from legislative proposals and policy innovations that they opposed (Schickler 2001, 163–74).

The Reform Coalition, 1958–1974

The committee-era Congress ended in the 1970s as a result of several factors. One was the influence of an interinstitutional reform coalition of legislators and interest groups that worked for decades to change the system. They began as a liberal coalition in the 1940s and 1950s, committed to extending New Deal liberalism in areas such as civil rights. Reformers included politicians such as Richard Bolling (Missouri), Hubert Humphrey and Donald Fraser (Minnesota), and Phil Burton (California) as well as organizations like the Americans for Democratic Action, the AFL-CIO, and the NAACP. They morphed into a "reform coalition" in the 1960s by absorbing organizations and individuals (such as Common Cause) who were devoted to broad institutional reform as a end in itself rather than primarily a means to a specific policy objective. The coalition dismantled the procedural foundations of the committee era by obtaining incremental reforms and by taking advantage of focusing events such as scandals and watershed elections.[1]

The coalition believed that institutional reform was essential to expanding the American state. Following three long decades where southern Democrats had used the design of Congress to block important measures, post-war liberals were convinced that if they wanted to create programs that appealed to suburban voters, such as environmental regulations, and to defend hard-fought gains, including civil rights, they needed to transform congressional norms and processes. Much of the policy success of liberalism in the 1960s, according to reformers, had depended on the unusually large Democratic majorities that emerged after the 1964 elections, as well as congressional reforms passed in the early 1960s, such as the expansion of the House Rules Committee.

The coalition obtained many important reforms in the first half of the 1970s. The reforms purposely strengthened decentralization and centralization in both chambers with the intention of creating a system that fostered strong partisanship while forcing party leaders to be responsive to the membership. As a result of the reforms adopted between 1970 and 1978, party caucuses gained power over committees in the House and Senate. They did so as a result of formal mechanisms, such as the adoption of procedures granting caucuses the ability to easily vote on each chairman, the enhancement of party fund-raising mechanisms that allowed leaders to lean on their members, the centralized budget process that protected certain legislation from a filibuster, and more. New informal norms were likewise important, such as the diminished deference exhibited toward committee chairs. At the same time, reformers strengthened the forces of decentralization—thereby curtailing the autonomy of party leaders and allowing individual legislators to influence debate—through a variety of changes. The reformers opened more congressional deliberations to the public and the media, created specialized caucuses, allowed television cameras to cover floor proceedings (although the Senate held off on this change until 1984), codified ethics rules that affected all legislators (including party leaders), strengthened regulations on campaign finance practices, and lowered the number of senators needed to end a filibuster. The Subcommittee Bill of Rights (1973) granted House subcommittee chairs the power to hire staff and ensured them the right to review legislation.

There was some early evidence that the reforms would fulfill the political objectives of liberals. Democrats who entered Congress in the 1970s used the process effectively. California Representative Henry Waxman, for instance, was one of the "Watergate Babies" elected in 1974. Waxman capitalized on the Subcommittee Bill of Rights to use his subcommittee chairmanship to push several important policies—often opposed by senior Democrats—such as national regulations to curb smoking, requirements that automobile manufacturers use tougher safety measures, and new environmental initiatives.

External Institutions and Electoral Change

There were likewise important changes in the institutions external to Congress that weakened the hold of committee chairmen while offering new opportunities for party leaders to enhance their influence, as well as for individual legislators who were outside the leadership. Foremost, the national news media was transformed with the success of adversarial journalism and advent of cable television technology. By the 1980s legislators faced a twenty-four-hour, adversarial media where it was difficult to control or respond to the flow of information. The media environment offered party leaders a way to promote their agenda, as well as a means for mavericks to attack those in power. The Supreme Court, moreover, issued its one-man, one-vote rulings in the early 1960s, which eroded the rural-based legislative districts upon which southern Democratic power had depended. Meanwhile, the proliferation and segmentation of professionally managed interest groups and trade associations made it more difficult for legislators to sustain coalitions. The presidency remained strong, despite the hopes of reformers in the 1970s that they would tame the institution.

In addition to the reforms and institutional changes, electoral transformations greatly impacted Congress. The most important was the success of the Republican Party in breaking the Democratic monopoly in the South. Dixiecrats lost their place in the Democratic Caucus. Republicans won conservative votes in the region. Migration into the South from northern states, facilitated by the advent of air conditioning and suburbanization, created a competitive partisan atmosphere in a region once dominated by Democrats (Polsby 2004). As Republicans gained a stronger foothold in the southern states, conservatives lost their centrality within the Democratic Party (Black and Black 2002). The result was that congressional Democrats moved further to the left. More dramatically though, the GOP moved sharply to the right as the party absorbed southern conservatives and abandoned northeastern liberals. The persistence of partisan gerrymandering resulted in a diminishing number of competitive seats. As primaries became the central contest for legislators in every region of the country, they played to the extreme elements of their constituency who tended to turn out to vote in the primaries. With moderates dwindling in both parties, the electoral incentives in the 1990s were for legislators to vote exclusively along party lines (Rohde 1991; Binder 1996, 36–39).

The Contemporary Congress

The contemporary Congress is quite different from the committee-era Congress. Since the 1960s, party caucuses have been the dominant force in the institution. Party leaders have a large number of institutional weapons at their disposal. This is true in the Senate, where the filibuster still offers individuals a tool to block legislative progress. Senate party leaders have used the post-1974 budget process to avoid filibusters and campaign funds to maintain party cohesion. Even the filibuster has turned into a tool of party warfare since the 1970s, as opposed to one primarily used by bipartisan factions or individual legislators. Scandal warfare has also become normalized in both chambers, as politicians have been willing to engage in the politics of personal destruction to achieve improved political standing (Ginsberg and Shefter 2002). Strong partisanship and scandal warfare—facilitated by the rules of the game and electoral incentives—have made it extremely difficult to devise durable compromises, as Nolan McCarty reveals in his chapter. Finally, both chambers are more open to public scrutiny as a result of sunshine reforms and the twenty-four-hour media environment.

While parties are strong in the contemporary Congress, party leaders continually encounter many threats and challenges. The legislative process crafted in the 1970s offered considerable political space for mavericks, specialized caucuses, the chamber minority, disaffected legislators, and others to challenge leaders through ethics rules, scandal warfare, and the media. Congress is much more open to public scrutiny in the current era, and that meant that it was far more difficult for leaders to shield themselves and control political outcomes. All legislators, including party leaders, are forced to maneuver within an endless and instant news cycle that could be perilous to politicians caught in a frenzy.

The Conservative Movement

The new legislative process turned out to be central to the fortunes of the conservative movement. The conservative movement that emerged in the 1970s constituted several networks, individual leaders, and organizations that had formed in response to liberalism. Conservatives defined themselves in opposition to Great Society liberalism. The continued growth of the American state in the 1970s belied the notion that Richard Nixon's election as president in 1968 had marked the defeat of American liberalism. "Looking back on the budget, economic and social policies of the Republican years," lamented Nixon's conservative speechwriter Pat Buchanan in 1976, "it would not be unfair to conclude that the political verdict of 1968 had brought reaffirmation, rather than repudiation, of Great Society liberalism" (Hayward 2001, 286). In domestic policy, the federal government was expanding in size and substance. In foreign policy, conservatives felt that politicians were hamstrung by the legacy of Vietnam. Nixon's presidency had been especially disappointing to conservative activists. The onetime darling of anti-communist conservatives had campaigned in 1968 by promising to represent the concerns of the right, yet he ended up presiding over a massive expansion of the federal government before resigning from office in 1974. He also introduced the policy of détente, whereby the United States negotiated with the Soviet Union and China over arms limitations and trade. Making matters worse, the Watergate scandal threatened to destroy the party vehicle through which conservatives hoped to reclaim control of government. The "New Right," as they were often called, hoped to reverse these trends by tapping into the conservative traditions of America and giving them organizational muscle: "The conservatism was always there," wrote direct-mail guru Richard Viguerie. "It took the new right to give it leadership, organization, and direction" (Viguerie 1981, 6).

The Meanings of Modern Conservatism

Within the broad context of opposing the growth of domestic programs and attacks on post-Vietnam foreign policy, the conservative movement included several factions. Neoconservatives were former New Deal Democrats who had grown disaffected with the Democratic Party as its members turned leftward on foreign policy and social issues in the 1960s. The religious right, consisting of individuals who had become frustrated with the dominant social and cultural norms of the country, was rooted in the South and Southwest. Members who identified with the religious right were concerned with a series of Supreme Court decisions in the 1960s and 1970s that outlawed school prayer, limited the power of the government to regulate obscenity, allowed for the sale of sexual contraception and the medical practice of abortion, and protected the rights of criminals. Furthermore, the movement included business and financial leaders whose main policy concerns were deregulation and lowering federal taxes.

Although there were many areas of disagreement within the conservative movement, the various factions did share certain common beliefs: these included the need for a strong military stand against communism and other international threats, the centrality of tax reductions to overcome stagflation and revive the economy, and the belief that the 1960s was a decade when American society moved in the wrong direction. The conservative movement defined itself through a distinct set of organizations that represented these concerns before members of Congress. Terry Dolan headed the National Conservative Political Action Committee, which was devoted to promoting the New Right. Campaign specialist Richard Viguerie taught conservatives to use direct mail to solicit small contributions from a broad base of citizens. Paul Weyrich organized the Committee for the Survival of a Free Congress, which assisted allied legislators in their rise to power through fund raising, propaganda, and grassroots organizing. Conservatives relied on certain think tanks, both new and old, such as the American Enterprise Institute and the Cato Institute, to promote ideas that could be used against liberal programs. One of the most influential of these think tanks was the Heritage Foundation, formed in 1973 by Joseph Coors, Paul Weyrich, Richard Scaife, and Edward Noble. Heritage abandoned the restrained approach of the Brookings Institution by packaging and promoting ideas aggressively and with the intention of providing political advocacy information.

The conservative movement was thoroughly partisan since its inception. To a greater extent than most twentieth-century social movements, conservatism not only linked itself to a political party (Republicans) but also committed a large amount of resources to improving the party's electoral standing. Although the movement reached out to the remaining southern conservative Democrats, most of the individuals and organizations associated with the movement staked their fortunes on the GOP. As Hodgson (2004, 38) wrote, "the conservative movement came of age. In the 1970s it captured the Republican Party."

CONGRESSIONAL CONSERVATIVES AND THE
POWER OF DECENTRALIZATION, 1978–1993

Because conservatives felt that they had been excluded from power for three decades, movement activists were keenly sensitive to the way in which institutions mattered. Although voters determined whether someone entered office, conservative Republicans believed that institutional politics held a key to success once a person was elected. The institutional reforms of liberals in the early 1970s, they were quick to see, offered opportunity structures for conducting attacks against the state, rather than just expanding it. Congress was a primary arena where conservatives felt as if they needed to thrive. The challenge was not simply to become a majority in both chambers, but to learn to use the institution more effectively even when they were a minority. There was a cohort of young Republicans who entered Congress between 1972 and 1982 who were closely linked to the conservative movement. Many were southern, southwestern, or western conservatives who came into Congress with a strong ideological mission, yet they were simultaneously committed to playing hardball politics so that they were not relegated to the margins. In the early years, they capitalized on the decentralizing reforms of the 1970s to cause enormous problems for Democrats. At first, the senior leaders of the party looked at them with suspicion and feared that their renegade attitude would subvert the effectiveness of the GOP at influencing legislation and isolate Republicans from the mainstream electorate.

The Young Turks, 1972–1982

The most prominent conservative Republicans came from the South and the West and were on a crusade to transform the GOP. They came from all walks of life. There were intellectuals in this group. One of them was Newt Gingrich, a brash and idealistic army brat who spent much of his youth traveling through the United States and Europe. Born in 1943 in Pennsylvania, his biological father was an alcoholic with a nasty temper who left the family when Newt was three years old. His mother remarried to Bob Gingrich, a tough disciplinarian. Gingrich earned his Ph.D. in history at Tulane University in 1971. He taught for several years at West Georgia College. It took Gingrich several attempts to win a seat in the House to represent the sixth congressional district of Georgia (which stretched from the Atlanta suburbs to rural west Georgia). After losing in 1974 and 1976, Gingrich won the seat when John Flynt, a southern conservative Democrat, vacated it in 1978. In his first two campaigns, Gingrich had run as a southern moderate. In the last campaign, he ran as a conservative. In contrast, Flynt had become alienated from the voters in his district as a result of suburbanization and redistricting (Fenno 2000). Gingrich was known for having a brilliant intellect. He could comprehend broad political trends in deep historical context. Critics, and allies, also knew that he suffered from a massive ego as well, as indicated in the tendency to overplay his hand. Furthermore, his emphasis on big ideas sometimes led him to overlook practical strategy. "If I have any criticisms of your style at all," Republican Dick Armey wrote Gingrich in October 1993, "it would be that you sometimes allow the forest to obscure the trees" (Garrett 2005, 281).

Other movement Republicans entered Congress through the traditional path of law. Trent Lott of Mississippi was born in 1941 and raised in Pascagoula, Mississippi. His father was a shipyard worker and a teacher. After graduating from the University of Mississippi law school, he practiced law at a private firm and worked for the notorious conservative southern Democrat, William Colmer (D-MS), Howard Smith's (D-VA) chief ally on the House Rules Committee. Symbolizing the regional shift that was taking place during this period, Lott replaced Colmer in 1972, who endorsed his protégé. As the youngest member of the House Judiciary Committee, Lott stood as one of Nixon's most ardent defenders during Watergate. Lott moved up the ranks of the party quickly, becoming whip in 1980. While he earned a public reputation for conservatism, he consistently showed his inclination to negotiate and make deals.

A few were journalists. John Vincent Weber (known as Vin Weber) grew up in Minnesota and studied political science at the state university. Weber spent a few years co-publishing his family's newspaper, the *Murray County Herald*, and managed the U.S. Senate campaign of Rudy Boschwitz in 1978. Constituents in the sixth district of Minnesota elected Weber to represent them in the House in 1980. He was skilled at using computers in fund raising and using television in politics.

Finally, there were many career politicians who, ironically, came to embody a movement that bashed politicians. The most famous example was Richard Cheney of Wyoming. Before entering Congress, Cheney had gained considerable experience in the executive branch, such as serving as chief of staff for President Gerald Ford in 1975 and 1976. Cheney had been greatly disappointed when Ford courted Republican moderates on issues such as détente, at the expense of pleasing the right-wing, who almost helped Ronald Reagan win the party nomination in 1976. When the representative of Wyoming, Democrat Teno Roncalio, retired in 1977 Cheney ran for the seat. Despite suffering a heart attack during the campaign, he won at thirty-seven years of age. Cheney avoided the spotlight, preferring to work behind the scenes. He was a conservative on both domestic and foreign policy.

Gingrich, Lott, Cheney, Weber, and other young Republicans kept close contact with conservative activists about the progress of "the coalition" in weakening Democratic power.[2] As a minority, they wanted to bring the Democrats to their knees and were determined to turn the GOP into a congressional majority. When Republicans took control of the Senate in 1980, their enthusiasm only grew in the anticipation of united government.

Not surprisingly, the young Republicans adopted similar legislative tactics as the Democratic Watergate Babies. Both cohorts had entered right as the committee-era Congress came to an end. Members of this legislative generation, both Republicans and Democrats, were comfortable with post-committee legislative politics because this was the process they experienced from the start. They were familiar with partisan decision making, using scandal warfare as a normal tactic of battle, maneuvering through the decentralized opportunity structures offered by subcommittees and specialized caucuses, and surviving in the news cycle of television. Regarding the importance of television, for instance, Gingrich explained that "television is the dominant medium of our society . . . the guys and gals in Congress who don't master it get killed" (Lamb 1998, 117).

Just like the Watergate Babies, young conservative Republicans made their voices heard immediately upon entering office. Elected in 1978, Daniel Lungren (R-CA), explained:

> We didn't come here accepting that things take time and compromise. We wanted to challenge the institution and raise issues that ought to be raised . . . we have to be willing to shake up the system in the House in ways that may make us uncomfortable . . . because there is a natural tendency to want to be liked. No one, for example, wants to read in the newspapers that the Speaker called us ruthless, as he did, or wants to call for votes that inconvenience other Members. (Cohen 1984, 413–17)

In 1979 and 1980 the new House Republicans held more than forty meetings to discuss pending legislation. Gingrich organized an informal strategy group to coordinate legislative and political action (Cohen 1980). While reaching out to the Republican leadership, the younger Republicans were simultaneously critical of House Minority Leader Robert Michel, a plainspoken Illinois representative whose proclivity was to work with Democrats when possible. Michel disapproved of Gingrich's tactics. Rejecting Michel's accommodationist approach, Gingrich explained in 1982 that "the best Republican strategy is to recognize that the Democrats run the House and will do all they can to butcher the budget. . . . We should point out their obstruction from now until November and emphasize the opportunities of the Reagan budget. Bob Michel should relax, concentrate on the impotence of Tip O'Neill and refuse to take up the burden of being Speaker himself" (Cohen 1982; see also Cohen 1981). Gingrich saw guerrilla warfare as a defensive tactic: "Liberal Democrats intend to act bipartisan before the news media while acting ruthlessly partisan in changing the rules of the House, stacking committees, apportioning staff and questioning the administration."[3]

Most young conservatives were devout followers of President Ronald Reagan, whose election in 1980 symbolized to them a watershed moment akin to the election of Franklin Roosevelt for liberals. They believed that Reagan could bring together the diverse coalition that constituted the conservative movement and articulate their ideas in a fashion that would attract broad-based support from the population. They perceived the historic tax cut that the Reagan administration moved through Congress in 1981 as a turning point in American politics. While the Republican Party had always tended to balance the demands of tax and deficit reductions, Gingrich's cohort was much more interested in tax cuts. A large number of the younger members, including Gingrich, had run on this issue in the 1978 congressional elections (Hayward 2001, 529–30). New York Representative, and former professional football player, Jack Kemp became an intellectual guru for the group by promoting a theory of economics whereby tax cuts for the wealthy would trickle down to help everyone and eliminate deficits by bringing money to the federal government through economic growth. Gingrich was even willing to freeze defense spending to save tax cuts (White and Wildavsky 1989, 359). He was not alone. In the 1980s Grover Norquist, president of a conservative advocacy group called Americans for Tax Reform, convinced more than 90 percent of House Republicans to sign a pledge stating that they would never vote to raise taxes under any circumstances (Gourevitch 2004).

Yet within a few years of Reagan's election, many movement conservatives were frustrated because so many of his policy promises seemed unfulfilled. For instance, the administration compromised by agreeing to sizable tax increases to reduce the federal deficit. The failure to restrain the federal tax system emerged as one of the central fault lines that divided these young conservatives from older members of the Republican Party. Responding to the 1983 tax increase, Gingrich (1983, 30–32) wrote: "From January to August of 1981, it [the nation] lived through a truly revolutionary period in the tradition of the early New Deal. We conservatives began to change the direction of federal spending, we changed the direction of national defense, we changed the pattern of regulatory bureaucracy, and we changed the pattern of taxation. But from that point to the present, we have essentially been muddling." Gingrich feared that the administration had been captured by moderates, who he defined as "people who articulate conservative goals and beliefs but who try to govern inside Washington. They believe that, in the end, you have to compromise inside Washington and that you have to govern within the values of that city, which is by definition impossible."

The Conservative Opportunity Society, 1983–1989

Exercising control in the House, Gingrich and his colleagues concluded, was essential if Republicans wanted to fulfill the Reagan revolution. After all, the House constituted a liberal bastion in a federal government now dominated by a Republican president and Senate. Like the persistence of a big federal government, the continued power of House Democrats—who used the centralizing procedures obtained in the 1970s to manhandle the GOP and isolate conservatives within their own ranks—greatly frustrated conservative Republicans. The young maverick Republicans formed the Conservative Opportunity Society (in 1983) as a vehicle to promote their message and to design legislative strategy. They defined the term in opposition to the liberal welfare state, which they hoped that they could replace through their bold policies (Broder 1983).

COS was created following a weekend conference in Baltimore, chaired by Newt Gingrich and freshman Connie Mack (Florida), where Republicans spent most of their time trading war stories about how Democrats used the procedural power of the majority to stifle their participation (Cohen 1984). During the Baltimore meeting, they divided themselves up with different tasks. Gingrich would be in charge of formulating policy and tactics. Vin Weber was named the coordinator because he was well liked by his colleagues. Robert Walker, another member of the group who represented Pennsylvania, was made floor leader because of his knowledge about parliamentary tactics and reputation for being willing to be aggressive when needed. "Oh, yeah, they think I'm a pain," Walker said in one interview. "But see, you don't win a lot of friends in my job" (Reid 1984). Following the conference, COS started to meet every Wednesday morning in the office of Vin Weber. COS realized that the procedures and norms of the post-committee House offered numerous methods for challenging the majority. Cheney, who had clout with senior GOP members as a result of his work in the Ford administration, served as a liaison between COS and the leadership. "I was the grease between the grinding gears to some extent," he said (Remini 2006, 463).

Just as the Democratic Study Group had offered young liberals assistance in the 1960s, COS worked with Republicans elected in 1984 who were seeking a different kind of conservative politics. Gingrich and his allies, for instance, were quick to embrace Tom DeLay, who was elected in 1984 to represent the suburbs of Houston and symbolized the rising power of affluent suburban conservative Republicans. This Texan was just the kind of legislator COS was looking for, one with a strong commitment to the ideological principles of modern conservatism and a brazen individual who was willing to use the toughest of tactics to combat Democrats and moderate Republicans. DeLay was born in Laredo, Texas, to a family that was in the oil business. He graduated from the University of Houston in 1970. While he was the owner of a pest control company, DeLay developed an intense dislike for federal agencies (particularly the Environmental Protection Agency). He served for six years in the state House of Texas before winning election to the U.S. House in 1984. A devout Baptist, DeLay's twenty-second district was a model of the new suburban South, filled with up-scale residential developments as well as churches and civic associations. While Anglo-Americans constituted the largest part of his solidly Republican district, there was a sizable percentage of Hispanics and Asians. If the 1960s counter-culture had redefined American culture, most of his constituents had missed the news.

COS conceived of numerous plans to achieve their objectives. Gingrich, for example, devised an elaborate media strategy for Republicans. He urged GOP legislators to coordinate their responses for national interviews on the evening news shows and on the Sunday morning talk shows in order to offer a consistent message. Gingrich implored Republicans to act as partisans in front of reporters by pinning blame on Democrats and claiming credit for themselves.[4] Although Michel and other senior leaders initially dismissed Gingrich's media ideas, they gradually embraced them as their own after they began to realize that COS was succeeding at influencing the agenda and building a following. For example, the GOP leadership adopted a central tactic of Gingrich's group when they launched a well-coordinated national media campaign depicting Democrats as corrupt.[5]

COS used the post-committee legislative process effectively. "It is my tactic to confront them so hard they have to respond," Gingrich said (Rogers 1984). As a minority, for example, the Republicans understood that the televised Congress (the House authorized televised floor proceedings in 1978, and C-SPAN was founded in 1979) could be used as an effective weapon for individuals and the minority to challenge the party in power. Although C-SPAN was a small station compared to the networks, Gingrich concluded that the small viewership still ranged between a quarter of a million to half a million people each day. "My test was very simple," Gingrich explained, "How far would you go to speak to five thousand people. The average politician would go around the planet" (Clift and Brazaitis 1996, 228). In 1984 COS coordinated televised one-minute and special-order speeches on C-SPAN where they attacked Democrats for various policy issues. The practice became the center of controversy

in May 1984, when COS members criticized the foreign policy positions
of Democrats. After each speech, Republicans would ask Democrats to
respond to the charges of their being weak on fighting communism. Viewers were unaware that the chamber was empty, so it appeared as if Democrats had nothing to say. David Obey (D-WI) compared this to the anti-
communist scares of the 1950s: "He may look prettier than Joe McCarthy,
but 'it still looks like a duck to me.' "[6] Speaker O'Neill was livid when
COS attacked his close friend Eddie Boland (D-MA). "What really infuri-
ated me about these guys," O'Neill later recalled, "is that they had no real
interest in legislation. As far as they were concerned, the House was no
more than a pulpit, a sound stage from which to reach the people at home.
If the TV cameras were facing the city dump, that's where they'd be speaking" (O'Neill and Novak 1987, 353–54). To retaliate for the attacks, the
Speaker ordered the cameraman to pan the chamber in order to show that
it was empty (thereby violating the rules of the House). Although at first
"CAMSCAM" seemed to reveal the tricks that COS employed, COS
turned the incident against O'Neill by launching television ads that depicted the Speaker as a corrupt boss who violated and manipulated the
rules. Jack Kemp wrote Republicans: "Since he has become Speaker in
1977, he has manipulated and maneuvered the system to insure his iron-
fisted control." With CAMSCAM, Kemp argued: "O'Neill alone altered
procedure and tried to use the televising of the House to embarrass the
Republicans."[7] All of the three major networks covered the events, so Gingrich's name gained national attention.

The incident established COS as a serious player in the Republican
Party. Understanding the irony of how events unfolded, O'Neill said to
Gingrich that "when I came out on the floor and attacked you, you were
nothing but backbench-rabble rousers. I made you" (Farrell 2001, 636).
In January 1984 the Conservative Opportunity Society drafted its own
budget, which included curtailing the growth of Medicare and across-the-
board freezes on domestic programs. Gingrich publicly criticized Reagan
for "feeding the liberal welfare state instead of changing it" (Birnbaum
1984). In the summer of 1984, the young Republicans shunted moderates
such as Robert Dole (Kansas) and Howard Baker (Tennessee) and rewrote
the Republican platform. Describing himself as a "visionary conservative," Gingrich wanted Reagan to launch a "dynamic, audacious first 100
days reminiscent of [Franklin] Roosevelt's first term" (Thomas 1984, 34–
35). Some moderate Republicans were angry. Jim Leach of Iowa, head of
the Republican Mainstream Committee, said of the revised platform: "I
do not identify with the Republican platform and view it as an embar-
rassment. I will run on my record" (*U.S. News and World Report* 1984,
23). But these kinds of activities gave the impression that House Republicans were now the source of ideas in the GOP. Former Indiana representa-

tive Dan Quayle, elected to the Senate in 1980, said of Gingrich and his allies: "They are conducting the intellectual work of the Republican Party" (Shribman and Rogers 1985).

In addition to televised proceedings, conservative Republicans also relied on the congressional ethics code that had been enacted in 1977 and 1978. The most infamous example involved the downfall of Speaker James Wright (D-TX). Wright had been elected as Speaker in 1987. Although he started his career as a centrist southern Democrat, Wright moved with the congressional base of the party to the left by the mid-1980s. By the time that Democrats elected him as Speaker, Wright understood that he had to push for the national agenda of the party or he would face retribution from the caucus. Therefore, Wright ruthlessly used the rules that the majority had gained in the 1970s. For instance, he worked closely with the House Rules Committee to make sure that party-based legislation received favorable treatment. As a result of the 1970s reforms, the Rules Committee had become an instrument of the caucus rather than an independent fiefdom, as it had been in the committee era (S. Smith 1998). Following the 1984 election, the Democratic majority voted to seat a Democratic legislator over a Republican, who had been certified by the Indiana state authorities to represent the eighth district, following a series of controversial and partisan recounts. Not only were young Republicans unhappy with the Democratic leadership but with senior Republicans as well for their apparent indifference (Evans and Novak 1985). Gingrich proposed civil disobedience. Richard Cheney complained "What choice does a self-respecting Republican have . . . except confrontation? If you play by the rules, the Democrats change the rules so they win" (Balz 1985). In 1987, moreover, the Speaker held open a vote on tax increase legislation beyond the allotted time just so that Democrats could find someone to switch his vote and thereby gain a victory. "Can we lock the damn door?" asked Trent Lott in protest. Republicans who had cheered when Wright initially declared that time had expired and the vote stood at 206–205 against the measure, started to boo and yell at him. "They had to cheat to win it," complained Minnesota Representative Bill Frenzel, who added that "it was a bad day for the speaker and for the country." The House approved the $12.3 billion tax increase by a narrow one-vote margin (Birnbaum and Langley 1987).

Gingrich perceived an opening to attack the Speaker through the ethics rules. Common Cause, an organization that had formed in 1970 to fight for government reform, accused Speaker Wright of ethics violations. Gingrich realized that Wright offered a perfect target: it seemed that he had really abused the laws, and he had so many enemies in both parties (many Democrats personally disliked Wright because of his gruff style). Gingrich called for a House Ethics Committee investigation with a professional staff that was granted subpoena powers.[8] Common Cause and Gingrich made several accusations. They charged the Speaker with having violated the rules regarding outside income by forcing trade associations to purchase copies of his book—a collection of floor speeches—when he made an appearance. William Carlos Moore, a friend of Wright from Texas whose business had received over $600,000 in consulting fees from the Speaker's reelection committee, published the book. Another accusation involved the claim that Wright once intervened with the Egyptian president to help a business friend obtain oil rights in the country and that he had approached the head of a savings and loan in Texas for special assistance. When Gingrich called this situation a crisis for the House,[9] Wright responded that he had "violated no rule and certainly violated no commonly accepted ethical standard" (Carlson 1988, 21). Importantly, most of the aforementioned activities would have been tolerated during the committee era (W. Schneider 1989). To spearhead his defense, the Speaker released a twenty-three-page pamphlet refuting each of the charges. He called this an inquiry being driven by partisanship and targeted the seventy-two Republicans mounting the attack, while ignoring the role of Common Cause (*Time* 1988, 31; Borger 1988, 20). Bill Alexander (D-AR), one of Wright's closest allies, took a different tack. He raised questions about Gingrich's ethics, claiming that he had engaged in inappropriate financial deals. Alexander also said that "Gingrich is clearly an extension of the Republican 'Southern Strategy' based on confrontational, demagogical politics that began with Richard Nixon and Harry Dent of South Carolina and is now being continued by Lee Atwater, Roger Ailes, and Ed Rollins. This strategy has established a political base for Republicans in the South."[10] Gingrich himself did not care about public perceptions that he was mean: "If voters see a race as a nice-guy Republican against a nice-guy Democrat, we lose" (Dionne 1991, 296).

The House Ethics Committee began an investigation into Wright on 9 June 1988. The Republicans pressured the Ethics Committee into conducting a thorough investigation. They also appeared regularly on the media to keep these chargers at the forefront of attention. Republicans elected Gingrich as minority whip in 1989, and then the partisan warfare accelerated into high gear. Gingrich told PBS's *MacNeil/Lehrer News-Hour:* "It is my honest belief as a citizen that you now have Tammany Hall on Capitol Hill . . . that it is a sick institution, and that it has no legitimate authority, has enormous power, and that it has no legitimate authority; it does not represent the constitutional government. It is, in fact, a subversion of the process of free elections" (*National Journal* 2001). In April 1989 the Ethics Committee released a full report stating that Wright had violated the ethics rules on multiple occasions.[11] Sensing that he would be removed, Wright decided to resign on 31 May 1989.

Before he stepped down, the Speaker warned his colleagues that they needed to stop the "mindless cannibalism" that was sweeping through the chamber as both parties eviscerated each other through scandal warfare.[12] As with CAMSCAM, the deposition of Wright revealed that COS was a force to be reckoned with. Not only had these mavericks gained a secure foothold in the GOP, but they had also toppled the most powerful legislator in the House.

A few years later, conservative Republicans would strike once again with their campaign to depict Democrats as a corrupt majority.[13] In 1991 the GOP pressured Democrats to launch an investigation following a report from the General Accounting Office in 1991 that showed 269 sitting representatives had bounced checks at the House Bank without having been required to pay a penalty. The scandal was complicated, because the House Bank was not actually a bank. Rather, it was a depositing service offered to legislators that covered bad checks. Republicans kept the issue in the spotlight, however, despite attempts by Democrats to quiet them down. Once the investigation began, Republicans pushed for an even broader inquiry. Representative James Nussle (R-IA), part of the notorious "Gang of Seven" who favored confrontational styles, wore a bag over his head before the C-SPAN cameras to indicate disgust with his colleagues.

In the spring of 1992, the House Ethics Committee released the names of the worst offenders, which included 252 sitting lawmakers. The Justice Department hired a special counsel to investigate the worst cases. The revelations seemed to have an effect, earning the House some of the worst press that the institution had faced in years. During the 1992 elections, voters produced the largest House turnover in forty years with 110 new members. Of the 269 sitting members implicated in the scandal, 77 retired or were defeated. The scandal also caused a significant number of retirements and primary defeats. While many accused survived, there were enough losses to vindicate the Republican campaign.

The Frustration with President George H. W. Bush, 1990–1991

When it came to public policy, however, the young Republicans were not as successful. Indeed, one of the factors that motivated congressional conservatives to maintain such high levels of discipline and energy was that, despite their increased political success, they were unable to curb the growth of the American state. Their disappointment was evident with the presidency of George H. W. Bush, who signaled to conservatives that Republicans were regressing. During Bush's presidency, there was a series of historic expansions in the scope of government, including the Civil Rights Act of 1989 and the Americans with Disabilities Act of 1990. The defining moment for congressional conservatives occurred in 1990 when, faced with pressure from Republican and Democratic budget hawks, Bush agreed to raise taxes in exchange for spending cuts. Upon hearing of the president's decision to renege on his famous promise in 1988 not to raise taxes, Gingrich lambasted it as "the fiscal equivalent of Yalta" (Critchlow 2004, 719).

Gingrich and his allies would not tolerate the tax hikes, as they had with Reagan, because they already did not trust Bush and believed he was an old-guard compromiser (Gould 2003, 448). Bush was so angry with Gingrich for defying him that he refused to shake his hand during a White House ceremony. Gingrich said that "there was a sense in the White House that the admiral of the fleet had made the decision and I was but a disloyal ship captain. . . . I think that is a total misunderstanding of politics. For me to have voted for that compromise would have destroyed my effectiveness" (Clift and Brazaitis 1996, 245). Many conservatives never forgave Bush for raising taxes. His opponent in the 1992 Republican primaries, Patrick Buchanan, said to fellow conservatives: "George Bush, if you'll pardon the expression . . . has come out of the closet as an Eastern Establishment liberal" (Hodgson 1996, 250).

Frustration with Bush further energized congressional Republicans to stifle President Clinton (although they were certainly prepared to attack, regardless of the experience with Bush). During the 103rd Congress, despite Democrats controlling both chambers of Congress, Republicans maintained tremendous discipline and made it difficult for Democrats to pass major legislative accomplishments. Congressional Republicans were even able to block Clinton's health care reform proposal in 1993, turning what was meant to be a centerpiece of his presidency into an electoral liability that would cost Democrats control of Congress in 1994 (Jones 1999, 82–87). Congressional Republicans worked together in the months running up to the midterm elections of 1994, relying on congressional investigations in the House and the Senate filibuster to block Clinton's agenda. Clinton was able to pass an economic stimulus package in 1993 that included a tax increase and other deficit-reduction measures, but he did so without Republican support.

CONGRESSIONAL CONSERVATIVES AND THE POWER OF CENTRALIZATION, 1994–2004

The election of 1994 had been a watershed year in congressional history. Republicans took control of both chambers of Congress for the first time since 1954. Senate Republicans increased their number to 52 by gaining 8 seats; 2 Democrats then switched parties. House Republicans took over the chamber with 230 seats. Importantly, the biggest Republican gains

were in the South, Midwest, and West. Most politicians and pundits credited Minority Whip Newt Gingrich for having orchestrated a national
campaign based on the conservative ideas (including a balanced budget,
term limits for legislators, capital-gains tax cuts, a policy to prevent U.S.
troops from being placed under the authority of the United Nations, and
requirements promoting personal responsibility and self-sufficiency for
citizens on welfare) that were outlined in the "Contract with America."
This was a slick document, published in *TV Guide,* that Republicans promoted through a sophisticated public relations campaign. As a result of
the election, the individuals who came from COS were now in control
of Congress and of the party. The Republicans showed themselves to be
children of the 1970s reforms and had little interest in turning back the
clock to the committee era. Most of the reforms that they passed in 1995
cemented, and accelerated, the trends of the 1970s.

The Republican Reforms in 1995

After years of using the decentralizing aspects of the legislative process
to their advantage, conservative Republicans switched course. Speaker
Gingrich continued to strengthen parties through a variety of methods.
He created task forces that reported directly to the Speaker to craft legislative proposals and committee agendas. Gingrich organized the Speaker's
Advisory Group (SAG) to meet every week and design policy (Dodd and
Oppenheimer 1997, 43; Wolfensberger 2000, 175–91). The Speaker and
others in House leadership also stacked the key committees with individuals and chairmen who were loyal to the new Republican agenda,
while imposing six-year term limits for committee chairs in the House
and Senate. House Republicans created a twenty-six-person Steering
Committee that obtained the responsibility of naming committee chairs.
The Speaker chaired the committee and had more votes than the other
members (S. Smith and Lawrence 1997, 174). Republicans did reverse
some of the 1970s changes by eroding the balance between centralization
and decentralization that reformers had hoped to achieve. For example,
the Republican leadership under Gingrich weakened the Subcommittee
Bill of Rights by granting committee chairs the power to name subcommittee chairs and to hire staff (Schickler 2001, 272). Republicans
also limited the number of subcommittees that most committees could
have to five. "In the Commerce Committee," lamented Henry Waxman,
"the subcommittees are practically irrelevant" (S. Smith and Lawrence
1997, 179).

Yet Gingrich understood that the decentralizing tools of the 1970s reforms were still in place and that he needed to remain responsive to his
membership. In this respect, the post-committee reforms worked by creat-

ing opportunities for strong party caucuses while leaving party leaders susceptible to attack. The forces of decentralization, though not as strong after 1994, were still very relevant. Gingrich depended on the seventy-three freshmen as a solid voting block, and he was always aware of the trouble they could cause him. This was a big challenge because the freshmen were a volatile bunch. While sharing the ideological outlook of the founders of COS, they were more extreme than their predecessors in their refusal to learn how to work in the political system or to build any kind of coalitions. Most of this class never intended to stay in politics. Only twenty-six of the freshmen had any previous legislative experience, and almost none of them envisioned themselves as career politicians. As a result, most were willing to put everything on the line.

The freshmen included South Carolina's Lindsey Graham, a single Baptist who was born in 1955 and raised in Pickens County by a family that owned a bar. He studied at the University of South Carolina following the early death of his parents, and he was the first person in his family to earn a college degree. Graham went on to earn a law degree at the University of South Carolina. He worked as an attorney for the Air Force. After practicing law in Seneca and serving in the Gulf War, he worked for two years in state government before being elected to the House in 1994. In his campaign, he ran against state senator Jim Bryan on a platform that emphasized increased military spending, term limits, and cultural conservatism. Another freshman was Mark Foley, who represented the sixteenth district of Florida that included beachfront resort communities, affluent suburban areas, and farmers. A Massachusetts native, Foley's family had moved to Florida when he was three. Unlike Graham, Foley did not do as well in school. He never completed his work at Palm Beach Community College and instead opened a restaurant. Before his election in 1994, Foley served in state politics for only four years. From the time he arrived to Washington, Foley became known for his independence and willingness to challenge any authority, including the Republican leadership. Then there was Mark Neumann, a self-made millionaire who had worked his way through undergraduate and graduate school at the University of Wisconsin by taking jobs in restaurants and coaching sports teams. Neumann had earned his millions through a real estate company; he financed much of his own campaigns. Despite his self-accumulated wealth, Neumann did not embrace the life-style of a millionaire. This workaholic maintained a cluttered and messy office on Capitol Hill, and he rejected most of the perks that came with working in Washington. Neumann developed a passion—bordering on an obsession—with the size of federal deficits. He entered office with a determination to cut the cost of federal spending, even when that meant that he would have to do battle with Republican leaders (Browning 1995).

Freshmen such as Graham, Foley, and Neumann made their voices heard. When Robert Livingston (R-LA) tried to remove Neumann from the defense appropriations subcommittee for voting against a piece of legislation, the freshmen intimidated Gingrich into placing Neumann on the Budget Committee instead. During one of the budget battles between President Clinton and the Republican Congress in 1995, Neumann added an amendment to an appropriations bill that would have blocked the $600,000 that was earmarked for the African Elephant Conservation Act and $200,000 that was to go to a fund to help developing nations protect certain animals that were headed toward extinction. Gingrich was angry because he supported the appropriations, especially the first measure that would have sent money to the Atlanta Zoo. Gingrich also felt that Neumann was practicing a kind of budget-balancing extremism that had little effect on the overall budget but earned GOP scorn among constituents. In response to criticism that $800,000 was a trivial amount of money, Neumann said: "Some people here in Washington would have us believe that $800,000 is not worth worrying about. Let me respond. . . . I understand it takes $1 per day to keep a starving child alive in some of these countries. That means we could use these same tax dollars to keep 2,100 starving children alive (for a year), rather than spend the money to preserve tigers, elephants and rhinos." Neumann moved forward with his amendment despite Gingrich's fervent opposition. Although the House rejected Neumann's measure, it was a bold sign of defiance. Neumann, was not the only young Republican willing to take on the leadership. At a retreat that followed the 1994 elections, some Republicans asked why the party shouldn't impose term limits on the Speaker as it had with committee chairs. The idea "caught on like wildfire," recalled Lindsey Graham, and the freshmen imposed an eight-year term limit. "Ain't nothing was off-limits, buddy. You could feed us, wash us, and comb us, but we'd still bite," Graham said (Baumann 2004).

Additionally, these conservative legislators used advocacy think tanks to gain ground in the battle over ideas (Ricci 1993; J. Smith 1991). Republicans likewise depended on the new campaign finance system to gain political advantage, capitalizing on their broader base of support to mobilize small contributions and political action committees. After years of exile, Republicans became prominent in the mainstream media. Besides gaining attention in the network news shows, they relied on talk radio shows, C-SPAN, Internet Web sites, and cable television.

The Travails of Conservatism, 1995–1999

In the coming years, Gingrich realized that lower-ranking Republicans could cause him enormous problems. As Speaker, Gingrich had to confront the tension between the strength of the conservative movement of which he was a part and the persistence, as well as entrenchment, of the American state. When Republicans squared off against President Clinton in 1995 over the federal budget for fiscal year 1996, attempting to obtain deep cuts in spending and complete Reagan's revolution, they found themselves in a bind. Republicans proposed over $1 trillion in spending cuts over a seven-year period, as well as $353 billion in tax cuts and increases in defense spending. They packaged most of their proposals within the budget process since the rules created in 1974 offered a means of avoiding the filibuster in the Senate (Sinclair 1997, 216). They also relied on a number of highly restrictive rules to limit debate. For instance, upon introducing the budget resolution in the House, Republican leaders required that any substitute show it would balance the budget in seven years. Until then, only narrow amendments had been barred from consideration when dealing with budget resolutions (Sinclair 1997, 185). Clinton responded by calling for $1.1 trillion in spending cuts over ten years and a much smaller tax cut that would only benefit the middle class. "The White House," Gingrich told his colleagues early on in the battle, "has crossed the line. We want them to understand that if they want a long-term stand-off, we are prepared to stay the course for as long as it takes" (Thurber 1997, 337).

During the budget battles, Republicans learned that it was extremely difficult to dismantle the American state. President Clinton was able to link the proposed Republican Medicare cuts to their proposed tax cuts, presenting this budget as an attempt by the GOP to transfer money from the poor to the rich. Clinton also honed in on specific cuts in the budget that affected programs that had public support, such as food stamps, school lunches, and health care (Witcover 2003, 676). Gingrich, however, had little room to maneuver since the freshmen remained adamant regardless of the political costs. As Clinton's top adviser said, "the freshman had become Newt's Frankenstein monster—and my new best friend" (Stephanopoulos 1999, 406). When the intransigence of both sides caused a series of government shutdowns in December 1995 and January 1996, the media turned on the Republicans by presenting them as unwilling to compromise and as prepared to abandon popular government services ranging from the National Zoo, to federal monuments, to travel visas. Republicans had not perceived that most voters would blame the Congress for a government shutdown—particularly after they spent so much time wielding this as a threat in public—rather than Clinton. The tension between Republicans and the White House became so severe that at one point during a shutdown, as House GOP leaders complained to the president about an insulting picture the White House had provided to *Time* magazine, Gingrich picked up the phone and cursed at Clinton, accusing him of being a "goddamn lying son of a bitch!" (Garrett 2005, 125).

In the end, Republicans agreed to a federal budget that did not significantly cut into the strength of the federal government. Kansas Senator Robert Dole was instrumental at reaching a compromise, in part because he was concerned about how the budget shutdown would affect his presidential campaign. Politically, Clinton emerged from the battles with renewed strength as congressional Republicans had lost some of the luster they gained following the 1994 elections. Gingrich personally suffered as the national media developed an unfavorable caricature of the Speaker as immature, mean-spirited, and out-of-control.

Nonetheless, congressional Republicans would score some important victories. In January 1996 Clinton sent a message to Congress with a plan to balance the budget by 2002, thereby adopting a central platform of the Republicans in the budget battles. Moreover, in 1996 Clinton agreed to sign legislation that ended the federal welfare program, Aid to Families with Dependent Children. Clinton also made the famous proclamation that the "era of big government is over," which seemed to confirm the ideological message of the conservative movement. In 1997 Clinton agreed to a budget that constrained discretionary spending below the predicted rate of inflation, opened the door for Medicare reform, and reduced income taxes. In exchange, Clinton ameliorated certain parts of the welfare reform and obtained a new health care program to cover low-income children. Republicans would also prevent programs from being updated to meet current conditions, an effective way to retrench programs without eliminating them (Hacker 2004). Despite the Republicans accomplishments in the second term, however, most parts of the American state remained intact throughout the 1990s, and spending did not decline in dramatic fashion.

Once again, the persistence of the American state inspired Republicans to remain aggressive in employing the tools of the majority to achieve their goals. Their political victories were not translating into the kind of policy victories that they desired, so many in the GOP did not feel as successful as they thought they should. The leadership continued to use House rules to curtail dissent within their caucus and to limit Democratic opposition. Republican investigations into the White House were a central tactic that they used to combat Clinton, culminating with the investigation of Clinton's affair with a White House intern named Monica Lewinsky. As the House of Representatives considered whether to impeach President Clinton in 1998, Majority Whip Tom DeLay prevented Democrats and moderate Republicans from offering a censure resolution that would likely have attracted the support of many legislators (Baker 2000, 217–37).

Exercising Majoritarian Power in an Era of United Government, 2000–2004

Once the era of divided government ended with the election of President George W. Bush in 2000, House Republicans accelerated their efforts to use the centralizing aspects of the 1970s reforms. With Gingrich out of office (he was forced by Republicans to resign during the Clinton impeachment), Tom DeLay stepped into the power vacuum. As whip and then majority leader, DeLay used House rules without restraint. One Republican colleague called DeLay's office "a cross between the concierge at the Plaza and the mafia. They can get you anything you want, but it will cost you" (*National Journal* 2003). The role of committees continued to decline, as was evident from the diminished number of committee meetings and hearings (*National Journal* 2001).[14] Between 2000 and 2004 Republicans also blocked Democratic participation in committee deliberations, refused to give Democrats access to the language of legislative proposals until hours before a vote, and made it hard for them to gain attention in the media. Even the tragedy of 9/11 did not stop House Republicans from employing their procedural power. Initially, Speaker Hastert tried to work across partisan lines. According to one report, shortly after 9/11 Congress was working on legislation to stimulate economic recovery. Senator Tom Daschle's (D-SD) and Richard Gephardt's (D-MO) staff convened with Hastert's staff in a conference room to work on an airline bailout package in the late hours of evening. After hearing about this, DeLay personally dashed into the conference room without announcement. In a fury, DeLay screamed at the Democratic staffers: "Who elected you to Congress?" He ordered the Republican staffers to leave immediately. Thereafter, he dismantled the work completed in the discussions. The Republican leadership removed all of the Democratic provisions the following day before the House voted on the legislation (Crowley 2003).

But with a Republican in the White House and fewer GOP centrists to stop them, the skill of conservatives at institutional politics started to reap big dividends. In 2001 the Republican Congress passed a massive tax reduction, the largest in postwar history, which made deep inroads into the fiscal capacity of the state. In 2003, in the midst of a war against terrorism, Congress passed a smaller tax reduction that nonetheless broke the historic tradition in the U.S. of increasing federal tax contributions when American troops were fighting abroad. The $350 billion tax cut of 2003 included lower rates for dividends and long-term capital gains, various benefits to individual taxpayers, and business tax benefits such as improved depreciation rates. The rules were important to a smooth passage. House Democrats, for example, were only granted one hour to debate their less costly and more progressive $150 billion alternative; Democrats were not even allowed to vote on their plan. Republicans were so successful at stifling Democratic proposals through restrictive rules that the media reported as if Democrats had agreed to the Republican plan rather than being shut out of debate (Crowley 2003).

House Republican leaders employed many tactics throughout other battles in Bush's first term. Republicans only allowed 15 percent of the bills in 2004 to be open for amendment (Milligan 2004). In numerous committee meetings, Republicans prohibited Democratic amendments. During a vote on a prescription drug benefit in 2002, Democrats were not allowed to vote on their plan. Republicans also have delayed omnibus spending legislation until the very last minute so that Democrats had to scramble to influence legislation without having much time to devise strategy. Frequently, Republicans prevented Democrats from obtaining access to critical information. Democrats have been denied meeting space on some occasions or locked out of conference committees. The House Rules Committee barely gave notification about meetings on important rules decisions, while the markup of most legislation has been handled by party leaders, administration staff, and lobbyists without the consultation of members on the conference committees (Mann and Ornstein 2006, 172–73).

With control of the White House and Congress secured, congressional Republicans also strengthened the K Street Project. Begun in 1994, this was an effort by conservative legislators to master the campaign finance and lobbying systems that had emerged in the 1970s. Conservatives understood that to thrive they needed command over the relationship between private contributions, interest-group lobbying, and governance. Congressional Republicans felt that so many decades of Democratic rule had biased the entire Washington community against them. The connections between Congress and lobbyists had become all that much more important after the 1960s as the number of trade associations exploded in Washington and the costs of campaigns skyrocketed. Through the K Street Project, Republicans attempted to make certain that top interest groups hired Republicans who had worked in Congress or the White House, thereby ensuring GOP dominance over money in politics. After 2001 Senator Rick Santorum of Pennsylvania met every Tuesday on Capitol Hill with carefully selected lobbyists. They discussed new job openings and the best candidates for the positions.

The lobbyists in the K Street Project were usually devoted Republicans, who had been working with activists in the conservative movement for more than a decade. Jack Abramoff, for example, had become involved in politics while he was an undergraduate at Brandeis University. In the 1980 election, he helped organize, along with Grover Norquist (who was then a graduate student at the Harvard Business School), Massachusetts college students who supported Ronald Reagan for president. After the election, Abramoff and Norquist moved to Washington where they worked with the activist Ralph Reed to transform College Republicans into a national force. Following his experience with the College Republicans, Abramoff directed a small grass-roots operation (Citizens for America), that lobbied for U.S. assistance to the anti-communist Nicaraguan Contras. The Republican takeover of Congress in 1994 convinced Abramoff to turn his energy toward lobbying. Abramoff met Tom De-Lay's fund raiser in 1995, and the two men would quickly form a strong alliance (Schmidt and Grimaldi 2005).

The Abramoff and DeLay relationship was not unique. Following the election in 1994, Tom DeLay had sent a strong message when he put together a list of 400 of the biggest political action committees along with the amount of money that they had contributed to candidates. Having asked the lobbyists to come to his office, DeLay revealed whether they were in the "friendly or unfriendly" column of his list. "If you want to play in our revolution," he told them, "you have to live by our rules" (Confessore 2003) According to Grover Norquist, "Ninety percent of the new top hires are going to Republicans; it should be 100 percent . . . it would be suicidal of them to go to a Democrat" (Chaddock 2003). The K Street Project was a well-orchestrated effort to solidify a machine with its own spoils system, namely jobs in the private sector, which was comparable to the urban Democratic machines from the Gilded Age that relied on public patronage (Confessore 2003; Drew 2005).

After the 2004 election, emboldened Republicans moved to further weaken the constraints on party leaders. When the new Congress convened, Republicans pushed through a rule change stipulating that the House would be required to dismiss an ethics complaint if the House Ethics Committee found itself in a deadlock. Previously, as a result of a 1997 modification, an investigation was automatically triggered if the ethics committee (which was split evenly between parties) did not act on a complaint within forty-five days. The change adopted in January 2005 diminished the chances for new ethics investigations. To be sure, Republicans decided against moving forward with other changes—including when the caucus decided to reinstate a party rule whereby an indicted member could not serve in the leadership (which they had just overturned a few weeks earlier to protect DeLay). The GOP reversed the decision, however, only after DeLay told them in closed-door session that he was confident he would not be charged and that the leadership feared the political costs of the recent decision. This change, which prevented an investigation if the ethics committee was deadlocked, was significant. As Zach Wamp, a Republican from Tennessee, said, the change removed "a ball and chain around our foot" (Allen 2005).

Yet even in an era of homogeneous parties, united government, and skilled legislative leadership, the American state has not disappeared. In fact it has grown. During President Bush's first three years as president, federal spending increased from 18 percent of the economy in 1999 to 20 percent in 2003. Discretionary spending, which rose at a rate of 2.4 percent a year during the 1990s grew by more than 27 percent in 2002 and 2003 (*Albany Times Union* 2003). Much of this money went toward nonmilitary items such as transportation, education, and farm subsidies. Despite the emphasis of the 1994 class on balanced budgets, the government was drowning in a sea of red ink by its ten-year anniversary. "If Bill Clinton had tolerated this," noted the *Wall Street Journal,* "Republicans would be shouting from the rooftops" (*Wall Street Journal* 2003; see also Rosenbaum 2003). When House Republicans gathered in Arizona in January 2004 to reminisce ten years after the Republican revolution, most of the talk was about what had gone wrong and why so many "revolutionaries" had compromised their principles. "After three years or so," said Michael Franc, vice president of the Heritage Foundation, "they went from revolutionaries to members of a committee or a state's delegation. . . . They shifted their senses of identity, and it became a lot easier for them to say, 'Well we have to get this project.' They lost their way with respect to the size and scope of government." The new Republicans in 2005 promised that things would be different. "They came back to their senses," said Thomas Fitton, president of Judicial Watch, "We returned to our moorings, to our foundations. . . . Those of us who remain are more committed to the reform agenda that brought us here" (Klein 2005).

Republicans, moreover, have been struggling with the dangers that the legislative process poses to leaders of any party. During the period of reform in the 1970s, liberal Democrats had created numerous mechanisms that could be used to bring down congressional leaders in order to make certain that the legislative system did not facilitate the type of long-term, unchecked power that had existed in the committee era. Young conservative Republicans had depended on these mechanisms to attack Democrats when they were in the majority of the House and Senate and to weaken GOP leaders who had played to the center in the 1980s. Now, conservative Republicans are finding themselves struggling on Capitol Hill. Majority Leader Tom DeLay was forced to resign in April 2006 after being indicted for campaign finance violations and implicated in a massive lobbying scandal. Senate Majority Leader Bill Frist of Tennessee has been under investigation for ethics violations involving his personal finances. A congressional sex scandal involving Mark Foley's interaction with underage pages—and evidence that the Republican leadership had failed to act on earlier warnings of this—wrought havoc on the GOP one month before the 2006 midterm elections. Key figures from the notorious K Street Group—including the lobbyists Jack Abramoff and Michael Scanlon and the legislators who they had worked with— came under intense scrutiny. Abramoff, the kingpin of the operation, pled guilty to criminal felony counts. Meanwhile, maverick Republicans and Democrats started to flex their muscle and cause serious problems for the GOP leadership.

As a result, one of the big questions today is whether conservative Republicans can survive the immense challenges that have emerged ever since the Bush administration stumbled in its response to Hurricane Katrina, faced its own ethics scandal with the indictment of Lewis "Scooter" Libby, and confronted questions about how it handled intelligence before starting the War in Iraq. "Conservatives are in power but out of sorts," complained the commentator David Brooks (2005). "Fifty years after the founding of the modern right, conservatives hold just about every important government job, yet the conservative agenda has stalled." Republicans lost control of Congress in 2006.

Conclusion

America's Congress underwent significant reform in the 1970s at the hands of liberals who hoped to make the institution more progressive and accountable. But reformers learned that it is impossible to control these kinds of changes as conservative Republicans proved to be extremely adept at operating in the new institutions to achieve political power. A new generation of Republicans who entered Congress in the 1970s and maintained close ties to the conservative movement, mastered the post-committee legislative process—both the decentralizing features that benefited the minority or mavericks, as well as the centralizing features that favored the majority leadership—and used the process to achieve influence in national politics.

But the political success of conservatism in Congress did not slay the dragon of the American state. Republicans watched as the state proved to be extremely durable in the conservative era—even as the GOP was able to chip away at its edges. Although there were some instances when retrenchment occurred, such as with welfare reform in 1996 and the federal tax intake after 2001, overall, the government remained substantial through 2006. Whether congressional conservatives can finally translate their political success into policy remains one of the most vexing puzzles of the twenty-first century. Republicans leaders must also find out if they can succeed in the volatile nature of the political process upon which they have depended as they climbed to the top.

NOTES

1. These arguments and issues are explored in much greater detail in my book *On Capitol Hill* (2004). For an outstanding history of the tensions conservatives faced between ideology and the needs of governing, see Donald Critchlow's essay in *The American Congress: The Building of Democracy* (2004).

2. Newt Gingrich to Paul Weyrich, 18 December 1980, Tip O'Neill Papers, Kirk O'Donnell Papers, box 1, file: Newt Gingrich, 1982–1985, Boston College, Boston, Massachusetts.

3. Newt Gingrich to Republican Colleagues, 8 February 1983, Tip O'Neill Papers, Kirk O'Donnell Papers, box 1, file: Newt Gingrich, 1982–1985.

4. Newt Gingrich to Fellow Republican, 18 March 1982, Tip O'Neill Papers, Kirk O'Donnell Papers, box 1, file: Newt Gingrich, 1982–1985.

5. "Republican Agenda for the Remainder of 1983," 17 October 1983, Robert Michel Papers, Press Series, box I, file: Memoranda 1981–1988 (2), Dirksen Congressional Center, Pekin, Illinois.

6. David Obey to Tony Coelho, 3 May 1984, Tip O'Neill Papers, Kirk O'Donnell Papers, box 1, file: Newt Gingrich, 1980–1989.

7. Jack Kemp to Friends, 1984, Tip O'Neill Papers, Kirk O'Donnell Papers, box 1, file: Newt Gingrich, 1982–1985.

8. Newt Gingrich to Colleagues, 15 December 1987, Jim Wright Papers, RC box 18–4, The Capital, Suite H 324, Steering and Policy Committee, file: Newt Gingrich, Texas Christian University, Fort Worth.

9. Newt Gingrich to Colleagues, 17 February 1988, Jim Wright Papers, RC box 18–4, The Capital, Suite H 324, Steering and Policy Committee, file: Newt Gingrich.

10. Bill Alexander to Colleague, 7 April 1989, Jim Wright Papers, RC box 18–4, The Capital, Suite H 324, Steering and Policy Committee, file: Newt Gingrich.

11. U.S. Congress, House of Representatives, Committee on Standards of Official Conduct, *Statement of Alleged Violation in the Matter of Representative James C. Wright, Jr.,* 101st Congress, 1st session, 13 April 1989.

12. U.S. Congress, House of Representatives, *Congressional Record*, 101st Congress, 1st Session, 31 May 1989, p. 10400.

13. Jerry Solomon to House Republican Leadership, 6 December 1990, Robert Michel Papers, Staff Series, K. Bullard, box 132, file: Legislative Agenda for 102nd Congress.

14. In the House, for instance, there were 5,388 House committee hearings in the 100th Congress (1987–88); 5,152 House committee hearings in the 102nd Congress (1991–92); 3,786 House committee hearings in the 104th Congress (1995–96); and 3,347 House committee hearings in the 106th Congress (1999–2000).

Chapter Six

Economic Insecurity, Party Reputations, and the Republican Ascendance

MARK A. SMITH

COMMON UNDERSTANDINGS OF AMERICAN domestic politics point to differences between the parties in their respective electoral strengths (Shafer and Claggett 1995). On social and cultural issues such as crime, moral values, drugs, abortion, homosexuality, pornography, and affirmative action, close observers believe, the public has usually preferred Republicans over the past three decades. Among political scientists, the concepts of priming and issue ownership have been enlisted to support the notion that the GOP wins if people vote based on those issues (Petrocik 1996). Meanwhile, according to conventional wisdom, Democrats enjoy higher public evaluations on economic and social welfare issues. When those matters form the focal point of campaigns, the reasoning goes, Democrats gain the upper hand. Thomas Frank's *What's the Matter with Kansas?* (2004) provides a popular version of this assessment. Republicans have supposedly pursued a "bait and switch," winning elections because of social and cultural issues but then governing with economic policies favoring the rich.

This interpretation certainly offers some insights into recent American political history. Beginning in the late 1960s and early 1970s in a backlash against the counter-culture, civil rights, and loosened sexual mores, and continuing up to the present with the rise of the religious right, social and cultural issues often bolstered the electoral prospects of the Republican Party (see, e.g., Campbell in this volume; Edsall and Edsall 1991). One should remember, though, that these gains were partially offset by flows the other way. As recently as the 1950s and 1960s, the Northeast and the West Coast were GOP strongholds, but the social liberalism of those areas now makes them fertile territory for Democrats. In the middle of the twentieth century, Republicans commonly attracted a third of the African American vote, but the corresponding vote percentages barely cracked double digits at the end of the century. The policy stances that brought the religious right to the Republican Party also pushed both secular voters—a relatively small but growing part of the population—and members of other religions toward the Democrats. On balance, the Republicans probably gained votes by upholding positions favored by social and religious conservatives, but those issues did not cut only in one direction.

This chapter examines the other side of the domestic divide and the accompanying assumption that the economy has provided one of the few long-term assets for Democrats. The Democrats supposedly encountered difficulties because economic matters were regularly pushed to the sidelines during elections. I argue that these understandings miss the mark in crucial respects. I begin by briefly surveying the changing economic landscape over the past half-century and the rising importance of economic issues beginning in the early 1970s and continuing into succeeding decades. These experiences, in turn, made the state of the economy a more pressing and salient concern to the American public. The parties did not respond by turning away from the economy and toward culture; to the contrary, economic questions have become more central to political debates and campaigns.

I next provide evidence of the striking divergence in the economic reputations of the two parties over the past three decades. With only limited exceptions, the GOP has gained a large and durable advantage on public perceptions of which party can better deliver strong economic performance. The shifting reputations of the parties cannot be attributed to superior economic performance under Republican administrations. Instead, explaining the gains requires an examination of the content and packaging of what each party had to offer. Aided by the GOP's commitment to tax cuts and the switching of the parties' positions on who held most tightly to fiscal responsibility, the Republicans' messages were clearer and more consistent than those of the Democrats. Complementing these attributes of the GOP's economic message, moreover, has been a stronger and more effective organizational infrastructure for developing and disseminating the party's stances. At the same time, GOP repositioning around tax cuts eventually led Democrats to reposition around a commitment to deficit reduction—which turned out, in time, to be a politically damaging step. In combination, superior message and organization, not performance, have contributed to the Republicans' long-term advantage in economic reputation.

THE RISE OF ECONOMIC INSECURITY

By the early 1970s, the rosy economic portrait that prevailed after World War II had vanished for many American workers. Falling rates of productivity gains ultimately meant slow wage growth. After seeing its real income rise by 38 percent in the 1950s and 37 percent in the 1960s, the median family witnessed real income growth of only 10 percent in the 1970s, 9 percent in the 1980s, and 12 percent in the 1990s.[1] Moreover, even the gains in family incomes that did occur in the later decades were primarily the result of a greater number of hours worked per family rather than increases in real wages (Levy 1998). In a striking documentation of economic insecurity, Jacob Hacker's (2006) investigation based on a lengthy data series reveals a trend of downward mobility for many citizens alongside a pattern of upward mobility for others. Family incomes over the past three decades have turned more volatile from year to year, with more people moving down the wage scale as others move up.

Pronounced shocks to the labor market accompanied the changes in wage growth and stability. Many of the factors that formerly had provided some measure of insulation from economic fluctuations diminished. Employers gained flexibility from a declining rate of unionization, greater international trade, and the availability of temporary workers and staffing services. As a result, the threat of job turnover was no longer confined to recessions, becoming instead a permanent feature of the labor market. Workers readily sensed the contours of the new environment: when comparing years with similar unemployment rates, surveys found larger numbers of people believing that they could be laid off in the next year during the 1990s than in the 1970s (Schmidt 2000). With job losses potentially just around the corner, workers invariably felt less secure.

Meanwhile, demands for consumption of goods and services continued to increase, creating a growing disparity for many people between what they had and what they desired. For a time, the day of reckoning could be postponed through lower savings rates and higher levels of debt. The debt-to-income ratio of households, calculated as total consumer, mortgage, and other debt divided by after-tax personal income, skyrocketed from .67 in 1973 to 1.07 in 2000.[2] With more Americans living paycheck-to-paycheck and making significant interest payments, they became vulnerable to unforeseen financial shocks. While families holding a cushion of savings might be able to absorb the lower income resulting from a job loss or the higher expenses stemming from a medical emergency or a divorce, large debt loads increasingly caused such problems to push people over the financial edge (Sullivan, Warren, and Westbrook 2000). The number of filings for personal bankruptcy more than doubled in the 1980s and then leaped by another 70 percent during the 1990s. In a startling indicator of families' weakened financial health, the first decade of the twenty-first century sees more filings for personal bankruptcy every year in the United States than there are bachelor's degrees awarded.[3]

On top of concerns over employment, consumption, and debt, the American population increasingly faced challenges over health insurance and retirement. Owing largely to a decline in employer-provided coverage, the number of Americans without health insurance rose from 23 million in 1976 to 44 million in 2002 (Miringoff and Miringoff 1999; Connolly 2003). At the same time, massive inflation in health care costs has made fears of unexpected and unpayable medical bills more pressing. Meanwhile, in the midst of continual discussion among political elites about the long-term funding of Social Security, public perceptions that "it won't be there when I retire" have increased. Relatively few people have built up personal savings or paid down debt to offset the concerns.

These various outcomes can be called "economic insecurity," a concept broader than, though related to, conventional understandings of a "sluggish economy." The economy can be growing steadily, but if people wonder whether layoffs are imminent due to downsizing or globalization, and they hold piles of debt and live a layoff away from bankruptcy, then they do not possess economic security. A robust economy as it is normally defined, then, is a necessary but not sufficient condition for pervasive economic security, which rests on not only typical measures like GDP growth and the unemployment rate but also wages, debt, job stability, and the scope of health insurance and retirement coverage. Moreover, economic security contains a strong subjective component, because people's fears about such matters as the threat posed by international competition, the actual likelihood of layoffs, and the prospects for a collapse in Social Security may not match the reality. The key point for the purposes of this chapter is that during the past three decades economic insecurity became, and remains, far more widespread than was the case from the end of World War II through the early 1970s.

PUBLIC AND PARTY RESPONSES TO ECONOMIC INSECURITY

Rising economic insecurity brought significant political consequences. Not surprisingly, public concern about the economy has grown markedly. Public attention to various problems can be measured through the Gallup polls that have regularly asked random samples of Americans, "What do you think is the most important problem facing this country?" These surveys provide a comprehensive picture of the shifting concerns of the American public over a long period. For a few years after World War II, the economy occasionally topped the list amid a burst of inflation and fears of another depression. During the next twenty-five years of employment security and consistent growth in real incomes, however, references to the economy seldom reached the number one position. Only 17 percent of the surveys conducted from 1946 to 1972 found the economy to be the dominant priority of the public. Those rare instances occurred during moments of economic troubles in 1958, 1961, and 1971.[4]

The succeeding decades looked very different. Beginning with the arrival of stagflation in 1973, Americans have regularly cited the economy
as their leading concern. Stagflation eventually receded but economic difficulties remained regarding international competition, job turnover,
downsizing, slow wage growth, and mounting debt. All of these factors
would be expected to make people more closely attuned to the wider
economy. During the 138 surveys from 1973 to 2004, various references
to the economy reached the top spot in the "most important problem"
surveys a remarkable 76 percent of the time.[5]

Political observers have often assumed that cultural issues like abortion, homosexuality, and guns dominate contemporary American politics,
but more often than not the leading concern of Americans has been
the economy. Even in the years following 9/11, economic matters remained noteworthy among the public's priorities. The cluster of issues
around terrorism and national security overshadowed the economy
from October 2001 through most of July 2002. Thereafter, however, public attention to the economy rebounded. During the long buildup, execution, and occupation of the second Iraq War and the continuing War on
Terror, a clear majority of the "most important problem" surveys from
mid-2002 through 2004 found that the economy occupied the number
one position. In this respect, the place of the economy on the minds of
American citizens stood close to where it had resided from 1973–2001
and remained far removed from the lesser attention the issue garnered in
the 1950s and 1960s.

How did the parties respond to the changed economic environment
and the higher levels of public attention to economic concerns? Rational
parties would be expected to move economic matters closer to the forefront of their rhetoric, and they did. One indicator comes from each party's quadrennial platform, where the opening section usually addresses
what the candidates and their supporters have defined as the most pressing issues. From 1946 to 1972, only 14 percent of the Republican platforms and 43 percent of the Democratic ones emphasized economic matters in the first section. The comparable figures for 1976–2004 were much
higher, at 75 and 88 percent (M. Smith 2007). Similarly, in state-of-the-
state speeches, governors of both parties gave economic matters much
more prominence in the 1980s, 1990s, and 2000s than in the 1950s and
1960s. The sample of years for the governors' speeches include both
strong and weak years such that apples-to-apples comparisons over time
are possible (M. Smith 2007). In other words, even when comparing the
best years from recent times to the best years in the immediate post–World
War II decades, the increasing amount of emphasis on economic issues
stands out. Given the trends summarized at the beginning of the chapter,
the governors seemingly recognized that even a "good" economy was not

"good enough" to alleviate the problems of economic security pervasive among the population.

Further evidence on recent elections can be found from campaign advertisements. Table 6.1 presents the results of a content analysis of each party's television advertisements, averaged across the six presidential elections from 1984 to 2004.[6] It indicates that the Republicans spent more time on foreign affairs than did the Democrats, who gave a higher priority to social welfare issues. Those results are consistent with what most observers of American politics would expect. For present purposes, one crucial finding is that social and cultural issues were relatively rare in the paid advertisements of both parties throughout this period. Averaged across the six campaigns, those matters formed only 9 percent of the issue references of each party.

The category attracting the most emphasis across the period under study was the economy, with 40 percent each of the Democratic and Republican references. Television viewers during recent presidential elections were exposed to innumerable claims and counter-claims about taxes, jobs, growth, inflation, and government spending. The related group of social welfare issues ranked second in the amount of attention, with social and cultural issues falling much lower in their representation within campaign ads. Of course, that focus does not imply that social and cultural issues were irrelevant to voters' decision making. To the extent that these matters affected American elections, though, the main sources of communication were interest groups, not the parties (see also Fiorina et al. 2005).

The second problem with the conventional account of the balance between culture and economics runs even deeper. The difficulty for Democrats was not that they shied away from economic issues; nor was it that Republicans successfully changed the subject to culture. Rather, the conundrum for Democrats was more fundamental: the public showed no eagerness to buy what the party had to sell. During most of the three decades after 1972, the economy proved to be a winning issue for Republicans rather than Democrats.

THE PUZZLE: SHIFTING PARTY REPUTATIONS ON THE ECONOMY

There is a simple way to determine which party people prefer on the economy: we can ask them. Several survey questions, repeated in the same form multiple times, measure Americans' perceptions of which party would produce better economic outcomes. The largest single source of observations comes from a Gallup question posed at regular intervals since 1951: "Looking ahead for the next few years, which political party

TABLE 6.1
Issue Priorities in Presidential Advertisements, 1984–2004 (percent)

	Democrats	Republicans
Foreign affairs	**13**	**22**
Military strength	1.4	10.3
Arms race/nuclear war	4.4	1.8
Iraq War (I and II)	3.4	1.1
Terrorism	2.7	4.1
Peace	0.0	3.6
Other foreign affairs	1.1	1.1
Economy	**40**	**40**
General	5.5	5.3
Deficit/balanced budgets	4.9	3.0
Taxes	11.4	11.2
Trade/international competition	2.5	0.8
Inflation/prices/interest rates	2.3	3.5
Jobs/unemployment/job training	9.1	7.2
Standard of living/incomes/minimum wage	3.4	3.1
Government spending/waste	0.4	4.9
Other economy	0.8	1.1
Social welfare issues	**31**	**23**
Social security/pensions	6.7	4.3
Medicare	4.1	3.8
Education	7.6	8.3
Child safety/care/nutrition	2.1	0.5
Welfare/poverty	2.6	1.0
Health care	7.3	4.7
Family and medical leave	0.7	0.4
Social and cultural issues	**9**	**9**
Crime	3.7	2.7
Illegal drugs	3.7	4.8
Church and state	0.5	0.1
Abortion	0.1	0.4
Gay rights	0.0	0.0
First Amendment	0.0	0.7
Gun control	1.3	0.1
Judicial appointments	0.0	0.1
Other	**6**	**5**
Environment	4.7	2.2
Stem cell research	0.8	0.0
Legal reform	0.0	1.3
Miscellaneous	0.8	1.3

do you think will do a better job of keeping the country prosperous—the Republican party or the Democratic party?" Tapping the same underlying concept, several related polls administered by Gallup and other survey organizations asked respondents which party would be better for "improving the economy," "dealing with the economy," "making sure the country is prosperous," "handling the economy," "keeping the economy strong and prosperous," "keeping the economy healthy," and "keeping the economy prosperous." The various wordings are treated here as equivalent.[7] By combining data from the various questions, the shifting balance between the parties can be observed.

Perceptions of respective proficiencies on the economy come into sharper relief when compared with the results from a second question, one designed to measure people's summary evaluations of the parties. The standard Gallup poll assessing people's partisan identification reads, "In politics, as of today, do you consider yourself a Democrat, a Republican, an independent, or what?" If the level of overall identification with a party is subtracted from public judgments of it in the economic area, a useful measure is created. The resulting variable captures the degree to which economic images help or hurt each party at each interval, relative to everything else in the political environment. If people view a party more positively on economics than they view it in general, then economic matters—for that moment—are a net winner drawing people into the party. Should the difference be negative, then the economy is a net loser dragging the party down by comparison to everything else affecting macropartisanship.

The difference measure resembles the concept of comparative advantage often employed in studies of international trade. The public may favor a certain party overall and on the economy, but the comparative advantage on the economy could still fall to its competitor. If a party has 55 percent support on the economy and 65 percent support in general, it would be better off directing people's attention away from economic questions and toward other issues for which its level of backing is higher. Likewise, the other party would benefit from steering the national political conversation toward the economy, for its disadvantage is smaller in that domain than in others.

Figure 6.1 presents the quarterly measure of the extent to which economic perceptions help or hurt the Republicans vis-à-vis the Democrats.[8] Higher scores for the data points indicate greater favorability for Republicans. The data show that from 1951 through 1972, economic matters moved back and forth from being a comparative advantage to a comparative disadvantage for Republicans. The average during that period was almost identical to zero, meaning that the issue did not consistently benefit either party.

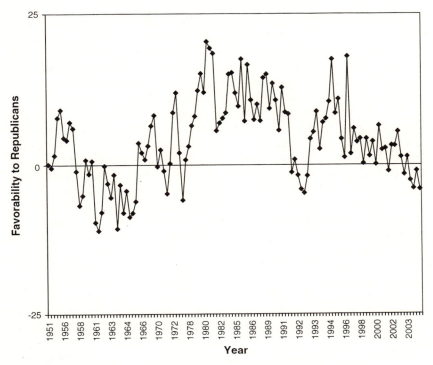

Figure 6.1 Comparative Advantage of the Parties on the Economy

After 1972 and especially after 1980, however, the figures changed dramatically—and, for the Democrats, badly. The powerful symbol of the "party of prosperity" became far more frequently attached to Republicans, thereby providing a valuable source of political capital. The Republican gains came on the measure of comparative advantage, it must be remembered. That is, they occurred over and above a shift toward the GOP in general partisan identification. The status of the economy as a net winner for Republicans was only rarely relinquished, with the Reagan era—including the campaign year of 1980—showing particularly strong results.

Except for a few brief moments, such as the period from 1991 to 1992, Republicans after 1972 would have improved their standing had people chosen their party identification simply by determining which one would supply superior economic outcomes. The Republicans thus turned a factor that did not consistently tilt in either party's direction in earlier decades into a persistent advantage. Moreover, this pronounced shift occurred under circumstances that highlighted the importance of economic reputations. Democrats have been doing worse on an issue that has become increasingly significant in the public's mind. Thus, for Democrats this dramatic shift in the economic reputations of the two parties is a major electoral problem. It is beyond the scope of this chapter to pinpoint the consequences for voting results, but the available evidence indicates that the Republican gains in economic reputation have yielded on average three points in presidential electoral margins (M. Smith 2007).

What happened to cause the shifts in how people viewed the economic competence of the two parties? Potentially one might interpret the movement toward Republicans as a reaction against the party in power at the onset of economic troubles in the early 1970s. The Democrats had controlled Congress since 1955, but many Americans were unaware of that fact. Public opinion polls over several decades indicate that the percentage of Americans who could correctly identify which party held the majority in the House of Representatives averaged 63 percent—a figure only marginally above the 50 percent that would be reached if everyone chose randomly from the two major parties (Delli Carpini and Keeter 1996, 316). Most Americans who think about which party runs the federal government consider the affiliation of the president, not Congress.

More leverage can be gained, then, by examining the health of the economy under each party's presidents. In accounting for rising evaluations of Republicans, one possible explanation involves the economic performance overseen by various occupants of the White House. Perhaps the more positive views of Republicans simply reflected mass prosperity under their leadership as opposed to stagnation when Democrats held power. Although the economic health of the nation in the 1990s under a Democratic president gives pause to anyone entertaining such a possibility, the idea merits closer examination.

The best summary measure of the economy is the rate of growth of real GDP, which incorporates not only increases in the production of goods and services but also inflation. Average real growth rates reveal a striking pattern in the post-1972 period. The Republican figures range from a low of 2.1 percent during George H. W. Bush's four years in office to a high of 3.8 percent under the second Reagan administration, with the average being 2.8 percent. On the Democratic side, the Carter and two Clinton administrations yield a low of 3.2 percent, a high of 4.2 percent, and an average of 3.6 percent. The raw numbers, then, favor Democrats. Introducing lags (so that the economy in an administration's first year is attributed to its predecessor) reduces the Democratic advantage but does not eliminate it. This pattern is difficult to reconcile with the usual Republican dominance in public views of economic prowess. Moreover, the figures are even more tilted toward Democrats when one considers changes in personal income rather than GDP. Families at the 95th percentile of the income distribution have done equally well under both parties, but fami-

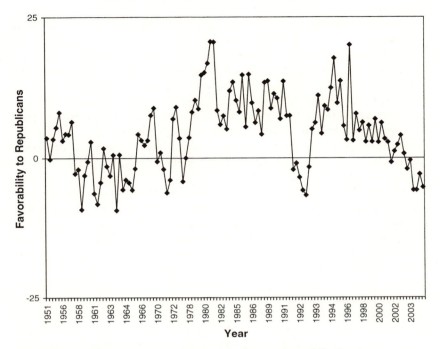

Figure 6.2 Performance-Adjusted Economic Reputation of the Parties

lies in all other income brackets have fared much better when Democrats hold the presidency (Bartels 2004).

If the GOP gained in economic perceptions during a period when its presidents delivered weaker economic outcomes than did Democrats, does that mean that party reputations are unaffected by changes in the objective economy? A straightforward statistical analysis indicates otherwise. The rate of growth of real GDP, as one would expect, bears a statistically significant relationship with the party reputations.[9] However, only a small share of the variation in the parties' reputations can be explained by variation in the economy, meaning that the key influences lie elsewhere. The measure of comparative advantage on the economy responds to economic reality but is not fully determined by it; reputations can be better or worse than the nation's economic profile warrants. Figure 6.2 shows the economic reputation of the parties, purged of the effect from the public's updating its opinions using new information on economic reality. Because it represents the part of perceptions that is purely a matter of reputation rather than performance, the resulting variable can be called the performance-adjusted economic reputation.[10]

The data in figure 6.2 essentially replicate the movements already seen in figure 6.1. When one subtracts from the scores on the parties' comparative advantage on economic reputation the portion explained by the state of the economy, most of the original variation remains. The peaks and valleys seen in figures 6.1 and 6.2 are sometimes different, but the overall trend benefiting Republicans appears starkly in both. In other words, the trend remains despite accounting for economic conditions during the parties' respective tenures in office. Although the patterns depicted by the two graphs are similar, figure 6.2 is easier to interpret because one need not wonder whether a given movement simply records the public reacting to a healthy or weak economy.

As seen in figure 6.2, the period from 1951 to 1972 yields many positive and negative data points, which combine for an average virtually indistinguishable from zero. A very different portrait emerges from 1973 to 2004 and particularly after 1980. This period witnessed a lasting decline in economic security, with a complicated series of rhetorical and programmatic responses and counter-responses by the parties. The Republican strategy usually prevailed in the court of public opinion. Figure 6.2 identifies, in effect, the bonus the GOP attained in recent decades that is independent of what happened in the economy. One cannot make this basic pattern vanish by incorporating additional economic indicators like the inflation rate or by including lags on the variables.[11] The graph does not imply that the economy has no real effects. The point, rather, is that Republicans gained even after taking those effects into account. In an unpleasant twist for the Democrats, their presidents must preside over a strong economy to receive the same benefits as Republicans holding office during a mediocre one.

This shift in partisan reputations thus poses an acute puzzle. It is not at all obvious why the deteriorating economic security described at the outset of this chapter should have worked against the Democrats. Indeed, the orientation of culture versus economics of many observers of American domestic politics builds from a starting assumption that the economy normally has represented a winning issue for Democrats. The data presented here indicate, to the contrary, that it was the Republicans who held the advantage on the economy for most of the past three decades.[12]

Sources of the GOP's Reputational Edge: Consistency of Message

Why did Republicans gain the upper hand on public perceptions of which party is better for the economy? One crucial factor was that their economic message of lowering taxes and improving incentives has been clear and consistent. The Democrats, by contrast, have changed their economic emphases repeatedly, have developed arguments more difficult to convey to voters, and have encountered difficulties settling on an agenda that satisfies important constituencies.

The consistency of the GOP's economic message dates back to Ronald Reagan's campaign of 1980. Reagan followed his predecessors like Barry Goldwater in demanding a balanced budget, but the means of achieving it were thoroughly transformed. Reagan's supply-side philosophy allowed him to reconcile his promises that, "We must balance the budget, reduce tax rates and restore our defenses" (Reagan 1980a). Proposing to cut taxes and open a major new line of expenditure would seem to make balancing the budget impossible—unless the tax cuts would actually increase, rather than decrease, federal revenues. During his convention acceptance address, Reagan (1980b) stated: "When I talk of tax cuts, I am reminded that every major tax cut in this century . . . ended up yielding new revenues for the government." His key difference with prior nominees lay in the supply-side philosophy, which, as a practical matter, meant that Reagan need not wait for action on the spending side of the ledger before moving on taxation.

Led by the tax issue forcefully championed by Reagan, the Republicans have embraced a limited set of principles and repeated them in election after election. Republican elites have linked the party's key policy stances clearly, directly, and repeatedly to a healthy economy. Instead of pushing for flatter taxation with claims that it is unfair for individuals to pay at unequal rates, which was the primary contention of Republican conservatives in the two decades after World War II, their successors argued that higher taxes on the wealthy decrease the incentive to work and save. Regulation of business, formerly often opposed as falling outside the proper responsibilities of government, was now challenged on grounds that it caused jobs to be lost. Social welfare programs became targeted for cuts based in part on the rationale that they crowded out private investment. Economic means of framing these issues had long been present but submerged in the rhetoric of conservative intellectuals and Republican politicians. The increased prevalence of economic insecurity beginning in the early 1970s invited a different rhetorical response. Republican stands on taxation, regulation, and the welfare state were increasingly marketed to the public as a means to promoting prosperity (M. Smith 2007).

The organizational components of the GOP's coalition have underpinned and reinforced its economic messages. With the onset of greater economic insecurity, Republicans gained because their allies in the business community were well positioned to articulate an effective response. Although the claims offered by corporations and business associations can easily be discounted when they rest on other rationales, those assertions acquire an inherent credibility when the basis of support involves which policies will facilitate job creation. Companies and industries, after all, can be presumed to have developed detailed knowledge about and firsthand understanding of employment levels. Republicans cooperated especially tightly with small business, which went from being relatively unorganized a few decades ago to being highly mobilized today. Small-business organizations have been active and vocal in attempting to block new regulatory and social welfare programs and in advocating the curtailment of existing ones (C. Martin 2000; Young 2004). It has not been lost on policymakers that small businesses create most of the new jobs in the United States, giving credence to their trade associations' claims about the policies needed to boost employment rolls and growth levels.

Republicans also worked cooperatively with conservative think tanks in advancing their economic programs and arguments. Beginning in the 1970s, executives and program officers of conservative foundations, along with many other leaders on the right, came to believe in the power of ideas. Convinced that they were overshadowed and outgunned in the dialogues and debates that inform policymakers and shape public opinion, conservative foundations began building an intellectual infrastructure comprising conservative magazines and journals, a scattering of academic programs at universities, student newspapers, and—most importantly for the purposes of this chapter—think tanks. Right-leaning think tanks quickly became a primary recipient of a sustained infusion of capital.

Funded primarily by patrons, think tanks can work on a variety of issues and adopt whichever arguments and appeals—economic ones among them—prove useful in promoting and defending their positions among policymakers and the general public. The importance of think tanks to the process of honing and disseminating ideas has been well known among scholars and journalists since the early Reagan years. What has not been appreciated, however, is the particular effectiveness of think tanks in the realm of economic policies and the barriers advocacy groups and social movements face in exerting a parallel impact. Working over many years, think tanks can put their proposals and the supporting arguments into circulation. Likewise, the policy institutes can use economic issues and arguments to influence the mass public, thereby marshaling the backing that manifests itself later in elections, polls, or other means that enter the stream of information shaping legislative decisions. As Steven Teles' chapter reveals, funding from patrons allows for long-term thinking and the patient development of proposals that may take years or even decades to gain a foothold.

The dominance of conservatives within the world of ideologically oriented think tanks does not guarantee policy success. It does, however, give them a critical mass of intellectuals who can create, nurture, and publicize economic ideas and express those ideas in a persuasive way. The conservative economic program since 1980 has made tax cuts the largest component but also included deregulation, privatization, and curtailing social spending. All of these elements have been assiduously promoted by conservative and libertarian think tanks. Those on the left who have documented foundations' funding of the research institutes often point to specific policy areas where the money seems to have paid some of its highest dividends, such as cuts in marginal income tax rates, welfare reform, deregulation, social security privatization, and school vouchers (Covington 1997; Callahan 1999). Nationwide policy changes have yet to be passed in the latter two areas, but it is nevertheless a measure of success that the ideas moved from the fringes of political debates three decades ago into the mainstream today.

The rise of economic insecurity thus played into the hands of the Republicans, for their organizational allies were ideally suited to capitalize rhetorically on enduring financial anxiety. These actors amplified and extended the Republicans' rhetoric in stressing the economic benefits of low taxes, minimal regulation, and a streamlined welfare state. This organizational capacity fostered consistency and repetition, which political consultants consider crucial components of a winning message. When political participants desiring similar policies use contrasting rhetoric, the likely result is to sow confusion among the broader public. Because of the innumerable diversions of people's time and the difficulty for any message to register, it is important to find the most effective arguments for a given policy and repeat them across time and in a variety of venues. With Republican politicians commonly promoting the same initiatives and framing as think tanks and segments of business, especially small business, the message enjoyed a greater opportunity to register an impact on the electorate.

The Democrats could not benefit from a similar level of consistency either within their own programs and rhetoric over time or from organizational allies. For much of the past three decades, the Democrats flitted from issue to issue without a core economic strategy. In the late 1970s, much of the party's economic attention flowed toward government guarantees of employment as reflected in the Humphrey-Hawkins bill that eventually passed Congress in a watered-down form. Moving into the early 1980s, many of the party's luminaries viewed industrial policy as a means to solve the problems with the ongoing restructuring of the nation's economy. As the luster of industrial policy faded, deficit reduction attracted support from Democratic presidential candidates, beginning in 1984 with Walter Mondale. Indeed, deficit reduction provides the only real thread connecting recent Democratic nominees; other policy areas continued to see little consistency. On trade, for example, Walter Mondale and Michael Dukakis, the 1984 and 1988 nominees, embraced some protectionist stands, whereas the campaigns of Bill Clinton, Al Gore, and John Kerry moved more firmly toward a stance of free trade. The larger point for present purposes is that with the exception of deficit reduction, most voters would have been hard-pressed to identify the Democrats' economic program.

Not only did the Democrats' platform and message change from election to election, it also lacked consistency with other forces in society. The Democrats' strongest organizational allies are in advocacy groups covering areas like environmental protection, minority rights, civil liberties, and the separation of church and state, and these allies have been effective in certain policy areas (Berry 1999). Advocacy groups, however, have played a limited role in economic areas and are generally uninterested in contesting conservative economic ideas. As a result, Democrats had the wrong kind of organizational allies for operating within a climate of a heightened prominence of economic matters. The traditional source of institutionalized support for Democratic economic policies came from unions, but they have shrunken in size and felt alienated from some of the policies—deficit reduction and especially free trade—characteristic of the Democratic Party in the Clinton-Gore years. The net result is that while Republican economic messages were complemented by other actors, the Democrats could not benefit from similar consistency and repetition from potential allies.

Sources of the GOP's Reputational Edge: Clarity of Message

The clarity of the GOP's economic message constituted a second major source of the party's reputational advantage. Research on congressional behavior finds that politicians are well aware that the clarity of the cause-and-effect chain from policies to their consequences shapes the distribution of accountability (Arnold 1990). The more visible are a policy's effects, and the more easily they can be traced to specific legislative votes, the more likely that politicians will become associated with them. Lawmakers sometimes write laws such that benefits materialize early but costs occur later, when the legislative decisions may have been forgotten. When a policy is claimed to produce simple and direct consequences, citizens find it easy to place the responsibility for legislative decisions; yet when policies create their effects only through many intervening steps in a complex causal chain, lawmakers are less likely to receive praise for positive outcomes or culpability for negative ones.

The Republican message from Reagan forward, especially its central component of tax cuts, had the formidable virtue of being clear and intuitive. Taxes are themselves an economic quantity, and the notion that putting money in people's pockets leads to greater investment and consumer spending is simple to understand. Because the connection between taxes and the economy seems direct to voters, it would be relatively easy for a president to attract credit for a strong economy after having followed a policy of tax cuts. Of course, should the economy be weak after the enactment of tax cuts, as was the case for most of George W. Bush's first term, then credit-claiming opportunities will be limited.

On the other side of the aisle, Democrats struggled to find a compelling message that would allow them to win the struggle over the allocation of credit and blame. Forced into a reactive posture by Reagan's success, Democrats shifted gears in seeking an effective response. Their most consistent message—deficit reduction—had neither the resonance nor the clarity of the GOP's appeals. Moreover, the decision to reposition the party around a posture of fiscal responsibility required its leaders to scale back or deemphasize potentially popular proposals that required new government spending. Because it represented the most persistent component of the Democrats' economic message, and because it was the one element the party actually had the opportunity to implement fully, it is worth examining in some detail the political consequences of the party's move toward fiscal responsibility.

Bill Clinton and the Democrats' Embrace of Deficit Reduction

Deficit reduction can become an appealing campaign issue under certain circumstances. While bringing few benefits to Walter Mondale in 1984, it did later assist both Paul Tsongas in the 1992 Democratic primaries and Ross Perot in the general election. Yet Bill Clinton's experience demonstrates the differences between sometimes-popular campaign pledges and the reality of allocating the pain once in office. To meet his promise to cut the deficit in half in four years, the former Arkansas governor needed to restrain any spending increases or tax cuts. Clinton's first-term decisions therefore developed under tight constraints that led him either to bypass entirely or propose in weakened form most of his economic agenda from the 1992 campaign that would add to the deficit. On education, the unfulfilled commitments included boosting funding of Head Start to cover all eligible children, guaranteeing a college education for everyone willing to devote two years to national service, and establishing a national apprenticeship program. For building new infrastructure, the abandoned pledge was a "Rebuild America" fund with $20 billion per year. On taxes, Clinton had campaigned on a middle-class tax cut—"giving working families a choice between a children's tax credit and a rate cut"—but this initiative too got left on the cutting room floor. Clinton's early budgets offered modest increases in spending on highways, Head Start, apprenticeships, and national service, but the allotted funding totaled nowhere near the levels he had promised while campaigning for the presidency.

By contrast, most of Clinton's actions that fulfilled promises from the campaign of 1992 were those that either had no direct and immediate impacts on the budget or actually helped reduce the deficit. In the former category, Clinton not only pushed the North American Free Trade Agreement (NAFTA) through Congress but also backed a new round of the General Agreement on Tariffs and Trade (GATT), U.S. entry into the World Trade Organization, and permanent most-favored-nation trading status for China. Among the elements of his economic platform consistent with reducing the deficit, Clinton signed a 1993 budget including three minor revenue sources along with higher marginal rates on corporations and high earners. The 1993 legislation raised the top marginal income tax rate on individuals to 39.6 percent, a change that generated the lion's share of the revenue increases in his administration.

In the end, Clinton's economic program included two primary pieces: shrinking the deficit (and, eventually, balancing the budget) and signing trade agreements. That combination proved deadly to Democratic prospects in the 1994 midterm elections. Interestingly, Clinton himself anticipated as much. In a meeting of administration officials early in the president's first year, he said that Democratic members of Congress were "crazy" for thinking they could run successfully for reelection on the 1993 budget and the NAFTA and GATT agreements (Woodward 1994, 165). Subsequent scholarly analyses indicated that support for the president's positions was a strong predictor of defeat for Democratic incumbents, and voting for the 1993 budget resolution was especially likely to incite a backlash in the electorate (Brady, Schlozman, and Verba 1996).

The 1990s Boom and the Campaign of 2000

The character of economic argumentation and political campaigning at the end of Clinton's second term provides a useful window into the long-term shifts in the parties' economic reputations. Although Clinton in the late 1990s presided over the strongest economy in thirty years, the public assigned responsibility for the nation's sparkling economic performance not only to the Clinton administration but also to the Republican Congress and the Federal Reserve. Near the end of the long boom in June 2000, a Gallup poll asked respondents, "to which one would you give more credit for the positive state of the economy in the past few years—the Clinton administration or Congress?" A tiny plurality—44 to 42 percent—actually chose Congress over the Clinton administration. In a separate question pitting the Clinton administration against the Federal Reserve, the nation's central bank amassed a sizable majority of 53 to 38 percent (Public Opinion Online 2004a).

These differences in attribution created important consequences for how people voted in the subsequent election. It is well known that a strong economy improves the electoral prospects of the incumbent party, but recent research has shown that the effects depend on how individual voters allocate responsibility. Holding all else equal, those who credited Clinton were much more likely to vote for Gore in 2000. In an undesirable turn for the vice president, large parts of the population chose either Congress or the Federal Reserve as the institutions most praiseworthy for the nation's positive economic conditions (Rudolph and Grant 2002).

How could the characteristics of Clinton's policies help explain his inability to garner more credit for the state of the economy? Addressing the budget deficit hindered Clinton's prospects for fulfilling the parts of his 1992 economic program involving education, training, and transportation. Unfortunately for Clinton, these were the parts of his program that, if enacted, would be the most visible to constituents and traceable to the president's actions. If people suddenly qualify for an apprenticeship program, Head Start for their children, or a college education to be repaid through national service, they will surely know it; new mandates on employers for job training would be similarly noticeable to workers; and building infrastructure such as highways, bridges, and airports leaves behind physical structures that the eye cannot miss. Had Clinton pursued these policies as the core of his economic program, he later could have pointed to them as a leading cause of the nation's prosperity.

By contrast, neither deficit reduction nor trade agreements possess properties that facilitate credit claiming. Deficits are an abstract accounting device rather than something tangible to ordinary citizens; without a concrete reference point, voters in the 1990s were slow even to notice that deficits were shrinking. A truly stunning public opinion poll in July 1996 asked people, "Compared to five years ago, is the budget deficit larger or smaller now, or is it about the same." The correct answer, of course, is that the deficit was smaller—much smaller. Yet 70 percent of the respondents replied that it was larger, compared to only 12 and 17 percent saying smaller and about the same, respectively (Public Opinion Online 2004b).

Moreover, the connection between deficits and economic performance is opaque. Probably not five citizens out of a hundred could explain why many economists believe that sustained deficits hurt the economy's long-run trajectory. That case rests on the linkage of deficits with interest rates, which then affect business investment and the amounts homeowners spend on mortgages, thereby affecting job creation through the demand for capital and consumer goods. Some economists doubt the existence of a causal nexus between deficits and macroeconomic performance, but in assessing the reaction among citizens the dissension within the economics

profession is beside the point. Voters are unlikely to retrace the steps in
the chain of effects, reasoning back from a robust economy to the level
of interest rates to the amount of borrowing, and then finally back to a
deficit reduction plan enacted a few years earlier.

Trade agreements are equally if not more unlikely to create credit-
claiming opportunities. NAFTA represented a major political victory
for President Clinton, but its electoral benefit was marginal at best.
After its provisions had been implemented and the results could be observed, the public was closely split. A very slight plurality of Americans
was favorably disposed toward the treaty, appearing willing to trade off
fewer jobs for workers for a gain of lower consumer prices (Public Opinion Online 2004c).

From seeing the results of public opinion polls, one can safely conclude
that if unemployment rose after the signing of a free trade agreement,
the public would be receptive to a critique that blamed the treaty. But if
unemployment reached a historic low—as it did in the late 1990s—the
public would be unlikely to identify the policies of free trade as a cause.
Just looking at the raw numbers of jobs, one would find little grounds for
concluding that NAFTA had led American jobs to exit for Mexico and
Canada. And yet even in the most favorable economic climate in recent
history, a majority of the public still believed that NAFTA weakened the
employment picture domestically. The notion that free trade allows employers to flee American shores for cheaper labor overseas cannot be easily shaken from public beliefs. Economists typically claim that free trade
brings lower prices at home *and* more jobs because money that otherwise
would have been spent on higher prices fuels production, and hence employment, elsewhere in the economy. Those effects, however, are indirect
and difficult to observe. When a plant closes and moves its operations to
the Third World, by contrast, the result is visible, tangible, and easy to
portray in the news media.

Clinton also lacked an organized base in society that could complement
his attempts to frame the consequences of his policies. The most likely
source of rhetorical support for a Democratic administration, labor
unions, found deficit reduction and especially free trade to be anathema.
Believing that the interests of workers lay in a different approach to governing, unions would have undermined their own agenda by retreating
and declaring that the policies had succeeded after all. Although some
business associations approved of the broad course Clinton charted on
economic policy, they could not easily speak for or represent groups of
voters. Clinton's policies thus enjoyed some elite backing but had no institutional support connected to a mass constituency, making it more difficult for him to be successful in asserting that positive outcomes followed
from his actions.

The president in the late 1990s nevertheless attempted to win public recognition for his administration's stewardship of a booming economy. In high-profile State of the Union addresses in 1999 and 2000 (B. Clinton 1999; 2000), he called attention to the broadly shared prosperity and identified his pursuit of fiscal discipline as a central determinant of prevailing conditions. But the message did not seem to register with the populace. In these speeches, arguably his most prominent during his final two years in office, he did not even *try* to assert that trade agreements had contributed to the robust economy—probably a wise rhetorical decision given the skeptical state of public opinion. Simply by being the incumbent during a period of prosperity, Clinton benefited from the halo effect that would accrue to whoever held office; yet he could not surpass this baseline amount of credit by pointing to policies that, being visible to ordinary citizens and traceable to his actions, accounted for the nation's economic conditions. Given this situation, it is unsurprising that polls showed that people were more likely to attribute responsibility to other governmental institutions. Perhaps the cult of personality that built up around Alan Greenspan in the 1990s could help explain Clinton's slipping behind the Federal Reserve in receiving credit, but the president could not even outshine Congress—an institution that normally attracts high levels of distrust among the public (Hibbing and Theiss-Morse 1995).

CONCLUSION

After taking office in 1992, Clinton made the fateful decision to fulfill his campaign promise of reducing the deficit by half. When Congress began deliberating over Clinton's proposed package of tax increases and spending cuts, the public immediately began shifting its economic evaluations away from the Democrats. Even with the strongest economy in thirty years that emerged during his second term, Clinton could not bring the Democrats' economic reputation back to parity with the GOP.

Indeed, by the time Clinton left office, the reverberations from Reagan's decision two decades earlier to overturn the traditional Republican position and to embrace tax cuts first without any certainty of spending cuts were evident. For decades leading Republican officeholders and candidates had advocated tax cuts, but the equally pressing desire for balanced budgets formerly served as a counter-balancing force. While its status as economic doctrine was a subject of skepticism, Reagan's supply-side economics achieved success as a political doctrine. Without producing improved economic performance, the GOP had boosted its economic reputation. This achievement stemmed from a message that was clear, consistent, and compelling—all qualities that the Democrats' economic messages lacked—and from the sustained backing of a strong organizational supporters. In a context of rising economic insecurity, these gains in reputation translated into enhanced electoral strength.

Some of Reagan's intellectual allies in the late 1970s, even as they doubted supply-side claims that tax cuts would not create massive budget deficits, had shrewdly anticipated the long-term political benefits. Irving Kristol described the appeal in an opinion piece published on 16 May 1980, shortly after Reagan offered a revised version of the Kemp-Roth tax cuts then circulating in Congress. The political logic for endorsing Kemp-Roth was irresistible despite, or even because of, the potential for causing gaping deficits:

> When in office the liberals (or social-democrats, as they should more properly be called) will always spend generously, regardless of budgetary considerations, until the public permits the conservatives an interregnum in which to clean up the mess—but with the liberals retaining their status as the activist party, the party of the "natural majority." The neo-conservatives have decided that two can play at this game—and must, since it is the only game in town. . . . And what if the traditionalist-conservatives are right and a Kemp-Roth tax cut, without corresponding cuts in expenditures, also leaves us with a fiscal problem? The neo-conservative is willing to leave those problems to be coped with by liberal interregnums. He wants to shape the future, and will leave it up to his opponents to tidy up afterwards. (Kristol 1980)

Within the strategic stance endorsed by Kristol, balanced budgets are for chumps. Why not let the other party take the tough stands and suffer the consequences at election time?

The series of events, policies, strategies, and responses that gave Republicans the upper hand on the economy began with Reagan's repositioning of the party to focus on tax cuts first and spending cuts of corresponding size, if at all, later. Reagan's rhetoric tying tax cuts to a future of prosperity was facilitated by the spread, brought about by the conservatives' invigorated intellectual infrastructure, of supply-side economics. The benefits of the shift in stance were twofold: the consolidation of a clear, consistent, and appealing Republican message on the economy, and the placement of Democrats in a less favorable position. The resulting deficits, along with new ones in the early part of the twenty-first century, brought strong temptations to Mondale, Dukakis, Clinton, and Kerry to highlight the issue, always a potent short-term means of criticizing the opposition for reckless financial management. Even though Reagan himself probably did not intend it, the genius of his political and rhetorical moves lay in leading the Democrats to believe that fiscal responsibility was both desirable on the merits and an effective stance for gaining political advantage.

Over a longer period, deficits amounted to irresistible bait that created precisely the effects Irving Kristol had expected. Fiscal restraint tied the hands of the Democratic Party, forcing it into what Kristol called the "liberal interregnum" that dealt with the budgetary problems it inherited rather than pro-actively offering an ambitious agenda of its own. With the exception of George H. W. Bush's unpleasant venture into deficit reduction, the Democrats rather than the Republicans were most often saddled with running on a platform of tax increases or spending cuts. Thus Reagan's repositioning of the Republicans around a clear and consistent economic message focusing on tax cuts not only constrained the maneuvering room of the Democratic Party but also produced a durable improvement in the economic image of the Republicans.

NOTES

1. Calculated from the Historical Income Tables, Current Population Survey, U.S. Bureau of the Census, "Families by Median and Mean Income: 1947 to 2000," www.census.gov.

2. Calculated from Federal Reserve Board, Flow of Funds Accounts of the United States, annual historical data, www.federalreserve.gov/releases/z1/current/data.htm.

3. Bankruptcy figures are from American Bankruptcy Institute, U.S. Bankruptcy Filing Statistics, www.abiworld.org/stats/newstatsfront.html. Figures on the number of bachelor's degrees awarded can be found in the *Digest of Education Statistics*, published annually by the National Center for Education Statistics at the U.S. Department of Education.

4. Most of these data (from 1946 to 2001) were collected and coded by Frank R. Baumgartner and Bryan D. Jones as part of the Policy Agendas Project. The data spanning 2001–4 were compiled by the author. The economic category, as defined here, includes not only mentions of such dimensions as unemployment, inflation, and interest rates but also energy production and prices, foreign trade, and labor unrest.

5. These data stand in opposition to the claim, advanced by Ronald Inglehart (1990), that mass publics in advanced industrialized nations have gravitated away from worrying about economic matters and toward a broader set of "post-materialist" concerns. While relatively new issues involving environmental protection, rights, and life-styles have certainly occupied space in the public agenda, in no way have they pushed aside basic matters of economic security.

6. Each advertisement broadcast after 1 September was coded according to its issue content, using fractions where more than one issue was mentioned. Vague appeals to families, children, the future, the middle class, or patriotism fall outside of the coding system, but linkages to specific issues—say, a program promoting

child nutrition—are included. The data for 2000 are incomplete, reflecting only the advertisements available as of this writing.

7. While question wording effects are prevalent in public opinion polls, the close similarity in the wording of those used here make any systematic biases unlikely.

8. Following Erikson, MacKuen, and Stimson (2002, 121), I apply a correction of 3.12 points to account for the greater number of Republicans that emerged when Gallup switched from using in-person to telephone surveys. Without the correction, an immediate Republican gain in partisan support of 3.12 points appears that can be shown to simply reflect a method artifact. Measures of perceptions of the parties on prosperity and total partisan identification both receive this adjustment when based upon polls conducted by Gallup.

9. The rate of growth of real GDP, measured quarterly and converted to an annual rate, is the independent variable in this analysis, while the dependent variable is the comparative advantage of Republicans as graphed in figure 6.1. The variables are measured contemporaneously to each other. The coefficient on the independent variable should be positive when Republicans hold the presidency, meaning that economic views of the GOP become more favorable in the presence of concrete proof of the party's bona fides. When the president is a Democrat, though, it is lower growth that should bolster the comparative advantage of Republicans—an expectation built into the model by recoding the GDP variable by multiplying it by (-1) when Democrats occupy the White House.

The results of an ordinary least squares regression correspond with these expectations. The coefficient on real GDP growth reaches statistical significance at the .001 level, and the parameter estimate indicates that a one-point change in real GDP growth leads to a 0.44 point change in the comparative advantage. That is, as the economy strengthens during a Republican administration or falters under Democratic control, the GOP rises in public esteem. Sluggish performance under Republicans or a robust economy overseen by Democrats, on the other hand, benefits the party of Jackson, FDR, and Kennedy. Clearly, people notice the fluctuations in the economy and sanction or reward the party in power. However, it should be recognized that the R^2 of the model is low at .09.

10. To determine whether a party fares better or worse than expected from economic performance, the statistical model developed above relating party reputations to the state of the economy can be put to use. Based upon the model's results, one subtracts from the dependent variable the portion explained by the independent variable. The resulting measure is conceptually similar but not identical to the residuals, which can be calculated by subtracting from the dependent variable the effects not only of the independent variable but also the constant. The residuals always carry a mean of zero by construction, whereas the measure desired for this chapter has no predetermined average. By following the procedure described here, the economic reputation of the parties is purged of the effect from the public updating its opinions using new information on economic reality.

11. Conceivably the economy affects economic perceptions of the parties in ways that the model summarized here has failed to capture. To address this possibility, I reestimated the model while including a wider array of economic variables

as explanatory factors. More specifically, I included as measures of the economy not only real GDP growth but also the unemployment rate, the inflation rate, and the growth rates of the index of lagging indicators and the index of coincident indicators. All variables were recoded (as before) by multiplying them by (-1) during periods when Democrats held the presidency. The coefficient on real GDP growth is the only one that reaches statistical significance at the .05 level. I also estimated a model with a full year's worth of data for each indicator, using lag 0 (the current quarter) as well as the first three lags. The purpose of this procedure is to attempt intentionally to "overfit" the model. In order to show that important variation remains unexplained by the state of the economy, one must give the economy every chance to explain the movements in economic perceptions of the parties. This approach borrows heavily from DeBoef and Kellstedt (2004). In this additional analysis, none of the individual coefficients are statistically significant, which would be expected because of the massive collinearity when including four lags of each economic indicator. More relevant, then, is the joint statistical significance of the lags on each variable. F-tests show that none of the variables' four lags are statistically significant as a group. Thus, the best model is the one used earlier that includes only real GDP growth, measured contemporaneously.

12. If economic issues are construed expansively to cover the various components of the welfare state, then the conventional wisdom holds up reasonably well. Despite the fact that Republicans are typically preferred on taxes, trade, and controlling government spending, surveys taken at various points over time typically find that majorities favor Democrats on Social Security, Medicare, education, health care, and assisting the poor (Petrocik 1996; Shafer and Claggett 1995). Dramatically different conclusions emerge, however, if the "economic" category is defined more precisely to refer to the economy rather than everything that contains a material dimension.

Chapter Seven

Conservative Mobilization against Entrenched Liberalism

STEVEN M. TELES

IN 1981 SOCIAL SECURITY PRIVATIZATION was a fringe idea in American politics, so marginal that even the most conservative president since Herbert Hoover did not actively support it.[1] Twenty-five years later, the president of the United States not only supported the idea, but made it the centerpiece of his second term agenda. In 1981 conservative public-interest law firms were poorly organized and ineffective, conservative lawyers and law students were isolated and unorganized, and conservative legal ideas were still weakly developed and intellectually marginal. Twenty-five years later, the Supreme Court regularly hears cases carefully groomed by conservative law firms, the Federalist Society has developed chapters in every major law school and across the country, and conservative legal ideas are close to the mainstream of legal thought.

How did this happen? Electoral shifts, while obviously of great importance, are not sufficient to explain such changes. Changes of this sort require both electoral success and effective organizational mobilization—and the latter does not evolve naturally in tandem with the former. Organizational development has its own timeline, requires different sorts of resources and skills, and faces different challenges than does electoral mobilization. Understanding conservative successes, therefore, requires that we pay close attention to the constraints that organizational entrepreneurs have faced and the strategies they have adopted to respond to them.

In addressing this problem, I ask two distinct questions. First, what explains the form that conservative organizational mobilization has taken? Here I put substantial weight upon the nature of the regime against which conservatives were mobilizing, what I call the modern activist state. In order to explain conservative strategies, therefore, I begin by describing the way that liberal accomplishments were insulated from direct electoral control—the essential background condition that led to conservative organizational mobilization. Second, what explains the pattern of conservative successes and failures? Here I pay greater attention to the fact that solutions to the problem of mobilizing against the modern activist state were not always obvious, and in some cases internal movement factors led conservatives to adopt less than optimal strategies. By combining these two questions, I produce an analysis that explains the structure of the conservative network as a combination of *inheritance* and *problem solving* and thus incorporates both structural constraints and creative strategic behavior.

This chapter begins with the general phenomenon that I will call "liberal entrenchment," focusing on the attenuation of electoral power in modern American politics. I then proceed to examine two cases that illustrate the challenge represented by entrenchment, and the ways that conservative organizational entrepreneurs have responded to it. I conclude with a brief discussion of what the case of conservative organizational mobilization might tell us about the possibilities and limits on political change in modern American politics.

The Path to Entrenched Liberalism

As impressive as conservatives have been in shifting the political ground in Social Security and the law, their effect on political and policy outcomes has been much less impressive, and less connected to Republicans' electoral breakthroughs, than in such areas as taxes and foreign policy. With the election of Ronald Reagan, conservatives were able to swiftly cut the federal tax take and rapidly shifted the direction of foreign policy to one of aggressive confrontation of the Soviet Union. But in Social Security the administration's efforts to make even relatively modest cuts in the program were rebuffed (Derthick and Teles 2003), and change in Supreme Court precedents of vital interest to the party's base were slow in coming. What explains the insulation of these policy areas from shifts in electoral power? In this chapter I argue that, in these areas, conservatives were confronted by a network of supportive interests, patterns of institutional control, and inherited liberal normative and intellectual advantage. To make change happen here, conservatives would have to couple their electoral power with efforts to weaken liberalism's insulated power in the universities, professions, media, and bureaucracy, while building their own nonelectoral network.

Political scientists have long argued that this insulation was not accidental but was a key objective of policymaking in the New Deal and Great Society era. In the case of Social Security, Martha Derthick (1979, 417) famously asserted that "executive leaders have sought to foreclose the options of future generations by committing them irrevocably to a program that promises benefits by right as well as those particular benefits that have been incorporated in an ever-expanding law. In that sense, they designed social security to be uncontrollable." In a similar vein, Sidney

Milkis (1993, 143) claims that, "The New Deal program had the objective of constructing an administrative loft for programmatic liberalism—once built, party politics would give way to a policy-making state. The emergence of that state meant that public deliberation and choice were reduced to, subordinate to, a 'second bill of rights' and the delivery of services associated with those rights." In essence, the goal of progressive politics was "depoliticization," in the sense that it sought to remove from political contention the fundamental normative choices in politics, emancipating professionals to initiate policies to further those choices, and foreclose their reconsideration.

This depoliticization was accompanied by the entrenchment of liberalism in the institutions of civil society. A more professionalized and less electorally driven policy process depended upon the expansion of knowledge, expertise, and credentialization. The expanding welfare state was accompanied by the growth of the fields of public policy, public finance, and social work, while the legalization of society was accompanied by the increasing influence of the legal profession and, with it, the law schools. Throughout the 1960s and 1970s, these professional networks became increasingly committed to norms of social justice, thereby implicitly mobilizing middle-class experts for the pursuit of political change. These professional networks all but monopolized expertise in their domains and, in the process, also mediated access to professions and the networks through which public ideas were discussed and legitimated.

Even as the liberal coalition's political tide ebbed in the late 1960s, new actors took advantage of this diffuse political system to produce policy change by courts, subcommittees, and bureaucrats, collaborating in a subtle game of low-visibility, incremental policy expansion (Melnick 1983; 1994). Conservatives found this system of policymaking frustrating, not only because of its effects on their core interests, but because it rewarded precisely the resources and networks conservatives lacked and was immune to attack even when conservatives were in power (Greve 1987). These frustrations sensitized conservative organizational entrepreneurs to the fact that electoral power could not be used as a crutch to compensate for their organizational disadvantages vis-à-vis those on the left: conservatives would have to develop a network of institutions, and long-term political strategies, that could magnify the power they derived from the ballot box. This meant shifting from a grass-roots- to a beltway-centered strategy. Hillel Fradkin, formerly of the Bradley Foundation, observes that the early Reagan administration produced a "discovery that you could do things, but also a discovery that there were things you couldn't do, or that would take a long time, which would mean that you'd have to settle into Washington" (Interview with Fradkin 2001). In that sense, conservatives were forced to adapt to the regime—centralized, profession-alized, insulated from popular mobilization—they sought to dislodge.

Conservatives recognized that not all of the levers of power in Washing-ton were immediately accessible to them on the basis of brute electoral power—as suggested earlier, previous waves of liberal policymaking had effectively placed many of them entirely out of the hands of elected offi-cials. Where those levers *could* be easily reached by elected politicians (as in tax and defense policy), conservative investments in electoral mobiliza-tion yielded large and immediate results. In other cases, such as unemploy-ment insurance and health care, conservatives could not retract liberal accomplishments, but could prevent changes necessary to maintain their effectiveness (Hacker 2004). But where those levers were hard to reach (either for institutional or normative reasons) and positive change was required, experience taught conservatives that they needed to think about political investment in a different way. Rather than making large short-term investments in elections, they had to make more sustained, long-term investment in approaches that would compensate for their deeply institutionalized disadvantages in highly entrenched policy domains.

Conservative opponents of activist liberalism developed six basic strate-gies for long-term political investment. First, they sought to develop insti-tutions that mirrored those on the left, providing the infrastructure through which strategic action could occur. Second, they used these insti-tutions both to produce critiques of existing government commitments and to spell out conservative alternatives to the status quo. Third, they shifted from an essentially reactionary approach to one that focused on seizing control of the intellectual and programmatic agenda from the left. Fourth, they attempted to demonstrate the (political and programmatic) efficacy of these alternatives, by identifying short-term changes that would alter the ground on which subsequent battles would be fought. Fifth, they created networks to facilitate collective action and to create a cadre of conservative activists. Sixth, and finally, they sought to shift the foundation of the conservative movement, putting ideologically moti-vated activists and intellectuals in the driver's seat, displacing the pre-viously dominant role played by business interests.

Most of these strategies emerged only incrementally, as a result of learn-ing from previous mistakes and taking advantage of opportunities as they presented themselves. In this process of organizational learning, charita-ble foundations—which provided much of the early funding for organiza-tional entrepreneurship—were the dominant force for dislodging failed approaches and encouraging those with the potential for greater impact. In explaining the increasing success of conservatives in the stickiest and most entrenched areas of social policy, the increasing strategic sophistication and organizational density of the movement is just as important as its effectiveness in winning elections.

Social Security and law are especially illuminating venues in which to examine these processes, because they represent areas with significantly, but differentially, entrenched liberal achievements. While both cases draw attention to the importance of idea generation in the process of counter-mobilization, they differ in illuminating ways. Whereas Social Security is a policy insulated by its own programmatic characteristics and the interests that have grown around it, the law is a profession insulated by the distance of so much of its decision-making apparatus from political control. To mobilize against entrenched liberalism, therefore, required that conservatives come to resemble, organizationally, the liberals they sought to dislodge. Focusing closely on the development of conservative strategies in these areas serves both to illuminate the low-profile sources of long-term change, but also to make clear both the obstacles to and opportunities for change in significantly entrenched policy and institutional contexts.

THE LONG MARCH TO SOCIAL SECURITY PRIVATIZATION

Not long ago, experts on the politics of Social Security had concluded that the program's pay-as-you-go financing structure, combined with the impressive organization of its elderly beneficiaries, foreclosed structural change in the program (Pierson 1994; Patashnik 2000). Although recent events may have proved these skeptics right in the short term (Teles and Derthick forthcoming), the success that conservatives have had in placing privatization at the top of the Republican Party's policy agenda forces us to look back at conservative strategies in this area, to ask how they have effectively neutralized many of the constraints that previous analysts found so daunting. A close examination of the past quarter century suggests that the obstacles to programmatic change in this area were never so constraining as to render all resistance futile. In a pattern that recurs in the area of the law, conservatives' first efforts to attack Social Security were strategically naïve and easily thwarted. This led to a rethinking of strategy across the movement and a recognition that, while their scope for effective action was substantially limited in the short term, viewed from the long term it was much wider.

The Entrenchment of Social Insurance

By the early 1980s any effort to scale back Social Security or substitute a private alternative faced a number of daunting obstacles. These obstacles provided the context within which any strategy to transform the program would have to operate.

First, the Social Security Administration (SSA) had a near monopoly on information and analysis, which gave its own proposals the authority of social science, as opposed to its opponents' relatively amateurish appeals to ideology. This meant that the agency, in the hands of supporters of the program's growth, controlled the agenda where social insurance was concerned. Control of the agency also gave the program's supporters an impressive capacity for long-run strategic planning and coordination, whereas its opponents were scattered and disorganized.

Second, the structure of Social Security's benefits ensured that the SSA could count on the existence of strong, mobilized organizations of recipients, organizations that would reinforce the agency's own strategic direction. For example, unions strongly supported Social Security for ideological reasons and because of its relationship to company pensions. Further, Social Security brought into being a durable, mass-based organization of seniors: in Jonathan Rauch's (1999, 60) shrewd formulation, "Fifty years ago, the elderly were a demographic category. Today they are a lobby." The American Association of Retired Persons (AARP) office is now large enough to require its own zip code, and its ability to communicate with its members weighs heavily on the mind of every member of Congress. Finally, generations of policy intellectuals were trained to produce analysis supportive of the expansion of social insurance, providing critical intellectual support for their allies in the SSA's policy network.

Third, the benefits of Social Security were relatively certain, and its long-term costs obscure, whereas any private alternative had relatively unknown benefits but highly concrete costs. The system's opponents would thus have to convince the public of the moral or economic failings of a system that regularly delivered checks to millions of seniors, had all but eliminated old-age poverty, and, at least in its early years, provided an impressive return on contributions. As a result, they had to emphasize the dire consequences that lay ahead, rather than those manifest in the present—an unenviable rhetorical position. On the other hand, they had to persuade that same public of the merits of an alternative with which they had no knowledge or experience. Opponents had to convince the public to surrender an existing, known and seemingly effective system for a hypothetical, unfamiliar, and questionably effective alternative.

Finally, once the program matured, there was a huge millstone around the neck of a funded, private alternative. Moving to an advance-funded system like private accounts created a "double payment problem": the working public would be asked to pay both the costs of funding existing retirees and those associated with funding their own account. These transition costs, in effect, imposed an enormous tax on innovation, thereby creating strong incentives to not even consider privatization and to work within the political constraints of the existing system.

Social Security would thus seem to be a textbook case of the claim by some political scientists that, over time and under certain conditions, some policy alternatives get "foreclosed" and alternative paths disappear. In fact, it was by recognizing these mechanisms of entrenchment that conservatives have been able to implement long-term strategies to dislodge them.

The Agency, Information, and Coordination

Critics of Social Security, while recognizing the agency's importance in preserving the system, never seriously attempted a direct challenge to the SSA's political role. Instead, they were able to take advantage of processes the SSA did not directly control, while leveraging their own resources to compete with it. The SSA's own power declined as its guiding elite retired and its reputation declined with the rocky addition of disability insurance (Derthick 1990; Stone 1984). Equally important, the agency's monopoly on information and analysis declined due to technological advances and increased public access to previously limited government information. As Stuart Butler, the vice-president of the Heritage Foundation, argues, "The sunk costs of large scale data analysis used to be a government monopoly. The economies of scale were so large that [only] large organizations that had capacity like the agencies of the federal government, at taxpayers expense, [or] universities . . . could compete effectively. So first of all you had a technological change, in that places like us could get the hardware to do this. It was unthinkable when I first came here" (Interview with Butler 2004). The erosion of the government's role as the monopoly supplier of sophisticated analysis in social insurance allowed "someone like Heritage to compete, which we did, directly with the Social Security Administration, in arguing policy such as rates of return and so on: forcing them into a debate, which they didn't have to do in years gone by" (Interview with Butler 2004). Whereas for the program's first sixty years the SSA was able to produce analyses that reflected its own assumptions and objectives, now critics of the program were able to present their own analyses, which reflected standards designed to cast Social Security in the least flattering light. Not only that, but the capacity to perform their own analysis allowed outsiders to conduct research directly comparing how Social Security and private accounts would treat politically sensitive groups. Expanded analytical capacity thus allowed conservatives to destabilize the dominant "social insurance" framing of Social Security through the introduction of a new, "rate of return" frame.

By the 1990s Heritage, Cato, and the American Enterprise Institute (AEI) all had serious Social Security programs up and running, and they could couple their own politically informed research with the more rigorous and academically oriented work of university-based privatization advocates, such as Harvard's Martin Feldstein and Boston University's Lawrence Kotlikoff. These organizations' increased technical capacity was made all the more effective by their presence in Washington, which sensitized them to the political constraints felt by working politicians. This allowed these organizations to shape policies cognizant of those constraints, develop rhetorical strategies, and push intermediate steps that would ease the way for larger steps in the future—exactly what the Social Security elite had done decades earlier. By the 1990s program opponents were able to coordinate behavior and plan for the long term, compensating—and attempting to correct—for the short-term bias of their allies in office.

A sign that the seeds of past investments were bearing fruit was the changing role of Social Security advisory councils. Until 1994 the SSA was able to control these councils' composition and agenda, which were regularly convened to suggest changes to the program (Derthick 1979, 89–131). By the early 1990s, however, advocates of privatization had become sufficiently organized and intellectually confident to prevent the stacking of that year's council and were able to put two strong privatization advocates, Sylvester Schieber and Carolyn Weaver, on the committee (Weaver had made a career as a critic of Social Security). The plurality report of the council supported an aggressive privatization plan, while advocates of the status quo were unable to build a majority. The combination of ideological ambition and political pragmatism that characterized conservatives by the mid-1990s is suggested in a letter from Weaver to Milton Friedman, written soon after the council released its report: "I just wanted to reassure you that I agree 100 percent on the need to have full social security privatization on the table—both to enhance the public understanding and to improve the likely political outcome. The opportunity to get 5 members of the Social Security Advisory Council on board partial privatization—with real potential for garnering a majority—was, in my judgment, just too important to pass up" (Letter from Carolyn Weaver to Milton Friedman, 18 March 1997).

By the 1990s conservatives had succeeded in weakening the dominant role of the Social Security Administration. They had succeeded in eliminating the agency's monopoly over information and agenda control, which the SSA had previously managed through its control of its advisory councils. As a result, the SSA is no longer an important player in the politics of Social Security reform.

Status Quo Bias: Uncertainty and the Idea of Social Insurance

Social Security had three fundamental advantages over any comprehensive alternative: Social Security recipients' mobilized expectations of unchanging benefits; future recipients' expectations, rooted in experience, of future benefits; and uncertainty about the effects of any alternative. In order to disentrench Social Security, conservatives needed to come up with answers to all three.

Conservatives attempted a frontal assault on Social Security in the early Reagan administration, hoping to use their electoral power and the need to reduce domestic spending to offset the Reagan tax cuts as leverage for direct, immediate cuts in the program. The failure of this direct strategy of attack, which arguably halted the advance of the Reagan domestic agenda, sensitized conservatives to the need to play Social Security as a long-term game, one that forced them to accept at least some of the program's assumptions in order to pave the way for structural change (Derthick and Teles 2003). Most important, to avoid leaving themselves open to Democrats' attacks, conservative politicians would have to accept that the program, as it related to existing and soon-to-be retirees, was sacrosanct and separate from the rest of federal spending. In 1982, soon after the failure of the Reagan Social Security cuts, Peter Germanis (1982, 80) of the Heritage Foundation concluded that, "Although it may have been highly irresponsible for the government to promise benefits that are becoming increasingly difficult to provide, these are, nevertheless, obligations that must be met. Rather than instilling widespread panic among our elderly, we should acknowledge these liabilities as a total write-off so that we can move on with reforming the system." As Germanis implied, serious long-term thinking was impossible until conservatives accepted the futility of changing Social Security in the present.

Second, conservatives recognized that waiting for the program to collapse under its own weight was not a viable strategy. As the Heritage Foundation's Stuart Butler and Peter Germanis put it soon after the passage of the 1983 Social Security bailout, criticizing the program's "inherent flaws" would not necessarily open the way for structural changes: "The public's reaction last year against politicians who simply noted the deep problems of the system, and the absence of even a recognition of the underlying problems during the spring's Social Security 'reform,' suggest that it will be a long time before citizen indignation will cause radical change to take place. Therefore, if we are to achieve basic changes in the system, we must first prepare the political ground so that the fiasco of the last 18 months is not repeated" (Butler and Germanis 1983, 545–46). "Preparing the political ground" meant reducing the certainty of future benefits, attacking the privileged status of social insurance, building up the social and political infrastructure for an alternative system, and undermining the financial accounting systems that create transition costs to a private alternative. In each of these cases, conservatives recognized the need to move from "normal" politics to a long-term strategy of disentrenchment.

Disentrenchment required that conservatives weaken the public's certainty of receiving benefits (thereby reducing the belief that future benefits were a right to which they were entitled) while simultaneously increasing their certainty in and experience with an alternative. Conservatives could take advantage of the fact that well-known moderates, many of them associated with the Concord Coalition, were successfully convincing the public that Social Security would go "bankrupt" if radical changes were not made (Peterson 1993). The coup de grace of this strategy was the poll by Third Millennium, a small conservative group, that claimed that 18 percent more young people believed that UFOs existed than that Social Security would pay benefits when they retired (Third Millennium 1994). Despite the survey's serious methodological problems, it received enormous attention beyond the Washington policy community, showing how politically salient future expectations were to the program's political viability.

As important as these steps were, none were as important as the development of private alternatives. By supporting the move from defined-benefit private pensions to 401(k)s and tax-subsidized IRAs, conservatives were able to shift decisively from critiquing Social Security to building the foundations of their own preferred alternative.

It is always difficult, in hindsight, to distinguish between long-term planning and good fortune. Almost certainly, few members of Congress who voted to expand IRAs saw their decisions as part of a long-term strategy to uproot Social Security. But explaining elected officials' short-term motivations is not necessary for our purposes. What is important is that significant actors outside of Congress did think about the policy in these terms and organized their agenda-setting behavior accordingly. About this there is ample evidence.

In the case of Social Security, conservatives had the advantage of a remarkable stability of commitment and personnel. The Cato Institute, for example, made Social Security one of its primary issues from its founding, keeping the issue alive even when it was considered the most hopeless of lost causes. Even more important was the Heritage Foundation, which has combined a strong interest in the issue with a close—one might even say "quasi-party"—relationship with House Republicans and their staffs (Rich 2004). This gave Heritage a more effective coordinating role than the detached image of a think tank would suggest.

Almost immediately after the debacle of 1983, staffers at Heritage, led by Stuart Butler, began discussing the importance of building up IRAs as the core of an alternative system to Social Security. Although IRAs were passed for reasons unconnected to Social Security (Zelinksy forthcoming), conservative activists quickly recognized the potential for linking IRAs to long-term structural change in Social Security.

IRAs can ease the transition toward structural reform of the Social Security system. This effort should begin with small legislative changes to make the present IRA system more comprehensive so that it becomes, in practice, a small-scale private Social Security system— supplementing federal Social Security. . . . The reason for designing a "Super IRA" law with these restrictions is primarily political. While in an economic sense, the current allocation of money for the various types of insurance may not be optimal, expanding the IRA system in this way would make it a mirror image of Social Security. Americans would be able to compare the two alternatives. As they gradually became more familiar with the parallel private sector option, they would find it easier to compare the private and public alternatives when deciding which plan to use as their principal guarantee of security. (Germanis 1983, 11)

As Stuart Butler observes, "this was a long-haul strategy and involved the creation of a parallel system in social security. And it has clearly paid off and it was conscious at the time. We felt that as people became more familiar with these kind of private retirement plans they clearly would feel less threatened with ideas of allowing people to privatize. When you say you should be able to take some of your Social Security payroll taxes and put it into IRAs or 401ks, they don't say, what's an IRA?" (Interview with Butler 1998). The creation and expansion of IRAs (along with the shift to 401(k)s in employer pensions) would reduce the uncertainty in conservatives' alternative. Instead of having to describe an abstract idea, widespread use of IRAs would allow conservatives to point to something a wide range of individuals were already using and encourage them to compare their returns from Social Security and their IRA. By the end of the 1990s, conservatives had come much of the way to implementing the strategy that Carolyn Weaver (1983, 379) had identified in the early 1980s: "Uncertainties, in other words, are what will make reform possible, even at a cost. Reforms that draw on non-familiar methods of supply (such as expanded use of IRAs) will be particularly attractive. . . . If the extreme (and costly) uncertainty about one's financial security in old age is recognized by an administration that has concrete ideas for expanding the options for young people, then—despite the transitional costs of reform—we could see real changes in our social insurance system."

Transition Costs: Privatizers' Most Daunting Obstacle

The final, and most daunting, obstacle to conservatives' goal of at least partially privatizing Social Security has been "transition costs"—the large, temporary costs associated with paying simultaneously for the benefits of existing recipients while funding individual accounts. Analysts, like Paul Pierson, who have been most impressed by the durability of Social Security's basic structure, have emphasized this feature, treating it as a hard constraint on change. Advocates of privatization have also focused on this feature, cognizant as they are that it would loom large the closer the policy came to realization.

The first, and oldest, response among conservatives was purely intellectual—to deny that transition costs are, in fact, a problem at all. As far back as Peter Ferrara's 1980 Cato Institute privatization proposal (Ferrara 1980), conservatives have argued that transition costs are merely an accounting fiction—they simply represent the program's unfunded future liabilities. This purely intellectual argument can only take conservatives so far, and they know it: arguments must be accompanied by long-term institutional arrangements.

The more mature approach to transition costs has been to transform the way that future liabilities are treated in government accounting, thus, in effect, eliminating transition costs as far as the federal budget is concerned. Stuart Butler describes the conservative approach to the problem as:

> What we're trying to do is to somehow put in people's minds that there is a huge cost in the current Social Security system that they will somehow have to pay. . . . We're very involved in the budget process, looking at the way that the budget is put forward. What we're doing is making the argument . . . that if you're a stockholder in a corporation, the law requires your corporation to give you in the annual report a notion of the cost of future liabilities for retirement. . . . We're trying to get into the budget process . . . that the liabilities of these programs, Social Security, Medicare, somehow show up just like they do in the FASB rules for corporations. . . . Ideally what we're trying to do, and we're working with CBO and other people on this, is it possible to use a present value approach to say, in the budget process, each year, there has to be a component, just like we have interest on the debt today, there's a component that is in fact, based on the present value of future unfunded liabilities. If that's the case, then in the budget process [and] in the way you talk to Americans, [you say] that's ok, we'll take on this obligation of the transition costs, and pay for it over the next few years, and that's a certain amount of money, and by doing that, we'll reduce the present value of the unfunded liability by a larger amount. That's a good deal. That's like, say, I pay points on my mortgage and it reduces my mortgage costs. People understand concepts like that, and so part of our challenge is to redefine transition costs to that kind of language

in a way that is generally accepted and they can understand. (Interview with Butler 2004)

This final component of conservative strategizing goes beyond merely reframing the problem of transition costs intellectually. By rewiring the process of government accounting (a change, like the creation of IRAs, that may seem at least one remove distant from Social Security policy), privatization advocates are seeking to expand the kinds of arguments that their allies can make in government by institutionalizing their position on transition costs—making their argument the new orthodoxy. This is another example of the importance of long-term actors in politics: making substantial changes in the budgetary process takes a long time and requires the coordination of a wide range of actors. For that reason, it will be organized by actors able to discount the short-term costs of such a measure, or not at all.

Although these changes might be helpful to a number of interests, for most the necessary investment is too marginal to be worth their time and energy—despite the potential for very large long-term gains. Actors like Heritage, which have long time horizons, can therefore manipulate issue framing, selling the idea to those who are not supportive of privatization as "good government" and to those who might be supportive but are afraid of electoral retribution as "good politics." As a result, they can attract a short-term coalition for a change with long-term consequences—just as with IRAs they were able to bring on board congressmen who wanted to increase national savings, or merely wanted an opportunity for credit claiming.

It is this combination of thinking carefully about the obstacles to reform and manipulating the short-term incentives of political actors for long-term objectives that defines strategic policy activism. The key question strategic actors ask is not how a proposal compares to their ideal, but whether it will so rearrange the politics of future periods as to make their ideal more politically viable. As Stuart Butler of Heritage observes,

There are a huge number of concessions we can make, if we get to stage one, if we get some kind of opt-out, we'll give all kinds of protections and requirements and anything to get to that, because once you've done that, you've made the decisive step in the right direction. Which is exactly what the left thinks, which is, we just want a program, we want a group of people who will run that program, interested in expanding it in the future, we want a committee on the Hill with jurisdiction, because once we get our foot in the door, it will expand, and that's how they [the left] think and it's how we think. (Interview with Butler 1998)

This approach is best understood as strategic pragmatism, an approach very different from incrementalism or "moderation": a willingness to compromise on details so long as a policy change realigns the political calculus of the future. It is precisely this sort of thinking that moved privatization from the outer margins of policy discourse to the core agenda of a second-term Republican president. Despite the president's failure to get traction on the issue in 2005, moving the issue from the outer margins of polite discourse to the top of a president's policy agenda is a political victory of the first order.

THE LONG STRUGGLE AGAINST LEGAL LIBERALISM

Along with resistance to communism, there has been no stronger glue holding the conservative movement together than opposition to liberal judicial activism. Businessmen angered by the use of courts to expand environmental and safety regulations, blue-collar white ethnics opposed to school busing, Christian evangelicals enraged by the use of the courts to restrict school prayer, to legalize abortion, and to support gay rights—all these groups, who otherwise share little, have been knit together through criticism of "the imperial judiciary."

But criticism is only one part of a long-term political strategy. Digging into the history of conservative efforts to restrict liberals' use of the courts reveals serious obstacles to disentrenchment that were only minor concerns in Social Security. In particular, the case of the law shows that the structure of the existing regime is not always the most important obstacle to change—in some cases it has been the difficulty conservatives have faced in diagnosing the weaknesses of that regime and organizing resources and allies in a way that is sensitive to them.

The most obvious mechanism of entrenchment in the law is federal judges' lifetime terms. A growing body of scholarship argues that the attempt to extend partisan regimes over time through the federal courts is a recurring pattern in American political development (Gillman 2004). Judges, these scholars argue, are "temporarily extended representatives of particular parties, and hence, of popular understandings about public policy and the Constitution" (Balkin and Levinson 2001, 1067). Because their terms typically extend past the partisan coalition that put them in office, conflict between the courts and elected officials is a structural feature of American constitutional government. Entrenchment, therefore, is nothing new.

Courts do not, however, exist in a vacuum. The scope of partisan conflict in the law ranges well beyond electorally rooted institutions (such as the Senate and presidency) that analysts of a "political court" usually assume drive long-term judicial change, into the institutions that feed the courts with ideas, personnel, and cases. Charles Epp has observed that the massive transformation of American law in the 1960s and 1970s was driven (and extended in time) not only by a newly sympathetic federal judiciary but also by a shift in the "support structure" of litigation. This structure is made up of "rights-advocacy organizations, willing and able lawyers, financial aid of various types, and, in some countries, governmental agencies" (Epp 1998, 19). Beyond the organizations bringing cases, it includes "the network through which information about rights litigation travels. Rights-supportive lawyers and law schools have also built a body of scholarship in individual rights and legal remedies, which aids others in learning how to successfully pursue rights-advocacy litigation" (Epp 1998, 20). Epp persuasively argues that to understand why the American rights revolution had the impact it did, we must recognize how the shift in the federal judiciary (along with a culture of rights) provided an "opportunity structure" that organizational networks could exploit.

One generation's support structure for change is another's entrenched establishment. In the early 1970s, when conservatives began organizing against the rights revolution, they faced institutions that were organized both to extend liberal legal accomplishments and to protect those they had already won. Liberal public-interest law firms, from Natural Resources Defense Council (NRDC) and Environmental Defense Fund (EDF) in the environment to Mexican-American Legal Defense and Education Fund (MALDEF) and the NAACP Legal Defense Fund (NAACP LDF) in civil rights to the wide-ranging panoply of Nader groups produced (along with allies in congressional subcommittees and the federal bureaucracy) a constant stream of challenges to corporations and government—all pressing for expansion in government activity (Melnick 1982). The law schools increasingly provided strategic analysis for this legal activism, as well as identifying and training future liberal legal activists. The organized bar, which had once been a conservative sinecure, began in the 1960s to support the rights revolution, and to lobby government to subsidize its infrastructure (such as legal aid for indigent clients and government support for "private attorneys general") (Teles forthcoming, chap. 2). Legitimating all of this organizational activity was the hallowed idea of rights, and implementing it was a federal judiciary that reflected the reigning legal ideas of the age.

COUNTER-MOBILIZATION WITHOUT IMPACT

Faced with this impressive combination of an increasingly liberal judiciary and a large, mobilized liberal support structure, conservatives responded in two ways: through the Nixon administration's efforts to appoint more conservative federal judges and by creating new, business-supported public interest law firms. Neither were notably effective.

Richard Nixon ran for president in 1968 promising to reverse the rule of "activist judges" and roll back "crime in the streets"; this provided a powerful appeal both to disaffected Democratic southerners and northern whites, essential elements in Nixon's "emerging Republican majority" (Phillips, 1969). Once in office, however, Nixon found that using his appointment power to reverse liberal control of the courts was easier said than done. With his first-term Supreme Court appointments, Nixon had every reason to believe that he had made good on his campaign promises. As his staunchest conservative staffer, Patrick Buchanan, argued soon after the 1972 election, "The president has all but recaptured the . . . [court] from the Left; his four appointments have halted much of its social experimentation; and the next four years should see this second branch of government become an ally and defender of the values and principles in which the President and his constituency believe" (Oudes 1989, 559: 10 November 1972). The president—and the conservative movement—discovered how limited the appointment power could be just two months later, when the Supreme Court handed down *Roe v. Wade*. This experience showed the conservative movement's weakness, for despite high-profile presidential support, its network was not able to effectively identify truly conservative judges, and when they did, those judges lacked the intellectual sophistication, professional standing, and compelling legal vision to be appointed (Yalof 1999). The Nixon administration's one significant conservative judicial success was, in retrospect, an accident: William Rehnquist was chosen haphazardly, after a string of other potential nominees fizzled (Dean 2001). In the law, it seemed, simply gaining political power—even the electorally rooted power of judicial appointments—was not enough to loosen liberal control of the federal courts.

The second conservative response to liberal legal entrenchment was the creation of a nationwide network of regionally based, business-supported public-interest law firms. Beginning with the founding of the Pacific Legal Foundation (PLF), these firms worked to counter the increasing influence of groups like the EDF and NRDC. Lee Epstein (1985, 133) accurately observes that PLF and other first-generation conservative public-interest law firms were created "not because they were disadvantaged in the legislative or executive arenas, but because they viewed conservatives as disadvantaged in the courts, where they believed that liberal firms had a 'moral monopoly' on the public interest." Their fundamental premise was that the left succeeded in court primarily because no one, other than the government or corporations that were being sued (and whose arguments were therefore assumed to be self-interested), was there to present the other side. As a consequence, these firms relied heavily on amicus briefs, which were relatively inexpensive, allowed them to participate in a wide range of cases, and seemed impressive to their donors.

By the end of the 1970s, conservative foundations were increasingly questioning the impact of their heavy investment in the regional public-interest law firms. In an illuminating report originally submitted to the Scaife Foundation but later widely distributed, Michael Horowitz argued that the fundamental assumptions behind those firms were misguided. By emphasizing amicus participation in order to weigh in on the widest possible range of cases, conservatives were simply reacting to cases brought by the left, thereby granting them the power to set the legal agenda. Further, this strategy ignored the larger battle over the direction of legal culture: "'Conservative' ideas can and must generate idealism and enthusiasm on the part of large numbers of young, able and motivated attorneys and can and must effectively challenge the moral monopoly still largely enjoyed by traditional public interest lawyers and their allies. Until that occurs, the conservative public interest law movement will at best achieve episodic tactical victories which will be dwarfed by social change in the infinite number of areas beyond the reach of its case agendas" (Horowitz 1979, 3).

In the battle for cultural transformation, conservatives were victims of their own strength. Conservative power in the 1970s was rooted in small and medium-sized businesses and in grass-roots, state-based organizations. These strengths were easily—and effectively—translated into electoral power (as the 1980 elections would demonstrate), but they were counter-productive in influencing the course of the law. Conservatives' power at the state level encouraged them to organize their law firms regionally, yet "in maintaining its regional orientation, the conservative public interest law movement has essentially confused wish with reality, for it is in being more effective in Washington that the conservative public interest law movement can more effectively erode the power of its agencies" (Horowitz 1979, 73). Conservative organizations needed to mirror the legal regime they hoped to undermine, rather than reflect their own movement's federal structure.

Second, the firms' close business supporters saw them simply as a more effective way to defend their corporate interests (with tax-exempt funds), rather than furthering the conservative movement's long-term strategic goals (Houck 1984). This relationship was especially problematic given that "there is likely to be an increasing number of situations where businesses will seek federal support and subsidies to insure survival and to maximize their short-run interests. In such situations, 'conservative' positions will often be adverse to those of the businesses in question" (Horowitz 1979, 26). To cite one instructive example, the Mountain States

Legal Defense Fund (MSLF), based in Denver, brought suit in the early 1980s against the city's plan to establish a private cable television monopoly. While exactly the type of case Horowitz believed conservatives should take, Chip Mellor, then a staff attorney at MSLF, recalls that "It gored the wrong ox, it gored very powerful interests there, well connected to the Republican party. The day we filed the lawsuit Joe Coors resigned from our Board. . . . while he didn't like the idea that it was going to gore the people it was going to gore, he had much more of a feeling that, this is not what I founded MSLF to do. I founded it to take on the Sierra Club, not to do this sort of thing" (Interview with Chip Mellor 2001). The case eventually collapsed, with Mellor convinced that conservatives needed to substantially diminish the role of business if their public-interest law firms were to succeed.

Conservatives were slowly recognizing that businesses could not be counted on to protect the free market: they would always take advantage of short-term opportunities, even when this expanded government control (P. Weaver 1989). Ultimately, conservatives needed to find nonbusiness constituencies to defend, ones that would allow them to claim the mantle of the public interest from the left. "It is clear that only law-action centers which speak for such unrepresented parties as taxpayers, ultimate consumers and small businessmen, and which take positions (which may or may not be joined in by large corporations) against the growth of federal power and expenditures, can sufficiently articulate principled 'conservative' positions with a requisite measure of staying power and consistency" (Horowitz 1979, 30). Defending these groups, and gaining the legitimacy that would come from them, meant finding funding sources with longer time horizons than corporations.

Ultimately, the structure of the law itself meant that conservatives needed to develop their own support structure, which could operate at every level of the law—in judicial selection, the production of ideas, the production of long-term legal strategies, legal education and culture, and the fostering of a network of practicing lawyers. Horowitz had provided a cogent critique and had pointed out the direction in which the movement would have to go, but it would take a decade for it to have its full effect.

The lessons of the Horowitz report found their most significant outlet in three general areas of organizational development: support for law and economics, both within the law schools and in programming for federal judges; the creation and expansion of the Federalist Society; and a revitalized group of conservative public-interest law organizations. These organizational developments provided the support structure that allowed conservatives to make the most of their increasing political power—a significant shift from the situation in the 1970s.

Law and Economics: Conservatives' Entrée
into the Judiciary and Universities

Law and economics as an intellectual movement substantially predated
the conservative organizational mobilization of the 1980s: in its modern
form it began at the University of Chicago in 1950s, with the appointment
of Aaron Director to run a program to support "private enterprise,"
funded by the Volker Fund. As Director recalls, "It was earlier decided
that Chicago was the only place that was likely to accept such a project,
and it was also decided that the law school was the only part of the University of Chicago that would accept such a project" (Kitch 1983, 181).
While not producing much tangible output, it did succeed in embedding
a strong free-market orientation in the law school. Director was, by all
accounts, a powerful teacher, and his influence, especially through the
course he co-taught with Edward Levi on anti-trust, helped to associate
law and economics with the law school. With the appointment of Ronald
Coase to the faculty and the creation of the *Journal of Law and Economics*, the University of Chicago became the movement's intellectual hub.
Most early leaders in the law and economics movement either went
through Chicago Law as students (including Robert Bork and Henry
Manne) or had their scholarship influenced by teaching in the school's
environment (including Richard Posner and Richard Epstein).

As a strategy of real counter-mobilization against legal liberalization,
however, Henry Manne's Law and Economics Center (LEC) takes pride
of place. Manne originally proposed creating a law and economics—oriented law school at the University of Rochester in the late 1960s; the idea
collapsed largely due to opposition from the local bar. As an alternative,
Manne created the Law and Economics Center, a highly mobile organization that began at the University of Miami and then moved to the Emory
University and George Mason University law schools. The LEC combined
research with a missionary purpose: increasing the supply of law professors trained in law and economics, and communicating these ideas to
federal judges. The LEC pursued the first goal by offering economics seminars for law professors—typically at luxurious locations—and subsidiz-
ing the legal training of economics Ph.D.s. Among the program's prominent graduates are Fred McChesney, now a chaired professor of law at
Northwestern University, and Henry Butler, who as professor of law and
economics at the University of Kansas established a series of economics
seminars for administrative law judges (De Alessi 1999, 344).

More important, however, were Manne's economics seminars for
federal judges. The seminars, begun in 1976, brought federal judges to
fashionable locations for two weeks of intense training in basic microeco-
nomics. This was eventually complemented by in-depth training in econo-

metrics and statistics, designed to increase the sophistication with which federal judges could evaluate expert testimony and evidence. Forty percent of sitting federal judges have now attended at least one seminar, which is remarkable given the time commitment involved. Although it is difficult to evaluate the impact of these seminars, the foundations' long-standing, generous funding indicates that the conservative network believes they have been highly successful. One 1993 Olin Foundation staff evaluation noted that:

> It is important to remember that Bill Clinton's election means that conservatives can no longer count on the changing composition of the federal judiciary to make judges more concerned with the economic implications of their decisions. For twelve years the Reagan and Bush appointments to the federal bench created a judiciary that was steadily more inclined to consider market processes and economic effects in the [sic] decision-making. With Bill Clinton making appointments to the court, even if they must be approved by a Senate committee chaired by Orrin Hatch, it is especially important that every sitting judge who is even slightly receptive to the law and economics approach be given the chance to become familiar with it. (Olin Foundation 1993)

Support for this program, like much of the conservative movement's programming in the law, was driven by the insight that investments in the conservative legal support structure might not only magnify the influence of conservative electoral successes but, in some cases, could be effective independent of them.

The experience with the LEC sensitized foundations to the idea that law and economics could give conservatives leverage over legal education and culture. In 1982 the Olin Foundation approached Gerhard Casper at the University of Chicago Law School, where law and economics already had a substantial presence, about the possibility of formalizing and expanding its programs in the area. Casper told foundation officials that Manne's programs, while valuable, needed to be complemented by cutting-edge academic research and law student education. This led to the creation of the Olin programs in law and economics, which the foundation quite consciously targeted only at the nation's most elite law schools—foundation officials assumed that, given the rigidly hierarchical nature of legal education, once the top schools got behind law and economics, it would only be a matter of time before the rest followed.

The foundation's most daring foray in law and economics came soon after formalizing its support of the University of Chicago, at Harvard Law School. By the early 1980s critical legal studies (CLS) had become a powerful force at Harvard, a fact that caused no small alarm to traditionalist professors in the law school (such as Philip Areeda), senior university administrators, and eventually members of the Olin Foundation board. Especially concerned was George Gillespie, a 1955 graduate of Harvard Law, a partner at Cravath, Swaine, John M. Olin's private lawyer, and a man not at all amused to hear that professors at his alma mater were encouraging law graduates to "reconceive the internal issues of firm hierarchy as an important part of one's political life, fighting the oligarchy of senior partners, opposing the oppression of secretaries by arrogant-young men who turn around and grovel before their mentors" (Kennedy 1981, 39).

By 1984 concerns that Harvard Law had gotten "out of hand" broke into the mainstream press (Trillin 1984), and the foundation—which had already been looking for opportunities to extend the reach of law and economics—moved rapidly. The 22 May 1984 minutes of the foundation indicate that George Gillespie "asked that staff consider what could be done in the area of critical legal issue studies at Harvard University and suggested that they confer with the most reputable scholars known to them in this field to prepare a presentation to the Trustees for discussion at May 31 meeting" (Olin Foundation 1984a). At that meeting, the board of trustees agreed that it should seek "To Support scholars at leading universities who are able to advance the intellectual case against the CLS movement through public lectures and debates, publication and research," as well as to "emphasize support of assistant law professors in the John M. Olin program of support for the untenured faculty" (Olin Foundation 1984b). Finally, the trustees instructed the staff to invite Professor Philip Areeda to the next board meeting, which was done. Plans were quickly drawn up for an ambitious law and economics program at Harvard Law, which over the next two decades was the foundation's largest investment in the area. Even Duncan Kennedy, the bête noire of CLS, acknowledges that the Olin program was one of the most important factors in turning back the movement's momentum at Harvard Law (Teles forthcoming, chap. 6). Unlike much of the foundation's programming, this was a program initiated by the foundation board itself, which points to the pro-active role that movement philanthropy played in organizational counter-mobilization.

The overall strategy in law and economics emerged through interaction between organizational entrepreneurs and foundations—in some cases, as at Harvard Law, foundations took the lead; in others, organizational entrepreneurs took the first step, with foundations encouraging subsequent replication. Law and economics became the principal source of conservative programming in the law schools not because it was seen as necessarily the most important area of the law, but because it was where the law schools' immune system was weakest. Most importantly, it brought conservatives onto the faculty who could provide support for the rest of the movement's law school—based programming:

> Eventually we did develop the idea that we could influence legal education more broadly this way by funding these programs. . . . I had the view that it was important to get into the law schools. . . . It was important to find some sort of presence there. Remember, at this time the Federalist Society had started, so you had student groups forming, so you had a way to bring speakers in and various activities. Law and economics seemed like a way to work on the faculty side and the curriculum side of this. As it turned out, the Federalist Society chapters did work very closely with the law and economics programs. They became their advisors and so on. . . . I would have preferred to have done something in constitutional law, but you couldn't really do that, you didn't have enough people . . . inside the law schools to do that. If you said, I want to do conservative constitutional law, well that would never work. If you say law and economics, that right away has some content, but it's kind of neutral, but you know where its headed. It was a good way into the law schools. Seemingly neutral but not really. (Interview with James Piereson 2004)

Because law and economics focused on areas outside the central axis of conflict in legal culture (such as constitutional interpretation, abortion, and, until recently, the rights of minorities and women), liberal faculty resistance was relatively muted. Regardless of the subject area, however, conservatives believed that representation on a major law school faculty was a critical asset for the movement. As a 1996 Olin Foundation evaluation of the UC-Berkeley Boalt Hall law and economics program suggests the programs' importance: "Staff believes it is important to maintain an intellectual beachhead at Berkeley. . . . At Berkeley, as at other eminent law schools, most of the faculty lean to the left; our Law and Economics Program is a strong counterweight" (Olin Foundation 1996, 3). While the foundation certainly thought that the purely intellectual work of law and economics practitioners was important, it was equally valued for the impact it might have on the balance of power in the law schools and, ultimately, in the university as a whole.

The Federalist Society: Creating a Legal Network

Establishing a "beachhead" in elite legal institutions was also the mission of the Federalist Society. While the Nixon administration's failure to change the character of the federal bench pointed to the weakness of the conservative legal network, the Horowitz report had sensitized conservatives to their limited influence over the legal profession's culture and framing ideas. The creation of the Federalist Society in the early 1980s helped alleviate both of these problems and has to be counted as the most effective case of conservative counter-mobilization examined in this chapter.

The Federalist Society began modestly, with a conference at Yale University in 1982. Steven Calabresi, one of the society's founders, recalls that the conference revealed the potential for a national organization. "Our conference was covered by *National Review* and suddenly conservatives at fifteen other law schools began calling us and telling us they wanted to attend the conference and they wanted to form chapters too. That was a process of almost spontaneous generation. It turned out there was an enormous demand at other law schools for the kind of thing we felt a demand for at Yale" (Interview with Calabresi 2002). While the organization's core mission has always been to encourage intellectual debate, its founders imagined it having a broader impact. The society's original grant proposals to conservative foundations made this longer-term goal clear: "Simply through its existence, the society can be expected to create an informal network of people with shared views who are interested in helping each other out in the placement sphere. It will in fact be one of the national organization's goals to develop key relationships with judges, legislators, governmental counsels and practitioners" (Federalist Society 1982).

The society was originally designed to fulfill three purposes: first, to encourage intellectual debate in the law, especially among law students open to conservative ideas; second, to establish a conservative presence in the law schools, to compensate for the lack of faculty representation through visiting speakers and debates; and, third, to create a network of legal conservatives who could direct or organize activities that the society itself would not. These were ambitious goals, but ones that required funders willing to invest in projects with potentially high, if difficult to measure, long-term payoffs. Eugene Meyer, the society's president, argues that:

> If you look at it as a whole, the conservative foundations have done a good job and that they've done it understanding that the long term matters and that is what foundations should be for. . . . You can understand that if you're doing a new group, a certain percentage of your grants will fail, the group won't work, and you have the same costs that any other entrepreneur in the business world has, that's the way business works. If you can choose intelligently, you'll start some really good businesses, or really good organizations. . . . Scaife [for example] had . . . the attitude that [if] it's really good and really promising, let's give it some more resources and see how much this opportunity can be exploited. (Interview with Meyer 2002)

Had conservatives been organizationally incapable of making such long-term investments (as they generally were in the 1970s and before), it is unlikely that their counter-mobilization in the law would have been anywhere near as effective as it has been.

Since its founding, the Federalist Society has rapidly expanded its activities, spreading out from the universities both geographically and functionally. Geographically, the society has followed its members out into the world of legal practice through its "Lawyers Division," which now maintains active chapters in every major city in the country. Functionally, the society has created practice groups across a wide range of legal areas, helping to cement a network of lawyers in areas like civil rights, administrative law, federalism, and telecommunications. More recently, the society has begun matching conservative lawyers with pro bono law cases, potentially mobilizing millions of dollars worth of conservative legal expertise. Taken as a whole, these expanded programs have transformed the society into a "quasi ABA," paralleling the networks and services that many members currently receive through the national bar organizations. With almost 40,000 members joined together through both functional and geographic networks, and serviced by an increasingly ambitious set of programs, the society has managed to expand its influence beyond the law schools into the core of legal culture and organization.

Conservative Public-Interest Law: Learning from Failure

As we saw earlier, the first generation of conservative public-interest law was not a success. Hampered by their division along regional lines and their excessively close relationships with business, these firms were unable to translate their supporters' resources into significant precedents. The contrast with the second generation of firms, beginning in 1989 with the Center for Individual Rights (CIR) and continuing two years later with the Institute of Justice (IJ), has been dramatic. IJ has successfully defended Ohio's private-school choice plan before the Supreme Court (in *Simmons-Harris v. Zelman*), as well as similar plans before lower courts. In addition, the Supreme Court recently decided in favor of IJ in *Swedenburg v. Kelly*, a challenge to restrictions on interstate commerce, as part of a much larger set of cases aimed at strengthening the constitution's protection of economic liberty. Even its most significant loss in the Supreme Court, *Kelo v. New London*, appears well on its way to success, as state after state has taken up the issue of eminent domain in the wake of the Court's refusal to second-guess local government. CIR has been even more successful in reaching the Supreme Court with major, precedent-setting cases. The most famous of these, *Gratz v. Bollinger* and *Grutter v. Bollinger*, challenged the constitutionality of affirmative action in university admissions. Even more successful than the Michigan cases were CIR's 1995 victory in *Rosenberger v. Rector and Visitors of the University of Virginia,* a landmark religious liberty case; *Reno v. Bossier Parish School District,* an important voting rights case; and *United States v. Morrison,* where CIR successfully challenged the constitutionality of provisions of the Violence against Women Act, in this process resuscitating the Commerce Clause. While it would be easy to dismiss these victories as the natural consequence of a changing judiciary, it is important to recall Epp's argument that significant legal change requires both a receptive audience and a support structure capable of putting strategically designed cases before them. With the creation of CIR and IJ, in conjunction with the Federalist Society network and the increasing prominence of conservative legal scholarship, the movement finally had this support structure in place.

The success of IJ and CIR rests on a few fundamental shifts in organizational design. First, both organizations avoided soliciting direct corporate support. Aware that conservatives would always operate under the suspicion of being "corporate tools," they sought support primarily from foundations and individual donors. What is more, the firms recognized early on that business could not be counted on to defend its own collective interests, something CIR discovered in its early efforts to address tort reform: "With the exception of a handful of prominent academic experts, no one has shown much interest in the idea of restoring and expanding contractual rights as a means of redressing the tort crisis. In our efforts to raise money for the project, those hit by the tort crisis—manufacturers, insurers, doctors and so on—informed us that they were not interested in legal principles or even considerations of economic efficiency; they cared solely about doctrines and practices that cause specific problems for their particular industries" (CIR 1990, 6–7). Both from necessity and design, therefore, both groups sought new cases, new legal issues, and new allies for the conservative legal movement.

With big business out of the picture, both groups sought out individuals whom they could claim to defend against the unprincipled machinations of large, faceless organizations—the same basic template used by the liberal public-interest law firms of the 1970s (McCann 1987). IJ has defended African American hairbraiders, shoeshiners, and other small businessmen against regulations that served as barriers to entry, while CIR has represented professors, Christian student groups, and white applicants to universities. The two organizations were able to draw upon the rhetoric— and, in some cases, the precedents—established by the liberal public-interest organizations, in particular a suspicion of concentrated power. This has given the groups a claim to speak for the "public interest" that their predecessors never had.

Second, both IJ and CIR have focused on controlling cases from start to finish. Although this is significantly more expensive than amicus participation, it permits conservatives to set the legal agenda, rather than responding to it. These firms are able to litigate strategically: identify cases with attractive litigants, build on their previous precedents, and complement their litigation with a determined effort to influence public perceptions. Doing this requires the existence of funders who are willing to accept the speculative, long-term nature of strategic litigation, and sophisticated enough to understand the groups' approach. Michael Greve recalls that in putting together their pitch to the foundations, "[What we said was] here's a model that reflects the insights of the Horowitz Report and the current thinking about this. There is significant start-up time on these things, so give us two or three years to try this out, this different model, and if it succeeds it's cool, if it doesn't we'll be the first to tell you, and you'll know it, and then we'll just shut our doors. You could do that at the time" (Interview with Greve 2001). As was also the case with the Federalist Society and law and economics, the resource-rich, multiyear litigation that both groups have specialized in would have been impossible without the type of funding foundations were able to provide.

Third, both firms recognized that strategic litigation required a much closer relationship with legal academics and elite practitioners than had characterized the first-generation firms. Detached from the conservative base in business and the Republican Party, both CIR and IJ developed much closer links with the legal academy. The early planning meetings for IJ involved the stars of the conservative academy, such as Jeremy Rabkin, Michael McConnell, Nathan Glazer, and Lilian BeVier—and no representatives of business. For its part, CIR put its links to academia at the core of its first grant proposals' legal strategy:

Liberal public interest law firms cooperate closely and in various ways with leading academic scholars. As a result, they have been able to gain access to legal and scientific expertise, to develop feasible litigation strategies; to secure a large amount of credibility in public policy forums and in court; and to draw upon a steady stream of talented law school graduates who will work for the firms. The conservative, free-market public interest law movement's connections to academic scholars have, on the whole, been rather tenuous. We are convinced that this is a serious weakness. Accordingly, the Center for Individual Rights maintains close contacts with legal scholars in the academic community. . . . Academic advisors are asked to identify potential litigation issues and to formulate a corresponding litigation strategy for the Center to pursue in court. They also give advice to the attorneys who litigate the Center's cases. (CIR 1989)

Academics were also critical to CIR's strategy as a source of free labor. CIR put at the core of its organizational strategy a dependence on outside, pro bono counsel, and law professors (such as Michael McConnell of the University of Utah and Michael Paulsen of the University of Minnesota) have always made up a large percentage of the firm's pro bono counsel.

CIR's use of outside counsel also required that the organization establish close relationships with the Federalist Society, which provided a network for identifying lawyers in private practice willing to do pro bono legal work. What is more, the Society also made CIR's job easier by familiarizing lawyers in its network with conservative legal ideas and bringing them to the attention of Republicans responsible for judicial nominations. Greve believes that it is the presence of members of the society network on both sides of the bench that has been at the core of most of its successes: "You need the Federalist Society not just as talent but on the bench. We couldn't have won *Hopwood* without [Fifth Circuit Court of Appeals Judge] Jerry Smith, or *Morrison* without [Fourth Circuit Court of Appeals Judge] Michael Luttig" (Interview with Greve 2004). This points to the links between investing resources in individual projects and funding organizational development across the board: the wider and deeper the network of organizations the conservative movement created, the greater the likelihood of creative synergies across them.

It might seem paradoxical that, at least in the law, the conservative movement grew stronger the greater the distance it put between itself and what many outsiders assume is its "natural" base in the business community. But this paradox dissolves when one considers the nature of the regime that conservatives were facing in law. It was only when the lawyers and intellectuals in the movement took control of the movement that conservatives developed organizational strategies that matched the terrain that they were fighting on. It was only when conservatives learned from and adopted the approaches to legal change that liberals had used to bring about the rights revolution that they were able to counter it effectively. And it was only when conservatives were able to ground their strategies in a funding source willing to invest in organizations with speculative, long-term goals that a full response to entrenched legal liberalism was possible.

Conclusion

In order to understand the way that conservatives formed organizations, defined their goals, and developed strategies to pursue them, we need to start not with the actors themselves but with the context in which they operated—in particular, the system they sought to undermine. In both

Social Security and law, conservatives were faced with an exceptionally well-entrenched policy regime, one that was highly insulated from frontal attack. Effectively countering policy entrenchment was an exceptionally challenging strategic problem, and conservatives' initial responses were not, for the most part, up to the task. The long-term strategies described in this chapter developed only incrementally, as a result of a process of political learning. It took time and experience for conservatives to recognize the necessity of building up an organizational infrastructure, and for them to adapt that infrastructure to the nature of the political challenge. Doing so required that they put less stress on leveraging their electoral strength and more stress on long-term efforts to weaken the structures of liberal policy insulation, by making political investments in the present that would yield returns in the future.

This story shows that, while the structures that political actors inherit from the past are essential to explaining policy outcomes, structures are not everything: actors do have meaningful scope for action, but only up to the point of their ability to orient their activities in the present to their effects on the future. Although there are good reasons to believe that this long-term political investment can yield significant returns, there are multiple reasons why those investments are often not made. First and foremost, while the return on political investment is likely to increase proportionately to the time horizon over which it is made, elected politicians and many of the interests that seek to influence them live in a world in which short-term incentives are very powerful. The pressure of impending elections on politicians, and of quarterly earnings on businessmen, make it hard for them to shift resources from the near term to the long term, and also make it unlikely that they will develop the strategic acumen to make such investments wisely. To the degree that such actors are dominant in an ideological movement, long-term political investment is unlikely to occur, no matter what the potential gains may be.

The power of this insight is amply demonstrated by the cases described here. It was only when control of the conservative movement shifted to actors embedded in institutions that were insulated from the pressure of short-term incentives (such as charitable foundations and think tanks) that intelligent strategic responses to the problem of liberal entrenchment emerged. Actors in these institutions had the freedom to think about political battles in the present in terms of their effect on conflicts in the future, and to make investments in political infrastructure even where their impact was distant and hard to measure. These investments allowed conservatives to maximize the influence of their victories in the electoral sphere and to reshape the political battleground even in those periods when they were at an electoral disadvantage.

The story of conservative counter-mobilization also points to the distortions that can enter into our understanding of political processes by foreshortening our time horizon. The conservative policy organizations that are taken-for-granted parts of the political universe today did not emerge automatically, spontaneously, or without trial and error. In the area of public-interest law, for example, it took two decades for conservatives to develop organizations capable of taking advantage of available opportunities. In part, this was due to the underdevelopment of conservative mobilization in other areas of the law, in particular the dearth of networks to connect conservative lawyers together and to produce ideas suitable for litigation. It was only when these networks were sufficiently mature, and when they were matched with skilled legal strategists with experience in the movement, that the breakthrough litigation strategies of the past fifteen years were possible.

Effective counter-mobilization thus requires that those disadvantaged by the dominant regime discover not only the optimal strategies for exploiting that regime's weaknesses, but also figure out how to create organizations capable of carrying those strategies to fruition. This involves not only identifying sources of funding but also aligning the interests of those supporters with the strategies most likely to have the largest long-term impact. As the example of the relationship between the conservative legal movement and business in the 1970s suggests, this is far from a hypothetical problem. Counter-mobilization is both an intellectual and an organizational problem—it is only when solutions to both problems are identified that effective long-term strategies can be deployed.

Counter-mobilization, therefore, is a process whose effects are likely to be measured in decades, not years—a lesson that should be kept in mind when evaluating the movements' failures, such as the failure of President Bush's Social Security privatization initiative in 2005. If the experience of conservatives is any indication, we should not be surprised if it takes liberals, now on the outside of a rising conservative governing coalition looking in, an equally long time to discover this regime's weaknesses and to develop organizations and strategies capable of countering it.

Note

1. The theoretical argument in this chapter, and most of the legal cases, draw from Steven Teles, *Parallel Paths: The Evolution of the Conservative Legal Movement* (Princeton, N.J.: Princeton University Press, forthcoming).

PART THREE
Policy and Politics in the
New American Polity

Chapter Eight

The Transformed Welfare State
and the Redistribution of Political Voice

SUZANNE METTLER

AT THE DAWN OF THE TWENTY-FIRST CENTURY, a deeply paradoxical relationship exists between the American national government and its citizens. The activist state spends more than ever on programs meant to elevate citizens' economic security and well-being, committing more than one-third of the federal budget—more than 15 percent of the gross domestic product—to social provision. Such programs affect the lives of vast numbers of citizens: a 2005 poll conducted nationwide found that 92.8 percent of Americans report that they have benefited from one or more programs administered by national government, and the average person has benefited from 3.4 such programs (Rank and Hirschl 2002; Maxwell Poll 2005).[1] Yet, at the same time, an anti-government spirit abounds.

Unlike Americans at the middle of the twentieth century, who exhibited high levels of confidence that government was responsive to people like themselves, citizens today have much less of a sense of connection to the political system, and the attitudes of many toward government are far more negative (Hughes and Conway 1997, 194; Orren 1997). Also, whereas citizens a half century ago demonstrated high levels of interest and participation in civic and political affairs, today, by most measures, they are considerably less attentive and less involved (Putnam 2000, 45; Verba, Schlozman, and Brady 1995, 69–74; Rosenstone and Hansen 1993). Not all have withdrawn from public life: in many ways, the political voices of the affluent and highly educated have grown louder and are heard more frequently. Less advantaged citizens, however, participate considerably less than they did in the midcentury, particularly in the most fundamental political act of all, voting (Freeman 2004).[2] Somehow, despite government's commitment of more resources than ever to social provision, it is failing to inspire citizens' confidence and to engage them as active and equal participants in the practice of democracy.

Understanding the sources of this paradox—citizens' disengagement from politics and antipathy toward government even amid high social spending—requires that we consider how changes in the welfare state may have affected the linkage between particular groups of citizens and government. Depending on their age, income, employment, and other circumstances, citizens experience programs with distinct policy designs: they vary in terms of their value, coverage, rules and procedures, political sustainability, visibility, and traceability (Peterson 1995; Schneider and Ingram 1993; Skocpol 1991; Arnold 1990). Although such distinctions themselves are known to generate particular effects on citizens' attitudes and participation, we do not know whether trends altering social programs over time may be compounding their impact.

Over the past few decades, the welfare state has weathered some crucial changes. If individual policies are viewed only in isolation, these alterations may seem fairly modest. Yet, if we peruse changes across a large number of programs, across time, three distinct patterns become evident. This chapter examines how these trends may be transforming government's relationship to different groups of citizens.

The first trend is one of status quo: government has remained a strong and effective presence in the lives of elderly citizens, as before. Key programs that benefit seniors have remained intact and continue to be relatively generous.

Second, and conversely, government makes less of a difference than in the past in the lives of many nonelderly citizens, particularly those who are nonaffluent. This is in part because some policies that affected large portions of this population previously no longer do so and in part because several policies that still reach many citizens have diminished in their real value. It is important to note that there are exceptions to this pattern: Medicaid and policies for the disabled have actually grown more inclusive and generous toward nonelderly citizens in recent decades (Mettler and Milstein 2003; Erkulwater 2006). Aside from those reached by these programs, however, many members of younger generations are likely less cognizant of government's positive role in their lives than were their forebears. The significance of this shift is likely amplified by the fact that it has occurred in the context of rising economic inequality, as the nation's economy slowed and the wages of less highly educated individuals deteriorated. Unlike European governments, which acted to offset the widening income gap with tax and transfer policies, the United States has done relatively little to alleviate such trends (Brandolini and Smeeding 2006). Neither has it responded to new risks borne by nonelderly Americans as they experience more frequent spells of unemployment and compensate for deteriorating wages with increased workplace participation, particularly by women (Burtless 1999; Gottschalk 1997; Hacker 2004; Scholz and Levine 2001; Warren and Tyagi 2003). The impact of government's reduced role in citizens' lives is likely more consequential in these times of greater financial need and increased stress.

The third trend is that, simultaneously, social policies of the "hidden welfare state," those delivered in the form of tax expenditures, have actually expanded considerably over the period (Howard 1997). Among these, the Earned Income Tax Credit is noteworthy in that it shifts funds toward the less well-off. Most such benefits, however, bestow their most ample benefits on the wealthiest Americans, through mortgage interest deductions and employer-provided retirement savings and health care plans (Hacker 2002).

Political scientists have long argued that new policies can, in turn, create new politics (Schattschneider 1935; Lowi 1964). Social policies may powerfully affect citizens' relationship to government because they typically provide them with their most personal and significant experiences of government in action. Both the extent to which policies extend economic security—or fail to do so—and the manner in which benefits are delivered speak volumes to citizens about the relevance of government to people like themselves. Through "resource effects," the funds, goods, or services offered through policies may elevate citizens' capacity for political action and their incentive to get involved (Campbell 2003). As well, policies may convey crucial messages or "interpretive effects," transmitted to citizens through the character of program rules and procedures, which affect their attitudes toward government and their inclination to be involved. For instance, policies may influence citizens' perceptions about whether government is relevant to their lives, whether their exercise of political voice is potentially worthwhile, and whether they have responsibilities and obligations toward the political community (Pierson 1993; Soss 1999a; Mettler 2005). Some programs may promote citizens' sense of belonging to the polity, heighten their inclination to be involved in civic life, and strengthen their participatory capacities; others may have no effect; and still others might undermine civic engagement (Mettler and Soss 2004; Schneider and Ingram 1993; 1997).

The transformations in social provision, in affecting the value and form of benefits extended to particular groups, may be influencing their political attitudes and behavior in ways that exacerbate the strained and troubled relationship between government and citizens. Such changes may help explain why some groups have become less engaged politically and why others continue to participate but through a politics that is increasingly anti-government in its message. Changes in the welfare state likely bear implications not only for the redistribution of public resources but also for the distribution of political involvement and hence for the well-being of democracy itself.

THE VIRTUOUS CIRCLE OF MID-TWENTIETH-CENTURY POLITICS

During the middle of the twentieth century, from the end of World War II until 1973, U.S. social programs and high levels of civic involvement flourished in tandem. In those years, through the expansion of existing programs and the creation of new ones, national government promoted economic security and opportunity in direct and visible ways. Increasing numbers of citizens experienced government making a difference in their own lives and those of their family members, enhancing their well-being and providing chances to better their circumstances. Simultaneously, citizens exhibited especially positive attitudes toward government and politics, and they took part in politics at high levels. Compared to their predecessors, they reported a growing sense of confidence in government and felt less alienation from government (Lane 1965, 874–95). During the Eisenhower era, 90 percent of the public concurred that they "usually have confidence that the government will do what is right." In 1960, 85 percent reported that they were aware of government's impact on their lives, and 76 percent agreed that the effects of such intervention were positive (Bennett 2001, 50–55). Most striking, citizens were highly active in public life. Memberships in federated civic organizations soared, reaching twentieth-century peaks, and citizens exhibited high rates of involvement in a wide range of political activities (Skocpol 2003; Putnam 2000, chap. 2).

The policies that constituted the pillars of the New Deal welfare state grew increasingly influential in citizens' lives during the midcentury, owing partly to increasingly effective implementation and partly to Congress's action to expand coverage and to raise benefit rates. Policymakers repeatedly enlarged the coverage of Social Security, including more sectors of the work force in Old Age and Survivors' Insurance and, in 1956, broadening the program to reach nonelderly disabled workers. By the mid-1970s, more than 14 percent of the population received benefits through the program. Benefit rates were increased repeatedly, and in 1972 lawmakers applied "cost-of-living adjustments" (COLAs) to the program so that henceforth rates would simply rise with inflation. Aid to Dependent Children (later called Aid to Families with Dependent Children, or AFDC) grew somewhat in 1950 when benefits were granted to mothers; the program expanded far more—reaching more than 5 percent of the population—after Supreme Court decisions in the 1960s forced states to abandon tactics used previously to exclude individuals from coverage (Melnick 1994). Average benefits under unemployment insurance also increased in real terms from about $138 per week in 1938 to $244 per week in 1972, in 2002 dollars (Mettler and Milstein 2003). Unions, sanctioned by the National Labor Relations Act of 1935 and offered at least tacit support by governing officials in the midcentury, grew in membership to include one-quarter of the work force (Moe 1987). Workers benefited from the higher standards of pay and working conditions that unions demanded (Mishel, Bernstein, and Boushey 2003, 189–96). The Fair Labor Standards Act of 1938, when first established, had extended minimum-wage guarantees, maximum-hours provisions, and overtime pay rules to only 34 percent of the population; by 1974 it had been expanded to cover most workers (Mettler 1998, 199). Beginning in 1949, Congress increased the minimum-wage rate several times; by 1968, its value crested at $8.28 per hour in 2002 dollars (Mettler and Milstein 2003).

Other programs were created anew during the midcentury period, expanding access to higher education and strengthening the safety net. The G.I. Bill, first created for returning veterans of World War II, extended generous education and training benefits, low-interest mortgages, and unemployment compensation. More than half of all veterans—5 percent of the general population at the time—utilized the education and training provisions, which paid for their tuition at any college, university, vocational school, or job-training program that admitted them and granted them subsistence allowances to help cover living expenses. Updated versions of the policy were extended to veterans of the Korean War and Vietnam War, such that a large portion of males who came of age during the midcentury—and fully 80 percent of those born in the 1920s, members of the renowned "civic generation"—gained access to such provisions, and nearly half utilized them (Mettler 2005). Congress proceeded to create other programs—such as student loans, work study, and Pell Grants—that extended the opportunity for advanced education to the general population (J. King 2000, 7). Policymakers established the Food Stamps program in 1962; after being broadened during the 1970s, it reached 8 percent of the population. Medicare and Medicaid became law in 1965 and quickly began to cover a significant percentage of the population (Mettler and Milstein 2003).

These programs, all of them highly visible instances of government making a difference in citizens' lives, coalesced with the century's lowest degree of income inequality (Goldin 1999; Burtless 1999). Not only did the economy soar in the postwar era, but equally significant, its fruits were widely distributed across the population, especially to those in the lower and middle classes. The nation's social structure was transformed from pyramid-shaped to diamond-shaped. Factory workers saw their incomes double, and they gained new health and retirement benefits that bolstered their standard of living (Solberg 1973, 248–49; Leuchtenburg 1973, 48; Gottschalk 1997, 43). Poverty rates fell dramatically (Scholz and Levine 2001, 196). While economic growth itself helped spur the enlargement of the middle class, government programs also played an important role in bolstering wages, insuring economic security in times of transition and job loss, and providing for the aged, disabled, and less advantaged (Goldin and Margo 1992; Plotnick et al. 2000).

This confluence of developments—the expansion of the American welfare state, the growth of the middle class and the reduction of economic inequality, and high levels of positive attitudes and civic involvement among citizens—begs the question of the relationship between them. To what extent should government's increased involvement in citizens' lives be credited with mitigating social and economic inequality, and to what extent did it help facilitate civic engagement? While a full answer to this broad question lies beyond what scholars know, research into the effects of one of the era's landmark programs—the G.I. Bill—offers evidence of a highly salutary relationship.

The G.I. Bill's education and training benefits were utilized by 7.8 million returning veterans of World War II, with more than one-quarter of them using the provisions for higher education and the remainder, for a wide array of non-degree programs. While college attendance had, previously, been limited primarily to white Protestants and children of the wealthy elite, the program ushered into the academy large numbers of Jews, Catholics, African Americans, immigrants and the children of immigrants, and members of working- and middle-class families. All else equal, the higher-education provisions boosted educational attainment among beneficiaries by an average of nearly three years (Behrman, Pollack, and Taubman 1989; Fligstein 1976). Meanwhile, the majority of G.I. Bill users utilized the non-degree programs, pursuing technical training in a wide array of fields. The skills they acquired enabled them to advance in their careers and to reach supervisory or managerial positions that, in the postwar economy, typically guaranteed middle-class wages and health, pension, and other benefits (Mettler 2005).

As it extended generous benefits, the G.I. Bill also prompted higher levels of subsequent involvement in civic and political activity. Comparing two nonblack male veterans with the same socioeconomic background and level of educational attainment, the veteran who used the G.I. Bill's education and training benefits joined 50 percent more civic organizations and participated in 30 percent more political activities during the postwar era. It is well known that advanced education fosters greater civic capacity and a stronger sense of civic duty, and thus leads to higher rates of political participation (Verba, Schlozman, and Brady, 1995). Yet, the G.I. Bill generated civic involvement even apart from the advanced educational attainment it facilitated. Its policy design and manner of implementation conveyed the message to beneficiaries that government was for and about people like them, making them more inclined to participate in civic and political activities. Recipients widely regarded the program to signify a "turning point" in their lives; they found the education and training it made possible to be highly valuable and consequential; they perceived government's role in granting the benefits to be clearly manifest; and they experienced fair and respectful treatment in the course of program delivery. These "interpretive effects" were most pronounced among those from low to moderate socioeconomic backgrounds: they experienced, often for the first time, incorporation into the polity as first-class citizens. Interpretive effects also proved strong among vocational education users as well as among African American beneficiaries, who became particularly active in the civil rights movement of the 1950s and 1960s and subsequently in electoral politics and political organizations (Mettler 2005). Civic engagement remained high thereafter among the G.I. Bill users who had gained the highest levels of formal education through the provisions. Advanced educational attainment generated resources, skills, and networks that continued to promote involvement in public life (Mettler and Welch 2004).

Conceivably, other social and labor policies of the mid-twentieth century may have yielded positive results for civic engagement as well. Highly visible programs may have generated a "virtuous circle" to the extent that they elevated and expanded social and economic well-being and enhanced democratic citizenship. As the nation entered the mid-1970s, however, circumstances began to change.

SELECTIVE RETRENCHMENT AND EXPANSION

Beginning with the first oil shock in 1973, the economy, which had been growing at an average annual rate of more than 4 percent during the postwar years, slowed considerably, producing far more modest increases of around 2.5 percent per year. High rates of inflation combined with the structure of the tax system such that individuals across the income spectrum found themselves paying considerably more than ever before in federal, state, and local taxes (Brownlee and Steurle 2003, 156). As well, Social Security matured, meaning that policymakers could no longer finance the program easily by including new groups, as in prior decades; rather, they faced tougher choices involving higher political costs. Quickly, a new politics of austerity began to take hold, commencing as the spirit of tax revolt spread among states and localities. In 1978 Californians gave overwhelming support to Proposition 13, establishing a constitutional amendment that limited local property taxation to 1 percent of market value (Sears and Citrin 1985). In the Republican Party, a conservative coalition gained momentum, calling for lower taxes and reduced government spending; it gained prominence at the national level with the election of President Ronald Reagan.

Reagan's presidency introduced, nationwide, a new public philosophy, one that made the overhaul and downsizing of the welfare state a central aim. In his first inaugural address in January 1981, Reagan (1981) announced, "Government is not the solution to our problem; government is the problem." Yet, although some insiders to the Reagan administration termed his presidency a "revolution," in fact major social programs survived intact (Pierson 1994), and most have continued to do so to the present.

The relatively generous direct-spending programs that are geared especially toward the elderly—Social Security, Medicare, and Medicaid—remain strong. Coverage rates for Social Security have held steady at about 14 percent of the population; Medicare coverage has grown to about 10 percent; and policymakers actually expanded Medicaid's reach in the 1990s to include more low-income families, such that it now covers more than 14 percent of the population (Mettler and Milstein 2003). As seen in figure 8.1, benefits under Social Security have retained their value, while Medicare and Medicaid increased in real terms. In short, these programs continued the trajectories established under post-war governance, and they remain highly effective. In 1996, 21.6 percent of the U.S. population had incomes below the poverty line before government transfers; such benefits cut poverty in half, to 11.5 percent, and Social Security alone was responsible for doing so in the case of nine out of ten individuals. Among the elderly, Social Security is particularly effective, lifting out of poverty more than three-quarters of those who would otherwise be poor, and reducing the elderly poverty rate from about 37 percent to less than 10 percent (Center on Budget and Policy Priorities 1998).

At the same time, however, government has receded from its visible role in the lives of nonelderly citizens who are lower or middle class. Some generous policies of the mid-twentieth century—such as the G.I. Bill—lack successors of comparable scope in recent decades. More typically, programs persist but their condition has deteriorated. Some of these changes result from actions taken by policymakers. During the Reagan administration, for example, policymakers reduced federal support for states' unemployment insurance trust funds, subsequently prompting states to curtail program benefits as well as coverage (Pierson 1994, 116–20, 128; Nathan 1983, 60; Peterson and Rom 1988, 226). But overt action by policymakers to scale back programs tells only part of the story. Many of the programs geared toward less advantaged citizens had already withered considerably in real terms due to policymakers' inattention during the high-inflation years of the 1970s. Then, by making a priority of tax cuts, Reagan pursued what amounted to an indirect but highly effective

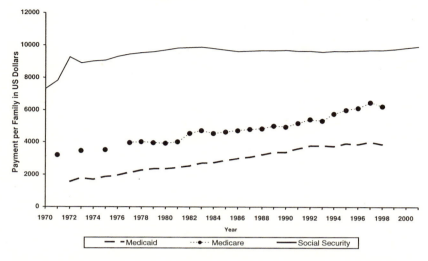

Figure 8.1 Average Annual Benefits for Social Security, Medicare, and Medicaid (in 2002 dollars), 1970–2000. *Sources:* Social Security Administration, *Annual Statistical Supplement to the Social Security Bulletin* (Washington D.C.: Social Security Board, U.S. Government Printing Office, 1971), 48; Social Security Administration, *Annual Statistical Supplement to the Social Security Bulletin* (Washington D.C.: Social Security Board, U.S. Government Printing Office, 1976), 95; Social Security Administration, *Annual Statistical Supplement to the Social Security Bulletin* (Washington D.C.: Social Security Board, U.S. Government Printing Office, 1981), 103; Social Security Administration, *Annual Statistical Supplement to the Social Security Bulletin* (Washington D.C.: Social Security Board, U.S. Government Printing Office, 1991), 189; Social Security Administration, *Annual Statistical Supplement to the Social Security Bulletin* (Washington D.C.: U.S. Government Printing Office, 2000), 124, 191; Social Security Administration, *Annual Statistical Supplement*, "Table 8.B: Medicare Enrollment, Utilization, and Reimbursement": http://www.ssa.gov/statistics/Supplement/2001/8b.pdf (2001); Annual Editions, 1981–2002, Social Security Administration, U.S. Department of Health and Human Services, *Social Security Bulletin: Annual Statistical Supplement* (Washington, D.C.: U.S. Government Printing Office); Social Security Administration, *Annual Statistical Supplement*, "Table 8.E: Medicaid Recipients": http://www.ssa.gov/statistics/Supplement/2001/8e.pdf (2001).

strategy of curbing spending over the long haul (Brownlee and Steuerle 2003, 160). Immense increases in budget deficits and the national debt ensued, thwarting efforts to increase program benefits to keep pace with inflation (Pierson 2001). President George W. Bush has achieved much bigger tax cuts than Reagan even as spending for war and counter-terrorism have vastly increased deficit spending; these factors combined further imperil domestic social programs.

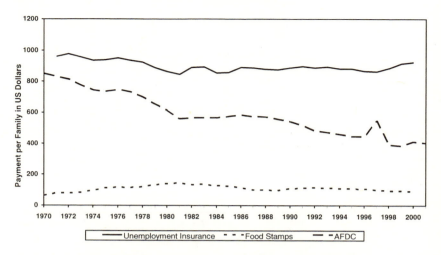

Figure 8.2 Average Monthly Benefits for Unemployment Assistance, Food Stamps, and Aid to Families with Dependent Children/Temporary Assistance to Needy Families (in 2002 dollars), 1970–2000. *Sources:* Council of Economic Advisors, *Economic Report of the President,* "B-45. Unemployment Insurance Programs, Selected Data, 1969–2000": http://w3.access.gpo.gov/usbudget/fy2003/erp.html (February 2003); U.S. Department of Health, Education, and Welfare, *Social Security Bulletin Annual Statistical Supplement and Bulletins, 1939–1972* (Washington, D.C.: U.S. Government Printing Office, 1973); United States Bureau of the Census, U.S. Department of Commerce, *Historical Statistics of the United States, Colonial Times to 1970,* Part 2 (Washington, D.C.: U.S. Government Printing Office, 1975), 354; Social Security Administration, *Annual Statistical Supplement,* "Table 9.G: TANF/AFDC and Emergency Assistance": http://www.ssa.gov/statistics/Supplement/2001/9g.pdf (2001); Social Security Administration, *Annual Statistical Supplement,* "Table 9.H Food Stamps": http://www.ssa.gov/statistics/Supplement/2001/9h.pdf (2001). According to the Department of Health and Human Services, the spike in the AFDC line for 1997 is a result of the fact that AFDC was replaced by TANF that year, and the federal government had to rely on states to provide the data. The new system led to some overlap in reporting as accounting shifted from quarters to calendar years. Conversation with Evelyn Mills, 3 November 2004.

As a result of such fiscal constraints, several of the most highly visible social programs that aided nonaffluent, nonelderly citizens have, to varying degrees, diminished in value over the period between the mid-1970s to the present, as seen in figure 8.2. In some cases, their coverage has also become less extensive. Average unemployment insurance benefits, in 2002 dollars, declined from $243 per week in the 1970s and hovered around $220 per week through most of the 1990s. At the same time, the percentage of the unemployed receiving benefits has diminished from about 50 percent, on average during the 1950s to 35 percent during the 1990s. Reasons for this shift include tighter state requirements, the decline of unionization, and the lesser likelihood that those in the growing ranks of the low-wage work force qualify for benefits (General Accounting Office 2000). Over the same period, the value of Food Stamps dropped from $144 monthly in 1981 to $91 in 2000. The most dramatic losses were experienced by AFDC beneficiaries, for whom benefits declined by more than half of their real value between the 1970s and 1990s. Then, in 1996, policymakers enacted the Personal Responsibility and Work Opportunity Act, terminating AFDC and signifying conservatives' most overt accomplishment thus far in transforming the welfare state. The new law replaced AFDC with Temporary Assistance to Needy Families (TANF); these block grants give states more authority over eligibility rules and procedures than they have known since 1935, but make federal funding contingent on states imposing strict work requirements and time limits on program beneficiaries. The dramatic decline in the welfare rolls—down by 50 percent between 1994 and 1999 alone—has been much celebrated by policymakers, but what remains unclear is what has become of those families no longer receiving benefits, as the new requirements may discourage them from making claims even in times of desperate need (K. Weaver 2000, 333–34).

Nonelderly lower- and middle-class Americans have experienced the diminishment of government's presence in their lives in other ways as well. Owing to a variety of economic, technological, and political factors, union membership fell precipitously from its midcentury levels of about one-quarter of the work force to about 13 percent presently. Inaction by policymakers explains government's receding presence in several other regards. For example, the value of the minimum wage deteriorated by nearly 40 percent, from $8.28 in 1968 (in 2002 dollars) to $5.15 currently (Social Security Administration 2000). The average award under Pell Grants, funds targeted to low-income students to assist with college tuition, also declined in value, despite the fact that tuition has increased far more rapidly than inflation (J. King 2000). Meanwhile, the United States has had what Jacob Hacker terms an "anemic" response to changing risks: policymakers have failed to take action to create new policies to address either the growth of inequality, pressures caused by both changes in family structure and rising numbers of hours worked by family members, or the fact that fewer workers receive employer-provided health and retirement benefits (Hacker 2004). Similarly, policymakers have neglected to respond to growing needs for affordable, quality child care for working families and long-term care insurance. Fiscal crises have deterred policymakers from creating new social policies; indeed, the long shadow of deficit spending during the Reagan era hindered efforts to create national health insurance in the 1990s (Skocpol 1996, 173–88), and soaring deficits of recent years will likely curb social spending for the foreseeable future.

Interestingly, however, other social policies, those in the form of tax breaks offered directly to families or individuals for social purposes, have not come under serious consideration as part of retrenchment efforts. Policy analysts identify these by using the term "tax expenditures" to convey that such provisions advance federal social policy goals—in the areas of health, housing, education, retirement security, and income security—by substituting targeted tax reductions for direct spending programs. Even in the Tax Reform Act of 1986, when policymakers slashed tax breaks for businesses, they left social tax expenditures for families and individuals untouched; in the case of the Earned Income Tax Credit (EITC), they expanded them (Brownlee and Steuerle 2003, 172–73; Howard 1997, 139–60). Even as many existing social programs have become inperiled, policymakers have increasingly used the template of tax expenditures to create new programs. In 1997, for instance, President Bill Clinton signed into law the child tax credit, as well as the HOPE Scholarship and Lifetime Learning Credits, which aimed to offset the costs of higher tuition.

Over recent decades, such social tax expenditures, which Christopher Howard has dubbed the "hidden welfare state," have actually increased in value, becoming a more substantial and generous component of U.S. social provision. As Eric Toder (1999) reports, between 1980 and 1999 the amount spent on social tax expenditures increased by more than 40 percent and came to represent 79 percent of all tax expenditures, up from 57 percent in 1980. The four most expensive of these programs are, from most to least costly, the exclusion from taxable income of contributions to and earnings from retirement savings plans; the exclusion of employer contributions for medical insurance premiums and medical care; deduction of income spent on mortgage interest for owner-occupied homes; and the deduction of income spent on state and local taxes. Citizens with privately provided health insurance and retirement accounts benefit from such tax breaks, which are in effect government subsidies for them and their employers. When we account for both tax expenditures and the private social spending that they help to subsidize, American social provision accounts for nearly one-quarter of GDP (Hacker 2002, 1–20; Howard 2003).

Likely the most publicized example among these policies is the Earned Income Tax Credit (EITC), which was expanded greatly during the Clinton administration and again during George W. Bush's first term. Notably, it is targeted to the working poor. Eighteen percent of beneficiaries in 2001 had incomes under $10,000, and 68 percent had incomes between

$10,000 and $30,000 (Joint Committee on Taxation 2002). The EITC can be credited with lifting 4.6 million people in working families out of poverty in 1998 (Center on Budget and Policy Priorities 1998). In redistributing wealth downward, however, the EITC represents an exception to the rule.

Distinct from other types of social programs, the most costly tax expenditures bestow their benefits disproportionately on the wealthiest citizens (Hacker 2002, 36–39), and do so increasingly. In 2001 those with incomes exceeding $100,000 comprised 60 percent of beneficiaries of the mortgage interest deduction and 65 percent of those gaining from the deduction for real estate taxes (Joint Committee on Taxation 2002). The more expensive a house or homes one can afford to buy and the larger a mortgage one qualifies to borrow, the greater the deduction. Since the late 1980s, employer-sponsored health and pension benefits, both of which constitute forms of nontaxable income, increasingly favor more affluent citizens as employers of the less advantaged have become much less likely to extend such provisions (Brady and Lin 2004, 4–5).

The tendency of most tax expenditures to redistribute resources upward—or, perhaps more accurately stated, to shift funds between the affluent, but in ways that reduce the progressivity of the tax code and reduce government revenues—owes to various dynamics. Not only do several of them reward activities that are pursued most easily by those who are relatively well-off, but furthermore they tend to be contingent on the submission of itemized tax returns. Only 30 percent of all returns are itemized, and they are most likely to come from the wealthiest Americans.[3] Less-advantaged citizens, furthermore, are less likely to know about the tax expenditures for which they qualify, as in the case of the Earned Income Tax Credit (Phillips 2001). Although the EITC does play an important redistributive role, low-income people who cannot or do not work are excluded. Other tax expenditures do considerably less to broaden access to economic security and well-being: the home mortgage interest deduction, for example, performs poorly as a means to expand home ownership; the child tax credit fails to cover many low-income families; benefits for the child care credit are not indexed to inflation and policymakers have only rarely increased them, and the program is not refundable, so those without tax liability cannot claim it (Glaeser and Shapiro, 2002, 7; Lee and Greenstein 2003; Maag 2003; Sammartino, Toder, and Maag 2002). All told, the growth of the welfare state through the tax system advantages affluent families most substantially. Some lower-income families do benefit significantly, but others are left out, and tax credits do not constitute a viable replacement for direct spending programs (Urban Institute 2002). Middle-income families, most notably, derive less than others from the hidden welfare state (Gitterman and Howard 2003).

Consequences for Political Voice

While the demise of civic engagement and the decline of citizens' sense of connection to government since the midcentury likely emanates from a complex variety of dynamics, the question here is whether changes in the welfare state may have played a contributing role. Granted, most of the attitudinal and participatory trends began earlier, in the late 1960s.[4] Conceivably, however, the negative messages about government that citizens derived from developments in the 1960s and 1970s—Vietnam and Watergate, for instance—yielded enduring effects because they were not deflected by visible activities that underscored government's positive role. Public programs were already receding in the lives of younger lower- and middle-class citizens. Possibly, too, subsequent changes in the welfare state exacerbated the effects on citizens' attitudes and participation.

Effects of Direct Social Provision

Among direct and visible forms of social provision, the policies geared especially toward the elderly—those which remained strong and generous over the last couple of decades—are known to boost senior citizens' involvement in political activity. Andrea Campbell (2003) has shown that benefits from Social Security and Medicare increase recipients' resources and elevate their interest in politics, and through both dynamics, they facilitate their political participation. Both programs bear the hallmarks of universality and are devoid of the stigma that characterizes some means-tested programs (Soss 1999b). Their relatively generous resources are highly valuable to beneficiaries and they link seniors' well-being to government in significant and obvious ways. For these reasons, program receipt prompts beneficiaries to engage in political action to preserve and bolster the program. In the case of Social Security, these effects have been especially pronounced among low-income seniors, as they derive a larger portion of their incomes from the program than those who are wealthier. Similarly, the less advantaged are more reliant on Medicare than are affluent citizens because they are less healthy and less likely to have supplemental insurance. Both programs are examples of "targeting-within-universalism" (Skocpol 1991), given that lower-income people receive higher financial returns to their investments than wealthier beneficiaries. Low-income people have a greater stake in both programs, and therefore they mobilize at higher levels to protect them (Campbell 2003). Given that rates of political participation are usually strongest among the most affluent citizens, this is a particularly noteworthy effect (Verba, Schlozman, and Brady 1995).

Conversely, Aid to Families with Dependent Children, the program for nonelderly citizens in which benefits deteriorated most drastically since the 1970s, is known to have undermined both beneficiaries' sense that public officials were responsive to people like them and their likelihood of voting. The value of welfare benefits pales by comparison to that of Social Security benefits, and recipients typically worked in order to make ends meet even prior to the creation of work requirements (Edin and Lein 1997). Benefits were administered through a highly demeaning process in which caseworkers retained a high degree of discretion and agencies proved unresponsive to client demands. Joe Soss found that unlike recipients of Social Security Disability Insurance (SSDI), who encountered a rule-bound but generally responsive agency, albeit encumbered with bureaucratic routines, welfare beneficiaries experienced "the assertion of grievances as both futile and unwise" and thus were discouraged from pressing their claims (Soss 1999a, 367). Recipients of both SSDI and AFDC experienced the program from which they benefited as a microcosm of the political system, one that conveyed critical lessons to them about their relationship to government. Not surprisingly, then, SSDI recipients were significantly more likely than AFDC recipients to view government as open and democratic and thus to have a greater sense of external political efficacy.[5] Such attitudes translated into different rates of political participation: controlling for several key variables, Soss found that AFDC beneficiaries were significantly less likely to vote in 1992, whereas voter turnout among SSDI beneficiaries did not differ significantly from that of other citizens (Soss 1999a; 2000; Lawless and Fox 2001).

Distinct policies, then, appear to engender different degrees of political participation (Campbell 2003, chap. 7). Now we can examine how the designs of these policies and the trajectories of their development—that is, whether they are growing more or less valuable and effective over time—affected citizens' political engagement over time, specifically in regard to voter turnout.

Voting deserves special attention because it is the most common form of political activity across socioeconomic groups, and because for citizens with lower incomes and less education, it is typically their only form of political participation (Schlozman 2004, 3–4, figs. 1, 2). It is especially significant, then, that over the past few decades, voter turnout has declined among citizens generally and rates have fallen most precipitously among the less advantaged (Wattenberg 2002; Freeman 2004). The electorate increasingly overrepresents citizens with college degrees and underrepresents those with high school degrees or less (Hughes and Conway 1997, 206–7). Most strikingly, among younger generations, those with less than a high school degree are far less likely to vote than were comparably educated members of older generations at the same point in their life cycle (Miller and Shanks 1996).[6]

Scholars have posed competing hypotheses for the decline of voter turn-out. Some note that large portions of the electorate have become disen-franchised. This owes in part to the rise in incarceration over the past quarter century and the fact that most states prohibit felons from voting and many prohibit ex-felons from voting (Uggen and Manza 2001). It also emanates from the increase in immigration, due to which more individuals lack voting rights. Others suggest that even controlling for these factors, nonvoting is on the rise (Freeman 2004). The point here is not to weigh these competing explanations but rather to explore whether policy receipt itself might also play a role in influencing turnout rates and their decline.

We can use data from the National Election Studies (NES) to speculate about this question, examining voter turnout among beneficiaries of the two groupings of direct social policies that we identified earlier in this essay.[7] We can group individuals according to whether they have benefited from Social Security, which remains strong and generous, or from any of a group of "weak policies" that have diminished to varying degrees in real value (Food Stamps, unemployment insurance, and AFDC), or from none of those policies.[8] We will also group individuals by whether their family income is low, medium, or high.[9] It is important to note that in the case of the weak-policy grouping, whereas eligibility for food stamps and AFDC were conditioned on means testing, unemployment insurance is available to citizens regardless of income, and thus many middle-income recipients are present in the samples. Yet, although some recipients of unemployment insurance appear among the high-income respondents, they number very few in the survey data and thus that category does not permit meaningful analysis. Finally, it should be noted that we are able to compare turnout by policy receipt only across three elections, a very limited number, and therefore we must be cautious in our interpretations.

Voter turnout rates in the midterm elections of 1982, held after the Reagan administration's tax cuts, budget cuts, and failed effort to alter Social Security dramatically, are illustrated by figure 8.3. The overall pat-tern shows that, as is generally expected, higher-income individuals vote at higher rates. At the low and medium income levels, however, the differ-ence between individuals who benefited from different policies—or from none of them—is quite striking. Recipients of Social Security participated at the highest rates, more than policy nonrecipients, and recipients of the weak policies voted at lower rates than either group. At the middle-in-come level, 79 percent of Social Security beneficiaries voted compared to only 51 percent of the recipients of weak policies. At the lower income level, 51 percent of Social Security beneficiaries voted compared to only

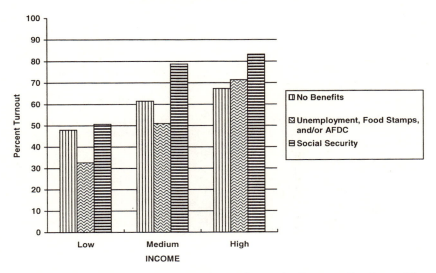

Figure 8.3 Voter Turnout in 1982 Midterm Election by Program Receipt and Income. *Source:* National Election Studies 1982.

33 percent of the weak policy beneficiaries. These differences are statistically significant when we control for both education and income.[10]

In the 1988 presidential election, when George H. W. Bush ran against Michael Dukakis, once again significant differences emerged in the voter turnout of citizens who were experiencing different forms of policy. Normally, we expect higher turnout in presidential elections than in mid-term elections. This was the case among low-income beneficiaries of Social Security, whose turnout increased by 15 percentage points compared to 1982. By contrast, among low-income citizens utilizing the programs that had been under attack, turnout rose by only 1 percentage point, from 33 to 34 percent.[11]

In the 1990 midterm election, voter turnout rates declined considerably compared to those of 1982. Yet they did not fall by comparable rates for all citizens, and, as illustrated by figure 8.4, citizens' experiences of different public programs remained a highly significant factor in determining the rate of their electoral participation. Among middle-income citizens, voter turnout by Social Security beneficiaries (66 percent) was more than double that of the beneficiaries of the weak policies (32 percent). Among lower-income citizens, Social Security beneficiaries, with a turnout of 48 percent, were more than three times as likely to vote as the beneficiaries of the weak policies, whose turnout plummeted to 15 percent. A more rigorous analysis that holds constant both income and educational attainment reveals that each of the two forms of policy receipt proved highly

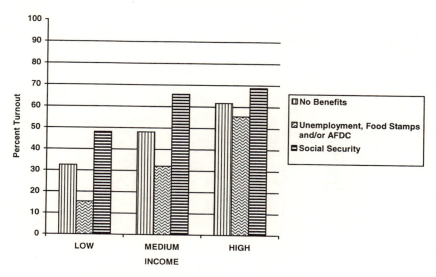

Figure 8.4 Voter Turnout in 1990 Midterm Election by Program Receipt and Income. *Source:* National Election Studies 1992.

significant as determinants of voting: those who benefited from Social Security were considerably more likely to vote, and those who utilized the weak policies were considerably less likely to vote.[12]

Now we can compare voter turnout among beneficiaries of individual policies, as seen in table 8.1. While the pattern of decline in voter turnout that has characterized the electorate generally is evident among all groups, considerable variation exists. Between the two midterm elections in 1982 and 1990, participation by Social Security beneficiaries declined the least, by 5.1 percentage points. By contrast, among the vast majority of nonelderly Americans, those who benefited from none of the direct, highly visible social programs, turnout slipped by 9.1 percentage points. Further, recipients of each of the policies that contracted over the time period voted at considerably lower levels in 1990 than in 1982, with turnout among recipients of unemployment insurance down by 13.5 percentage points; among recipients of food stamps, down by 17.7 percentage points; and among AFDC recipients, down by 25.5 percentage points.[13]

In short, citizens' voter turnout appears to be related to the condition of the portion of the social safety net on which they depend. Those who benefited from a program that has remained strong over time continued to vote at higher rates than citizens who benefited from none of the major social programs examined here. Conversely, those who depended on policies that have atrophied over time—unemployment insurance and Food

TABLE 8.1

Voting Participation in Elections among Beneficiaries of Various Government
Programs and Nonbeneficiaries, across Three Elections (percent)

Program Benefit	1982	1988	1990	Change between Midterm Elections 1982 and 1990
Social Security	63.8	75.1	58.7	−5.1
None in either grouping	60.8	66.7	50.0	−9.1
Unemployment insurance	50.8	58.1	37.3	−13.5
Food Stamps	38.2	38.4	20.5	−17.7
Aid to Families with Dependent Children	44.4	33.3	18.9	−25.5

Source: National Election Studies 1982 and 1992.

Stamps—withdrew considerably from electoral participation. The beneficiaries of the most severely weakened program, AFDC, nearly vanished among the electorate. The worse the extent of the retrenchment in the portion of the safety net on which citizens relied, the more they withdrew from what is typically considered the most fundamental act of exercising political voice.

How can we explain why these policy feedback effects changed over time, with negative effects accumulating among the beneficiaries of the weak policies, while the positive effects among beneficiaries of a strong program declined relatively little? From the evidence, it appears that a primary explanation involves the extent to which political leaders and groups mobilize program beneficiaries: notably, beneficiaries of the strong policies are much more likely to be mobilized by political parties and candidates than are beneficiaries of the weak policies. Generally, affluent citizens are contacted more than other citizens (Rosenstone and Hansen 1993; Verba, Schlozman, and Brady 1995). Analysis of National Election Study data reveals, however, that policy receipt can make for an exception: Social Security recipients were contacted at much higher rates than others with the same income or education.[14] Among middle-income individuals in 1992, beneficiaries of Social Security were contacted at three times the rate of beneficiaries of the weak programs, and 50 percent more than those benefiting from neither program. In fact, they were contacted at even higher rates than high-income citizens who lacked program benefits. Similarly, low-income recipients of Social Security were contacted nearly twice as much as others in their income group. The fact that senior citizens have been well organized by the American Association of Retired Persons (AARP) has made it clear to legislators that they are a potent political force; beneficiaries of weak policies lack such organizations. Mobilization by elected officials fosters a circular dynamic to the policymaking process as those who benefit most from it are invited to participate more, thus reinforcing their influence, while those who benefit less are barely mobilized, with the result that policymakers barely hear from them and thus can continue to ignore them (Rosenstone and Hansen 1993, 115–17).

Certainly the beneficiaries of the weak policies are not without advocates. Among the citizen advocacy groups that have formed since the 1960s are numerous organizations that speak on behalf of less-advantaged Americans. They include such organizations as Center on Budget and Policy Priorities, Center for Law and Social Policy, Children's Defense Fund, and numerous others, many of which belong to the Coalition on Human Needs (Coalition on Human Needs 2005; K. Weaver 2000, 142, 199–205). These groups have Washington offices and paid staff that often include lobbyists, but they typically lack a grass-roots membership of individuals who associate in local chapters, face-to-face. Their Web sites welcome "donors" and offer legislative alerts to citizens who wish to contact members of Congress on timely issues. As Theda Skocpol's chapter in this volume makes evident, to the extent that such organizations have members, they tend to be highly educated people but not members of the affected groups themselves. The problem is that such features of advocacy organizations make them far more easily ignored in the political process than civic groups of the past, those featuring large, widespread memberships that could exercise sufficient organizing muscle to hold politicians accountable (Skocpol 2003).

The divergence, over time, in the value of benefits in the strong and weak programs may also have contributed to the growing disparity in the political activity of beneficiaries of such programs. Indeed, Social Security recipients were significantly more likely than others to believe, in 1992, that federal policy made them better off. This was reasonable, given that Social Security benefits, by contrast to benefits of the weak policies, held their real value throughout this period.[15] Such resources likely conveyed to beneficiaries that they had an important interest or stake in government, thus prompting them to participate at higher levels.

The manner in which policymakers depicted and responded to beneficiaries of different policies may also have communicated interpretive effects to them about the status of people like themselves in the polity. Following the Reagan administration's ill-fated 1981 proposal to scale back Social Security, policymakers responded to senior citizens in a manner that conveyed that they are a respected, important, and effective political group and thus further reinforced their inclination to take political action (Campbell 2003; 2004). By sharp contrast, throughout the period policymakers depicted adult welfare beneficiaries as, at best, pitiable and in need of greater resources and more often as individuals in need of reform, for whom an altered incentive structure might stimulate a stronger work ethic and discourage out-of-wedlock births (Teles 1996, chap. 8). The program provided politicians with a potent political group—"welfare mothers"—that was easily castigated and about which they could make powerful political appeals to the general electorate (Mettler and Soss 2004, 61). Possibly, such distinct messages to and about the different groups further reinforced the inclination of the Social Security beneficiaries to participate in politics and made welfare beneficiaries increasingly disinclined to do so.

All of these dynamics, combined, help explain why Social Security has, until this point, remained resistant to retrenchment, and why, conversely, particular policies for the nonelderly have atrophied. Senior citizens, throughout the 1980s and 1990s, proved quite effective in protecting their programs from retrenchment. Over that period, the rate at which senior citizens contacted public officials grew sharply, and policymakers began to refer to the program as the "third rail of politics," meaning "touch it, and you die" (Campbell 2003). As the Bush administration attempted to restructure Social Security into a system that includes private individual accounts invested in the stock market, its proposals were premised on leaving intact the benefits for current beneficiaries, those who are most highly mobilized. By the same token, beneficiaries of the weak programs have been relatively powerless to protect their programs, as epitomized best by welfare recipients. As low-income individuals, they were lacking from the start in the resources and skills that help facilitate political action, and AFDC, with its meager resources, proved insufficient to strengthen their participatory capacity. As benefits deteriorated, the vast majority of these low-income recipients of weak policies gradually disappeared from the electorate. Their voices went unheard as their program remained under attack politically throughout the 1980s and 1990s and finally met with its demise and replacement in 1996 by the far more restrictive TANF program. Most states responded by quickly enacting highly restrictive new eligibility rules and more punitive procedures than had existed under AFDC, further underscoring welfare beneficiaries' weak political status and emphasizing that they are not rights-bearing citizens but rather are indebted by obligations to the polity (Mettler 2000). Importantly, in states in which lower-class voter turnout was higher, policymakers were less likely to adopt restrictive welfare rules (Avery and Peffley 2005).

Many have argued that rates of civic engagement and voter turnout are strongly related to the generation of which one is part (Putnam 2000, chaps. 2, 14; Wattenberg 2002, chap. 4). While this is undeniable, it does not tell us *why* members of younger generations participate so much less than the generations that came of age with World War II and the Korean War. Members of the older generation, when they were young, saw government intervene in their lives in highly significant ways, boosting their educational opportunity and social and economic circumstances. They benefited from the G.I. Bill, from a period of government's stronger support for labor unions (and of stronger and considerably larger labor organizations than exist presently), and from more generous support in public programs geared toward the nonelderly. Such experiences likely elevated citizens' sense of connection to government and, in turn, promoted their political participation. Then, as they grew older, these same citizens received generous Social Security and Medicare benefits, and, as we have seen, remained active politically as a result. Younger citizens, by contrast, have been much less likely to experience government making a highly visible and powerful difference in their economic security and life opportunities.[16] Not surprisingly, then, the benefits on which the older generation depend have remained intact even as they have continued to be highly involved politically, whereas the benefits affecting younger generations have diminished as they have failed to become equally active members of the polity.

Effects of the Hidden Welfare State

Use of the tax code to create and expand social policies has been in vogue during the past quarter century's conservative era of governance, and not surprisingly. The approach extends benefits through a technique that simultaneously reduces the size of government, by cutting revenues. While such policies redistribute primarily upward, bestowing government largesse especially on affluent citizens, the design of such programs obscures this impact and makes it unlikely that other citizens will trace and find fault with their effects. Neither is their cost typically listed among public expenditures nor do politicians tend to cite their effectiveness as chief aims of government or to refer to beneficiaries themselves as a politically meaningful group.[17] Indeed, experimental research has found that citizens do not realize the extent to which tax deductions for the reimbursement of private expenditures undermine the progressivity of the tax system (Baron and McCaffery 2004). Such dynamics allow tax expenditures to grow undeterred by public attention or conflict.

Tax expenditures likely do less than other entitlements to instill positive attitudes toward government. Granted, in structure, such benefits function like entitlement programs: qualification is automatic, not subject to the more invasive procedures involved in qualifying for public assistance or unemployment insurance, and thus beneficiaries likely perceive themselves as rightful beneficiaries (Hacker 2002, 48). Yet the lack of visibility and traceability in their design makes them less likely than direct social benefits to offer citizens a sense that they are government beneficiaries. Given the complexity of filing taxes (and the fact that more affluent citizens are likely to have accountants perform the task for them), beneficiaries may be unaware of how much they actually gain from policies. Unlike beneficiaries of direct forms of social provision, tax expenditure beneficiaries—with the exception of those receive the EITC and some who get advance payments for the child tax credit—do not receive a check from government, but rather they simply owe less than they would otherwise. Claimants may not perceive the tax breaks to be social benefits at all, but rather as rightful opportunities to reduce what they may already perceive as undue or burdensome financial obligations to government.

The fact that the most expensive tax expenditures—the nontaxable status of workplace benefits for retirement savings and health insurance—are delivered by employers likely further obscures government's role. Such arrangements may prompt citizens, increasingly, to understand such functions as the legitimate province of private-sector organizations rather than of government and may thus impede possibilities for reform (Hacker 2002, 24, 43, 283; 1998, 122).

The National Election Study of 2002 permits us to examine a few instances of how policies of the hidden welfare state and private social provision may affect citizens' attitudes. These data are not ideal as they require that we use proxies to infer what the effects of such policies might be. The findings should be considered as suggestive rather than as definitive.

Tax expenditures appear to evoke little awareness among recipients that they are gaining social benefits and paying considerably less in taxes than nonbeneficiaries. This becomes evident when we compare homeowners' and renters' attitudes about whether they pay the right amount in federal income taxes. Homeowners, unlike renters, benefit from both the home mortgage interest deduction and property tax deduction. Yet, as figure 8.5 illustrates, there is no significant difference between the two groups in their attitudes toward the tax system. Income is a highly significant determinant of individuals' attitudes about taxes, but tax benefits—inasmuch as homeownership confers them—are not significant.[18] In fact, despite the fact that the wealthiest homeowners derive the largest benefits from such tax breaks, they appear to be slightly more likely than renters to feel that they pay too much in taxes. Similarly, as shown in figure 8.6, no significant difference in attitudes about taxes exists between those with retirement pensions and accounts and those without, despite the fact that

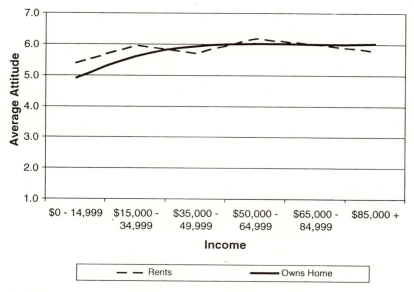

Figure 8.5 Attitudes Regarding Fairness of Federal Income Taxes, by Home Ownership and Family Income, among Nonelderly. *Source:* National Election Studies 2002. *Note:* Question asked, "Do you feel you are asked to pay more than you should in federal income taxes, about the right amount, or less than you should?" Responses are coded as follows: 1, don't pay; 3, less than should; 5, about right; 7, more than should.

the former receive ample benefits through the tax system.[19] This suggests that despite the generous resources bestowed through the hidden welfare state, they may do little to engender positive attitudes toward government.

Social provisions granted through the intermediary of private employers, in which public subsidization is largely hidden, may actually serve to undermine citizens' support of other social programs. As shown in figure 8.7, higher-income individuals with pensions or retirement accounts are significantly less supportive of increased Social Security spending than citizens lacking pensions or accounts.[20] Conceivably, government's role in enabling them to acquire such ample savings free of taxation is so obfuscated that the process undermines collective attitudes of obligation toward the polity and reinforces perceptions of individual identity and autonomy. If this is the case and if it is indicative of beneficiaries' perceptions of tax expenditures generally, such policies may have the effect of further eroding support for the welfare state, particularly among the wealthiest citizens: those who gain the most from them and who are overrepresented in the electorate.

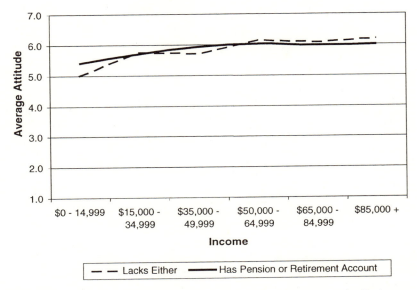

Figure 8.6 Attitudes Regarding Fairness of Federal Income Taxes, by Retirement Accounts and Family Income, among Nonelderly. *Source:* National Election Studies 2002. *Note:* Question asked, "Do you feel you are asked to pay more than you should in federal income taxes, about the right amount, or less than you should?" Responses are coded as follows: 1, don't pay; 3, less than should; 5, about right; 7, more than should.

Other programs that effectively hide government's role by channeling benefits through private providers may have a similar impact. Many beneficiaries of Medicare managed care plans are already under the impression that they are no longer in a government program (Bernstein and Stevens 1999, 184). The Medicare Prescription Drug, Improvement, and Modernization Act of 2003 privatized the program further by extending drug benefits through private firms rather than through traditional Medicare and by extending substantial subsidies to private plans in order to urge them to cover senior citizens. Andrea Campbell suggests that such a policy design will divide the constituencies of the program and may thus weaken their collective power, and that "seniors enrolled in private plans rather in traditional Medicare may no longer recognize the government's role in their health care" (Campbell 2004, 10–15). Among those of greater means, incorporation under more privatized policy arrangements may eventually erode support for government's role in social provision.

Ironically, however, at the same time as the hidden and private forms of the welfare state may obscure their redistributive qualities and undermine citizens' support for direct social provision, they may also actually

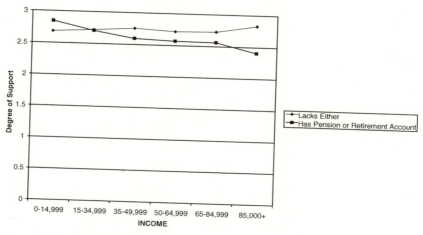

Figure 8.7 Support for Social Security Spending, by Retirement Savings and Family Income, among Nonelderly. *Source:* National Election Studies, 2002. *Note:* Question asked, "Should federal spending on Social Security be increased, decreased or kept about the same?" Responses are coded as follows: 1, decreased, 2, kept same, 3, increased.

heighten the political participation of its most advantaged beneficiaries. Citizens who were homeowners or who had a pension plan or an IRA proved significantly more likely to vote in the 2000 election than others of the same education level or income level. As we would expect, education is the most powerful determinant of voting, but other factors being equal, homeowners voted with considerably greater frequency than renters, and those with retirement savings more than those lacking such funds.[21] Scholars have long observed higher levels of civic involvement among homeowners and have reasoned that it owes to their greater sense of rootedness in their communities (Putnam 2000, 204). Yet possibly the tax benefits associated with homeownership themselves play a role. Despite the fact that beneficiaries of tax expenditures may neither consider them to be social benefits nor develop more positive attitudes toward government through receiving them, nonetheless such benefits may elevate beneficiaries' sense of a stake in the continuation of such policies and pique their interest in politics, thus bolstering their inclination to be involved politically in order to ensure that their interests will be protected.[22] As Jacob Hacker and Paul Pierson (2003, 11) report, "knowledge of the tax code and of policy changes to it is sharply skewed by income"; wealthy citizens are far more knowledgeable on such matters than others. To the extent that such dynamics operate in the contemporary polity, the expansion of tax expenditures and limits of private social provision may be exacerbating the overrepresentation of advantaged citizens in the exercise of political voice. At the same time, they may make these highly vocal citizens more inclined to articulate messages of antipathy toward the direct and public forms of social provision that traditionally have undergirded the welfare state and granted economic security to lower- and middle-class citizens.

THE RETRENCHMENT OF DEMOCRACY

For too long, scholars have treated public policies strictly as the results of citizens' participation and attitudes and not considered whether they may themselves, in turn, influence political behavior. When contemporary government spending consumes one-third of the gross domestic product, surely it no longer makes sense to treat citizens as if they exist in a "state of nature" prior to governance. Far more research is needed so that we may better understand the dynamics underlying the kinds of policy feedback effects identified here, as well as how a wide range of other policies might be affecting civic engagement. For example, we might investigate whether the interpretive effects of the shrinking value of welfare might have been offset among low-income families by the simultaneous expansion of Medicaid coverage for children and increases in EITC benefits (K. Weaver 2002, 15). It is possible that individuals gained a more powerful sense of government's relevance to their lives from higher welfare checks that boosted their income on a regular basis than from what for most are less frequently utilized medical benefits or lump-sum annual payments. Alternatively, might the Earned Income Tax Credit, which functions more as an entitlement for those who qualify, encourage low-income citizens to become more interested or active in politics? And might TANF, in promoting self-reliance, generate more positive effects on civic engagement than did AFDC? The different impact of such provisions awaits scholarly investigation. Likewise, it would be helpful to know whether the new rights and social provision extended to disabled nonelderly Americans provide a countervailing force to some of the patterns identified here (Erkulwater 2006), and whether student loans bear participatory consequences analogous to or different from those of Pell Grants or the G.I. Bill. In short, much research is needed so that we can begin to specify more clearly the effects of various policies and the mechanisms through which they operate.

The broad overview conducted here, in noting transformations in public policy and considering what we do already know about their effects on political behavior, does permit us to discern some important trends. Contrary to the hopes of some and fears of others, the American welfare state has survived a quarter century of conservative politics with most programs still relatively intact and with some even larger and more generous than ever. And yet, years of policymaking guided by an anti-government public philosophy and conducted amid severe fiscal constraints have yielded far-reaching consequences. They have set in motion path-dependent processes that are, slowly but surely, transforming the linkages between citizens and government. Elderly citizens have benefited from a virtuous circle of policies that generate civic engagement, responsiveness from policymakers, and mobilization efforts by party officials to further encourage their electoral participation. By contrast, many lower- and middle-class nonelderly and nondisabled citizens, even in the midst of rising employment insecurity and financial stress, find that government does little to improve their economic security. Many such individuals, relying on programs that have been shrinking in value and coverage over time, have disengaged from politics. At the same time, tax expenditures offer increasingly generous benefits especially to wealthy citizens, with the effect of exacerbating their already strong advantage in the exercise of political voice; the associated realm of privately provided social provision appears to further extend their lead. This growing sector of social policies, in obscuring government's role, threatens to undermine citizens' support for more redistributive forms of social provision by offering them the illusion that they gain economic security solely through their own individual efforts rather than as citizens and members of a polity with a shared set of obligations to each other.

Just as investments in individuals' education early in life yield the greatest impact on their socioeconomic well-being (Carniero and Heckman 2003), political experiences in childhood and early adulthood have an especially large impact on citizens' subsequent civic involvement and orientation toward government (e.g., Verba, Schlozman, and Brady 1995, chap. 15; Jennings and Niemi 1981). For these reasons, it is deeply consequential that members of an earlier generation of Americans—those who came of age with World War II and the Korean War—saw government intervene in their lives during the impressionable period of their early adulthood, in ways that were powerful and sometimes transformative. They learned that government was for and about people like them. In response, they became active and involved citizens. Today, by contrast, the welfare state is most effective primarily in the lives of the oldest citizens—many of the same individuals who also benefited earlier in their lives—and for whom programs at this juncture greatly reduce poverty rates and once again elevate democratic participation. Nonetheless, given their timing so late in citizens' lives, programs for the elderly cannot by themselves reap the long-term returns for civic engagement of those experienced far earlier in life.

In the lives of many—though not all—lower- and middle-class members of younger generations, government has been less present and less effective as a source of economic security and educational opportunity. Conceivably, such citizens may associate membership in the polity less with benefits and more with the imposition of burdens and restraints. They may be more persuaded by anti-tax arguments given that they themselves directly experience less in return for their taxes than did members of an earlier generation, for whom consciousness of the burdens imposed by government may have been matched or surpassed by awareness of the valuable benefits that government bestowed on them.

Across American history, laws and public policies have shaped and reshaped the status of groups of citizens relative to each other, the extent to which they participate in politics, and the form such participation takes. Likewise, the trends we have observed here may be imposing new patterns of stratification on the American citizenry. During the middle of the twentieth century, the welfare state helped moderate class divisions, moving individuals out of poverty and broadening the middle class. Over the past three decades, by contrast, U.S. government has failed to counter economic trends that are expanding inequality, leaving market forces to restratify citizens once again according to a new class-based hierarchy, one in which educational attainment is particularly significant. As a result, patterns of political participation appear to be becoming more stratified as well, amplifying the voice of the affluent over that of the less well-off. The fact that Social Security has such a different effect—both elevating the incomes of less advantaged elderly and boosting their political involvement—suggests that the exception proves the rule.

In addition, these trends in social provision appear to be curtailing the ability of the rights revolution to equalize citizenship in terms of race and gender. In the early 1970s, in the wake of the policy achievements of the civil rights and feminist movements, it would have been reasonable to expect that by the early twenty-first century, divisions of race and gender would be far less prevalent. Yet, while progress has certainly been achieved, it has been less than what could have been expected at that juncture. Arguably, the rise of economic inequality and the failure of the American welfare state to impede its effects have restratified the citizenry by class along cleavages that bear striking similarity to the old divisions of race and gender (Hacker, Mettler, and Pinderhughes 2005).

In his first term, President George W. Bush responded to the voices of the wealthiest citizens by promoting tax cuts that deliver their most ample benefits to them. The message that government is responsive to the interests of the affluent appears to have been conveyed effectively enough to highly mobilized wealthy citizens to widen Bush's margin of victory in the 2004 (Klinkner 2004). At the same time, such policies continue to undermine possibilities for extending greater economic security and educational opportunity to the vast majority of Americans, compounding the dynamics that discourage them from political engagement.

Perhaps what has suffered the most severe retrenchment over these past three decades is not the welfare state itself so much as it is the institutions of representative government for which it offers a crucial source of linkages between citizens and elites. Over time, policymakers have come to hear less and less from average citizens aside from the elderly, while the voice of the privileged has increased in both its volume and its clarity.

NOTES

For helpful comments, I wish to thank Andrea Campbell, Kay Schlozman, Jeff Stonecash, and two anonymous reviewers. In addition, I am grateful to Wagaki Mwangi and Andrew Milstein for excellent research assistance.

1. Among the most commonly used programs are the Earned Income Tax Credit, from which 42.3 percent of Americans have benefited; followed by student loans, 39.7 percent; mortgage interest deduction, 36.9 percent; unemployment insurance, 33.6 percent; and Social Security, 30.6 percent. These results come from the Maxwell Poll 2005, which surveyed a national, random sample of U.S. population. Results weighted by age, sex, and race to accord with U.S. population.

2. For further analysis, see Brady et al. 2002; also Verba, Schlozman, and Brady 1997.

3. Glaeser and Shapiro (2002) found that more than slightly less than one-half of the itemizers are in the top two income deciles, whereas the poorest 40 percent of the population contains only one-tenth of the itemizers.

4. Accordingly, the demise in citizens' political efficacy and trust are often attributed to such factors as the emergence of modern media, the Vietnam War, and Watergate, as well as the long line of ethics scandals that gained center stage in its wake (Lawrence 1997; T. Patterson 1994; Ginsberg and Shefter 2002); these attitudinal shifts, in turn, are thought to bear a relationship to the demise in voter turnout (Hughes and Conway 1997).

5. Interestingly, the program experience actually boosted beneficiaries' sense of internal political efficacy, their own capacity to make a difference. However, at the same time, it convinced them that such action would be futile. See Soss 1999a.

6. It should be noted that there is some dispute about this trend: Leighley and Nagler (1992) and Shields and Goidel (1997) argue that voter turnout has diminished evenly among income groups over time, leaving class bias in the electorate unchanged since 1960. McDonald and Popkin (2001) argue that the size of the population ineligible to vote has grown, not the nonvoting population. By contrast, Rosenstone and Hansen (1993) and others argue that inequality in voting has grown. Freeman (2004, 78) offers the most recent and rigorous assessment of the issue, and suggests that "The drop in turnout has occurred largely among the less educated, lower income, less skilled, and younger persons, increasing the inequality in voting among those groups."

7. Surveys that include both indicators of policy receipt and measures of political attitudes and behavior are extremely rare. They include the Civic Participation Study of 1990 and the National Election Studies of 1982 and 1992, all of which include indicators of usage of direct social programs. I use the two NES surveys in order to make comparisons over time. The policy questions are phrased as follows: "Do you (or any family member living with you) currently receive x"; each question asks about benefits from a specific program.

8. Individuals who benefited from both Social Security and any of the weaker policies will be grouped with the former, given that their treatment under it is likely more consequential for them. Medicare and Medicaid receipt are not included in the analysis for two reasons: the 1982 NES asked about receipt of the two programs in one question, making it impossible to distinguish between them when we look at policies individually; and the vast majority of AFDC beneficiaries benefited from Medicaid also, but it is less clear in that instance whether they should be grouped with beneficiaries of strong or weak policies.

9. In order to make these groups comparable across the two time periods, I have coded them so that the low income category includes the quarter of the population with the lowest incomes, the high-income group includes the top 18–19 percent, and all others are in the medium-income group.

10. Logistic regression results, with voting in 1982 as the dependent variable, yielded the following results (coefficients and significance, $*p < .05$; $**p < .01$; $***p < .001$ [two-sided] , standard error in parentheses): Social Security receipt, $.89***$ $(.16)$; weak policies receipt, $-.48**$ $(.19)$; income, $.08**$ $(.03)$; education, $.20***$ $(.03)$. Cox & Snell R^2, $.08$; N = 1,418.

11. Logistic regression results, with voting in 1988 as the dependent variable, yielded the following results (coefficients and significance, $*p < .05$; $**p < .01$; $***p < .001$ [two-sided] , standard error in parentheses): Social Security receipt, $1.3***$ $(.17)$; weak policies receipt, $-.39*$ $(.18)$; income, $.05***$ $(.01)$; education, $.45***$ $(.05)$. Cox & Snell R^2, $.16$; N = 2,485.

12. Logistic regression results, with voting in 1990 as the dependent variable, yielded the following results (coefficients and significance, $*p < .05$; $**p < .01$; $***p < .001$ [two-sided] , standard error in parentheses): Social Security receipt, $.98***$ $(.15)$; weak policies receipt, $-.78***$ $(.19)$; income, $.05***$ $(.01)$; education, $.24***$ $(.04)$. Cox & Snell R^2, $.12$; N = 2,485.

13. Changes in the composition of recipients of those policies likely explain little of their diminished turnout: over that time period, the percentage of the population utilizing unemployment insurance and Food Stamps declined slightly, but it remained constant in the case of AFDC, in which voting dropped off most substantially (Mettler and Milstein 2003, figs. 6, 12).

14. Logistic regression results, with being contacted by a political party official as the dependent variable, yielded the following results (coefficients and significance, $*p < .05$; $**p < .01$; $***p < .001$ [two-sided] , standard error in parentheses): Social Security receipt, $.68***$ $(.16)$; weak policies receipt, $-.46$ $(.07)$; income, $.03*$ $(.02)$; education, $.12*$ $(.05)$. Cox & Snell R^2, $.03$; N = 2,485.

15. Correlation between Social Security and the view that federal policy made respondents better off is $.06*$ $(.02)$ whereas correlation between weak policies

and same attitude is –.05 (06); correlations between Social Security and how much better or worse off is .06* (.03), whereas correlation between weak policies and same attitude is –.02 (39). Significance levels shown in parentheses, *p < .05. Data from 1992 National Election Study.

16. Hence, the regression results reported above do not control for age. By including age, we would inadvertently negate the differences in policy experiences between generations, most of which we cannot control for because we lack sufficient data.

17. We are used to appeals based on the notion that "taxpayers" are deserving citizens, but do not hear about "tax break dependents," though analogous derogatory constructions of businesses that received tax breaks were invoked prior to tax reform in 1986.

18. Ordinary least squares regression results, with attitudes about paying taxes (from "less than should" to "more than should") as the dependent variable, yielded the following results (standardized coefficients and significance, *p < .05; **p < .01; ***p < .001 [two-sided]): homeowner, –.04; income, .18*** ; education, –.03. Adjusted R^2, .02; N = 1,370. In order to explore whether owners with particularly expensive homes and thus bigger deductions might have noticeably different attitudes, I also tried including a variable to account for average housing cost by state, but it proved insignificant and did not change the results of the model.

19. Ordinary least squares regression results, with attitudes about paying taxes (from "less than should" to "more than should") as the dependent variable, yielded the following results (standardized coefficients and significance, *p < .05; **p < .01; ***p < .001 [two-sided]): has family retirement account or pension, .05; income, .15*** ; education, –.03. Adjusted R^2, .03; N = 1,379.

20. Ordinary least squares regression results, with attitudes about Social Security (1 = decrease it, 2 = keep same, 3 = increase it) as the dependent variable, yielded the following results (standardized coefficients and significance, *p < .05; **p < .01; ***p < .001 [two-sided]): has family retirement account or pension, –.07*; income, –.08*; education, –.10**. Adjusted R^2, .03; N = 1,379.

21. Logistic regression results, with voting in 2000 as the dependent variable, yielded the following results (coefficients and significance, *p < .05; **p < .01; ***p < .001 [two-sided] , standard error in parentheses): homeowner, 1.11*** (.20); has retirement account or pension, .51** (.21) ; income, –.05 (.05); education, .53*** (.07). Cox & Snell R^2, .12; N = 1,511.

22. This becomes evident by including a political interest variable, in which respondents indicate, on a scale of 1 to 4, whether they "follow what's going on in government and public affairs most of the time, some of the time, only now and then, or hardly at all." Logistic regression results, with voting in 2000 as the dependent variable, yielded the following results (coefficients and significance, *p < .05; **p < .01; ***p < .001 [two-sided] , standard error in parentheses): homeowner, 1.03*** (.23); has retirement account or pension, .44 (.23); income, –.04 (.06); education, .48*** (.08); political interest, –.86***(.42). Cox & Snell R^2, .17; N = 1,511. By comparison to the regression without political interest, having retirement income is no longer significant, suggesting that its effects are a function of the elevated political interest associated with it.

Chapter Nine

The Policy Effects of Political Polarization

NOLAN MCCARTY

THE DISPERSION OF AUTHORITY in the American political system makes it extraordinarily hard for any governing party to make effective policy without cooperation and support of members of the other party. In his seminal study of lawmaking in the U.S. from 1946 to 1990, David Mayhew (1991) finds that more than 70 percent of the most important enactments of the post–World War II era passed with bipartisan majorities in both chambers of Congress. More importantly, many of these bills would not have passed without bipartisan support.

Given the role of bipartisanship in forging the coalitions responsible for many of Congress's legislative landmarks, it should be noted with some alarm that this glue is drying and cracking. Whether gauged from the decline of cross-party voting in Congress, the acrimony of its debates, or the testimony of its members past and present, bipartisanship is almost a thing of the past. Although "polarization" became the buzz word for the 2004 elections, its congressional manifestation predates this election by at least a quarter of a century. Polarization on Capitol Hill escalated over sharp disagreements concerning the priorities of economic and social policy, cabinet appointments and Supreme Court justices, and the nature of impeachable offenses.

Speculating as to the causes of this recent polarization has become a cottage industry both among political scientists and pundits. Relatively less attention, however, has been paid to how this breakdown in bipartisanship has affected public policy and the routine functioning of our national government.[1] If, as Mayhew's data clearly show, most of the policy achievements of the post-war era are the result of bipartisan compromise, then what types of new policies, if any, can Americans expect in an era when partisanship is the dominant political emotion?

The most important effect of polarization may also be the most obvious: it makes it harder to build the legislative coalitions necessary to undertake ambitious new policies. Because of the supermajority requirements imposed by bicameralism, the filibuster, and the presidential veto, the majority party is rarely large enough or sufficiently cohesive to go it alone. By exacerbating the difficulty of bipartisan cooperation, polarization lowers the capacity of Congress to enact new laws.

Polarization and its consequent gridlock not only prevents the enactment of new policies but affects the trajectory of existing ones. Many important policies, especially in areas of tax, entitlements, and social policy, require frequent legislative adjustments to remain stable in the face of inflation and other economic and demographic shifts. Existing programs must be reauthorized. Without these legislative adjustments and reauthorizations, policy drift ensues. These drifts are not politically neutral. Sometimes gridlock allows policy to drift in a liberal direction such as when eligibility and benefit levels for certain entitlements get locked in despite the increasing costs of those programs. In other cases, the majority I believe, the effect is a conservative one, such as the deterioration in nonindexed social benefits and the minimum wage.

Of course, polarization does not inhibit all policymaking. In spite of a polarized political system, recently Congress has passed large tax cuts (see Hacker and Pierson in this volume), a new Medicare drug benefit, and an overhaul of the federal bankruptcy code. But I argue that, even in these rare legislation achievements, polarization greatly distorted both the policy process and the outcomes.

Beyond its effect on specific policies, polarization is likely to have profound effects on the operation of American political institutions. In particular, it is likely to weaken Congress vis-à-vis the other branches of government. Polarization provides presidents with the incentive and an excuse for circumventing Congress and governing by executive order. Because of its decreased ability to address new issues, the venues of policymaking are moving away from Congress to the courts and to the states.

WHY HAS AMERICAN POLITICS POLARIZED?

Before fleshing out my arguments, it is important to consider the arguments that have been proffered as to why American politics has become more polarized. One of the most important things to keep in mind is that polarization is primarily an elite phenomenon, not one that affects the mass public (DiMaggio, Evans, and Bryson 1996; Fiorina et al. 2005). The attitudes of the mass public have been stable, centrist, and converging in many issue areas. The story of elected officials and party activists is entirely different. Evidence across a number of indicators reveals that political elites, especially those in Congress, became more polarized as early as the mid-1970s. One indicator of this shift is the fact that cross-party coalitions on congressional roll call votes were becoming rarer.[2] Figure 9.1 shows how the frequency of close votes dividing both political parties has changed over time.

The sophistication and precision with which scholars measure such shifting voting patterns has improved dramatically. In the most widely accepted of these new methodologies, political scientists use roll call votes to estimate the positions of individual legislators on one or more policy dimensions. Essentially these techniques use information on who votes with whom and how often to locate these positions. For example, if Arlen Specter votes with either Hillary Clinton or Bill Frist much more frequently than Clinton and Frist vote together, then these techniques position Specter as moderate in between those more extreme senators. Using this logic across hundreds of votes and legislators produces fairly fine-grained estimates of legislators' positions. The DW-NOMINATE algorithm (McCarty, Poole, and Rosenthal 1997) estimates these positions for all legislators on two dimensions.[3] The first dimension is closely related to the liberal-conservative dimension that has organized American politics since Reconstruction whereas the second dimension captures variation on racial, regional, and social issues. Figure 9.2 shows the estimates of the positions of the 107th House and Senate where R tokens mark the location of Republican legislators and D tokens mark those of Democrats. Polarization is revealed by the large gulf separating the two clouds of tokens on the first dimension.

Once these measures are computed, it is straightforward to estimate polarization by computing the average distance between Democratic and Republican legislators. Figure 9.3 provides measures of polarization along the liberal-conservative dimension for each congressional term since the end of Reconstruction. This figure reveals remarkable variation in the level of partisan polarization over the past 125 years. The recent upward trend in polarization began after a very long decline. By 2003 the difference between the parties on the DW-NOMINATE scale has reached levels not witnessed since the 1920s. Whereas much of the twentieth century was characterized by heterogeneous legislative parties with large numbers of conservative Democrats and liberal Republicans, those two ideological species have all but disappeared.

Importantly, the polarization of the recent era has not been a symmetric one of each party moving from the political center. Rather it is the result of changes in the Democratic Party in the South and the Republican Party across the nation. These changes are seen in figure 9.4, which plots the mean position of northern Democrats, southern Democrats, and Republicans over time. Clearly, congressional polarization reflects two shifts: one to the left by southern Democrats and a shift of the Republicans to the right. Northern Democrats have held steady since the 1970s.[4]

The patterns of Figures 9.3 and 9.4 present a formidable intellectual puzzle. Why did a political system based on heterogeneous and moderate parties suddenly reverse course to produce very divided and distinct politi-

The 107th House of Representatives

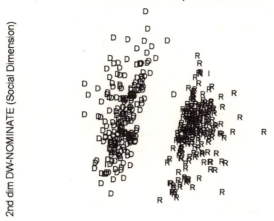

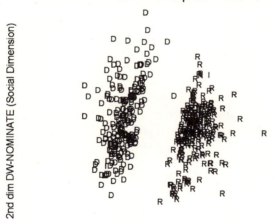

Figure 9.2 Estimates of Positions of the 107th House of Representatives and the 107th Senate

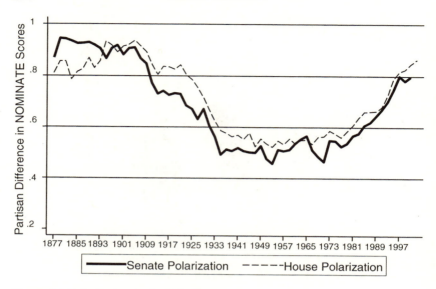

Figure 9.3 Polarization in the U.S. Congress

cal parties? One obvious source of these changes is the "southern realignment" in which southern whites began to shift from the Democratic Party after the passage of the 1964 Civil and 1965 Voting Rights Acts. A direct consequence of this shift is that many of the moderate and conservative Democrats in Congress were replaced by conservative Republicans, while newly enfranchised African Americans elected liberals. But the patterns of figure 9.3 are not solely the consequence of realignment. First, even if I completely exclude southern representatives from the calculations, the pattern of polarization is almost identical. Second, although realignment explains the departure of conservative Democrats, it does not explain an equally dramatic exodus of liberal Republicans from the Northeast and Midwest. Third, a focus on southern realignment produces few clues as to why polarization declined for much of the twentieth century during a period in which the regional basis of the party system was reasonably stable.

Although the direct effects of realignment clearly do not explain all of the changes, it is still possible that the realignment led to changes in the organizational structure of the parties that in turn triggered the polarization increase. For example, Rohde (1991) argues that realignment plus the influx of northern liberals to congress in the aftermath of Watergate made the Democratic caucus much more homogeneous. This allowed it to pursue much more partisan legislative strategies in Congress. These included a number of reforms to enhance the majority party leadership's capacity to discipline members, leading to even greater homogeneity of behavior.

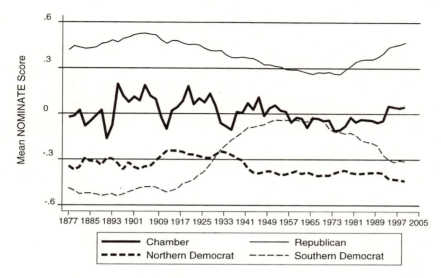

Figure 9.4 Party Means in the U.S. House

Rohde's argument is focused on the Democrats, however. And as we have seen, the recent spate of polarization has been largely a phenomenon of the Republicans moving to the right. This movement began well before the Republicans become the majority party. Why the minority Republicans became more homogeneous is less clear. Moreover, the argument that polarization resulted from party-strengthening reforms of the 1970s is a much more compelling explanation for changes in the U.S. House than it is for the Senate where there have been fewer party-enhancing reforms and the rules for debate necessitate some level of bipartisanship.

Many political commentators have focused on the role of redistricting congressional seats following each decennial census as an explanation for both declining electoral competition and partisan polarization.[5] This explanation has focused on a number of factors, such as mandates for majority-minority districts and greater technical proficiency in drawing districts for partisan advantage, that are believed to have led to greater partisan heterogeneity of districts and consequently to greater polarization. Although this story seems consistent with the amazing dearth of competition in the 2002 House elections (the first following the 2000 reapportionment), like the other explanations, it is also incomplete.[6] First, the increases in the polarization measure following redistricting are not exceptional. Since 1979, polarization in the U.S. House (as measured by DW-NOMINATE) has risen an average of .023 per biennial congressional term. In the first election following the last three reapportionments, the increases were .030, .044, and .017, respectively. The average of the post-apportionment elections is scarcely greater than the overall average. Second, such explanations do not explain the fact that the U.S. Senate (which, of course, is not redistricted) has polarized. One could imagine that the effects of racial and partisan gerrymanders spill over into the Senate by changing the pool of Senate candidates. There is no evidence, however, that House polarization causes Senate polarization.[7] Finally, like many other explanations, it fails to provide an account of the decreasing polarization through most of the twentieth century.

Another explanation for political polarization lies in the role of primary elections to nominate congressional candidates.[8] It is widely assumed that moderates have an increasingly difficult time winning their party's contests. Such outcomes present increasingly stark choices to the general electorate. This is not a compelling story either. The widespread adoption of the primary as a nomination device for Congress took place at the end of the nineteenth and the first half of the twentieth century. As we have seen, this corresponds to an era of declining polarization. By the time polarization began escalating, primaries were nearly universal. So any general claim that primary elections are the major cause of polarization seems weak. Gerber and Morton (1998) provide evidence that laws dictating the ease with which independent voters can participate in partisan primaries have an important effect on the divergence of the general election candidates in congressional districts. They argue that those states with "closed" primaries that allow registered partisans to vote in their party's primary produce much more polarized general elections than states that allow independents to vote in primaries and for partisans to vote in any party's primary. But the number of closed primaries has been falling over time.

Perhaps the source of the effect of primaries on polarization is not institutional but is rooted in changes in participation and behavior of the electorate. David King (2003) argues that the decline in participation in legislative primaries is the major culprit. He speculates that declining participation has made each party's primary electorate more ideologically homogeneous resulting in more extreme candidates. There are a number of reasons to be skeptical of this explanation. The first is that the claim that primary electorates have become more partisan over time is hard to verify directly as the National Election Study has not consistently queried voters specifically about their participation in primaries. Second, if small primary electorates caused polarization, polarization would rise more following midterm elections (when turnout is generally lower) than it does following general elections. There is no evidence for such a pattern (McCarty, Poole, and Rosenthal 2006, chap. 2).

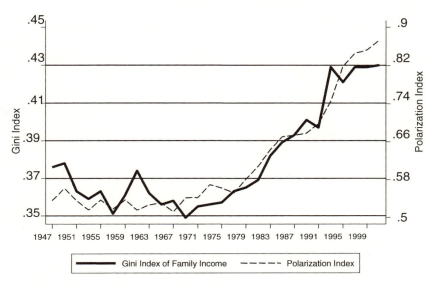

Figure 9.5 Polarization and Income Inequality

Changes in the media environment of politics may also have played an important role. Many observers have noted that the style of American journalism changed markedly following Watergate in a manner that may have contributed to a more confrontational style of politics. There is little debate that the introduction of cameras into the House chamber and the broadcast of its proceeding on C-SPAN gave the minority Republicans led by Newt Gingrich a powerful new weapon against the majority party (see Zelizer in this volume). It has also been argued that the proliferation of media outlets through cable television and the Internet has created an additional impetus for polarization. Recently Markus Prior (2007) has found that partisan voters increasingly self-select into news outlets that confirm their basic partisan and ideological biases (Republicans watch Fox and Democrats listen to National Public Radio). Perhaps more troubling is the finding that independents increasingly prefer Seinfeld reruns to any news outlet.[9]

Given that none of the preceding accounts explain completely the patterns of figures 9.3 and 9.4, many scholars have offered explanations rooted in more fundamental changes in the U.S. social and economic structure. The emphasis in many of these accounts has been the rising economic inequality experienced by the United States since the 1970s.[10] Figure 9.5 lends a great deal of credibility for such a linkage by plotting polarization and the Gini index of family income, a standard measure of income inequality. The two series correlate very highly, and they both experience reversals at almost exactly the same time.[11] Unfortunately, a limitation of these accounts is that the mechanism that translates inequality into polarization remains unclear, and it is even possible that the causality is reversed such that polarization generates inequality.[12] Clearly the most direct way that inequality might translate into polarization would be if the increasing gap between rich and poor voters led their respective parties to pursue divergent economic policies. Just as the current polarization is a phenomenon of the Republicans moving right with the Democrats holding steady, the recent growth in inequality is the result of rapid growth of incomes for the upper end of the distribution and stagnant incomes at the bottom. McCarty, Poole, and Rosenthal (2006) show that partisanship and voting are increasingly tied to income with income levels enjoying economic growth becoming more Republican while low-income voters have remained Democrats. These changes represent not only the voters' increased sensitivity to income but also their response to the polarization of the elite partisans.

Finally, some authors stress increasing divisions within the electorate on race and social issues are the culprit.[13] The first reason to discount such explanations as the whole story is that Congress rarely takes direct votes on these issues. The overwhelming majority of the votes used to construct the polarization indices in figure 9.3 are over taxes, budgets, and other economic policies especially after the issue de jure, civil rights for African Americans, left the congressional agenda at the end of 1960s. Second, several studies have failed to find evidence that the mass electorate is indeed more polarized on these issues now that it was twenty-five years ago.[14] These studies do, however, find that *partisan* voters are divided on these issues, but that the mass polarization begins after the elite polarization. Thus, the polarization of partisan voters may be more a reflection of voters being better able to sort themselves into parties based on racial and social issues after the party elites diverged.

THE LINK BETWEEN POLARIZATION AND GRIDLOCK

Why should polarization have an effect on policy outcomes? In a purely majoritarian legislature it would not. Imagine we can represent policy alternatives on a single left-right spectrum and that every legislator has an ideal policy on this spectrum. If each legislator votes for the alternative closest to her ideal choice, the median voter theorem says that the outcome of an open legislative process, where any legislator can offer amendments, is the ideal policy of the *median* legislator—the one whose ideal point lies to the right of half of the legislative ideal points and to the left of the other half.[15] The implication of this model for polarization is clear:

it shouldn't matter. The distribution of legislative preferences can become very bipolar, yet if the median preference is unaffected, the outcome is the same. In extreme cases where the two parties are completely distinct, polarization might affect the position of the median legislator so that policy outcomes move in the direction of the larger party. There would be no legislative gridlock, however, as any policy that deviated from the median position would soon be corrected.

Although the majoritarian theory is an important benchmark, its predictions about the consequences for polarization depend on its assumptions about legislative procedure, majority rule, and electoral politics. If we consider more realistic alternatives, a very different picture emerges. It is precisely those features of the American political system that depart from this idealized model that give polarization its bite.

Political Parties

Arguably, one of the limitations of the majoritarian model is that it neglects the role that legislative parties and their leaders play in the policy process. Many scholars argue that legislators have strong electoral incentives to delegate substantial powers to partisan leaders to shape the legislative agenda and to discipline wayward members. To the extent that parties can successfully pursue such strategies, policymaking becomes the interaction of parties.

In such a world, polarization becomes something of a mixed bag. American political scientists have long suggested that more cohesive, distinct, and programmatic political parties would offer a corrective to the failures of policymaking in the United States. Enamored with the "party responsibility" model of Westminster-style parliaments, they have argued that a system where a cohesive majority party governs encumbered only by the need to win elections would provide more accountability and rationality in policymaking. As formulated by the American Political Science Association's Report on the Committee for Parties (1950, 1), "An effective party system requires, first, that the parties are able to bring forth programs to which they commit themselves and, second, that the parties possess sufficient internal cohesion to carry out these programs."

Any benefits of polarization are offset, however, when control of the executive and legislative branches is split among cohesive parties. Unfortunately for the Responsible Party model, political polarization has occurred in an era in which divided governments occur with increasing frequency. Before World War II there is no positive association between divided government and polarization, but the two phenomena have frequently occurred since then.[16]

In situations of divided government with cohesive parties, party theories predict that policymaking represents bilateral bargaining between the parties. The predicted consequences of polarization in this environment are not so salutary. Just as a house cannot be sold when the buyer values it less than the price the seller is willing to accept, increased policy differences shrink the set of compromises that both parties are willing to entertain. The increased policy differences have a second effect on bargaining that endangers even feasible compromises. Returning to the analogy of a home buyer, consider the case when the buyer is willing to pay slightly more than the seller is willing to accept. Under such circumstance, the buyer is more willing to make a "low-ball" offer as her only risk is losing out on a transaction in which she stands to gain little. Returning to the political context, increased policy differences exacerbate the incentives to engage in brinksmanship in bargaining so that even feasible policy compromises might not be reached.[17] Thus, polarization leads to more gridlock and less policy innovation during periods of divided government. Polarization might lead to more policy innovation during unified governments, however, because of increased party responsibility. But, as I discuss later, this positive effect of polarization in unified governments may be fleeting.

Supermajoritarian Institutions

Institutions such as the presidential veto and the Senate filibuster also inhibit majority rule and allow polarization to cripple the policymaking process.[18] Because of these supermajoritarian obstacles, policymaking is driven not by the median legislator but by the preferences of those actors whose support is *pivotal* in overcoming vetoes and filibusters.

To see how supermajoritarianism produces gridlocked policy, suppose again that all policy alternatives and legislator ideal points can be represented as points on a spectrum from left to right such as the liberal-conservative scale. An important concept here is that of the *pivot*. The pivot is an agent in the policy process whose support is necessary for the passage of a new law. Consider for example, the effects of the Senate's rules for debate and cloture. Under its current rules, debate on most legislation cannot be terminated without a vote on cloture, which must be supported by three-fifths of those senators present and voting.[19] Thus, if all 100 senators vote according to their ideal points, the senators located at the 40th and the 60th most leftward position must support any new legislation, as no coalition can contain three-fifths of the votes without including these legislators. Thus, any policy located between these pivotal senators cannot be altered or is *gridlocked*. Prior to reforms in 1975, the requirement for cloture was a two-thirds vote so the *filibuster pivots* were located at either the 33rd or 67th position.

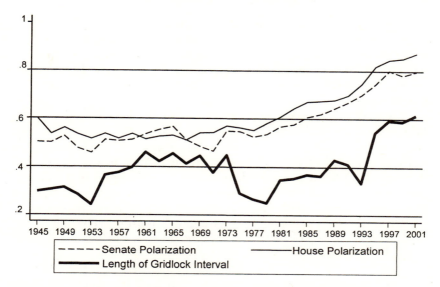

Figure 9.6 Partisan Polarization and the Width of the Gridlock Interval

Additionally, we can also take account of the presidential veto. Either the president must support new legislation or a coalition of two-thirds of each chamber must vote to override. Suppose the president is located toward the left of the policy spectrum. Then he or the legislator at the 33rd percentile must support any policy change. This legislator is dubbed the *veto pivot*. If the president is a rightist, the 67th percentile legislator becomes the veto pivot.

Putting these institutional requirements together, a rough measure of the propensity for legislative gridlock is the preference distance between the 33rd senator and the 60th senator when the president is on the left and the distance between the 40th senator and the 67th senator when the president is on the right.[20] When these distances are large, new legislation should be harder to come by.

Using the same DW-NOMINATE scores that were used to measure party polarization, I can measure this gridlock interval, which I plot over time in figure 9.6. Although the width of the gridlock interval and party polarization are conceptually distinct, we can see that empirically they go hand in hand. These two measures are closely related because the filibuster and veto pivots are almost always members of different parties. Thus, as the preferences of the parties diverge, so do those of the pivots. In fact, more than three-quarters of the variation in the width of the gridlock interval in the post-war period is accounted for by polarization and the 1975 cloture reforms. Thus, this "pivotal politics" model of supermajoritarianism suggests that polarization is a legislation retardant. These supermajority requirements may also lead to polarization-induced gridlock even during periods of unified government. So long as the majority party is not large enough to satisfy all of the supermajority requirements, cross-party bargaining and coalition building is necessary for policy change.

This pivot perspective also underscores why the Senate's cloture rules have come under such scrutiny and call for reform. Once an infrequently used tool reserved for the most important legislation, the filibuster has during the period of increasing polarization become one of the central features of American politics. Filibusters, both threatened and realized, have been used to kill a number of important pieces of legislation. Perhaps even more consequentially, it has led the Senate to rely greatly on legislative tricks to avoid its effects. One such gimmick is using the budget reconciliation process to pass new legislation because reconciliation bills cannot be filibustered. This was the approach taken to pass the major income and estate tax cuts in 2001 (see also Hacker and Pierson in this volume). To avoid points of order under the so-called Byrd Rule, however, such legislation can only have deficit-increasing fiscal effects for the term of the budget resolution (five to ten years). Thus, many important pieces of fiscal policy have become temporary artifices built on a foundation of budgetary gimmicks.[21]

Strategic Disagreement

Another mechanism that transforms polarization into legislative paralysis is the incentives of politicians to engage in *strategic disagreement*. Strategic disagreement describes a situation where a president, party, or other political actor refuses compromise with the other side in an attempt to gain an electoral advantage by transferring the blame for the stalemate to the other side. Classical instances include attempts to bring up controversial legislation near an election in the hopes that a president will cast an unpopular veto such as was done with the Family and Medical Leave Act in 1992 and the partial-birth abortion bill before the 2000 election. Such electoral grandstanding lowers legislative capacity because it not only diverts resources into an unproductive endeavor but also makes both sides less willing to engage in the compromises required by successful legislation.[22]

Polarization exacerbates the incentives to engage in this type of behavior for several reasons. As the parties have become more extreme relative to voters, making the other side appear to be the more extreme becomes more valuable. If a veto of a family leave bill can make the president look like a heartless panderer to the pro-business lobby, why exclude small firms from its provisions to get it passed? If a veto of partial-birth abortion can make the president look like a heartless panderer to NARAL, why make an exemption for women's health to get it passed? Strategic disagreement leads to the erosion of the remaining strands of common ground.

Exacerbating these incentives further is the contemporary media environment of politics. Especially since Watergate and Vietnam, the media covers policymaking much as they would a heavyweight boxing match, scoring the winner and loser round by round. In such an environment, both sides are loath to make any compromises for fear of having it scored as a losing round. The result is policy stagnation.

Citizen Trust

Another potential pathway from polarization to gridlock lies in how voters respond to polarized elites. David King and Marc Hetherington have separately argued that a primary consequence of partisan polarization is that it undermines citizens' trust in the capacity of government to solve problems. Such claims are bolstered by the fact that the polarization measures in figure 9.3 track survey evidence of citizen trust in government fairly closely.[23]

It is not hard to see how declining trust can lead to policy stalemate. If the two parties cannot agree how to solve problem x, it is hard to mobilize the public around a policy response. It is even worse when one party says policy y alleviates problem x while the other says it exacerbates it.

Having discussed many reasons why polarization should retard policymaking, I now turn to the evidence to bolster my claim.

POLARIZATION AND LEGISLATIVE ACTIVITY

Despite the strong case that can be made for a relationship between polarization and policy gridlock, few scholars have addressed the issue. For example, in his seminal work of post–World War II lawmaking, David Mayhew (1991) considers the important question of whether divided party control of the executive and legislative branches produces legislative gridlock but not the effects of polarization and declining bipartisanship. Indeed, he attributes his "negative" findings about divided government to the fact that during the post-war period, bipartisanship was the norm.

Despite Mayhew's neglect of polarization, his data on landmark legislative enactments can be used to assess polarization's effects on the

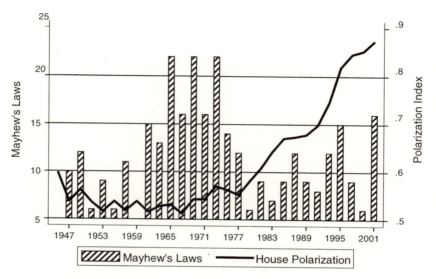

Figure 9.7 Polarization and Legislative Production

legislative process. Figure 9.7 plots the number of Mayhew's significant legislative enactments by congressional term against the DW-NOMI-NATE polarization measure.[24] The figure reveals a striking pattern. Congress enacted the vast majority of its significant legislation during its least polarized period. The ten least polarized congressional terms produced almost sixteen significant enactments per term whereas the ten most polarized terms produced slightly more than ten. This gap would be even bigger except for the enormous legislative output following the September 11 terrorist attacks during the most polarized congressional term of the era.

To control for other factors that contribute to legislative productivity, I developed a multivariate model of legislative output, presented in the appendix to this chapter. In this model, I attempt to isolate the effect of polarization by controlling for unified party control, the election cycle (congressional terms preceding presidential elections are not very productive), changes in party control of the presidency, and secular trends. These models produce a variety of estimates for the effect of polarization—these estimates depend on how a number of data issues are handled—but I consistently find substantively large and statistically significant effects.[25] At the upper end of the range, the least polarized congressional term produces a whopping 166 percent more legislation than the most polarized. For the lowest estimate, the figure is a still large 60 percent difference in legislative output.

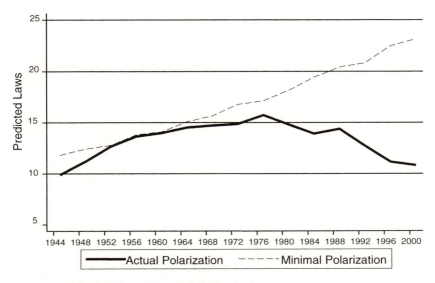

Figure 9.8 What If There Was No Polarization?

To get at the magnitude of these differences, figure 9.8 presents a coun-
terfactual analysis of Congress's output if polarization had remained the
level of the 1960s using the estimates of the multivariate model. Even
though this figure uses the lowest estimate of the effect of polarization,
the effect is substantial. Without polarization, a substantial upward trend
in legislative output would likely have continued. Polarization not only
dampened this trend, but reversed it.

One potential objection to these findings is that Mayhew's enactments
are only the tip of the legislative iceberg. Perhaps polarization affects only
the landmark but not the merely important. Data collected by William
Howell and his colleagues (2000) can address this issue. They code thousands of post-war statutes according to their "legislative significance"
grouping them into four levels. Their A-level statutes roughly correspond
to Mayhew's enactments. B-level statutes are statutes with significant policy changes that do not quite reach "landmark" status, whereas C statutes
are the remaining broad and substantive enactments. The lowest level,
D, contains the remainder—trivial and narrow legislation. I estimate a
separate multivariate model for each of these sets of statutes, identical to
the one I ran on Mayhew's data. The results show that polarization
has very large effects for the top three categories of legislation with the
largest effect on type B. The estimated effect on type D suggests that
polarization may increase the output of the trivial, but the effect is not
statistically significant.

One might also object to these findings on the grounds that they are solely the consequence of the historical coincidence of the Great Society with polarization's nadir. To alleviate these concerns, I marshaled data collected by a number of scholars on the legislative output of the late nineteenth and early twentieth centuries.[26] Estimates based on these data also confirm the negative effects of polarization on legislative output.

EFFECTS OF POLARIZATION ON SOCIAL POLICY

Given the evidence that polarization has reduced Congress's capacity to legislate, I turn to the question of how this has affected public policy outcomes. The most direct effect of polarization-induced gridlock is that public policy does not adjust to changing economic and demographic circumstances.

Various reasons could lead one to believe that these effects are most pronounced in the arena of social policy. Given that one of the aims of social policy is to insure citizens against the economic risks inherent in a market system, it must be responsive to shifts in these economic forces. If polarization inhibits these responses, it may leave citizens open to the new risks created by economic shifts brought on by deindustrialization and globalization. For example, consider the political response in the United States to increasing economic inequality since the 1970s. Most economists attribute increasing inequality to a number of economic factors such as the rise in the returns to education, exposure to trade, immigration, and changes in family structure. Nevertheless, many Western European countries faced with many of the same economic forces developed policies to mitigate the consequences so that the level of inequality changed only marginally.[27] Similarly, Jacob Hacker (2004) has recently argued that polarization was an important factor in impeding the modernization of many of the policies designed to alleviate social risks.

A second issue concerns the ways in which social policies in the United States are designed. Many policies, especially those aimed at the poor or near poor, are not indexed with respect to their benefits.[28] Therefore, these programs require continuous legislative adjustment to achieve a constant level of social protection. In the following sections, I argue that polarization has had a conservative effect on two important nonindexed social policies: the minimum wage and Temporary Assistance to Needy Families.

The Minimum Wage

Since its enactment in 1938, the federal minimum wage has been one of those issues that divides the Democratic and Republican parties. Both because of their desire to redistribute income to low-wage workers and to avoid competition with non-unionized labor, the Democrats have tended to favor a high minimum wage covering large segments of the work force. Alternatively, many Republicans have sought to keep the minimum wage low and to limit its scope as they believe that it creates unemployment by artificially inflating the cost of labor and that it imposes too great a burden on small businesses.

Despite these general differences, however, increases in the minimum wage and expansions of scope have tended to generate a fair amount of bipartisan support. For example in 1949, Republicans overwhelmingly supported an almost doubling of the wage. Moreover, Republican support was pivotal in the 1961 and 1966 amendments that increased the wage and extended it to new groups of voters.

This bipartisanship disappeared, as it did on so many other issues, in the 1970s. When Congress passed increases in 1977, it did so with a majority of Republicans voting against them in each chamber. Given Reagan's election and the Republican takeover of the Senate, increasing Republican opposition to the minimum wage meant that it would not be raised again until 1989. Although Republicans did support the bill on final passage, the three-step increase was so modest that the real value of the wage returned only to its 1986 level, doing little to reverse the long decline of the 1980s. In 1996 the minority Democrats were able to force a minimum-wage bill onto the agenda with a deft combination of obstruction of the Republican agenda and symbolic election-year politics. The result, however, was again a very modest increase at the cost of $20 billon in new business tax breaks.

To take a closer look at how partisan polarization has affected the trajectory of the minimum wage, figure 9.9 plots the real value of the minimum wage against the polarization of the U.S. House. Clearly, the real minimum wage tracks polarization closely. It begins to rise as polarization is going down after the war and begins to decrease as polarization begins rising in the 1970s. The mechanism behind the fall seems apparent. When there was little polarization, the effects of inflation were combated by frequent, large adjustments to the wage. After polarization escalated, however, adjustments became both less frequent and smaller.

Temporary Assistance to Needy Families

As another example of how polarization affects important social policies, consider the Temporary Assistance for Needy Families (TANF) program which was created by the 1996 Welfare Reform Act. This program was designed to replace the Aid to Families with Dependent Children (AFDC) program with a series of block grants to states to implement their own

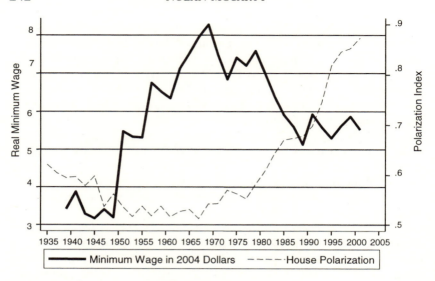

Figure 9.9 Polarization and the Real Minimum Wage

welfare programs. Under TANF, benefits are no longer an entitlement, and it is left up to the states to determine the various aspects of eligibility and the level of benefits. Given that no state has indexed the level of TANF benefits, polarization-induced gridlock should allow the real level of benefits to deteriorate.[29] To evaluate this claim, I look at data on real benefit levels for a family of four for each state from 1996 to 2000.

Unfortunately, good measures of polarization for state legislatures are not available except for a handful of states. Existing evidence seems to show that state legislatures are at least as polarized as the U.S. Congress, however. Table 9.1 presents DW-NOMINATE polarization measures for a sample of states from different regions for the late 1990s and early 2000s. These measures have been normalized against the 2003–4 U.S. House so that a score of 1 equals the polarization level of the House and scores greater than 1 imply more polarization. By way of comparison, the normalized measure for the 1973–74 U.S. House was only .691.

Most contemporary state legislatures are quite polarized. Because few states have supermajoritarian requirements other than the executive veto, we should expect polarization to be more important during periods of divided government. Thus, because of the lack of specific data on state polarization, I focus primarily on the effects of divided party government on TANF benefit levels.

Because they are not indexed, the real value of TANF benefits should fall more sharply over time when there is divided government in the state.

TABLE 9.1
Polarized Measures from a Sample of States

State	Normalized Polarization Measure
Alaska	0.944
Colorado	0.972
Connecticut	1.013
Iowa	1.018
Maine	0.921
Minnesota	0.956
Missouri	0.983
New Hampshire	0.913
New Jersey	0.977
Rhode Island	1.063
South Carolina	0.911
Texas	0.959
Utah	0.959
Vermont	0.872
Wyoming	0.940

Table 9.2 confirms this point by showing the annual percentage change in real benefits for a family of four for each form of party control.

Clearly, the declines in real benefits are larger for the two forms of divided government than for the forms of unified government. The drops are especially large in states where Democratic governors face Republican legislatures. Most importantly, the declines for divided governments exceed those of Republican unified governments.

In the appendix, I describe a multiple regression analysis designed to see if these differences hold up when other factors such as the racial and ethnic composition, income level, and economic inequality are controlled for. The results show that the average declines in unified governments and divided governments with Republican governors are statistically indistinguishable, but that benefits have dropped 13 percent more per year in divided governments with Democratic governors.

Although the evidence about the effects of polarization on the minimum wage and TANF benefits are far from conclusive, it does seem to point strongly in the direction of a conservative effect of polarization on social policy.

TABLE 9.2
Percentage Real Changes in TANF Benefits

	Unified Republican	Unified Democrat	Divided, Democratic Governor	Divided, Republican Governor
1997	−.025	−.023	−.296	−.237
1998	−.041	.092	−.079	.016
1999	−.015	−.012	−.098	−.015
2000	−.028	−.027	−.018	−.022

THE QUALITY OF POLICY IN A POLARIZED ERA

Thus far I have focused on the ways in which polarization-produced gridlock forestalls the creation of new legislative enactments. Congress has produced many important pieces of legislation even at the height of polarization, however. Although it would be easy to dismiss many of these as exceptions to a general rule or the result of extreme policy status quos, there is reason to believe that polarization affects even the legislation that passes.

Successful legislative enactments in a polarized environment share a number of important attributes. First, these policies must generate overwhelming support within the majority party. Unless such consensus can be imposed by party discipline, all wings and factions of the party become pivotal in the success of the new bill. In such a polarized environment, the power of extreme party factions may be enhanced most. Because it is difficult to replace the votes of more extreme elements with those of moderates from the other party, rebellions at the extremes can kill new legislation. Thus, policy outcomes may be more extreme relative to the political center when polarization is high. Governing parties succeed in a polarized environment only on those issues on which they are internally homogeneous, such as the Republican tax cuts (see Hacker and Pierson in this volume), and not on those where there are dissenting voices (Social Security privatization).

A second feature of new policies in a polarized environment is that they are more likely to be built upon distributive coalitions. One way to overcome disputes over policy principles is to resort to vote buying, side payments, and the "pork barrel." Thus, polarization may lead to a greater reliance on distributive spending. This was the pattern observed with the 1996 minimum-wage increases where Republican support was purchased by business tax breaks. It is also a plausible explanation for the explosion of domestic discretionary spending during George W. Bush's first term. In order to maintain cohesion among the Republicans and to get the support of the occasional Democrat, Bush had to be a willing accomplice in the congressional pork barrel. Even though domestic discretionary spending increased more than 30 percent, he was the first president in 175 years not to invoke his veto power during a four-year term.

Finally, models of strategic disagreement predict that new policies might emerge from electoral incentives to take issues off the agenda for future elections. Often a party supports an important piece of its opponent's agenda as a signal to voters that it cares about the issue as well. In principal, such strategic moderation is a good thing; indeed, its one of the reasons for having elections. These incentives often go too far, however, leading to "bidding wars" in which each party escalates its proposals to convince voters that it cares the most about the issue. The result of this pandering to uninformed voters could be policies on a scale that neither party would legislate on its own.

The recent addition of a prescription drug benefit to the Medicare program reveals many of these incentives at work. George W. Bush and Republican leaders were anxious to deny the Democrats the opportunity to focus on the issue of drug affordability for seniors. Because it was further determined that a limited or means-tested benefit would still leave the party vulnerable to campaign attacks, the decision was made to match the Democrats call for a near-universal benefit under Medicare. Because of the electoral motivations involved, the administration could count on few Democratic votes for its bill. Consequently, the administration had to prevent defections within the conservative ranks. To appeal both to free-market conservatives opposed to price controls and to drug industry interests, the administration's bill explicitly prohibited the Medicare program from using its purchasing power to negotiate cheaper drug prices, denying the government an important tool in cost control. Without these controls, the expected cost of the benefits has mushroomed from $400 billion over ten years when it was passed to more than $700 billion. Given the established benefit formulas, the inflation in the cost of pharmaceuticals will wipe out the monetary value of the benefit to seniors in just over two years. Perhaps gridlock would have been the better outcome.

OTHER POLICY CONSEQUENCES OF POLARIZATION

Perhaps one of the most important long-term consequences of the decline in legislative capacity caused by polarization is that Congress's power is declining relative to the other branches of government. A number of recent studies by political scientists have shown that presidents facing strong partisan and ideological opposition from Congress are more likely to take unilateral actions rather than pursuing their goals through legislation.[30] This effect is perhaps best exemplified by the large number of executive orders issued by Bill Clinton at the end of his second term. Many, if not most of these, lacked any chance of passage through Congress. The consequence of not getting statutory authorization was that George W. Bush was able to reverse many of these, even though legislative repeal would have been filibustered in the Senate. The result is government by executive order rather than statutes.

Not only are presidents likely to become more powerful, but polarization also increases the opportunities of judges and courts to pursue their policy goals because such judicial activism is unlikely to be checked by legislative statute.[31] The courts have become the dominant arena for a wide swath of policy from tobacco regulation to firearms to social policy.

Although most of this essay has concentrated on the effects of polarization within the legislative process, contemporary work in bureaucratic and judicial politics suggests that polarization has detrimental effects at the policy implementation stage. First, polarization decreases Congress's willingness to delegate authority to administrative agencies. In a systematic study, Epstein and O'Halloran (1999) show that Congress is far less willing to delegate policymaking authority to agencies when there are large ideological disagreements between the president and congressional majorities. Because party polarization has exacerbated these disagreements (especially during divided government), Congress relies far less on the expertise of the bureaucracy in the implementation and enforcement of statutes. The result is often excessive statutory constraints or the delegation of statutory enforcement to private actors and courts rather than agencies (Farhang 2003). These outcomes further weaken the executive and legislative branches vis-à-vis the judiciary. Also polarization has now distorted the confirmation process of executive branch officials and judges. In studies of all major executive branch appointments over the past century, Rose Razaghian and I find that increased partisan polarization is the major culprit in the increasing delays in the Senate confirmation process. Consequently, long-term vacancies in the political leadership of many departments and agencies have become the norm. As these problems are exacerbated at the beginning of new administrations, presidential transitions have become considerably less smooth.[32] Polarization has also clearly contributed to the well-documented conflicts over judicial appointments, leading to an understaffing of the federal bench.

Conclusions

"Politics ain't beanbag." It is the arena of contestation of fundamental values. Citizens expect their elected representatives to take strong stands on behalf of those policies that promote the citizens' conception of the good and just. But while it is not a child's game, it should not be a blood sport either. It should be carried on in a way that makes compromise and problem solving possible.

Unfortunately, events of the past thirty years have produced an elite political culture in the United States where compromise and problem solving have fallen dramatically on its list of virtues. No doubt some of these conflicts are rooted in principled disagreements about the welfare of the nation. But too often the conflicts originate from baser motives of narrow group interests or cynical electoral calculation.

As I have argued, increasing levels of polarization have led to a number of undesirable changes in the American policy process. By making compromise and consensus building substantially more difficult, polarization has weakened the capacity of Congress and state legislatures to engage in policymaking. Consequently, policy is less and less responsive to new economic and social problems. This dissipation in the ability of legislative bodies to wield public authority has opened the space for other, less representative and accountable institutions, to assert even grander claims of authority. Contemporary debates about executive and judicial power often fail to recognize that much of the problem lies in the legislative weakness wrought by polarization and partisanship.

Given the evidence of this problem, what can be done about it? To paraphrase Madison, we can only cure the mischiefs of polarization by removing its causes or by controlling its effects. Neither will be easy.

Though it would be facile to suggest that polarization could be reduced simply by wishing that the parties put their differences aside, it is worth recalling that the polarization of elected officeholders far exceeds that of the electorate. Thus, electoral reform may help take the edge of partisan conflict. Many politicians, scholars, and journalists have touted reforms of campaign finance and congressional districting to alleviate partisanship and polarization, but because expensive interest-group-financed campaigns and gerrymandered districts are not primary causes of polarization, such reforms are likely to have minimal effects.

Reforms to alleviate the effects of polarization will also be quite difficult to implement. At the national level, the obvious candidate is cloture reform to make it easier for Senate majorities to legislate. Reforms of the confirmation process might be required as well. Given that both of these reforms involve the granting of significant power from the minority party to the majority party, they are unlikely to happen in such a polarized environment.

Appendix: Multivariate Analyses

Significant Legislation

The details of the collection of his time series on significant legislation are discussed by Mayhew (1991). The main dependent variable for my analysis is the combined Sweep I and Sweep II laws from his original analysis supplemented by his subsequent lists of significant laws from 1990 to 2002. His supplemental lists are available at http://pantheon.yale.edu/~dmayhew/datasets.html.

One data issue to consider when using Mayhew's series is the possibility that his standards for inclusion changed significantly between the publication of his book and his subsequent updates. To be on the safe side, I include a dummy variable *post-publication* that takes on a value of 1 for each congressional term that he coded post-publication. Another issue is that the 107th Congress (2001–2) is a rather large outlier because of the legislation passed in response to the September 11 terrorism attacks. More than half of the significant legislation passed by that congress directly concerns the 9/11 attacks. No other one-time exogenous event is associated with such a large cluster of enactments in Mayhew's series. So in the models that I report here I handle this outlier in two ways: I ignore the 107th Congress altogether and omit 9/11 legislation from the 107th's total.[33]

The main independent variables in the analysis are measures of party polarization derived from DW-NOMINATE scores. I variously used polarization in the House, polarization in the Senate, the average of polarization for both chambers, and the maximum of polarization across chambers. The substantive results are very similar across measures. I report the results using polarization in the House.

I also include a number of other control variables. *Unified* is a dummy variable that takes on the value of 1 in congressional terms in which the presidency and both chambers of congress are controlled by the same party.[34] The variable *new regime* takes on a value of 1 during the first congressional term following a switch in party control of the presidency. Higher than average productivity in such terms is an implication of pivotal politics models. *Presidential election* takes on a value of 1 during terms preceding presidential election. Finally, *year* is the year in which

TABLE 9.A1
Polarization and Legislative Productivity

	Model 1	Model 2	Model 3	Model 4
	Laws	Laws –9/11	Laws	Laws –9/11
Polarization	–2.11	–3.21	–4.12	–5.71
	(1.27)	(1.27)	(1.96)	(1.88)
Unified	–.008	.018	–.069	–.051
	(.161)	(.154)	(.162)	(2.01)
New regime	–.019	–.150	–.084	–.231
	(.191)	(.186)	(.191)	(2.07)
Presidential election	–.313	–.324	–.372	–.398
	(.166)	(.159)	(.167)	(.157)
Year	.012	.016	.014	.019
	(.009)	(.008)	(.009)	(.008)
Post-publication			.496	.604
			(.378)	(.353)
Constant	–20.49	–27.36	–24.66	–32.82
	(17.47)	(16.86)	(17.26)	(16.41)
N	28	28	28	28
Log-likelihood	–78.82	–77.13	–77.99	–75.76

the congressional term begins. This is to account for an upward trend in legislative output.

Because the number of laws per congressional term is always a non-negative integer, ordinary least squares estimation is inappropriate. Therefore, I use negative binomial regressions to estimate all of the models I report in this section. Negative binomial regressions are appropriate when the dependent variable is a non-negative integer and when the data are overdispersed due to clustering.[35] Because these models are log-linear, the proper interpretation of coefficients is the percentage change in the dependent variable given a unit change in the independent variable.

The results of this model are presented in table 9.A1 where the standard errors are given in parentheses. The first two specifications do not control for any shift in coding standard while the third and fourth do. The coefficient on *polarization* is large and statistically significant in all specifications at the .05 level for one-tailed tests. The estimated effect is largest when both coding bias and the 9/11 laws are accounted for. The results for the other control variables are generally consistent with other studies. Although partisan theories suggest an interaction between polarization and gridlock, the coefficient on such an interaction was never significant and often had the wrong sign.

TABLE 9.A2
Legislation and Legislative Productivity: Howell et al.'s Measures

	A Laws	B Laws	C Laws	D Laws
Polarization	−5.111	−6.22	−3.885	.257
	(1.70)	(2.04)	(1.088)	(.783)
Unified	.319	.131	.124	−.127
	(.147)	(.178)	(.097)	(.069)
New administration	−.362	−.079	−.549	−.029
	(.189)	(.234)	(.129)	(.092)
Presidential election	−.414	−.154	−.429	−.039
	(.161)	(.200)	(.106)	(.075)
Year	.028	.036	.013	−.012
	(.008)	(.010)	(.005)	(.003)
Constant	25.827	45.347	229.6	814.936
	(8.893)	(15.52)	(66.54)	(438.25)
N	25	25	25	25
Log-likelihood	−55.89	−72.80	−102.79	−148.42

Robustness Checks

To verify the robustness of the findings derived from Mayhew's data, I estimate similar models using Howell et al.'s data (2000). These data provide counts of legislation coded by varying levels of legislative significance. Their highest level A is roughly identical to Mayhew's laws. Level B includes very important pieces of legislation that rank just below A. Levels C and D include correspondingly less significant legislation. Their series run from 1945 to 1994 so that there are no issues surrounding 9/11. The results of this analysis are shown in table 9.A2. These results show that polarization significantly retards legislation at levels A–C but has slightly positive but insignificant effect on the most trivial legislation.

To test whether polarization has the same effect on legislation prior to the 1940s, I also estimate models using two other series of laws that cover the period from Reconstruction to the end of World War II. One source of data is from Clinton and Lapinski (2006) who use a sophisticated econometric procedure to pool assessments of significance from eleven historical and contemporary sources. Their procedure produces significance scores for more than 30,000 pieces of legislation from 1877. As a dependent variable, I use the number of laws in each congressional term that score in the top 500 for the period of 1877–1948. As a second dependent variable I use a list generated by Petersen (2001), who attempts to replicate Mayhew's procedure for the period of 1881–1945. The first two

TABLE 9.A3
Pre–World War II Estimates of Effect of Polarization on Legislative Productivity

	Clinton and Lapinski	Peterson	Mayhew and Peterson
Polar	−2.96	−2.28	−1.56
	(.778)	(.569)	(.618)
Unified	.463	.210	.009
	(.240)	(.193)	(.122)
New administration	−.002	.407	.163
	(.275)	(.193)	(.141)
Presidential election	.446	−.350	−.330
	(.281)	(.199)	(.131)
Year			.005
			(.004)
Constant	4.814	3.81	−6.039
	(.727)	(.518)	(7.91)
N	36	33	60
Log-likelihood	−119.01	−85.36	−162.69

columns of table 9.A3 report the results using each of these dependent variables. One difficulty in evaluating the results on the earlier period is that polarization is consistently decreasing over the whole period. Thus, I cannot separately estimate the effect of polarization and a time trend. It is possible that the estimates of the effect of polarization are simply capturing the effects of a secular increase in legislative output. As a partial solution to this problem, I combined the Mayhew and Petersen data, on the premise that at least they have a common set of coding rules, to estimate a single model encompassing 1880–2002.[36] Although the estimated polarization coefficient on the combined series is smaller than that of other models, it is still substantively large and statistically significant.

State-Level TANF Benefits

To test for the effects of divided government on TANF benefits, I regress the percentage change in the benefits for a family of four on the current level of benefits, indicators for each pattern of party control, indicators for each year, and economic and demographic factors within each state (see table 9.A4). The monthly benefit levels for a family of four by state from 1996 to 2000 were obtained from the Urban Institute's *Welfare Rules Database*. The nominal values were converted to real values using a CPI-U series. The average real benefit levels were $828, while

TABLE 9.A4
Polarization and Percentage Change in State TANF Benefits

Unified Democratic	−.014	.045
Divided, Democratic governor	−.137	.049
Divided, Republican governor	−.043	.038
Black %	.059	.180
Hispanic %	.109	.187
Gini family income	−.028	.020
Median family income	.001	.022
1998	.141	.0421
1999	.124	.043
2000	.128	.044
Benefit levels	.0002	.00005
Constant	−.099	.178
R^2	.185	
N	197	

the average annual real change in benefits is −$38. The economic and demographic controls include data on the racial and ethic composition of the state as well as its per capita income. These are all obtained from the U.S. Census. Finally, I use a measure of economic inequality, the Gini Index of Family Income, estimated by Bruce Western, Josh Guetzkow, and Jake Rosenfeld from the Current Population Survey available at http://inequality.princeton.edu/.

NOTES

Many, if not all, of the ideas contained in this essay originate in my long-term collaboration with Keith Poole and Howard Rosenthal. I would also like to thank seminar participants at Harvard and Berkeley and Michelle Anderson for research assistance. The Center for Advanced Study in the Behavioral Sciences provided time off and a great intellectual atmosphere for undertaking this research.

1. An exception is the review essay of Rosenthal (2004).

2. Or conversely, the number of "party" votes in Congress was escalating.

3. Alternative, but closely related, procedures include Heckman and Snyder 1997 and Clinton, Jackman, and Rivers 2004.

4. Some care must be taken in interpreting figure 9.4 because nominate measures relative, but not absolute, positions of legislators. The interpretation that the Republican shift to the right is larger in magnitude than the Democratic

shift to the left is confirmed by studies of the content of party platforms (see Gerring 1998).

5. For the political science, see McDonald and Grofman 1999; Carson, Crespin, Finocchiaro, and Rohde 2003. For the commentary, see Toobin 2003.

6. This lack of competition carried over into the 2004 elections, where almost all partisan turnover in the House was the result of the controversial redistricting plan enacted in Texas in 2003.

7. See McCarty, Poole, and Rosenthal 2006, chap. 2.

8. See Gerber and Morton 1998; King 2003.

9. One could imagine the analogous argument that the drastic reduction in the number of daily newspapers may have reduced polarization before the take-off of the new media exacerbated it. The number of newspapers did not begin to decline until about 1980, however.

10. See McCarty, Poole, and Rosenthal 1997, 2005; Stonecash, Brewer, and Mariani 2003; Phillips 2002; Hicks 2003; Rosenthal 2004.

11. While the Gini index is only available from the 1940s onward, Rosenthal (2004) and McCarty, Poole, and Rosenthal (2005) show that over the longer run the polarization measure moves with a number of other indicators of economic and social inequality.

12. I consider the possibility of reverse causality in some detail later in this chapter. Of course, the correlation may even be spurious. For example, Krugman (2002) hypothesizes that there are recurring eras of "permissive" capitalism that produce both high levels of inequality and support for conservative economic policies (see also Schlesinger 1986).

13. See Carmines and Stimson 1989.

14. See DiMaggio et al. (1996); Evans (2003); and Fiorina et al. 2005.

15. Any other policy can be defeated by a majority coalition. Suppose the policy outcome was to the left of the median voter's ideal point. Then the median and every legislator located to her right would form a majority willing to overturn it in favor of the median's ideal point. The same logic precludes outcomes to the right of the median voter's preferred policy.

16. The average level of polarization during post-war divided governments is .64, whereas the average for unified governments is .55. The difference is statistically significant at the .0246 level (one-tailed test). Such a correlation is predicted by "party balancing" models of voter behavior (e.g., Fiorina 1996; Alesina and Rosenthal 1995; Sekhon and Mebane 2002). These theories argue that moderate voters have incentives to split their tickets in order to force polarized parties to bargain toward moderate policies.

17. See Cameron 2000 for the application of bargaining theory to policymaking.

18. See Krehbiel 1997 and Brady and Volden 1998.

19. The most prominent exceptions are budget reconciliation bills, which require only a majority vote.

20. This formulation embeds a couple of additional assumptions: that the president is generally more extreme than the veto pivots; and that the preferences in the U.S. House are similar enough to those of the Senate that obtaining cloture

or an override in the Senate is sufficient to ensure a majority in the House. These are all reasonable approximations.

21. The Byrd Rule, named for Senator Robert Byrd (D-WV), specifies that a point of order may be called on any provision in a reconciliation bill that authorizes discretionary appropriations and provisions that increase entitlement spending or cut taxes beyond a window of five (or more) years provided for in the reconciliation directive. Because it takes sixty votes to waive the rule, failure to abide by its terms essentially removes the parliamentary protections otherwise afforded reconciliation bills.

22. See Gilmour 1995; Groseclose and McCarty 2000.

23. The lack of data on trust before the 1970s makes it difficult to evaluate the ability of this hypothesis to explain longer-term trends in polarization.

24. See Mayhew 1991 for the details of his compilation of significant statutes. Figure 9.6 uses both the data published in his original study as well as his subsequent updates. It also combines Mayhew's series based on contemporary judgments with his series based on retrospective judgments.

25. Consistent with supermajoritarianism, I never find a significant effect for the interaction of unified government and polarization.

26. These data are from Petersen 2001 and Clinton and Lapinski 2003.

27. Many political economy models of redistribution predict that there is more redistribution following increases in pre-tax and transfer income inequality (e.g., Meltzer and Richard 1981 and Romer 1975). My arguments about polarization and gridlock may explain why this did not happen in the United States.

28. This is generally not true of programs with large middle-class constituencies such as Social Security and Medicare. For some tax policies such as the Alternative Minimum Tax, the lack of indexing has negative effects on portions of the upper middle class.

29. One reason states have not indexed the benefits is that the federal block grants are not indexed.

30. Howell (2003) documents such an effect with respect to the overall issuance of executive orders, while Lewis (2003) finds that presidents are more likely to create agencies by executive order rather than statute when there is interbranch policy conflict. Moreover, Lewis finds that agencies created by presidential order are often short-lived and underfunded.

31. Such arguments are consistent with the "separation of powers" model of judicial decision making. See Ferejohn and Shipan 1990 and Spiller and Gely 1992 for the theory and evidence.

32. That the September 11 terrorist attacks occurred just eight months into a new administration may not be coincidence.

33. The results of simply dropping the 107th from the analysis are very similar to those dropping just the 9/11 laws.

34. The 107th Congress poses another coding challenge because there was unified government until the party switch of Vermont Senator James Jeffords that shifted Senate control to the Democrats. Mayhew's list includes one piece of legislation in the unified period, the 2001 tax cuts. Because the unit of analysis in my models is the congressional term, I code the entire term as divided. This is reason-

able given that the tax bill passed after Jeffords's announcement, though before his official switch. The other alternative would be to drop the tax cut from the 107th output. The results are identical under both approaches.

35. See Cameron and Trivedi 1998 for a discussion of count models.

36. I make the adjustment for 9/11 legislation in the combined series.

Chapter Ten

Tax Politics and the Struggle
over Activist Government

JACOB S. HACKER AND PAUL PIERSON

In May 2006 Republicans in Congress, urged on by President George W. Bush, squeezed through the House and Senate a tax-cut package estimated to cost $70 billion over the next five years. The centerpiece of the bill was a continuation of Republicans' 2003 cuts in the dividends tax and capital gains tax—cuts that mostly benefited the wealthiest of Americans. Also included was short-term relief for upper-middle-class taxpayers hit by the ballooning Alternative Minimum Tax (AMT), whose future reach had been dramatically expanded by the tax-cut legislation enacted by the GOP Congress back during President Bush's first year in office in 2001. Even as the ink was drying on the 2006 tax-cut bill, Republicans vowed that they would come back and pass another string of tax cuts before the 2006 midterm elections, in which they found themselves facing their most serious electoral challenge since capturing Congress in 1994.

In the news media, the 2006 tax cuts were treated as mostly unremarkable—perhaps because they paled in size and significance to those passed in previous years, or perhaps because "Republicans pass tax cuts" had become the ultimate "dog bites man" story in American politics. Yet the tax cuts signaled the continuation of a striking and historically anomalous chapter in U.S. fiscal policy. Since President Bush had entered office in 2001, he and congressional Republicans had engineered a major shift in federal taxation that had dramatically reduced the overall tax burden and shifted it away from asset holders and the wealthy. In his first year in office, Bush had successfully championed massive income-tax reductions and eventual elimination of the estate tax. The 2001 law had a ten-year price tag that was estimated at $2.1 trillion (Orszag 2001). No less striking, however, was the bill's distribution: 36 percent of the cuts accrued to the richest 1 percent of Americans and 63 percent to the top 20 percent, while just over 20 percent when to the bottom 60 percent (CTJ 2002).

The 2001 law was a dramatic policy reversal, but not, it turned out, an isolated accomplishment. In each of the next three years, President Bush successfully pushed for additional cuts—first for businesses in 2002, then for individuals in 2003, and then again for individuals in 2004. The biggest of these post-2001 bills, the tax revision of 2003, was the most remarkable of the three. Roughly as tilted toward the affluent as the 2001 bill, its estimated price tag exceeded $1 trillion over ten years—at a time when budget projections showed a mounting tide of red ink. All told, if the 2001–3 tax cuts were extended as advocates desired, they would cost more than $4 trillion through 2013. In that year, the revenue loss would exceed 2.4 percent of GDP. To put this staggering figure in perspective, the long-term costs of fixing the shortfall in Social Security—often described as catastrophically large—is under .75 percent of GDP (Gale and Orszag 2003).

These numbers are so large they may be difficult to grasp. But in the simplest terms, they mean the federal government's fiscal capacity has declined sharply. On the eve of the 2004 presidential election, the tax cuts of the first Bush term had helped reduce income-tax revenues to their lowest level as a share of the economy since *1942* and to their lowest level as a share of all federal taxes since *1941*. Meanwhile, total federal revenues as a share of the economy—at a bit over 16 percent—were lower than at any point since 1950. Because federal spending obviously did not drop to the level of five decades ago, the result has been large deficits. Between 2000 and 2004, the federal balance sheet underwent an astonishing reversal, from officially projected surpluses of more than $5 trillion over ten years to projected deficits of more than $4 trillion (Kogan and Kamin 2004). In four years, Republicans had slashed federal revenues by nearly a quarter, yet left federal spending virtually untouched.

The success of the Republican assault on taxes raises two interrelated puzzles. First, how were Republicans able to achieve such large shifts in policy within America's famously fragmented system of checks and balances—and in a polarized climate that Nolan McCarty's contribution to this volume suggests should reinforce gridlock? This puzzle is all the more mysterious because, as will become clear, public views were strikingly at odds with the basic thrust of the GOP's anti-tax initiatives. Second, why did Republicans choose this particular means of taking on activist government? Why tax cuts, and why tax cuts of the character that GOP leaders sought and achieved? Answering these two questions turns out to be central to understanding the renewed conservative attack on activist government—its sources, its character, its achievements, and, ultimately, its limits.

Answering these two questions also turns out to demonstrate the analytic advantages of a long-term perspective on political and policy development. Republicans' strategies and success hinge on processes of political learning and strategic fine-tuning that played out over the two decades that separate the election of Ronald Reagan and the ascendance of George W.

Bush. Reagan's semi-successful attempt to choke off the hose supplying tax revenues to Washington grew out of a powerful grass-roots movement against taxes, but eventually it ran afoul of both public opinion and centrists in Congress and thus failed to secure a powerful GOP advantage. Bush's so-far-successful attempt to clamp down on the revenue hose, by contrast, lacks much of a true popular base. It has, however, enjoyed the support of an extensive network of conservative anti-tax organizations capable of enforcing anti-tax positions and pulling centrists within the Republican Party away from the middle. Perhaps more important, the Bush tax cuts depart from the Reagan tax cuts in the degree to which they were consciously crafted to minimize short-term political risks while maximizing gains down the road. For this reason, the Bush tax cuts are poised to have effects on American politics and policy that are much greater—and much more supportive of Republican aims—than even the Reagan Revolution was.

RADICAL CHANGE WITHOUT RADICAL SHIFTS IN PUBLIC PREFERENCES

Given the impressive string of Republican-engineered tax cuts, it would be natural to assume that Americans have been loudly clamoring to have their taxes slashed. But this is not the case—not now, and not in 2001, either. To be sure, when asked about tax cuts in the most abstract of terms without any mention of trade-offs or drawbacks, Americans are modestly supportive. But when the question becomes "Where do tax cuts rank in the list of public priorities for limited federal funds?" tax cuts consistently end up at or near the bottom of the heap. Immediately after the 2004 election, for example, a *New York Times* poll found that reducing the deficit trumped tax cuts as a public priority by more than a two-to-one margin (Nagourney and Elder 2004). What is more, Americans have repeatedly told pollsters that any tax cuts should benefit all Americans in roughly equal proportion, rather than being heavily tilted to the top in the manner that President Bush and congressional Republicans have pushed.[1]

Nor do Americans think that the economy or their own pocketbooks have benefited much from recent tax cuts. In August 2004, for instance, 63 percent believed that the tax cuts of 2001 and 2003 had either hurt the economy or not made much difference (TIPP Poll conducted 6–10 July 2004 for *Investor's Business Daily* and the *Christian Science Monitor*). Meanwhile, only a third of respondents said they had personally benefited from the tax cuts. When asked in March whether the "tax cuts [of the first Bush term] were too large" and needed to be scaled back to pay for social programs or "the right size" and needed to be made permanent to help the economy, 55 percent chose the first option, 39 percent the second (*NBC News/Wall Street Journal* Poll conducted 6–8 March 2004).[2]

If a dramatic public groundswell in favor of tax cuts cannot be the magic explanation for the tax-policy reversal of the past six years, neither will it do to treat this episode as merely a temporary departure from some sort of fixed political equilibrium, destined to be overturned as the negative effects of the tax cuts on the budget or their disproportionate benefit to the well-off finally come into view. *Despite the absence of general public support for their goals, Republicans have fundamentally dislodged the old tax-policy equilibrium.* And they are well on their way to establishing a *new* tax-policy equilibrium that is significantly more favorable toward tax cuts than that which reined during the Clinton and first Bush presidencies. If they achieve this, Republicans will have also succeeded in endangering the activist government role that even conservative icon Ronald Reagan found himself unable to challenge. In short, in six years Republican leaders in Congress and the White House have undone decades of established tax and budget policy, propelled the nation toward an epic showdown on terrain highly favorable to their cause, and set in motion political and fiscal forces that are at least as likely to enhance their power as endanger it.

Of course, these six years of active lawmaking were by no means the beginning of the Republican struggle against taxes. Rather, they are more appropriately seen as the culmination of a longer historical saga in which Republicans learned to live reluctantly with big government while abhorring, and increasingly assaulting directly, the tax system that funds it. Indeed, as will become clear, the politics of taxation is the cusp that links the two major transformations that dominate post-war American politics: the maturation of the activist state, and the emergence of a more powerful and aggressive conservative movement. Understanding how Republicans were able to take on the modern tax state, without appearing to threaten the activist government orientation that Americans by and large support, is central to understanding the success of the modern conservative movement—not just in winning office but in reshaping public policy in ways that are likely to prove difficult to reverse.

THE NEED FOR A LONG-TERM PERSPECTIVE

The reason for taking the long view of this saga is simple: as other chapters in this volume have convincingly shown, tracing the development of government policy over an extended period offers considerable analytic advantages over the shorter-term approaches that dominate most discussions of the subject. Explaining changes in any policy area requires that one think about how the efforts of multiple actors, operating in multiple institutional venues and sometimes over considerable temporal spans, "add up" to particular outcomes. Exploring development over time also encourages one to think systematically about major structural changes in the American polity, rather than fixating on the (often conjunctural) determinants of outcomes at each step along the way. And taking the long view also makes transparent the deeper roots of major policy shifts and shows why they enabled dramatic breakthroughs when they did. All of this is typically missed when analysts restrict their temporal focus to a single policy episode.

This is especially true with regard to taxes, which have played a pivotal role as both a cause and a consequence of political action on the right, gradually setting the stage for the policy explosion of 2001. Taxes have been a major catalyst for conservative mobilization and increasingly central to the conservative agenda. In fact, it is not too much of an exaggeration to say that taxation has become the essential policy glue that holds together the contemporary Republican Party. In assuming this integrative role, however, taxation has migrated from an issue based mostly on mass mobilization to one based mostly on elite policing. What was once a movement grounded in real, if diffuse, popular anger is now a movement grounded in the targeted recruitment, direction, and sanctioning of Republican officeholders. This strategic and social shift is central to understanding how the conservative movement has seized so much power, and how it has been able to hold it so successfully.

In tracing this transformation, what becomes clear is that many of the crucial factors that are typically taken as given in "snapshot" (Pierson 2004) analyses of a single policy episode are, in fact, the product of political strategy and manipulation over the longer term. In the snapshot view, President Bush succeeded because his party was so unified around tax cuts and so willing to use aggressive presentational and policy strategies to achieve them. But this unity and these strategies were, as we shall see, only possible because of the slow, steady, and active transformation of the tax-cut movement—its representatives, its resources, its network, and its capacity for coordination. Although taxes have proved an effective political issue for the right, it is fair to say that until recently at least those political benefits were not translated into large and enduring policy achievements. That has started to change, and yet, even after multiple rounds of tax cuts, the right's achievements remain tenuous in important respects. Most obviously, the conservative movement's success in reducing taxes has not been matched by success in controlling government spending. Many see this as the great Achilles' heel of the tax-cut movement. To these commentators, we have simply drifted back into the temporary fiscal insanity of the early 1980s, and when the true fiscal realities become unavoidable, the tax-cut crusade will die once again.

This chapter presents a less sanguine verdict. Although, as other contributions to this volume demonstrate, many of the actions that modern government takes require little in the way of taxation, tax capacity nonetheless represents a powerful proxy for state capacity. And Republicans have significantly undermined the tax capacity of American government. No less important, they have done so through policy means that may insulate the party and its officeholders from direct blame when the inevitable fiscal crunch takes place. The anti-tax agenda is based on a high-stakes gamble—that, in coming battles over taxation, Republicans will be in a stronger position because of their aggressive action today. Once one appreciates how well Republicans have insulated themselves from the fallout that the coming fiscal squeeze will produce, it becomes clear that the Republicans' gamble is one they have good reason to think they will win.

From Mass Mobilization to Elite Coordination

Tax cuts are scarcely a fledgling political goal of the American right. They have been a central part of the conservative agenda at least since the Reagan era. Taxpayer revolts were a crucial catalyst to Reagan's rise to power. No domestic issue was as central to his campaign, and in no domestic policy area were his initiatives as visible or substantial.

And yet, if one contrasts the politics of taxes in the early years of the Reagan presidency with that of George W. Bush, the differences are as striking as the continuities. Two important changes stand out in particular. First, both the strategies of political mobilization and the goals of influential conservatives are much more focused on elites now than was the case twenty-five years ago. Second, and partly as a result of this shift, key political elites have become significantly more radical on the tax issue.

These two changes are inextricably linked to a third—the failure of the American right to convince middle-of-the-road voters that tax cutting should be as high a priority as Republicans officeholders believe it to be.[3] Indeed, the divorce between elite and public opinion on this issue expresses a more general phenomenon: with the ascendance of the Republican Party, ruling political elites in the United States have become much more conservative—and the gap between the political parties has grown much larger—*even as public opinion has remained comparatively stable.* As Morris Fiorina and colleagues (2005, 213) sum up the evidence (with a particular emphasis on polarization, though the findings speak to opinion change more broadly), "There is little indication that voters are polarized now or that they are becoming more polarized. . . . If anything, public opinion has grown more centrist." Republicans have become radicalized on taxes without popular radicalization. In fact, their agenda has advanced despite a great deal of public skepticism toward the tax-cut agenda and public concern about its effects. The move to strategies of elite mobilization and coordination is a reflection of this basic reality. In turn, a chief measure of the success of these strategies is the failure of normal sources of accountability—in particular, elections—to bring Republicans' tax aims back to the center.

Ronald Reagan and the Taxpayer Revolt

Ronald Reagan's tax-cut agenda was popularly rooted. To be sure, powerful organized interests provided essential support for the Reagan campaign and its 1981 tax cuts (White and Wildavsky 1989). But the push for tax cuts was a mass phenomenon (Sears and Citrin 1982). Rapid inflation during the 1970s, combined with property and income-tax systems that had been designed for a low-inflation environment, led to rising real tax burdens for middle-income Americans. Polling data from the late 1970s indicate the high salience of tax cuts for a broad swath of the electorate. Key focusing events, like the success of the Proposition 13 campaign in California, also sent a powerful signal about mass sentiments. Reagan made tax cuts the centerpiece of his campaign, and survey data suggest that this call resonated strongly within the electorate. Although it is hazardous to speak of elections producing "mandates" for specific policy initiatives, it seems appropriate to consider the 1980 election results a mandate for lower taxes.

In the wake of Reagan's rise, conservative elites embraced his call for tax cuts. The depth of that commitment, however, was less certain. Midwestern and northeastern moderates made up a much larger share of the Republican coalition twenty-five years ago than they do today. Views about government spending were also more tempered. Reagan's rise to power, after all, was less than a decade removed from a Republican administration that had advanced proposals for both universal health care and something close to a guaranteed annual income.

Moreover, desire for tax cuts competed with concern for fiscal prudence as a priority. Although the Reagan campaign's embrace of supply-side economics (or, as GOP traditionalist George H. W. Bush termed it, "voodoo economics") temporarily finessed this conflict, it quickly rematerialized. Reagan's first—and only—success in cutting taxes, the massive reductions contained in the 1981 Economic Recovery and Tax Act, combined with recession to generate unprecedented deficits. What followed was, in retrospect, a remarkable about-face, accomplished with the support of moderate Republicans. Alarm about the deficit led to tax increases in 1982 and 1984. A major tax reform in 1986 was revenue neutral. Most striking of all was the 1990 budget agreement, signed by George H. W. Bush, which combined tax increases and spending cuts in a major effort to reduce the budget deficit.

Revolt of the Tax-Cut Turks

At the time, 1990 seemed to be just one of what would be a long series of deficit reduction packages from 1982 and continuing through 1997. Repeatedly, these packages combined tax increases (painful for Republicans) and spending cuts (painful for Democrats). In retrospect, however, 1990 was as much of a watershed in tax politics as the much more politically successful (and thus much better remembered) gambits of Reagan in 1981 and George W. Bush in 2001. It was a watershed because it triggered a realignment among Republican elites.

Here again, a long-term view is essential. Shifting structures of political influence are often virtually invisible for extended periods of time. Early on, they have not yet developed to the point where they allow ascending groups to mount an effective challenge. Later, new power relations may have sufficiently consolidated so that open conflict is no longer to be expected. Furthermore, the internal identity of Congress changes only slowly, as old members retire or (less often) are defeated and new members replace them. These slow-moving changes are as fundamental as the rapid shifts that usually catch analysts' attention.

In this instance, 1990 was the midway point in the transition from an old to a new Republican Party in Washington. The past two decades have witnessed the gradual replacement of an older generation of political moderates and fiscal conservatives with a new generation of hard-line conservatives and radical tax cutters. Like tectonic plates, the new breed of conservative elites was gradually pushing up against (and over) the old. The moment when this pressure finally led to an open rupture occurred in 1990. The trigger was the decision of George H. W. Bush, an old-line Republican, to meet mounting deficits with a package that included substantial tax increases. Ronald Reagan had agreed to similar packages, but only after he had made his mark as an energetic tax cutter. Bush, furthermore, had issued his famous "read my lips" pledge not to raise taxes just two years earlier. And, most important, Bush faced a very different Republican caucus in Congress.

The story is well known. In the face of a Republican president's appeal for compromise to reduce the deficit, Newt Gingrich instead instigated a revolt. Gingrich and his allies led more than half the Republicans in the House to inflict a humiliating defeat on their party's ostensible leader. In the short run, Bush was able to regroup. Congress eventually passed a revised—and, given the need to gain more Democratic votes in place of the rebels', slightly more liberal—package. The long-term effect on the Republican Party, however, was profound. Bush's relations with the conservative wing were permanently damaged. As his son, George W., was to become acutely aware, this rupture proved to be very costly when he sought reelection two years later. Equally important, Republican moderates in Congress never recovered. Gingrich's rebellion put House Minority Leader Robert Michel on notice: his tenure at the top was nearing an end. When Michel announced his retirement, Gingrich and his allies swept into the leadership and (and as Julien Zelizer's chapter recounts) rapidly signaled a much more aggressive and radical posture.

The New Republican Party

The trends that led to this leadership revolution have accelerated since 1992, leading to a thoroughgoing transformation of the Republican elite. The central mechanism has been replacement. Bastions of Republican moderation in the Northeast slowly ceded ground to Democrats. More important, as southern Democrats in Congress were defeated or retired, intensely conservative southern Republicans took their places. Less frequently noted but equally significant was what happened to the rest of the Republican caucus. As Republicans outside the South retired, they too were typically replaced by much more conservative Republicans.

This transformation is often summed up with a single word, "polarization"—the division of American politics into two sharply opposed groups. This formulation implies that the parties are running away from each other roughly at an equal gait. After all, if the parties were not moving away from each other at the same pace, the party that strayed farthest from the lodestar of the center would get clobbered at the polls. Fiorina and his colleagues (2005), whose careful dissection of trends in public opinion we cited earlier, make the claim explicitly: "So long as only one party moves away from the center . . . electoral punishment results. . . . But if both parties move away from the center and locate at more or less equal distances away from the mainstream, then electoral punishment need not result."

This formulation is comforting, in that it suggests that electoral accountability would bring policymaking back to the middle if only one party would offer centrist alternatives. Unfortunately, however, it is also questionable. The evidence is overwhelming that Republicans have moved farther right than Democrats have moved left. Sean Theriault (2004) has exhaustively studied the transformation of the preferences of Republican and Democratic members of Congress over the past three decades. His big innovation is to divide the causes of preference change into its component parts: the *replacement* of members of Congress through mechanisms of retirement, electoral defeat, and the like; and the *adaptation* of the positions of existing members of Congress over time. Although Theriault frames his analysis around the issue of partisan polarization, his data show conclusively that polarization has been far from symmetrical. Over the 1970–2002 period, the Republican Party has become twice as conservative, while the Democratic Party has become only about 50 percent more liberal. Moreover, the increasing liberalism of the Democratic Party is accounted for almost entirely by the replacement of moderate Democrats in the South by fiercely conservative Republicans. Outside the South, the median Democrat is scarcely more liberal than he or she was thirty years ago. The same is not true, however, of the Republican Party. Even outside the South, Republican legislators are markedly more conservative today than in prior decades.

Shifting preferences regarding taxation provide a striking illustration of this rightward shift. Although Republicans have long fought against higher taxes, this goal was always in tension with a commitment to fiscal conservatism. The traditional attitude was well summarized in Gingrich's derisive description of Senate leader Robert Dole as "the tax collector for the welfare state." As noted, throughout the 1980s and into the 1990s the basic dynamic of deficit politics revolved around bipartisan compromises that required each side to accept "second best" solutions (White and Wildavsky 1989). Republican deficit cutters would have preferred more spending cuts, Democrats more tax increases. They compromised grudgingly by doing some of each.

That the continuation of this compromise triggered Gingrich's rebellion revealed a fundamental transformation. In brief, the new-line Republicans reversed the priority between fiscal conservatism and tax cuts. For this generation of politicians, reducing taxes was absolutely central.

Explaining the Shift: The Race to the Base

Why has replacement in the Republican Party led to far more militant positions on taxation (as well as a host of other issues)? The most obvious answer would be that elite priorities tracked shifts in public opinion—that newer politicians are more receptive to popular demands for lower taxation. As noted already, however, there is very little evidence in survey research to suggest a strong rightward shift—indeed, any shift at all—on tax issues, or for a fundamental altering of the priorities between tax reductions and deficit reduction. To take the most striking example, at the time George W. Bush assumed the presidency, fewer than one in twenty Americans described taxes as the most important issue facing the country. When pressed, huge majorities expressed a preference for debt reduction and spending on key programs like Social Security, Medicare, and education over tax cuts. What was the electorate's biggest complaint about the income-tax system? That the well-to-do did not pay their "fair share" (Hacker and Pierson 2005a). These basic contours of public opinion were well recognized inside the Bush White House: one revealing internal memorandum, written in early 2001, warned bluntly that *"The public prefers spending on things like health care and education over cutting taxes."*[4]

A full alternative explanation for the scale of this rightward shift by Republican elites is beyond the scope of this chapter.[5] Briefly, we would point to several broad structural changes that have strengthened the role of "the base" in Republican politics. Political observers have long recognized the electoral tension between party activists and middle-of-the-road voters. Yet today's politicians have considerably enhanced incentives to cater to their base. Rising ideological unity of districts and sophisticated partisan gerrymandering have increased the relative importance of primaries. Campaign money matters more than it once did, and money flows disproportionately from the affluent and ideologically extreme. Equally important, parties in government have become more powerful as agenda setters, disciplinarians, and financers. They have also increased their ability to provide political cover for rank-and-file members who take positions that are out-of-step with their constituents. The result is not just increasing polarization, but also increasing need, desire, and capacity to respond to the base.

In the electoral realm, the major development is the growing relative importance of processes that precede the general election—both the initial vetting of candidates by party leaders and allied groups, and the crucial primary stage, where party champions are selected. Thanks to geographic polarization and increasingly sophisticated partisan gerrymandering, the overwhelming majority of congressional districts are safe for one party or the other. Incumbency advantages show no sign of eroding even as politicians have become more extreme. Despite the very close overall partisan balance, a record 99 percent of incumbents were reelected to the House in 2002. Few races are seriously contested, and even contested races are typically noncompetitive, with only fifteen races in 2002 decided by 4 points or less.

The insulation of so many seats means, in turn, that the greatest electoral risk faced by many current or aspiring officeholders is likely to come in primaries, rather than general elections. And in these races, marked by limited and intensely partisan turnout, responsiveness to one's base becomes of paramount importance. Barry Burden (2004) estimates that a credible primary challenge pulls a typical congressional candidate a remarkable 10 points toward the ideological poles on a scale of 0 to 100. Moreover, primary challenges do not need to be common to strike fear in politicians' hearts. Just their prospect—especially if unmatched by comparable concern about assaults from the other side of the aisle—may be sufficient to push politicians closer to the party line.

Rising Elite Coordination: The New Tax-Cut Power Brokers

Electoral pressures to adopt a strong and consistent anti-tax stance are reinforced by a complementary trend: the emergence of a much more institutionalized network of organizations, heavily funded by the most affluent elements of American society, with a strong commitment to tax cuts. A crucial feature of this changing organizational universe has been a shift in the focus of anti-tax activity. Put crudely, efforts have shifted from mass mobilization to elite mobilization, and the central strategy has changed from creating broad public support to recruiting and monitoring politicians. Well-funded organizations now play a key role in producing like-minded candidates—or at least candidates who face strong incentives to behave as if they are like-minded.

Two groups have played a central role in the radicalization of tax politics: Grover Norquist's Americans for Tax Reform (ATR) and Stephen Moore's Club for Growth (CfG).[6] It is worth underscoring at the outset just how radical the objectives of these two groups are. Norquist has described his goal as a 50 percent reduction in government (and taxes) as a share of GDP ("down to the size where you could drown it in the bathtub")—roughly the state of American government before World War II. Stephen Moore is a committed supply-sider and strong advocate of a flat tax—an idea that was beyond the pale fifteen years ago but is receiving increasing support within the GOP.

In addition to their radical positions on taxes, these advocacy groups share three striking similarities. First, they are relatively recent creations—each emerged well after the Reagan tax cuts of 1981. ATR began as a White House operation, headed by Norquist, in the run-up to the (ironically, given ATR's evolution, revenue-neutral) Tax Reform Act of 1986. Astonishingly, given its current significance, the Club for Growth really started only in 1999 (although formally it succeeded a virtually moribund predecessor). Moore, following work at the Heritage Foundation, on Dick Armey's staff, and the CATO Institute—a revealing career path—founded the organization with backing from conservative think tanks and media figures, as well as Wall Street financial interests.

Second, as these founding stories attest, both ATR and CfG are elite rather than mass operations. They have small memberships, and they have relied heavily on large donations (including, in ATR's case, sizable contributions from the Republican Party). The "mass" element of these influential organizations is largely confined to electioneering, rather than grass-roots mobilization. Indeed, by the standards of mass membership organizations, CfG is Lilliputian: it boasted around 10,000 members in 2003. Yet its affiliates are unusually well heeled: during the 2002 midterm elections, the club's $10 million in contributions made it the leading source of campaign funds for Republicans outside of the GOP itself. It was on pace to spend considerably more in 2004. In that year its efforts included a staggering $2.3 million contribution to a single *primary* campaign, in which it backed Pat Toomey in his almost-successful effort to unseat incumbent Republican Senator Arlen Specter in Pennsylvania.

Third, each of these organizations has developed strategies that are well tailored to the shifting political opportunity structures just outlined. In particular, each has focused its energies on ensuring that the gradual process of replacement within the Republican Party will facilitate a strategy of aggressive tax reduction. For ATR, a central tool has been the introduction of tax pledges, in which elected officials and candidates for office make specific pledges not to support tax increases.[7] Some Republican politicians, mostly moderate incumbents, resisted these pledges for a time. But the logic of contemporary Republican primaries is clear. For nonincumbents, agreement to these pledges has become a necessary component of any Republican run for Congress (and, in many places, state office as well). Moderates wishing to shore up their position have generally signed as well—if not, their successors do. By the end of 2003, ATR had signed pledges from 216 members of the House (just two short of a majority), and 42 U.S. senators, as well as President Bush. Notably, signers of the pledge also make up an absolute majority of members of Congress on the two crucial House committees that shaped the 2001–4 tax cuts: Ways and Means, and Budget (Gale and Orzag 2004b).

Like ATR, the Club for Growth has focused its energies on increasing the ranks of committed tax cutters in Congress. The preferred technique is candidate recruitment for open seats, combined—strikingly—by efforts to challenge "RINOs" (Republicans in Name Only). Club president Stephen Moore joked that when he threatens a primary challenge against wayward Republicans "they start wetting their pants."[8] In fact, while the CfG has had success in getting its candidates elected to open seats, it was not until 2006 that it won a primary challenge to a RINO, defeating Joe Schwarz in Michigan. On several occasions it has, however, come close. And it may well have hastened some retirements. More significant, its efforts serve to set moderates on notice of the potential costs of defection on tax issues. As club-supported House Republican Jeff Flake colorfully noted: "When you have 100 percent of Republicans voting for the Bush tax cut, you know that they are looking over their shoulder and not wanting to have Steve Moore recruiting candidates in their district."

The New Republican Strategy

If advocacy groups seeking radical changes in tax policy have played an important role in recruiting and monitoring politicians, they have also been participants in the development of a more sophisticated, coordinated, and effective conservative strategy for actually changing policy. ATR, in particular, has played a role in the formulation and execution of the Republican tax-cut agenda. Indeed, a crucial piece of the anti-tax story has been a striking shift in both the goals and strategies of tax reduction.

Like the accounts offered in Steve Teles' chapter, this is a story of political learning—again, something that is much easier to identify in an analysis that examines events unfolding over an extended period of time. Policy battles reverberate through the political system, and key actors derive lessons from those battles. Rounds of political conflict provide a series of experiments with different strategic and tactical approaches to achieving a coalition's objectives. Over time, these experiences may lead groups to redefine their goals, while they adjust their formulas for political success.

The broadest and most bitter lesson that tax cutters derived from the experience of the 1980s and early 1990s was that deficit reduction too often trumped tax reduction. Many on the left argued that the deficit was a Trojan Horse to launch an assault on social spending. To the right's dismay, however, it served at least as much to undercut the tax-cutting agenda. No major tax cuts passed after 1981. Instead, significant increases were introduced in 1982, 1984, 1990, and 1993. Indeed, it was this track record that triggered the creation of the Club for Growth. Co-founder Richard Gilder, an influential stockbroker, philanthropist, and ardent supply-sider put it this way: "We would hear these great growth ideas about how [the candidates] were going to cut taxes and push for growth, and then they'd get down there [to Washington] and vote to raise taxes" (Newlin 2002).

With the strengthening of "supply-side" advocacy groups and a more radicalized Republican caucus, tax cuts became the essential priority regardless of whether they produced deficits or not. In this respect, the contrast between the aftermaths of 1981 and 2001 could not be more striking. Republicans in Congress eagerly embraced the Reagan tax cuts, but many of them were willing to change course once large deficits appeared. Twenty years later, however, a ballooning deficit has had nothing like the same effect. Republican politicians seem more strongly committed than ever to holding the line on taxes. Indeed, they have continued to work energetically to push the revenue line lower. Sizable tax cuts were introduced in 2003 and 2004, overriding Republican moderates' muffled expressions of concern over deficits.

Along with this broad reformulation of goals came important strategic opportunities. Once the notion that budgetary rectitude required that tax cuts be "paid for" was rejected, Republicans learned that there were enormous opportunities to push for tax cuts that were both larger and more (upwardly) redistributive than anyone had previously thought possible. Again, policy development reflected a process of political learning, in which advocates experimented with various tactics. The goal was to maximize their capacity to pursue their ambitious policies in an institutional setting widely understood to require compromise.

This process began on a limited basis in the 1997 budget deal reached with President Clinton. It expanded radically in the tax cuts of 2001 and had been perfected by the time of the 2003 tax cuts. What tax-cut advocates found was that once fealty to deficit control was allowed to lapse, opportunities to reconfigure tax policy expanded considerably. This shift in goals coincided with new opportunity structures that accompanied unified control of Congress and the White House, as well as the development of an unusually disciplined and coordinated Republican coalition. In combination, these developments led to surprisingly successful efforts to escape from the fiscal gridlock evident in American politics for two decades.

The 2001 Breakthrough

The feasibility of these ventures rested on three broad tactics.[9] The first was to use unified Republican command over the House, Senate, and White House to dominate agenda setting. As both polls and prior experience suggested, the biggest obstacle to successful tax cutting stemmed from its unfavorable implications for deficits and popular government programs. Procedural rules, like the "paygo" system that had previously governed congressional budgeting (which required that all spending and tax cuts be financed), made the opportunity costs of tax cuts visible. So did competing Democratic agenda setters, especially during President Clinton's time in the White House. Indeed, it was Clinton's success in emphasizing the high opportunity costs of tax cuts (combined, of course, with his veto power) that had held previous tax cut initiatives in check (Balz and Brownstein 1996). Bush's ascension to the White House eliminated this factor.

Yet, while Bush's arrival triggered a sharp increase in agenda control, the preconditions for this powerful tactic had in fact been accumulating for almost two decades. As Julian Zelizer's chapter documents, party leaders in Congress had greatly increased their capacity to control the legislative agenda during this period. They now exert tremendous influence over the issues that receive legislative consideration and the specific proposals that come to a vote. They largely control the often highly restrictive rules governing debate, which limit or prohibit the consideration of meaningful alternatives. And they dictate the participants in conference committees, which in turn control the proposals that will be brought to the floors of the House and Senate for a final up or down vote. Robert Van Houweling (2003) has persuasively argued that interventions of this kind have increased for a very specific reason: they enable legislators to enact extreme policies without courting electoral backlash. Parties adopt procedural strategies, in other words, precisely to make it more difficult for voters (but not highly informed partisans) to recognize and respond to policies they might otherwise regard as extreme.

In both 2001 and 2003, congressional Republicans worked effectively, especially in the increasingly centralized House, to translate narrow legislative majorities into effective agenda control. In both cases, they pushed successfully for large tax cuts. Each time, these initiatives were strikingly well insulated from serious contemplation of the implications for deficits and government programs.

The second tactic that was used extensively in the tax-cut rounds that followed Bush's election was a systematic exploitation of previously untapped political potential buried within the complex and obscure processes of policy formulation (Arnold 1990). Over time, tax-cut advocates have learned how to design policies in ways that make tax cuts look much smaller and more equitable than they actually are. By employing phase-ins and "sunsets" of key provisions, legislators could make the "official" cost of their proposals much lower than the actual cost was likely to be. By front-loading benefits to average Americans while back-loading benefits for the well-to-do, tax laws could be presented as far more responsive to middle-income voters than they really were. For example, in its first year the 2001 tax cut was estimated to provide "only" 7 percent of its benefits to the top 1 percent of the income distribution. By year 10, however, when the new tax design has fully phased-in, that percentage rises to 51 percent (CTJ 2002).

Third, tax-cut advocates discovered new and powerful techniques to control not just today's policy agenda but tomorrow's. Policy features in the new legislation were designed not only to put the best initial face on these initiatives. They were also structured to create opportunities for legislators to set the agenda for further tax cuts down the road. The 2001 tax cuts, remarkably, included a "time bomb" that would make the Alternative Minimum Tax much worse over the medium-run—intentionally exacerbating a problem that, by 2004, was estimated to require a further $800 billion tax cut to fix. At the same time, by scheduling features to "sunset" at a future date, tax-cut advocates were essentially pre-scheduling votes that could be framed as up-or-down decisions on raising people's taxes.

The effectiveness of this strategy is already evident. In 2004, despite a deficit of almost half a trillion dollars, provisions of the 2001 bill scheduled to expire were instead extended, by votes of 339–65 in the House and 92–3 in the Senate. It is not coincidental that these provisions—the least skewed toward the rich of the 2001 and 2003 cuts—were set to expire right before the election. Nor, given what we have shown, is it surprising that Republicans still managed to include *new* tax breaks for higher-income groups in the legislation.

The story of the 2006 tax cuts mentioned at the outset of this chapter is substantially different but still revealing of the agenda-setting power of Republican leaders and their continuing commitment to top-heavy tax cuts. As was noted, the main elements of the 2006 legislation were extensions of the 2003 cuts in the dividend and capital gains taxes. These extensions were far more controversial than the 2004 extensions just discussed, and they occurred in a much more difficult political context for Republicans, whose popularity had been plummeting in response to congressional scandals, the anemic response to Hurricane Katrina, and public disillusionment with the ongoing war in Iraq.

Nonetheless, Republicans managed to pass the 2006 cuts on a narrow and mostly party-line vote, using the budget reconciliation process to avoid a Senate filibuster. To take advantage of the expedited budget process, they engaged in a series of gambits that will by now be familiar. Because the dividend and capital gains tax cuts were certain to exceed the $70 billion cap that Republicans had set for themselves, Republican leaders came up with tax-cut provisions that raised money in the short term but lost money in the long term. Then they insisted that these undeniable long-term costs should not be considered under Senate rules because they fell outside the 2006–10 budget window. Finally, they moved all the tax cuts they thought they could enact without threat of a filibuster into a separate tax-cut package estimated to cost about $20 billion a year. Not surprisingly, they said they planned to bring up these additional tax cuts, all of them completely unfinanced, just before the 2006 elections.

These developments suggest, as the next section argues, that Republicans have undermined the previous policy equilibrium. Whether that shift is sustainable remains the great question. But the effectiveness of conservative strategies to shape the preferences of members of Congress, to control the agenda of policymaking, and to limit the ability of Americans to hold Republican officeholders accountable give strong reason to believe that the tax-cut crusade could well survive the coming fiscal reckoning.

The Erosion of Federal Tax Capacity

As noted at the outset of this chapter, the tax cuts of the first Bush term have helped reduce federal tax revenues to their lowest level in decades. Table 10.1 makes the scale of this reversal clear. It would be a mistake, however, to see this huge drop as solely a result of the tax cuts of recent years. The bursting of the stock-market bubble and the economic downturn that followed both contributed to the large decline in revenues after 2000. What is notable about the present state of affairs in any case is not merely the decline in revenues, which has in fact continued even through the economic recovery. It is that this decline has occurred without any restraint on federal spending and on the brink of a major explosion of social program costs. The coincidence of continued high spending and big revenue drops is immediately evident when one looks at changes revenues and outlays from 2000 to 2004 (Gale and Orzag 2004a). Adjusting for business-cycle effects (which automatically reduce revenue and increasing public spending), revenues dropped by more than 3 percentage points of GDP in the 2000–4 period, while spending increased by more than 1 percentage point. By contrast, during the Clinton presidency, the pattern was almost exactly the reverse: revenues increased by nearly 2 percentage points of GDP, while spending dropped by more than 2 percentage points.

Before moving on, a common misperception should be cleared away. Notwithstanding Senator John McCain's evocative complaints about Congress acting like a "drunken sailor," the Republican leadership has not suddenly embraced rampant public spending. Nearly all of the spending increases of recent years are in three distinct areas: increased costs for existing mandatory programs and tax breaks (the largest), spending on national defense and homeland security (a good deal of it justified as a response to 9/11), and a small handful of new spending initiatives, most notably, the Medicare prescription drug bill. Historically speaking, as table 10.1 shows, current spending levels are not remarkably high. Rather than go on an indiscriminate spending spree, Republicans have increased spending specifically on the ends they value (national defense in particular) while failing to act to rein in built-in spending pressures within popular social programs that as recently as the early 1990s they directly tried to cut.

What explains this studious noninterference with built-in spending pressures? Here again, an account based on political learning is the most persuasive. In the mid-1990s, the Gingrich assault on social programs fizzled when President Clinton was able to link specified spending cuts with specified tax breaks. Whether the two were all that deeply related in reality was immaterial. What mattered is that Clinton and Democrats

TABLE 10.1
The Federal Balance Sheet as a Share of GDP (percent)

	2004	Average, 1962–2001
Expenditures	19.8	20.4
Revenues	16.2	18.3
Deficits	3.6	2.1

were able to link two policy changes (cuts in taxes, spending cuts) within a single, persuasive temporal story. The current Republican strategy is to divorce these two sides of the budgetary coin as much as possible. Tax cuts are to be pursued first and separately. Spending cuts are to come only later, when their link to tax cuts will be much less temporally proximate and therefore less transparent.

This is most evident in a key Republican policy technique mentioned earlier: the systematic deferral of many tax-cut provisions, as well as their political repercussions, well into the future. In recent tax bills, Republicans have implemented nearly all of the most important and costly (and regressive) provisions several years after adoption. They have also, on an unprecedented scale, decided to schedule other provisions to "sunset" as much as a decade after enactment. No one believes that most of these tax-cut "sunsets" will be honored—that, for example, the estate tax will go back into full effect in 2011, one year after it is eliminated, as is the schedule under present law. But the use of sunsets has two primary benefits for Republican tax cutters: it greatly lowers the official cost of tax-cut bills, and, no less important, it allows Republicans to frame the expiration of tax provisions as a "tax hike" that must be forestalled.

The increasing turn to back-loaded tax expenditures is another important example of deferral techniques. Almost without exception, these tax expenditures have little or no up-front cost. By encouraging wealthy citizens to shift money from traditional tax-favored accounts into these new policy instruments, in fact, back-loaded accounts are often projected to raise money in the short term. Yet these accounts almost always have large long-term costs, which conveniently come due only *after* the typical ten-year window of budgetary projections expires. This is true, for example, of the backloaded provisions that Republicans included in the 2006 tax-cut package to keep its five-year cost at $70 billion—they raise money in the short term, but they actually reduce revenues in the long term, after the close of the official budget window. In the past decade, in sum, Republicans have filled the tax code with time bombs that are primed to

explode in the fullness of time. Rather than fund tax cuts by cutting spending, they hope to create pressures for cutting spending by establishing tax
cuts that, in the decades ahead, must be funded.

The risk of this second strategy is that the significant drop in federal
revenues will merely create a gaping budget hole, which will eventually
be filled by a return to pre-2001 levels of income taxation. At the moment,
this outcome seems unlikely. In his failed presidential bid, Senator John
Kerry called only for repealing the recent tax cuts that benefit the richest
of Americans. Given a shift in party control of Congress, that outcome is
no longer remote. Still, there can be no gainsaying that Republicans have
set the stage for an epic battle, the outcome of which may well determine
the future of activist government in the twenty-first century.

Prospects for the Future: Starve the Beast versus Tax-Cut and Spend

A facetious law of economics, widely attributed to the economist Herbert
Stein, holds that "if something can't go on, it won't." Tax cuts without
spending cuts cannot go on forever. At some point, the tolerance for debt
will end. The deficit and the interest payments it requires will grow too
large. The market will balk. The American public or foreign creditors,
or both, will decide that enough is enough. When that point is reached
something will have to give. Revenues will have to go up, spending will
have to go down. And because every day of delay means higher interest
costs and greater public attachment to current spending and tax rates, the
adjustment will be all the more painful the longer it takes to arrive.

This day of reckoning is feared by many, but it is welcomed by those
conservatives who hope to "starve the beast" of the federal government.
In this view, aggressive defunding of the state will inevitably lead to a
conservative revolution in spending policy: with tax cuts locked in, the
only piggybank to raid will be the huge middle-class programs that make
up the vast bulk of federal spending. As President Bush declared in 2001,
tax cuts will help create a "fiscal straitjacket for Congress."[10]

Yet a wholesale assault on popular spending programs will face extremely rough sledding, as President Bush's failed attempt to restructure
Social Security suggests. For one, these programs remain overwhelmingly
popular, and not just in comparison with tax cuts. For another, their main
constituency—the elderly—is large, growing, attentive, and well mobilized. Finally, the least painful way in which conservatives could supplant
these programs would be to offer lavish subsidies for private alternatives
and aggressively finance the transition of younger Americans into the private sector. Yet the funds needed to permit this have already been spent,
several times over, on tax cuts.

The current trajectories of taxes and spending thus represent two huge and seemingly immovable forces about to collide. There is little prospect that this collision will produce the complete restructuring of public policy that conservatives desire. But neither is it likely to play out as the struggle over deficits did in the late 1980s and 1990s. With the benefit of hindsight, that struggle produced serious deficit reduction only because of a specific constellation of forces that are almost certain to remain elusive today. Perhaps the most important was the continued presence of moderate forces within the Republican Party—most prominently, in the personage of the now reviled George H. W. Bush. Those moderates are gone, and they are probably not coming back. The GOP establishment has been transformed, especially on the issue of taxation.

The struggle over the budget in 2006 suggests how conflictual this new environment is likely to be. Pressed on by fiscal conservatives within the party, Republican leaders in the House pushed for broad spending cuts. But Senate GOP leaders were more cautious, and the package eventually negotiated within the party reduced outlays for Medicaid, student loans, and other benefits for low- and middle-income families by around $40 billion—$30 billion less than the GOP's planned tax cuts. To get even these cuts passed, Republican leaders had to use every play in their playbook. For the first time in the history of the modern budget process, they split the tax cuts from the spending part of the bill so that they could talk about a "deficit-reduction" package even as they planned to cut taxes by nearly twice as much. In the House, they introduced the nearly 800-page bill at one o'clock in the morning; they held the vote four hours later. To get around the normal requirement that members of Congress have at least a little time to read what they are voting on, they invoked an expedited procedure that is known as "martial law." In the Senate, Vice President Dick Cheney rushed back from a trip to the Middle East to cast the decisive vote, breaking a 50–50 tie barely forty-eight hours after the conference report was revealed and pressed through the House.

Given public concerns about the plight of the disadvantaged provoked by the aftermath of Hurricane Katrina and the continued GOP insistence on large tax cuts, the nearly $40 billion in cuts pursued in 2006 should not be dismissed as small beans. But they nonetheless indicate how hard it will be to slash public spending even if Republicans retain control of the White House. More quickly than many Republicans probably expected, the room for fiscal maneuver is constricting, and the result is likely to be rising levels of conflict over increasingly difficult budget choices.

How will these choices be made? Before considering this, it bears emphasis that even if recent tax cuts are not further extended, they will represent a remarkable—and remarkably costly—interlude in federal tax policy, one that has distributed enormous largesse to already very well-to-do segments of the citizenry and added huge sums to the deficit (in turn, driving up the cost of servicing the debt). Even in the extremely unlikely event that tax policy were returned to the status quo ante sometime in the next decade, Americans will have experienced a substantial and sustained shift in the distribution of our economy's fruits and a deterioration of the nation's fiscal health that will have long-lived consequences.

Yet the prospect of returning to the status quo ante remains slim, for the very reasons that we have outlined in this chapter. The tax-cut agenda of the Republican Party has been premised on transforming the tax code and the structure of debate over taxes in ways favorable to the GOP's long-term goals of a smaller fiscal state. To be sure, Republicans have always had multiple motives for cutting taxes—they are a common denominator that links social conservatives and economic libertarians, they deliver substantial benefits to key constituencies, and they are much less divisive than other elements of the Republican agenda. Still, of an even greater importance for an influential wing of conservatives has been the conviction that cutting taxes is the key to restraining the activist state. Government may not inevitably shrink when taxes are cut, but tax cuts stack the deck in favor of that outcome.

The measure of the success of this strategy is not short-term fiscal maneuvering; it is long-term changes in the agenda and content of public debate and public policy. And on this measure, the signs remain good, if not altogether rosy, for the larger tax-cutting strategy. Despite the dramatic increase in the budget deficit, there is little willingness among Republicans to reconsider the tax cuts of the past decade. By making the frame for all future tax debates "If we don't act, we are raising taxes," Republicans have also put themselves in a favorable strategic position for future political struggles. To be sure, the scale of the fiscal gap that has arisen—and is slated to grow dramatically in the coming decades—is so large and the difficulty of cutting popular programs so great that it is hard to think that it will begin to be closed without tax increases of some sort. But even budget deals that "split the difference" between tax increases and spending cuts will leave many of the tax cuts of recent years in place. They will lead to more substantial cutbacks in government programs than were being contemplated before President Bush entered office. On the available evidence, the gamble Republicans have taken has placed them in a stronger strategic position than they would be in had they not taken it.

It is nonetheless a gamble with very high stakes and risks. The greatest risk is highlighted by the split that occurred in the GOP coalition at the start of our account of the recent anti-tax movement. Back in 1990, the decision of moderate Republicans to break with anti-tax pledges that looked increasingly unrealistic in the face of rising deficits led to the revolt of Newt Gingrich. This fissure weakened President George H. W. Bush and helped to usher in the presidency of President Clinton (but also hastened the arrival of a Republican Congress). With so many Republicans now tied to anti-tax positions that are ever more at odds with fiscal realities, Republicans could soon be faced with intense cross-pressures again. However these pressures are resolved, they remain an ever-present risk for a party so dependent on unity around tax cuts for its larger policy ambitions.

In short, the coming fiscal crunch is not likely to return us anywhere near where we were before 2001. The tax-cut movement may lose momentum, but many of its major gains are likely to be preserved. The fallout, both political and economic, will be broad and deep. But it will not be limited in reach to the Republican Party, and it could well favor an anti-government agenda. Like a man in shackles, American government will hobble toward the next century, hemorrhaging money and morale as it goes.

LESSONS AND LEGACIES

If our image of the future remains hazy, the lessons that emerge from our survey of the past are clear. The first and most important is that the tax-cut breakthroughs of the early 2000s owe as much to slow but steady changes in the identity and strategies of the Republican Party as they do to the leadership of President George W. Bush. Indeed, we would go farther and say that any analysis that links the tax cuts to the "preferences" of current officeholders misses the essential story: the way in which party elites and conservative organizations have used the recruitment and monitoring of politicians and the coordination of policymaking to build up a reliable cadre of tax-cut enthusiasts and protect them from possible backlash. Put differently, the greatest area of success for conservatives has been in shaping the raw material of the policy process—who is in office and what they are seeking to do—rather than in shaping the specific machinery of decision making through which that material is transformed into policy.

This may seem self-evident, but it is in fact fundamental. Most analyses of American politics take policy preferences as essentially given and ask how they add up to outcomes. The role of parties and elite organizations is measured by the degree to which policymakers depart from their "true" preferences in backing legislation. But a long-term view makes clear that a more effective, if more slowly realized, strategy for achieving major policy goals is to reshape the preferences of policymakers themselves. Looking at politics only at a point in time often means missing its most important aspects.

The deeper story that we have told has two essential parts: the increasing pull of the Republican base, and the increasing willingness and ability of political elites to hide the most extreme of their actions from average voters. The first part—increasing conservatism—is the more familiar, though we have tried to show how it is rooted in the increasing *coordination* of the conservative movement both inside and outside government. Our claim that Republicans have sought (so far, successfully) to limit their accountability on tax cuts is a more novel (and, no doubt, controversial) contribution. What we want to stress here is that there are two components of Republican strategy. The first, which is familiar to any observer of politics, is deliberate manipulation of rhetoric and policy presentation (Jacobs and Shapiro 2000). Yet we think that the importance of this kind of manipulation has been greatly overstated relative to a second: the manipulation of policy design. By crafting policy in ways that hide its true effects and create political pressures down the line, today's Republicans have made much greater progress in de-funding the state than any previous conservative leadership.

Nonetheless, their progress remains much less than fully complete. The contest between tax cutters and their opponents is a story with no tidy ending but only an ongoing series of clashes taking place on terrain profoundly shaped by Republicans' past tax-cut victories. In one such clash, in June 2006, Senate Republicans fell just three votes short of winning a cloture vote that would have allowed them to proceed with legislation to make a drastic curtailment or abolition of the estate tax permanent.[11] Only two Republicans voted to support a filibuster. One, George Voinovich of Ohio, declared that "repealing the estate tax during this time of fiscal crisis would be incredibly irresponsible and intellectually dishonest." Voinovich, however, looks to be one of a dwindling old guard. In his inimitable way, Grover Norquist summarizes the big picture: "What do these so-called [Republican] moderates have in common? They're seventy years old. They're not running again. They're gonna be dead soon. So, while they're annoying, within the Republican Party our problems are dying" (Gourevitch 2004). Tax-cut advocates have clearly been playing a long-term game, and they have reason to hope that time is on their side.

Notes

1. Extensive documentation of these claims are contained in Hacker and Pierson 2005a and 2005b.

2. All poll results cited are available at the National Journal's *Poll Track* website: http://nationaljournal.com/members/polltrack/2004/issues/04taxes.htm#13.

3. The American right and the Republican Party are, of course, not synonymous. As this chapter demonstrates, however, they are more nearly so than at any point in recent memory.

4. Cited in Hacker and Pierson 2005a (emphasis in original).

5. Several chapters of this volume take up important aspects of this problem. We develop our own views in detail in Hacker and Pierson 2005b.

6. After the 2004 election, Pat Toomey replaced Moore as head of the Club for Growth.

7. Again, it was the violation of such a pledge that precipitated George H. W. Bush's debacle in 1990. After meeting with Norquist, his son (along with every other Republican contender) committed to such a pledge in writing early in the 2000 presidential campaign.

8. The Club for Growth board replaced Moore with Toomey after the 2004 election—reportedly one of their complaints about Moore was that he was too friendly with some GOP moderates.

9. All of these issues are explored in much more depth in Hacker and Pierson 2005a.

10. White House Office of the Press Secretary 2001.

11. A cloture vote would have led to a contest between two competing proposals, one for abolition and one "compromise" that would have led to an estimated 84 percent of the revenue loss produced by abolition.

Conclusion

Chapter Eleven

Political Development and
Contemporary American Politics

PAUL PIERSON AND THEDA SKOCPOL

THE COMMON THEME OF THIS VOLUME'S essays is the need to take a long view. Students of American politics often separate the study of "the present" from the study of "the past." Yet political change is typically the result of processes unfolding over decades. The activities and events that are most visible at any moment often distract us from the deeper currents of a political system that is always in flux.

A long view allows us to identify and appreciate features of the political environment that shift only slowly. Never dramatic enough at any particular moment to call attention to themselves, these slow-moving shifts may nonetheless have profound effects on a political system. They may themselves represent important changes that cry out for explanation, or they may constitute important sources of other shifts that are too easily attributed instead to more proximate but superficial events.

A long view also gives us a richer sense of the contours of political action. Most of the individuals playing a prominent role in American politics participate over an extended period of time. They are engaged not in a single political episode, but in a series of encounters that may stretch over decades. This is even more the case for politically relevant organizations. Indeed, one of the principal purposes of organizations is to bring some coherence and continuity to the activities of overlapping generations of individuals.

In forcing us to connect seemingly separate events, the long view gives us an appreciation for the sophistication of much political action—as well as its characteristic limitations. Investigating activity over time draws attention to the significance of political learning. Serious, long-term participants in politics gain insights and skills from their experience, and they incorporate those lessons and capabilities into their practices. At the same time, a long view heightens our sensitivity to the unexpected or even perverse effects of political action. Even the most skilled and strategic political actors commonly produce results they had not anticipated. Often we will not see these effects unless we follow the story long enough to watch them unfold.

Finally, tracking political activity over time, even as it shifts across multiple sites of political contestation, helps focus our attention on the substance of politics rather than its form. Democratic politics is not just, or even primarily, about horse-race contests among individuals for office. It is about struggles to exercise authority. Those who are successful gain some control over the reins of government. With that control comes the opportunity to issue commands that others must follow (or ignore at considerable cost).

Because politics involves struggles to exercise authority, it attracts the enduring interest of those who care about the purposes for which that authority is exercised. Thus, much of this volume has centered on two subjects: the evolution of the two broad coalitions that have competed over political authority, one in decline and one ascendant, and the object of their contestation—the activist state. We wish to return briefly to these themes here to highlight how our long-term perspective brings some of the critical elements of American politics into sharper view.

PLACING POLITICAL COALITIONS IN TIME

Throughout this volume we have traced the development and evolving interaction of two broad political coalitions. Although these coalitions are loose and extend well beyond the confines of partisan politics, they are very broadly coordinated by the two major political parties. A long-term perspective provides a distinctive and useful vantage point for understanding the evolution of these two coalitions.

Too often, political analysts treat the major political parties as essentially mirror-images of each other. Both the election-focused, "horse-race" analysis that dominates political punditry and the sparse, economistic models that are prevalent in political science yield a surprisingly similar image of the parties. They are two basically similar teams of elites engaged in a competition for votes. All these politicians operate under the same rules. At least potentially they can access the same political resources. Politicians may join together for some purposes to form a "team," but they remain individual, entrepreneurial figures, who will adapt relatively fluidly if circumstances change. Indeed, within political science this flexible, "plastic" view of parties and politicians has become a cornerstone of expectations that American democracy will function well. Like two competing firms in the economic marketplace, each seeks to give the customers what they want. If it is not succeeding in that competition, the very survival of the firm (or party) depends on adjusting course. Thus, elections and party competition assure responsiveness and accountability.

There is considerable force in this vision of partisan politics, but significant distortion as well. Political parties are huge, complex, and long-lived. They involve long-term, ongoing relationships with voters, multiple powerful organizations, and elites. These relationships draw on and, in turn, reinforce complex social networks. For both individuals and organizations, they induce patterns of extensive investments—in organization building and repertoires of action, in reputation, in the development of expertise, in personal relationships, and in political and ideological commitments. In short, party organizations and their constituent parts are deeply embedded in particular social contexts. While they are constantly changing as party influentials attempt to adjust to evolving pressures, demands, and opportunities, they are far from plastic.

This "thicker" image of parties and their surrounding coalitions suggests that a party's historical path of development is enormously important. The constituent parts of a party respond to the events and circumstances they encounter along the course of their development, and these responses will include the patterns of investments just described. Although not carved in stone, these patterns will have enduring consequences and will be difficult to change in a hurry. Parties are shaped by their experiences—and their current structures carry forward important consequences of those experiences.

In this fundamental sense the Democratic and Republican parties are not mirror images of each other. They are instead distinct organizational constellations with different resources and capacities. Of course, these historical experiences are endlessly complex and could be traced back into the mists of time. A central argument of our book, however, is that the rise of activist government that began in the early 1960s represented a particularly profound political transformation. In a relatively brief period, the federal government's role in American society changed dramatically. Washington came to address concerns that previously had been the province of local government or private actors. Large areas of domestic life became simultaneously or in rapid succession both public issues and national ones. This shift represented a major alteration of the character of the American state. With that alteration came broader changes in the nature of American politics—the stakes for political actors, the resources and opportunities available to them, and the institutional terrain on which their conflicts would play out.

As the contributors to this volume demonstrate, the rise of the activist state had lasting effects on the two parties and their supporting coalitions. The effects on each party, however, were fundamentally different. These differential effects stemmed from two major sources. First, and most obviously, the two parties took different stances with respect to the expansion of federal authority on domestic matters. Second, and equally important, the Democratic lock on Congress throughout the 1960s and 1970s meant that the two parties were differentially positioned to influence and respond to that expansion. From these basic differences have flowed a series of distinctive adaptations in the two parties that continue to influence their contributions to governance and political contestation.

Broadly speaking, the Democratic Party was both more sympathetic to this transformation of the political landscape and better positioned to shape it.[1] As the majority party, Democrats were able to exploit incumbency advantages that were growing in American politics (indeed, some of the most often-criticized features of current Republican rule, such as widespread use of gerrymandering and other tactics of incumbency protection were evident on the Democratic side before 1994). They were able to fashion appeals to powerful interests, especially within the business community, that relied heavily on their majority status. Any group that wanted something from Washington—and as government activism increased, virtually every group did—knew that they needed help from at least some elements within the majority party. As the political journalist Nicholas Confessore (2003, 33) has written, this relationship contained "an inherent tension. For the most part, [business] groups supported Democrats because they had to and Republicans because they wanted to."

The Democrats' majority status also had tremendously important implications for the broader constellation of interests that made up their coalition. As Skocpol's chapter shows, the universe of modern interest groups is less the source of government activism than its product. As policy activity in Washington increased, a wide range of groups sprung up to take advantage of the new opportunities (Walker 1991). Predictably, they took forms and made investments in practices designed to exploit the new political landscape. For groups likely to get a sympathetic ear from the majority party, this meant organizing to leverage the enactment of their policy agendas. They needed concentrated expertise in particular issue areas, combined with the skills to promote the groups' goals either through legislation or through appeal to the courts, where sympathy for government activism was also ascendant (Melnick 1994). In short, the organizational universe supporting the Democratic Party became emblematic of what Theodore Lowi famously termed "interest group liberalism"—a network of organized advocates dedicated to the pursuit of discrete issues through appeals for ongoing government activism (Lowi 1979).

If interest-group liberalism aptly summarizes the basic contours of this majority coalition and its practices, it is equally important to stress what this formula left out—namely, organizational features designed to integrate or encompass the multiple rather than singular concerns of citizens.

Traditionally, two types of organizations have provided the main "encompassing" or integrative elements of the Democratic coalition: unions and local party machines. Whatever their limitations might have been, each of these organizations faced incentives to recognize and respond to a wide range of considerations that might animate or concern their constituents, rather than to fixate on any single dimension. Both these organizational forms, however, were in decline by the 1960s—and their retreat accelerated thereafter.

Equally absent from modern liberalism was any capacity to develop and sustain a public philosophy that could flourish in the political marketplace. Ideas and claims organized around particular issues were abundant, but little in the party's organizational infrastructure led it to focus on developing a more overarching set of justifications for its approach to governance. Ascendant and seemingly unassailable after its decisive victory in 1964, liberalism saw little need to explain itself. A clear sign that this confidence was misplaced can be found in the decline of its electoral fortunes after 1968. And it is striking that the decline was most rapid and pronounced in the presidential contests that come closest to offering a popular referendum on broad approaches to government. Mark Smith's chapter provides more detailed evidence of this failing. On broad issues of economic management that are of critical concern to ordinary voters, the Democratic Party over the past few decades has done a demonstrably poor job of explaining itself.

In short, the modern Democratic coalition adapted to the political contours of the activist state in a manner that suited its majority status and favorable stance toward that activism. Well equipped to exploit the political opportunities of that environment over the short run, it was less focused on developing the capacity to renew those conditions over the long run. And it would turn out to be equally ill-prepared to cope with the political realities that came with long periods during which Democrats did not control the machinery of the activist state.

The transformation of American politics that accompanied the rise of government activism had equally far-reaching effects on the Republican coalition. Given that coalition's more oppositional stance toward government activism and its initially more "outsider" status, however, these effects were very different. As Teles, Zelizer, and Hacker and Pierson all detail in different ways, what emerged on the Republican side was a movement organized precisely to reject much of the activist state.

For both the economic and cultural wings of the conservative movement, government activism itself was the major catalyst for political mobilization. Conservative Christians reacted vigorously against much of the rights revolution—a movement that nationalized policy on a range of hot-button social issues on terms they found unacceptable if not unconscionable. In the economic sphere, business during the 1970s confronted major expansions of government intervention, especially in the regulatory arena. Having initially attempted to ward off these encroachments by constructing ad hoc defensive coalitions as issues arose, business learned from painful defeats. In time employers responded by ramping up their political capacities at every level, but especially by taking a more coordinated and pro-active approach to politics (Vogel 1989). Over time, this course tightened their attachments to the Republican Party.

Some of this conservative organizational response involved the creation of issue-specific advocacy groups that mirrored their political competitors. At least three differences were critical, however. The first was a significantly greater emphasis on grass-roots mobilization. Especially among Christian conservatives, organization meant more than the liberal advocacy group formula of mailing lists plus litigators plus policy specialists—it meant mobilizing mass memberships for political action.

The second difference was a greater focus on ideational contestation. Conservatives devoted substantial organizational resources to refining and advancing broad arguments about governance. Perhaps the clearest indication of this difference comes in conservatives' virtual invention of a new kind of political organization—the unapologetically partisan "think tank." These idea factories drew on generous funding from patrons with strong political convictions. Clear advocacy of a broad ideological agenda supplanted norms of bipartisanship and open, evidence-based inquiry. Technocratic frames of refining "solutions" to policy "problems" gave way to the aspiration of winning in the political marketplace. Considerable resources were devoted to message, presentation, and dissemination of ideas.

Finally, befitting its outsider status, the organizational efforts of conservatives were increasingly oriented toward the long term. The advantages of an entrenched majority—its capacity to dictate the political agenda, to extract political resources, and to use its institutional control to structure policy and advantage its candidates—were formidable. This was a lesson that had to be learned through often painful setbacks, such as the rollback of the Reagan tax cuts, the heavy electoral losses incurred in 1982 after an unsuccessful effort to trim Social Security benefits, and the bitter internal fissures between the GOP's old guard and its ascendant elements that surfaced after George H. W. Bush's decision to raise taxes.

Many conservative political entrepreneurs gradually recognized that success required a strategy directed toward establishing the organizational and intellectual infrastructure necessary to craft a majoritarian appeal. As Zelizer's chapter observes, no single individual encapsulated the essence of this strategic shift more clearly than Newt Gingrich. Other chapters of this volume suggest, however, that he was far from alone in his efforts to construct a more coordinated movement with a broad and reasonably coherent vision of governance. Campbell's chapter, for instance, reveals the GOP's remarkably expanded capacity to reach out not just to traditional supporters but to demographic groups that had previously supported the Democrats.

Thus, the two political coalitions were shaped in important ways by their initial experiences with the vast expansion of federal policy activity that occurred between the mid-1960s and mid-1970s. Reflecting their different circumstances and aspirations, each developed a distinctive repertoire of organizational responses that gave them different capacities for particular types of political action. In turn, these repertoires have had enduring effects even as other elements of the political landscape have been transformed.[2]

The lasting repercussions are clearly evident on the Democratic side. The Democrats' "pillarized" structure of groups fiercely committed to particular issues but only weakly coordinated created characteristic strengths and weaknesses. It was well suited to develop policy in discrete areas where the relevant groups had access to sympathetic officials. It also retained a substantial capacity to mobilize defenses of programs facing direct challenges. On the other hand, it was much less effective at facilitating efforts to develop a coherent image for the party. Nor could it respond well to broad concerns of voters unless those happened to dovetail with the particular agenda these organized groups wished to advance.

The heavy reliance of Democrats on their majority status prior to 1994 also had long-term liabilities. Limited resources were devoted to the arduous task, often involving no immediate electoral payoff, of updating, articulating, and disseminating a broad philosophy of governance that would give voters a positive sense of what the party stood for. Equally problematic in the long run was the party's adaptation to the escalating financial demands of electoral competition: to use incumbency as the main basis for its appeal to those with the greatest financial resources. Although this strategy allowed Democrats to keep pace in the campaign spending arms race, it meant they could do so only as long as they kept their majority.

For Republicans as well one can see the lasting effects of its encounter with the rise of an activist state ushered in during an era of Democratic ascendance. Responding to its outsider status the party effectively galvanized—and was in turn reshaped by—those elements of American society most angered by the rise of government activism. Indeed, while it is common to observe the huge differences between the two main foundations of the Republican coalition—cultural conservatives and business—these two elements share an antipathy to the activist state constructed in the years after 1960. As the outsider party, Republicans found themselves driven to devote substantial energy to crafting both a philosophy of governance (drawing heavily on a critique of the status quo) and to developing the organizational infrastructure that would allow them to disseminate this message and operate in a coordinated fashion.

The lasting impact of these long-term processes of party formation can be seen in the aftermath of the reversal of fortune that took place in 1994. The parties would prove to be remarkably competitive over the next decade, with a closer electoral balance than during any similar length of time in modern American political history. Yet the advantages of the Republicans in that close competition were evident for a decade.

For Democrats, the fall from congressional power in 1994 was very costly. It immediately undercut the party's strongest claim for the attention of business interests who provided critical financial support (and the GOP's development of the K Street Project under the leadership of Tom DeLay amplified the shift). Party structures, moreover, were poorly adapted to the task of fighting to recapture majority status. The "pillarized" organizations of interest-group liberalism worked hard to protect their own programs, but were ill-equipped to advance an encompassing and coordinated push to regain the party's electoral edge. The party lacked the ideational infrastructure needed to develop such a message, and now it would find it doubly difficult to assemble the resources needed to create such an infrastructure.

By contrast, many of the distinctive organizational features of the GOP could be put to effective use in its new majority status. The party had developed a powerful message machine and a high capacity for coordination, features that translated into very high levels of unity. This unity could be combined with the party's enormous (and now enhanced) fundraising capacity and the trappings of incumbency to generate a formidable edge in electoral competition. Although Republicans' electoral advantage has been narrow, it proved resilient for many years.

The GOP's structure, developed over an extended period in opposition, has not been perfectly adapted to its new governing role, of course. The biggest limitation of an apparatus constructed around fierce opposition—perhaps the flip side of its strengths—was been a consistent temptation to overreach. In 1995, 1998, and 2005, encouraged by the strong and aggressive movements that constituted its "base," Republican initiatives courted backlash and tested the limits of its organizational advantages. In 2006, with an unpopular war adding to the Democratic wave, congressional Republicans finally paid the price. In short, both the contemporary strengths and weaknesses of each major party can be seen more clearly when we examine their development over an extended period of time.

THE EVOLVING STRUGGLE OVER THE ACTIVIST STATE

A long-term analysis not only gives us a clearer sense of the development of the major participants in political contestation. It also helps us understand what is happening to the complex set of government activities that these coalitions vie to control. Like our concentration on the evolution of political actors, our emphasis on policy development both enforces a focus on the substance of politics and an appreciation for the multiple and complex pathways through which political struggles are carried out.

As Pierson suggests in chapter 2, despite the resurgence of a conservatism openly dedicated to rolling back much of the activist state, it is difficult to find aggregate evidence that suggests major progress toward that aspiration. "Plateau" effects are clear—the expansion of government activism seems, on the whole, to have been halted—but substantial rollbacks are less apparent. Other contributions to this volume both help to explain this observation while complicating the picture in constructive ways. Previous work on policy development has led to a greater appreciation for how government activities may produce "feedback effects" that entrench particular arrangements (Skocpol 1992; Pierson 1993; Hacker 2002). As Mettler's chapter demonstrates, program designs can create mass bases of support that transform the political landscape and make reversal difficult. Teles shows how some elements of government activism not only enhanced mass support but carved out policy niches that were insulated from shifts in public opinion. Much of the activist state is popular, and even those elements that are not may be difficult to dislodge.

Resurgent conservatives have had to deal with these political realities. Confronting them effectively has required trial-and-error and adaptation. By concentrating on the long term, we are able to see how this struggle over the activist state has played out through multiple rounds of contestation in multiple venues, under shifting political circumstances, and under conditions that allow major participants to refine or shift their strategies on the basis of experience. The result is a better appreciation for the factors that contribute to success or failure in an ongoing conflict played out over uneven terrain.

Consistent with earlier research, we find that the popularity of particular elements of government activism combined with the political strength of their supporters helps to account for the difficulties conservatives have faced. Yet other conditions matter as well. In line with conventional thinking about institutions, the presence of veto points contributes to the protection of the policy status quo. Different forms of government activism vary in the level of these institutional protections. Policies that can be changed by unilateral executive action are more vulnerable than those that require legislation. Programs that can turn for protection to a Senate filibuster are less vulnerable than those that cannot.

For a deeper understanding of this central political conflict in contemporary American society, however, we need an analysis that takes change over time more seriously. As McCarty demonstrates, it is not just the presence of institutional veto points but their coupling with an increasingly polarized politics that can make policy reform difficult. Supermajoritarian institutions put a premium on consensus. The evolution of the two dominant political coalitions, especially with respect to their growing discord over the activist state, makes such consensus elusive. The result is often gridlock (Binder 2003).

Tracking policy conflicts and strategies over time, however, reveals why stopping here would be a mistake. More precisely, it would lead one to seriously underestimate the conservative movement's capacity to engineer policy change. As an important analysis by Jacob Hacker (2004) has demonstrated and McCarty's work in this volume confirms, one often must look more closely at the substance of a policy conflict to discover who is "playing offense" and who is on defense. In many cases—say, where the legally required minimum wage is not indexed to the cost of living—those seeking to preserve the content of a policy must play offense rather than defense. They must repeatedly win efforts to update the content of government activism. Otherwise the result is what Hacker calls "policy drift," with the substance of policy eroding over time. As he demonstrates, much of the activist state is vulnerable to this kind of drift. For instance, substantial elements of the American system of social insurance (with its reliance not just on public benefits but employer-sponsored and state-subsidized private benefits) have eroded considerably in recent years.

The same point applies broadly across the spectrum of government activity. The "activist state" constructed prior to 1980 remains, but as the world changes, government has failed to keep up. "Old" initiatives are preserved but new and often pressing problems meet with no significant response. Traditional workplace safety rules may remain, but ergonomics rules that would meet newly recognized risks in a greatly transformed world of work are blocked. The Clean Air Act survives but new challenges like global warming meet with indifference. Traditional social insurance programs like Medicare and Social Security continue but government responds not at all to the strains associated with two-earner households and rising economic insecurity. In short, the role of government in American society is changing. Yet this is mostly not a result of major legislative enactments, but rather the success of conservative efforts (facilitated, as McCarty suggests, by growing polarization) to thwart government adaptations to slow-moving but profound changes in social conditions.

Other contributions suggest additional alternatives to a direct assault on government activism. Teles notes that conservatives learned through experience that strategies of indirection could greatly enhance the prospects for success. These strategies were often dependent upon a long-term approach requiring not just patience in the absence of immediate returns but the organizational and financial capacity to sustain such efforts over time. Political entrepreneurs sought either to erode popular support for the policy status quo, to build up "parallel paths" of policy more consistent with conservative aspirations, or gradually to replace personnel in critical institutional sites with those more sympathetic to conservatism.

All of these strategies have had some success. Here we mention only the conservative effort to remake the Supreme Court. This is a slow-moving process of tremendous significance. Moreover, it is one where Teles' chapter reveals a considerable conservative capacity to take the long view. So far, the policy fruits of this strategy have been disappointing to many conservatives. Yet this process of replacement, or gradual turnover in membership, is still in motion. We have not yet seen the full swing of the court's pendulum to the right. Even a few weeks before the remarkable election of November 1994, the full implications of a very gradual process of replacing southern Democrats with southern Republicans were not yet visible. Similarly, the capacity of the Supreme Court to remake the activist state is not yet in full view.

An equally significant slow-moving challenge to the activist state takes the form of mounting fiscal imbalances. As Hacker and Pierson suggest, Republicans have recalibrated their strategies for taking on major public expenditure commitments. Instead of challenging these programs head-on, they have committed their political resources to tax cuts. These are much easier to sell, especially when they are carefully designed to take advantage of opportunities to defer pain to a later point in time. This strategy represents a high-stakes gamble, essentially putting the revenue and spending components of the American state on a collision course. At a minimum, however, conservatives seem to have succeeded in creating a new context in which advocates of public spending will have to meet them halfway. In other words, over the long run they have reconfigured the political terrain in ways that are likely to lead to big cuts in major spending programs and block the emergence of bold new programs even when Democrats regain seats in Congress.

Again, this investigation of the activist state highlights the benefits of examining long-term processes of change in American politics. Ascendant conservatives inherited a complex system of public authority, constructed over decades. As is now well understood, that system could not easily be turned to conservative purposes. Yet it is equally mistaken to reduce the past quarter century to a series of conservative failures. Failures often

REFERENCES

SECONDARY SOURCES

Abramowitz, Alan I., and Kyle L. Saunders. 1998. "Ideological Realignment in the US Electorate." *Journal of Politics* 60: 634–52.

Adams, Greg D. 1997. "Abortion: Evidence of Issue Evolution." *American Journal of Political Science* 41: 718–37.

Albany Times Union. 2003. "Big Spenders." 24 November.

Aldrich, John. 1995. *Why Parties? The Origin and Transformation of Political Parties in America.* Chicago: University of Chicago Press.

Alesina, Alberto, and Howard Rosenthal. 1995. *Partisan Politics, Divided Government, and the Economy.* New York: Cambridge University Press.

Allen, Mike. 2005. "GOP Shifts Gears on Ethics Rules." *Washington Post,* 5 January.

Almond, Gabriel A., and Sidney Verba. 1963. *The Civic Culture: Political Attitudes and Democracy in Five Nations.* Princeton, N.J.: Princeton University Press.

American Political Science Association. 1950. "Toward a More Responsible Two-Party System: A Report on the Committee on Political Parties." *American Political Science Review* 44 (3) (Supplement): 1–44.

Ansolabehere, Stephen, Jonathan Rodden, and James M. Snyder Jr. 2005. "Purple America." Unpublished manuscript, Massachusetts Institute of Technology.

Arnold, Douglas. 1990. *The Logic of Congressional Action.* New Haven, Conn.: Yale University Press.

Avery, James M., and Mark Peffley. 2005. "Voter Registration Requirements, Voter Turnout, and Welfare Eligibility Policy: Class Bias Matters." *State Politics and Policy Quarterly* 5 (1): 47–67.

Baker, Peter. 2000. *The Breach: Inside the Impeachment and Trial of William Jefferson Clinton.* New York: Scribner.

Balkin, Jack, and Sanford Levinson. 2001. "Understanding the Constitutional Revolution." *Virginia Law Review* 87 (October): 1045–1104.

Balz, Dan. 1985. "Frustrations Embitter House GOP." *Washington Post,* 29 April.

Balz, Dan, and Ronald Brownstein. 1996. *Storming the Gates: Protest Politics and the Republican Revival.* Boston: Little, Brown.

Baron, Jonathan, and Edward J. McCaffery. 2004. "Masking Redistribution (or Its Absence)." Social Science Research Network Paper Collection. http://ssrn.com/abstract=528165.

Bartels, Larry M. 1988. *Presidential Primaries and the Dynamics of Public Choice.* Princeton, N.J.: Princeton University Press.

Bartels, Larry M. 2000. "Partisanship and Voting Behavior, 1952–1996." *American Journal of Political Science* 44: 35–50.

———. 2004. "Partisan Politics and the U.S. Income Distribution." Unpublished manuscript, Princeton University.

———. 2005. "What's the Matter with *What's the Matter with Kansas?*" Paper presented at the annual meeting of American Political Science Association, Washington, D.C., 1–4 September.

Baumann, David. 2004. "Grading the Class of '94." *National Journal,* 1 May.

Baumgartner, Frank R., and Bryan D. Jones. 1993. *Agendas and Instability in American Politics.* Chicago: University of Chicago Press.

Baumgartner, Frank R., Beth L. Leech, and Christine Mahoney. 2003. "The Co-evolution of Groups and Government." Paper presented at the annual meeting of the American Political Science Association, Philadelphia, 28–31 August. polisci.la.psu.edu/faculty/Baumgartner/Baumgartner-et-al-2003.pdf. Accessed June 2003.

Baumgartner, Frank R., and Christine Mahoney. 2004. "Social Movements and the Rise of New Issues." In *Routing the Opposition: Social Movements, Public Policy, and Democracy,* ed. David S. Meyer, Valerie Jenness, and Helen Ingram, 65–86. Minneapolis: University of Minnesota Press.

Beer, Samuel H. 1978. "In Search of a New Public Philosophy." In *The New American Political System,* ed. Anthony King, 5–55. Washington, D.C.: American Enterprise Institute.

Behrman, Jere, Robert Pollack, and Paul Taubman. 1989. "Family Resources, Family Size, and Access to Financing for College Education." *Journal of Political Economy* 97: 398–419.

Bell, Daniel. 1976. *The Cultural Contradictions of Capitalism.* New York: Basic Books.

Bennett, Michael J. 1996. *When Dreams Came True: The G.I. Bill and the Making of Modern America.* Washington, D.C.: Brassey's.

Bennett, Stephen Earl. 2001. "Were the Halcyon Days Really Golden? An Analysis of Americans' Attitudes about the Political System, 1945–1965." In *What Is It about Government That Americans Dislike?,* ed. John R. Hibbing and Elizabeth Theiss-Morse, 50–55. New York: Cambridge University Press.

Bergan, Daniel E., Alan S. Gerber, Donald P. Green, and Costas Panagopoulos. 2005. "Grassroots Mobilization and Voter Turnout in 2004." *Public Opinion Quarterly* 69: 760–77.

Bernstein, Jill, and Rosemary A. Stevens. 1999. "Public Opinion, Knowledge, and Medicare Reform." *Health Affairs* 18 (1): 180–93.

Berry, Jeffrey M. 1977. *Lobbying for the People: The Political Behavior of Public Interest Groups.* Princeton, N.J.: Princeton University Press.

———. 1997. *The Interest Group Society.* 3rd ed. New York: Longman.

———. 1999. *The New Liberalism: The Rising Power of Citizen Groups.* Washington, D.C.: Brookings Institution Press.

Berry, Jeffrey M., and David F. Arons. 2003. *A Voice for Nonprofits.* Washington, D.C.: Brookings Institution Press.

Bibby, John F. 2002. "State Party Organizations: Strengthened and Adapting to Candidate-Centered Politics and Nationalization." In *The Parties Respond:*

Changes in American Parties and Campaigns, ed. L. Sandy Maisel, 19–46. 4th ed. Boulder, Colo.: Westview Press.

Binder, Sarah. 1996. "The Disappearing Political Center." *Brookings Review* 14 (Fall): 36–39.

———. 2003. *Stalemate: Causes and Consequences of Legislative Gridlock.* Washington, D.C.: Brookings Institution Press.

Binder, Sarah, and Forrest Maltzman. 2002. "Senatorial Delay in Confirming Federal Judges, 1947–1998." *American Journal of Political Science* 46 (1):190–99.

Birnbaum, Jeffrey H. 1984. "GOP Conservatives Join to Assail Reagan on Budget Strategy." *Wall Street Journal,* 24 January.

Birnbaum, Jeffrey H., and Langley, Monica. 1987. "House Passes Bill to Increase Taxes by $12.3 Billion." *Wall Street Journal,* 30 October.

Black, Earl, and Merle Black. 1987. *Politics and Society in the South.* Cambridge, Mass.: Harvard University Press.

———. 1992. *The Vital South: How Presidents Are Elected.* Cambridge, Mass.: Harvard University Press.

———. 2002. *The Rise of Southern Republicans.* Cambridge, Mass.: Belknap Press, Harvard University Press.

Bosso, Christopher J. 1995. "The Color of Money: Environmental Groups and the Pathologies of Fund Raising." In *Interest Group Politics,* ed. Allan J. Cigler and Burdett A. Loomis, 101–30. 4th ed. Washington, D.C.: Congressional Quarterly Press.

———. 2003. "Rethinking the Concept of Membership in Nature Advocacy Organizations." *Policy Studies Journal* 31 (3): 397–411.

Borger, Gloria. 1988. "The GOP's Sleaze Pinup: For Jim Wright and His Party, What Goes Around Comes Around." *U.S. News and World Report,* 20 June, 20.

Brady, David W., and Craig Volden. 1997. *Revolving Gridlock.* Boulder, Colo.: Westview Press.

Brady, Henry E., Kay Lehman Schlozman, and Sidney Verba. 1999. "Prospecting for Participants: Rational Expectations and the Recruitment of Political Activists." *American Political Science Review* 93: 153–68.

Brady, Henry E., Kay Lehman Schlozman, Sidney Verba, and Laurel Elms. 2002. "Who Bowls: The (Un)Changing Stratification of Participation." In *Understanding Public Opinion,* ed. Barbara Norrander and Clyde Wilcox, 219–42. Washington, D.C.: Congressional Quarterly Press.

Brady, Peter, and Emily Y. Lin. 2004. "Employment-Based Health Insurance and Pension Benefits: Trends and Inequalities in Accessibility and Participation, 1987–2001." Unpublished manuscript, Office of Tax Analysis, U.S. Department of Treasury.

Brandolini, Andrea, and Timothy M. Smeeding. 2006. "Patterns of Economic Inequality in Western Democracies: Some Facts on Levels and Trends. *PS: Political Science and Politics* 39 (1): 21–26.

Brint, Steven. 1994. *In an Age of Experts: The Changing Role of Professionals in Politics and Public Life.* Princeton, N.J.: Princeton University Press.

Broder, David. 1983. "Opening GOP Minds." *Washington Post,* 23 October.

Brooks, David. 2005. "Running Out of Steam." *New York Times,* 8 December.

Browning, Graeme. 1995. "Congress: On a Mission." *National Journal*, 30 September.

Brownlee, W. Elliot, and C. Eugene Steuerle. 2003. "Taxation." In *The Reagan Presidency: Pragmatic Conservatism and Its Legacies*, ed. W. Elliott Brownlee and Hugh Davis Graham, 155–81. Lawrence: University Press of Kansas.

Bryce, James. 1895. *The American Commonwealth*. 3rd ed. Vol. 2. New York: Macmillan.

Burden, Barry. 2004. "Candidate Positioning in U.S. Congressional Elections." *British Journal of Political Science* 34: 211–27.

Burke, Thomas F. 2002. *Lawyers, Lawsuits, and Legal Rights: The Battle over Litigation in American Society*. Berkeley: University of California Press.

Burnham, Walter Dean. 1970. *Critical Elections and the Mainsprings of American Politics*. New York: W. W. Norton.

Burns, Nancy, Kay Lehman Schlozman, and Sidney Verba. 2001. *The Private Roots of Public Action: Gender, Equality, and Political Participation*. Cambridge, Mass.: Harvard University Press.

Burtless, Gary. 1999. "Growing American Inequality: Sources and Remedies." In *Setting National Priorities: The 2000 Election and Beyond*, ed. Henry J. Aaron and Robert D. Reischauer, 137–40. Washington, D.C.: Brookings Institution Press.

Butler, Stuart, and Peter Germanis. 1983. "Achieving Social Security Reform: A 'Leninist' Strategy." *Cato Journal* 3 (Fall): 547–56.

Callahan, David. 1999. *$1 Billion for Ideas: Conservative Think Tanks in the 1990s*. Washington, D.C.: National Committee for Responsive Philanthropy.

Cameron, A. Colin, and Pravin K. Trivedi. 1998. *Regression Analysis of Count Data*. New York: Cambridge University Press.

Campbell, Andrea Louise. 2003. *How Policies Make Citizens: Senior Political Activism and the American Welfare State*. Princeton, N.J.: Princeton University Press.

———. 2004. "The Political Consequences of Program Design: The Case of Medicare." Unpublished paper, Massachusetts Institute of Technology.

Carlson, Margaret. 1988. "The Foul Stench of Money; in Congress the Scandal Is Not What's Illegal—It's What's Legal." *Time*, 4 July, 21.

Carmines, Edward G., and James Stimson. 1989. *Issue Evolution: Race and the Transformation of American Politics*. Princeton, N.J.: Princeton University Press.

Carniero, Pedro, and James Heckman. 2003. "Human Capital Policy." Working Paper 9495, National Bureau of Economic Research. http://www.nber.org/papers/w9495.

Carson, Jamie L., Michael H. Crespin, Charles J. Finocchiaro, and David Rohde. 2003. "Linking Congressional Districts across Time: Redistricting and Party Polarization in Congress." Paper presented at the annual meeting of the Midwest Political Science Association, Chicago.

Center for Individual Rights. 1989. "A Brief Description of Program Activities." Document in possession of Steven M. Teles.

———. 1990. "A Proposal and Request for Funding." Submitted to the John M. Olin Foundation, February.

Center on Budget and Policy Priorities. 1998. "Strengths of the Safety Net: How the EITC, Social Security, and Other Government Programs Affect Poverty." http://www.cbpp.org/snd98-rep.htm.

Chaddock, Gail Russell. 2003. "Republicans Take Over K Street." *Christian Science Monitor,* 29 August.

Charles, Jeffrey A. 1993. *Service Clubs in American Society: Rotary, Kiwanis, and Lions.* Urbana: University of Illinois Press.

Clemens, Elisabeth S., and James M. Cook. 1999. "Politics and Institutionalism: Explaining Durability and Change." *Annual Review of Sociology* 25: 441–66.

Clift, Eleanor, and Tom Brazaitis. 1996. *War without Bloodshed: The Art of Politics.* New York: Simon and Schuster.

Clinton, Bill. 1999. State of the Union address. Transcript from "My Fellow Americans. . . State of Our Union Is Strong." *Washington Post,* 20 January, A12.

———. 2000. State of the Union address. Transcript from "President Clinton on State of Union: 'The Strongest It Has Ever Been.'" *New York Times,* 28 January, A16.

Clinton, Joshua, Simon Jackman, and Douglas Rivers. 2004. "The Statistical Analysis of Roll Call Data." *American Political Science Review* 98: 355–70.

Clinton, Joshua, and John Lapinski. 2006. "Measuring Legislative Accomplishment, 1877–1994." *American Journal of Political Science* 50 (1): 232–49.

———. Forthcoming. "Measuring Significant Legislation, 1877–1948." In *Process, Party and Policymaking: Further New Perspectives on the History of Congress,* ed. David Brady and Matthew McCubbins. Palo Alto, Calif.: Stanford University Press.

Coalition on Human Needs. 2005. "Members of the Coalition on Human Needs." http://www.chn.org/pdf/chnmembers.pdf. Accessed on 13 February.

Cohen, Richard. 1980. "House GOP Conflicts May Surface If Party Gains in Fall Elections." *National Journal,* 12 July.

———. 1981. "The 'Revolution' on Capitol Hill: Is it Just a Temporary Coup?" *National Journal,* 29 August.

———. 1982. "His Troops Restless over the Budget, GOP Leader Michel Is on the Spot." *National Journal,* 20 February.

———. 1984. "Frustrated House Republicans Seek More Aggressive Strategy for 1984 and Beyond." *National Journal,* 3 March.

———. 2003. "In the House, a Fleeting Cease Fire." *National Journal, 26 July.*

Confessore, Nicholas. 2003. "Welcome to the Machine." *Washington Monthly* 35, nos. 7–8 (July–August): 30–37.

———. 2004. "The Myth of the Democratic Establishment." *Washington Monthly* 36, nos. 1–2 (January–February): 22.

Connolly, Ceci. 2003. "Census Finds 5.7% Rise in Number of Americans without Health Insurance." *Washington Post,* 5 October, A3.

Conway, M. Margaret. 2000. *Political Participation in the United States.* 3rd ed. Washington, D.C.: Congressional Quarterly Press.

Conway, M. Margaret, and Joanne Connor Green. 1995. "Political Action Committees and the Political Process in the 1990s." In *Interest Group Politics,* ed.

Allan J. Cigler and Burdett A. Loomis, 193–214. 4th ed. Washington, D.C.: Congressional Quarterly Press.

———. 1998. "Political Action Committees and Campaign Finance." In *Interest Group Politics*, ed. Allan J. Cigler and Burdett A. Loomis, 155–73. 5th ed. Washington, D.C.: Congressional Quarterly Press.

Cordes, Joseph. 1996. "The Yoke of Prior Commitments: How Yesterday's Decisions Affect Today's Budget and Fiscal Options." In *The New World Fiscal Order*, ed. C. Eugene Steurle and Masahiro Kawai, 95–116. Washington, D.C.: Urban Institute Press.

Costa, Dora L., and Matthew E. Kahn. 2003. "Understanding the American Decline in Social Capital, 1952–1998." *Kyklos* 56 (1): 17–46.

Costain, Anne N. 1992. *Inviting Women's Rebellion: A Political Process Interpretation of the Women's Movement*. Baltimore: Johns Hopkins University Press.

Covington, Sally. 1997. *Moving a Public Policy Agenda: The Strategic Philanthropy of Conservative Foundations*. Washington, D.C.: National Committee for Responsive Philanthropy.

Crawford, Susan, and Peggy Levitt. 1999. "Social Change and Civic Engagement: The Case of the PTA." In *Civic Engagement in American Democracy*, ed. Theda Skocpol and Morris P. Fiorina, 249–96. Washington, D.C.: Brookings Institution Press; New York: Russell Sage Foundation.

Crenson, Matthew A., and Benjamin Ginsberg. 2002. *Downsizing Democracy: How America Downsized Its Government and Sidelined Its Citizens*. Baltimore: Johns Hopkins University Press.

Critchlow, Donald. 2004. "When Republicans Become Revolutionaries." In *The American Congress: The Building of Democracy*, ed. Julian E. Zelizer, 703–31. Boston: Houghton Mifflin.

Crowley, Michael. 2003. "Oppressed Minority." *New Republic*, 23 June.

CTJ. 2002. Year-by-Year Analysis of the Bush Tax Cuts Growing Tilt to the Very Rich. Washington, D.C.: Citizens for Tax Justice.

Danziger, Sheldon, and Peter Gottschalk. 1995. *America Unequal*. New York: Russell Sage Foundation; Cambridge, Mass.: Harvard University Press.

Davis, Richard S. 1948. "Fifty Years of Service." *Eagle* 36 (2): 7–9.

Dawson, Michael C. 1994. *Behind the Mule: Race and Class in African-American Politics*. Princeton, N.J.: Princeton University Press.

De Alessi, Louis. 1999. "The Emergence of Law and Economics as an Academic Discipline: The John M. Olin Fellowship Program in Law and Economics." *Case Western Reserve Law Review* 50 (Winter): 341–45.

Dean, John. 2001. *The Rehnquist Choice*. New York: Free Press.

DeBoef, Suzanna, and Paul M. Kellstedt. 2004. "The Political (and Economic) Origins of Consumer Confidence." *American Journal of Political Science* 48: 633–49.

Delli Carpini, Michael X., and Scott Keeter. 1996. *What Americans Know about Politics and Why It Matters*. New Haven, Conn.: Yale University Press.

Derthick, Martha. 1979, *Policymaking for Social Security*. Washington, D.C.: Brookings Institution Press.

———. 1990. *Agency Under Stress*. Washington, D.C.: Brookings Institution Press.

———. 2005. *Up in Smoke: From Legislation to Litigation in Tobacco Politics.* 2nd ed. Washington, D.C.: Congressional Quarterly Press.

Derthick, Martha, and Steven M. Teles. 2003. "Riding the Third Rail: Social Security Reform." In *The Reagan Presidency: Pragmatic Conservatism and Its Legacies,* ed. W. Elliott Brownlee and Hugh Davis Graham, 182–208. Lawrence: University Press of Kansas.

DiMaggio, Paul, John Evans, and Bethany Bryson. 1996. "Have American's Social Attitudes Become More Polarized?" *American Journal of Sociology* 102 (3): 690–755.

Dionne, E. J., Jr. 1991. *Why Americans Hate Politics.* New York: Touchstone.

Dodd, Lawrence C., and Bruce I Oppenheimer. 1997. "Revolution in the House: Testing the Limits of Party Government." In *Congress Reconsidered,* ed. Lawrence C. Dodd and Bruce I. Oppenheimer, 29–60. 6th ed. Washington, D.C.: Congressional Quarterly Press.

Dowie, Mark. 2001. *American Foundations: An Investigative History.* Cambridge, Mass.: MIT Press.

Drew, Elizabeth. 2005. "Selling Washington." *New York Review of Books,* 23 June.

Edelman, Marian Wright. 1987. *Families in Peril: An Agenda for Social Change.* Cambridge, Mass.: Harvard University Press.

Edin, Kathryn, and Laura Lein. 1997. *Making Ends Meet: How Single Mothers Survive Welfare and Low-Wage Work.* New York: Russell Sage.

Edsall, Thomas Byrne, and Mary D. Edsall. 1991. *Chain Reaction: The Impact of Race, Rights, and Taxes on American Politics.* New York: W. W. Norton.

Epp, Charles R. 1998. *The Rights Revolution: Lawyers, Activists, and Supreme Courts in Comparative Perspective.* Chicago: University of Chicago Press.

Epstein, David, and Sharyn O' Halloran. 1999. *Delegating Powers: A Transactions Cost Approach to Policymaking under Separate Powers.* New York: Cambridge University Press.

Epstein, Lee. 1985. *Conservatives in Court.* Knoxville: University of Tennessee Press.

Erie, Steven P. 1988. *Rainbow's End: Irish-Americans and the Dilemmas of Urban Machine Politics, 1840–1985.* Berkeley: University of California Press.

Erikson, Robert S., Michael B. MacKuen, and James A. Stimson. 2002. *The Macro Polity.* Cambridge: Cambridge University Press.

Erkulwater, Jennifer L. 2006. *Disability Rights and the American Social Safety Net.* Ithaca, N.Y.: Cornell University Press.

Esping-Andersen, Gosta. 1990. *The Three Worlds of Welfare Capitalism.* Princeton, N.J.: Princeton University Press.

Evans, John. 2003. "Have American Attitudes Become More Polarized: An Update." *Social Science Quarterly* 84 (1): 71–90.

Evans, Peter, Deitrich Reuschemeyer, and Theda Skocpol, eds. 1985. *Bringing the State Back In.* Cambridge: Cambridge University Press.

Evans, Rowland, and Novak, Robert. 1985. "The Michel/Gingrich Split." *Washington Post,* 11 March.

Fallows, James M. 1996. *Breaking the News: How the Media Undermine American Democracy.* New York: Pantheon Books.

Farhang, Sean. 2003. "The Litigation State: Public Regulation and Private Lawsuits in the American Separation of Powers System." Unpublished manuscript, Columbia University.

Farrell, John Aloysius. 2001. *Tip O'Neill and the Democratic Century.* Boston: Little Brown.

Federal Election Commission. 2004. "Party Financial Activity Summarized, 12/14/2004." www.fec.gov/press/press2004/20041214party/20041214party.html.

Federalist Society. 1982. "Proposal to Form a National Conservative Legal Organization." 15 October.

Fenno, Richard F. 2000. *Congress at the Grassroots: Representational Change in the South, 1970–1998.* Chapel Hill: University of North Carolina Press.

Ferejohn, John, and Charles Shipan. 1990. "Congressional Influence on Bureaucracy." *Journal of Law, Economics, and Organization* 6: 1–21.

Ferrara, Peter. 1980. *Social Security: The Inherent Contradiction.* Washington, D.C.: Cato.

Fiorina, Morris P. 1996. *Divided Government.* 2nd ed. Boston: Allyn and Bacon.

———. 1999. "Extreme Voices: A Dark Side of Civic Engagement." In *Civic Engagement in American Democracy,* ed. Theda Skocpol and Morris P. Fiorina, 395–425. Washington, D.C.: Brookings Institution Press; New York: Russell Sage Foundation.

Fiorina, Morris P., with Samuel J. Abrams and Jeremy C. Pope. 2005. *Culture War? The Myth of a Polarized America.* New York: Pearson Longman.

Flanigan, William H., and Nancy H. Zingale. 1998. *Political Behavior of the American Electorate.* 9th ed. Washington, D.C.: Congressional Quarterly Press.

Fligstein, Neil. 1976. "The G.I. Bill: Its Effects on the Educational and Occupational Attainment of U.S. Males, 1940–1973." CDE Working Paper 76–9. Center for Demography and Ecology, University of Wisconsin, Madison.

Foundation Center. 2002. Statistics on Foundations. fdncenter.org/fc_stats. Accessed 29 September 2003.

Fox, Sherwood Dean. 1952. "Voluntary Associations and Social Structure." Ph.D. diss., Harvard University.

Frank, Thomas. 2004. *What's the Matter with Kansas? How Conservatives Won the Heart of America.* New York: Metropolitan Books.

Freeman, Richard B. 2004. "What, Me Vote?" In *Social Inequality,* ed. Kathryn Neckerman, 703–28. New York: Russell Sage.

Frymer, Paul. 1999. *Uneasy Alliances: Race and Party Competition in America.* Princeton, N.J.: Princeton University Press.

Gale, William G., and Peter R. Orszag. 2003. "Sunsets in the Tax Code." *Tax Notes,* 9 June, 1553–61.

———. 2004a. "Bush Administration Tax Policy: Starving the Beast?" *Tax Notes,* 15 November, 999–1002.

———. 2004b. "The 'No New Taxes' Pledge." *Tax Notes,* 12 July, 197–209.

Gamm, Gerald, and Robert D. Putnam. 1999. "The Growth of Voluntary Associations in America, 1840–1940." *Journal of Interdisciplinary History* 29 (4): 511–57.

Garrett, Major. 2005. *The Enduring Revolution: How the Contract with America Continues to Shape the Nation.* New York: Crown Forum.

General Accounting Office. 2000. "Unemployment Insurance: Role as Safety Net for Low-Wage Workers Is Limited." GAO-01–181. http://www.gao.gov/new.items/d01181.pdf.

Gelb, Joyce, and Marian Lief Palley. 1982. *Women and Public Policies*. Princeton, N.J.: Princeton University Press.

Gerber, Alan S., and Donald P. Green. 2000. "The Effects of Canvassing, Telephone Calls, and Direct Mail on Voter Turnout: A Field Experiment." *American Political Science Review* 94 (3): 653–63.

Gerber, Elisabeth R., and Rebecca B. Morton. 1998. "Primary Election Systems and Representation." *Journal of Law, Economics, and Organization* 14 (2): 304–24.

Germanis, Peter. 1982, "Epilogue." In *The Heritage Lectures*, no. 18. Washington, D.C.

———. 1983. "Increase the IRA Advantage." *Heritage Foundation Backgrounder*, 24 August.

Gerring, John. 1998. *Party Ideologies in America, 1828–1996*. Cambridge: Cambridge University Press.

Gillman, Howard. 2004. "Courts and Regime Politics: A New Institutionalist Typology." Paper presented at the annual meeting of the American Political Science Association, Chicago, September.

Gilmour, John. 1995. *Strategic Disagreement: Stalemate in American Politics*. Pittsburgh: University of Pittsburgh Press.

Gingrich, Newt. 1983. "Battle Plan for Business in Politics: Stand Firm." *Nation's Business*, April, 30–32.

Ginsberg, Benjamin, and Martin Shefter. 2002. *Politics by Other Means: Politicians, Prosecutors, and the Press from Watergate to Whitewater*. 3rd ed. New York: W. W. Norton.

Gitterman, Daniel P., and Christopher Howard. 2003. "Tax Credits for Working Families: The New American Social Policy." Discussion paper. Washington, D.C.: Brookings Institution Center on Urban and Metropolitan Policy.

Glaeser, Edward L., and Jesse M. Shapiro. 2002. "The Benefits of Home Mortgage Interest Deduction." NBER Working Paper no. 9284 (October). http://papers.nber.org/papers/w9284.

Godwin, R. Kenneth. 1992. "Money, Technology, and Political Interests: The Direct Marketing of Politics." In *The Politics of Interests: Interest Groups Transformed*, ed. Mark P. Petracca, 308–25. Boulder, Colo: Westview Press.

Godwin, R. Kenneth, and Robert Cameron Mitchell. 1984. "The Implications of Direct Mail for Political Organizations." *Social Science Quarterly* 65 (3): 829–39.

Goldin, Claudia. 1999. "Egalitarianism and the Returns to Education during the Great Transformation of American Education." *Journal of Political Economy* 107: S65–S92.

Goldin, Claudia, and Robert A. Margo. 1992. "The Great Compression: The Wage Structure in the United States at Mid-century." *Quarterly Journal of Economics* 107 (February): 1–34.

Gottschalk, Peter. 1997. "Inequality, Income Growth, and Mobility: The Basic Facts." *Journal of Economic Perspectives* 11 (2): 21–40.

Gould, Lewis. 2003. *Grand Old Party: A History of the Republicans.* New York: Random House.

Gourevitch, Philip. 2004. "The Fight on the Right." *New Yorker,* 12 April.

Granberg, Donald, and Donald Denny. 1981. "The National Abortion Rights Action League and the National Right to Life Committee: Initial Report of Comparisons of Two Opposing Social Movement Organizations." Unpublished manuscript, Center for Research in Social Behavior, University of Missouri—Columbia.

Green, Donald, Bradley Palmquist, and Eric Schickler. 2002. *Partisan Hearts and Minds: Political Parties and the Social Identities of Voters.* New Haven, Conn.: Yale University Press.

Green, John C. 1996. "The Republican Victories in 1994: A View from the Grassroots." In *The State of the Parties: The Changing Role of Contemporary American Parties,* ed. John C. Green and Daniel M. Shea, 140–48. 2nd ed. Lanham, Md.: Rowman and Littlefield.

Greve, Michael. 1987. "Why 'Defunding the Left' Failed." *Public Interest* 89: 88–96.

Groseclose, Timothy, and Nolan McCarty. 2000. "The Politics of Blame: Bargaining before an Audience." *American Journal of Political Science* 45 (1): 100–119.

Guth, James L., John C. Green, Lyman A. Kellstedt, and Corwin E. Smidt. 1995. "Onward Christian Soldiers: Religious Activist Groups in American Politics." In *Interest Group Politics,* ed. Allan J. Cigler and Burdett A. Loomis, 55–76. 4th ed. Washington, D.C.: Congressional Quarterly Press.

Hacker, Jacob S. 1998. "The Historical Logic of National Health Insurance: Structure and Sequence in the Development of British, Canadian, and U.S. Medical Policy." *Studies in American Political Development* 12: 57–130.

———. 2002. *The Divided American Welfare State: The Battle over Public and Private Social Benefits in the United States.* New York: Cambridge University Press.

———. 2004. "Privatizing Risk without Privatizing the Welfare State: The Hidden Politics of Social Policy Retrenchment in the United States." *American Political Science Review* 98 (2): 243–60.

———. 2006. *The Great Risk Shift: The Assault on American Jobs, Families, Health Care and Retirement—and How You Can Fight Back.* New York: Oxford University Press.

Hacker, Jacob S., Suzanne Mettler, and Dianne Pinderhughes. 2005. "Inequality and Public Policy." In *Inequality and American Democracy: What We Know and What We Need to Learn,* ed. Lawrence R. Jacobs and Theda Skocpol, 156–213. New York: Russell Sage.

Hacker, Jacob S., and Paul Pierson. 2003. "Abandoning the Middle: The Revealing Case of the Bush Tax Cuts." Paper presented at annual meeting of the American Political Science Association, Philadelphia, 28–31 August.

———. 2005a. "Abandoning the Middle: The Bush Tax Cuts and the Limits of Democratic Control." *Perspectives in Politics* 3 (1): 33–53.

———. 2005b. *Off-Center: The Republican Revolution and the Erosion of American Democracy.* New Haven, Conn.: Yale University Press.

Hansen, John Mark. 1991. *Gaining Access: Congress and the Farm Lobby, 1919–1981*. Chicago: University of Chicago Press.

Hausknecht, Murray. 1962. *The Joiners: A Sociological Description of Voluntary Association Membership in the United States*. New York: Bedminster Press.

Hayes, Michael T. 1986. "The New Group Universe." In *Interest Group Politics*, ed. Allan J. Cigler and Burdett A. Loomis, 133–45. 2nd ed. Washington, D.C.: Congressional Quarterly Press.

Hayward, Steven F. 2001. *The Age of Reagan: The Fall of the Old Liberal Order, 1964–1980*. Roseville, Calif.: Forum.

Heckman, James, and James Snyder. 1997. "Linear Probability Models of the Demand for Attributes with an Empirical Application to Estimating the Preferences of Legislators." *Rand Journal of Economics* 28: S142–89.

Heclo, Hugh. 1978. "Issue Networks and the Executive Establishment." In *The New American Political System*, ed. Anthony King, 87–124. Washington, D.C.: American Enterprise Institute.

Herrnson, Paul S. 2002. "National Party Organizations at the Dawn of the Twenty-First Century." In *The Parties Respond: Changes in American Parties and Campaigns*, ed. L. Sandy Maisel, 47–78. 4th ed. Boulder, Colo.: Westview Press.

Hibbing, John, and Elizabeth Theiss-Morse. 1995. *Congress as Public Enemy: Public Attitudes toward American Political Institutions*. Cambridge: Cambridge University Press.

Hicks, Alexander. 2003. "Back to the Future? A Review Essay on Income Concentration and Conservatism." *Socio-Economic Review* 1: 271–88.

Hinckley, Barbara. 1971. *The Seniority System in Congress*. Bloomington: Indiana University Press.

Hodgson, Godfrey. 1996. *The World Turned Right Side Up: A History of the Conservative Ascendancy in America*. Boston: Houghton Mifflin.

———. 2004. *More Equal Than Others: America from Nixon to the New Century*. Princeton, N.J.: Princeton University Press.

Horowitz, Michael. 1979. "The Public Interest Law Movement: An Analysis with Special Reference to the Role and Practices of Conservative Public Interest Law Firms." Prepared for the Scaife Foundation, Washington, D.C.

Houck, Oliver. 1984. "With Charity for All," *Yale Law Journal* 93 (8): 1415–1563.

Howard, Christopher. 1997. *The Hidden Welfare State: Tax Expenditures and Social Policy in the United States*. Princeton Studies in American Politics. Princeton, N.J.: Princeton University Press.

———. 2003. "Is the American Welfare State Unusually Small?" *PS: Political Science and Politics* 36 (3): 411–16.

Howell, William. 2003. *Power without Persuasion: The Politics of Direct Presidential Action*. Princeton, N.J.: Princeton University Press.

Howell, William, Scott Adler, Charles Cameron, and Charles Riemann. 2000. "Divided Government and the Legislative Productivity of Congress, 1945–1994." *Legislative Studies Quarterly* 25 (2): 285–312.

Huber, Evelyn, and John Stephens. 2001. *Development and Crisis of the Welfare State*. Chicago: University of Chicago Press.

Huckfeldt, Robert, and John Sprague. 1992. "Political Parties and Electoral Mobilization: Political Structure, Social Structure, and the Party Canvass." *American Political Science Review* 86: 70–86.

Hughes, John E., and M. Margaret Conway. 1997. "Public Opinion and Political Participation" In *Understanding Public Opinion*, ed. Barbara Norrander and Clyde Wilcox, 191–210. Washington, D.C.: Congressional Quarterly Press.

Imig, Douglas R. 1996. *Poverty and Power: The Political Representation of Poor Americans*. Lincoln: University of Nebraska Press.

Inglehart, Ronald. 1990. *Culture Shift in Advanced Industrialized Societies*. Princeton, N.J.: Princeton University Press.

Jacobs, Lawrence R., and Robert Shapiro. 2000. *Politicians Don't Pander: Political Manipulation and the Loss of Democratic Responsiveness*. Chicago: University of Chicago Press.

Janofsky, Michael. 2004. "Advocacy Groups Spent Record Amount on 2004 Election." *New York Times*, 17 December, A25.

Jenkins, J. Craig. 1998. "Channeling Social Protest: Foundation Patronage of Contemporary Social Movements." In *Private Action and the Public Good*, ed. Walter W. Powell and Elisabeth S. Clemens, 206–16. New Haven, Conn.: Yale University Press.

Jenkins, J. Craig, and Abigail Halcli. 1999. "Grassrooting the System? The Development and Impact of Social Movement Philanthropy, 1953–1990." In *Philanthropic Foundations: New Scholarship, New Possibilities*, ed. Ellen Condliffe Lagemann, 277–99. Bloomington: Indiana University Press.

Jennings, M. Kent, and Richard G. Niemi. 1981. *Generations and Politics: A Panel Study of Young Americans and Their Parents*. Princeton, N.J.: Princeton University Press.

Johnson, Paul E. 1998. "Interest Group Recruiting: Finding Members and Keeping Them." In *Interest Group Politics*, ed. Allan J. Cigler and Burdett A. Loomis, 35–62. 5th ed. Washington, D.C.: Congressional Quarterly Press.

Joint Committee on Taxation. 2002. *Estimates of Federal Tax Expenditures for Fiscal Years 2002–2006*. Washington, D.C.: U.S. Government Printing Office.

Jones, Charles O. 1999. *Clinton and Congress, 1993–1996: Risk, Restoration, and Reelection*. Norman: University of Oklahoma Press.

Jordan, Grant, and William Maloney. 1997. *The Protest Business? Mobilizing Campaign Groups*. Manchester: Manchester University Press.

Kagan, Robert A. 2001. *Adversarial Legalism: The American Way of Law*. Cambridge, Mass.: Harvard University Press.

Katznelson, Ira, Kim Geiger, and Daniel Kryder. 1993. "Limiting Liberalism: The Southern Veto in Congress, 1933–1950." *Political Science Quarterly* 108 (June): 283–302.

Kaufmann, Karen M., and John R. Petrocik. 1999. "The Changing Politics of American Men: Understanding the Sources of the Gender Gap." *American Journal of Political Science* 43: 864–87.

Kennedy, Duncan. 1981. "Rebels from Principle: Changing the Corporate Law Firm from Within." *Harvard Law School Bulletin* 36 (Fall): 36–40.

Key, V. O., Jr. 1949. *Southern Politics in State and Nation*. New York: Knopf.

———. 1955. "A Theory of Critical Elections." *Journal of Politics* 17: 3–18.

———. 1964. *Politics, Parties and Pressure Groups*. New York: Crowell.

Kiger, Joseph C. 2000. *Philanthropic Foundations in the Twentieth Century*. Westport, Conn.: Greenwood Press.

Kinder, Donald R., and Lynn M. Sanders. 1996. *Divided by Color*. Chicago: University of Chicago Press.

King, David C. 2003. "Congress, Polarization, and the Fidelity to the Median Voter." Unpublished manuscript, Harvard University.

King, Jacqueline E. 2000. *2000 Status Report on the Pell Grant Program*. Washington, D.C.: American Council on Education.

Kitch, Edmund. 1983. "The Fire of Truth: A Remembrance of Law and Economics at Chicago, 1932–1970." *Journal of Law and Economics* 26: 163–233.

Klein, Rick. 2005. "House GOP Seen Straying from Pledges in 'Contract.'" *Boston Globe*, 10 January.

Klinkner, Philip A. 1994. *The Losing Parties: Out-Party National Committees, 1956–1994*. New Haven, Conn.: Yale University Press.

———. 2004. "Money Matters." *New Republic Online*. 10 November. http://www.tnr.com/doc.mhtml?pt=uaFGC74E%2FqSak8UrjSFNlR%3D%3D.

Kogan, Richard, and David Kamin. 2004. "New Congressional Budget Office Estimates Show Continued High Deficits and Further Fiscal Deterioration." Washington, D.C.: Center for Budget and Policy Priorities.

Krehbiel, Keith. 1998. *Pivotal Politics: A Theory of U.S. Lawmaking*. Chicago: University of Chicago Press.

Kristol, Irving. 1980. "The Battle for Reagan's Soul." *Wall Street Journal*, 16 May, A22.

Krugman, Paul. 2002. "For Richer." *New York Times Magazine*, 20 October.

Lakoff, George. 2002. *Moral Politics: How Liberals and Conservatives Think*. 2nd ed. Chicago: University of Chicago Press.

Lamb, Brian. 1998. *C-SPAN: America's Town Hall*. Washington, D.C.: Acropolis Books.

Lane, Robert E. 1965. "The Politics of Consensus in an Age of Affluence." *American Political Science Review* 59 (4): 874–95.

Lange, Mathew, and Deitrich Reuschemeyer, eds. 2005. *States and Development: Historical Antecedents of Stagnation and Advance*. London: Palgrave/Macmillan.

Lawless, Jennifer L., and Richard L. Fox. 2001. "Political Participation of the Urban Poor." *Social Problems* 48 (3): 362–85.

Lawrence, Robert Z. 1997. "Is It Really the Economy, Stupid?" *Why People Don't Trust Government*, ed. Joseph S. Nye Jr., Philip D. Zelikow, and David C. King, 111–32. Cambridge, Mass.: Harvard University Press.

Layman, Geoffrey. 2001. *The Great Divide: Religious and Cultural Conflict in American Party Politics*. New York: Columbia University Press.

Lee, Andrew, and Robert Greenstein. 2003. "How the New Tax Law Alters the Child Tax Credit and How Low-Income Families Are Affected." Center on Budget and Policy Priorities, Washington, D.C.

Leighley, Jan E., and Jonathan Nagler. 1992. "Socioeconomic Class Bias in Turnout, 1964–1988: The Voters Remain the Same." *American Political Science Review* 86 (3): 725–36.

Leuchtenburg, William E. 1973. *A Troubled Feast: American Society since 1945.* Boston: Little, Brown.

Levy, Frank. 1998. *The New Dollars and Dreams: American Incomes and Economic Change.* New York: Russell Sage Foundation.

Lewis, David E. 2003. *Presidents and the Politics of Agency Design.* Stanford, Calif.: Stanford University Press.

Loomis, Burdett A., and Allan J. Cigler. 1998. "Introduction: The Changing Nature of Interest Group Politics." In *Interest Group Politics,* ed. Allan J. Cigler and Burdett A. Loomis, 1–32. 5th ed. Washington, D.C.: Congressional Quarterly Press.

Lowi, Theodore J. 1964. "American Business, Public Policy, Case Studies, and Political Theory." *World Politics* 16: 677–715.

———. 1979. *The End of Liberalism.* 2nd ed. New York: W. W. Norton.

Maag, Elaine. 2003. "Recent Expansions to the Child and Dependent Care Tax Credit." *Tax Notes,* 27 October, 539. Tax Policy Center, Urban Institute and Brookings Institution.

Majone, Giandomenico. 1997. "From the Positive to the Regulatory State: Causes and Consequences of a Change in the Mode of Governance." *Journal of Public Policy* 17 (2): 139–67.

Mann, Thomas E., and Norman J. Ornstein. 2006. *The Broken Branch: How Congress Is Failing America and How to Get It Back on Track.* New York: Oxford University Press.

Mare, Robert D. 1995. "Changes in Educational Attainment and School Enrollment." In *State of the Union: America in the 1990s,* vol. 1, *Economic Trends,* ed. Reynolds Farle, 155–213. New York: Russell Sage Foundation.

Martin, Cathie Jo. 2000. *Stuck in Neutral: Business and the Politics of Human Capital Investment Policy.* Princeton, N.J.: Princeton University Press.

Marwell, Gerald, and Pamela Oliver. 1993. *The Critical Mass in Collective Action: A Micro-Social Theory.* Cambridge: Cambridge University Press.

Matthews, Donald R. 1960. *U.S. Senators and Their World.* Chapel Hill: University of North Carolina Press.

Maxwell Poll. 2005. Campbell Institute of Public Affairs, Maxwell School of Citizenship and Public Affairs, Syracuse University, Syracuse, N.Y. http://www.maxwell.syr.edu/campbell/Poll/MaxwellPoll.htm.

Mayer, William G. 1996. *The Divided Democrats: Ideological Unity, Party Reform, and Presidential Elections.* Boulder, Colo.: Westview Press.

Mayhew, David R. 1986. *Placing Parties in American Politics: Organization, Electoral Settings, and Government Activity in the Twentieth Century.* Princeton, N.J.: Princeton University Press.

———. 1991. *Divided We Govern: Party Control, Lawmaking, and Investigations, 1946–1990.* New Haven, Conn.: Yale University Press.

———. 2002. *Electoral Realignments: A Critique of an American Genre.* New Haven, Conn.: Yale University Press.

McAdam, Doug. 1982. *Political Process and the Development of Black Insurgency, 1930–1970.* Chicago: University of Chicago Press.

McCann, Michael. 1987. *Taking Reform Seriously: Perspectives on Public Interest Liberalism.* Ithaca, N.Y.: Cornell University Press.

McCarthy, John D. 1987. "Pro-Life and Pro-Choice Mobilization: Infrastructure Deficits and New Technologies." In *Social Movements in an Organizational Society: Collected Essays,* ed. Mayer N. Zald and John D. McCarthy, 49–67. New Brunswick, N.J.: Transaction Books.

McCarty, Nolan, Keith Poole, and Howard Rosenthal. 1997. *Income Redistribution and the Realignment of American Politics.* Washington, D.C.: American Enterprise Institute.

———. 2006. *Polarized America: The Dance of Political Ideology and Economic Inequality.* Cambridge, Mass.: MIT Press.

McCarty, Nolan, and Rose Razaghian. 1999. "Advice and Consent: Senate Response to Executive Branch Nominations, 1885–1996." *American Journal of Political Science* 43 (3): 1122–43.

McDonald, Michael P., and Bernard Grofman. 1999. "Redistricting and the Ideological Polarization of the House of Representatives." Paper presented at the annual meeting of the Midwest Political Science Association, Chicago, April.

McDonald, Michael P., and Samuel I. Popkin. 2001. "The Myth of the Vanishing Voter." *American Political Science Review* 95 (4): 963–74.

McFarland, Andrew S. 1984. *Common Cause: Lobbying in the Public Interest.* Chatham, N.J.: Chatham House.

McGir, Lisa. 2001. *Suburban Warriors: The Origins of the New American Right.* Princeton, N.J.: Princeton University Press.

McKinnon, John D. 2005. "Big Government's Changing Face." *Wall Street Journal,* 4 April, A4.

Mebane, Walter R., and Jasjeet S. Sekhon. 2002. "Coordination and Policy Moderation at Midterm." *American Political Science Review* 96 (1): 141–57.

Meffert, Michael F., Helmut Norpoth, and Anirudh V. S. Ruhil. 2001. "Realignment and Macropartisanship." *American Political Science Review* 95: 953–62.

Melnick, R. Shep. 1983. *Regulation and the Courts.* Washington, D.C.: Brookings Institution Press.

———. 1994. *Between the Lines: Interpreting Welfare Rights.* Washington, D.C.: Brookings Institution Press.

———. 2005. "From Tax-and-Spend to Mandate-and-Sue: Liberalism after the Great Society." In *The Great Society and the High Tide of Liberalism,* ed. Sidney M. Milkis, 387–410. Amherst: University of Massachusetts Press.

Meltzer, Allan H., and Scott F. Richard. 1981. "A Rational Theory of the Size of Government." *Journal of Political Economy* 89: 914–27.

Mettler, Suzanne. 1998. *Dividing Citizens: Gender and Federalism in New Deal Public Policy.* Ithaca, N.Y.: Cornell University Press.

———. 2000. "States' Rights, Women's Obligations: Contemporary Welfare Reform in Historical Perspective." *Women & Politics* 21 (1): 1–34.

———. 2002. "Bringing the State Back In to Civic Engagement: Policy Feedback Effects of the G.I. Bill for World War II Veterans." *American Political Science Review* 96: 351–65.

———. 2005. *Soldiers to Citizens: The G.I. Bill and the Making of the Greatest Generation.* New York: Oxford University Press.

Mettler, Suzanne, and Andrew Milstein. 2003. "'A Sense of the State': Tracking the Role of the American Administrative State in Citizens' Lives over Time."

Paper presented at the annual meeting of the Midwest Political Science Association, Chicago, 3–6 April.

Mettler, Suzanne, and Joe Soss. 2004. "The Consequences of Public Policy for Democratic Citizenship: Bridging Policy Studies and Mass Politics." *Perspectives on Politics* 2 (1): 55–73.

Mettler, Suzanne, and Eric Welch. 2004. "Civic Generation: Policy Feedback Effects of the GI Bill on Political Involvement over the Life Course." *British Journal of Political Science* 34 (March): 647–67.

Milkis, Sidney. 1993. *The President and the Parties.* Oxford: Oxford University Press.

Miller, Warren, and J. Merrill Shanks. 1996. *The New American Voter.* Cambridge, Mass.: Harvard University Press.

Milligan, Susan. 2004. "Back-Room Dealing a Capitol Trend." *Boston Globe,* 3 October.

Minkoff, Debra C. 1995. *Organizing for Equality: The Evolution of Women's and Racial-Ethnic Organizations in America, 1955–1985.* New Brunswick, N.J.: Rutgers University Press.

Miringoff, Marc, and Marque-Luisa Miringoff. 1999. *The Social Health of the Nation: How America Is Really Doing.* New York: Oxford University Press.

Mishel, Lawrence, Jared Bernstein, and Heather Boushey. 2003. *The State of Working America 2002/2003.* Ithaca, N.Y.: ILR Press, an imprint of Cornell University Press.

Mitchell, Robert C., John D. McCarthy, and K. Pearce. 1979. "The National Abortion Rights Action League: Report on a Membership Survey." Unpublished report, Washington, D.C.

Moe, Terry M. 1980. *The Organization of Interests: Incentives and the Internal Dynamics of Political Interest Groups.* Chicago: University of Chicago Press.

———. 1987. "Interests, Institutions, and Positive Theory: The Politics of the NLRB." *Studies in American Political Development* 2: 236–302.

Morris, Aldon D. 1984. *The Origins of the Civil Rights Movement: Black Communities Organizing for Change.* New York: Free Press.

Nagourney, Adam, and Janet Elder. 2004. "Americans Show Clear Concerns on Bush Agenda." *New York Times,* 23 November, A1.

Nash, George H. 1976. *The Conservative Intellectual Movement in America since 1945.* New York: Basic Books.

Nathan, Richard P. 1983. "The Reagan Presidency in Domestic Affairs." In *The Reagan Presidency: An Early Assessment,* ed. Fred I. Greenstein, 48–81. Baltimore: Johns Hopkins University Press.

National Center for Education Statistics. 2001. *Digest of Education Statistics, 2000.* Washington, D.C.: U.S. Government Printing Office. nces.ed.gov/pubs2001/digest/. Accessed March 2003.

National Journal. 2003. "Representative Tom Delay." 14 July.

———. 2001. "The Mean Season at Ways and Means." 20 October.

Newlin, Eliza. 2002. "Right on the Money?" *National Journal,* 26 October.

Olin Foundation. 1984a. Minutes, John M. Olin Board of Trustees Meeting. 22 May.

———. 1984b. Minutes, John M. Olin Board of Trustees Meeting. 31 May.

————. 1993. John M. Olin Foundation Grant Proposal Record. George Mason University Law and Economics Center, 21 December. Document in possession of Steven M. Teles.

————. 1996. Grant Proposal Record. Boalt Hall School of Law. 23 September.

O'Neill, Thomas P., and Novak, William. 1987. *Man of the House: The Life and Political Memoirs of Speaker Tip O'Neill*. New York: Random House.

Ornstein, Norman J., Thomas E. Mann, and Michael J. Malbin. 2000. *Vital Statistics on Congress, 1999–2000*. Washington, D.C.: AEI Press.

Orren, Gary. 1997. "Fall from Grace: The Public's Loss of Faith in Government." In *Why People Don't Trust Government*, ed. Joseph S. Nye Jr., Philip D. Zelikow, and David C. King, 77–107. Cambridge, Mass.: Harvard University Press.

Orszag, Peter R. 2001. *The Bush Tax Cut Is Now about the Same Size as the Reagan Tax Cuts*. Washington D.C.: Center on Budget and Policy Priorities.

Oudes, Bruce, ed. 1989. *From the President: Richard Nixon's Secret Files*. New York: Harper and Row.

Paget, Karen. 1990. "Citizen Organizing: Many Movements, No Majority." *American Prospect*, no. 1 (June): 115–28.

Patashnik, Eric. 2000. *Putting Trust in the U.S. Budget*. Cambridge: Cambridge University Press.

Patterson, James. 1967. *Congressional Conservatism and the New Deal: The Growth of the Conservative Coalition in Congress, 1933–1939*. Lexington: University of Kentucky Press.

Patterson, Kelly. 1998. "The Political Firepower of the National Rifle Association." In *Interest Group Politics*, ed. Allan J. Cigler and Burdett A. Loomis, 119–44. 5th ed. Washington, D.C.: Congressional Quarterly Press.

Patterson, Thomas E. 1994. *Out of Order*. New York: Vintage.

Perlstein, Rick. 2001. *Before the Storm: Barry Goldwater and the Unmaking of the American Consensus*. New York: Hill and Wang.

Petersen, R. Eric. 2001. "Is It Science Yet? Replicating and Validating the *Divided We Govern* List of Important Statutes." Paper presented at the annual meeting of the Midwest Political Science Association, Chicago, April.

Peterson, Mark A. 1993. "Political Influence in the 1990s: From Iron Triangles to Policy Networks." *Journal of Health Politics, Policy and Law* 18 (2): 395–438.

Peterson, Paul E. 1995. *The Price of Federalism*. Washington, D.C.: Brookings Institution Press.

Peterson, Paul E., and Mark Rom. 1988. "Lower Taxes, More Spending, Budget Deficits." In *The Reagan Legacy: Promise and Performance*, ed. Charles E. Jones, 213–40. Chatham, N.J.: Chatham House.

Peterson, Peter. 1993. *Facing Up*. New York: Simon and Schuster.

Petrocik, John R. 1996. "Issue Ownership in Presidential Elections, with a 1980 Case Study." *American Journal of Political Science* 40: 825–50.

Petrocik, John R., William L. Benoit, and Glenn J. Hansen. 2003–4. "Issue Ownership and Presidential Campaigning, 1952–2000." *Political Science Quarterly* 118: 599–626.

Phillips, Katherin Ross. 2001. "The Earned Income Tax Credit: Knowledge Is Money." *Political Science Quarterly* 116 (3): 413–24.

Phillips, Kevin. 1969. *The Emerging Republican Majority.* Garden City, N.J.: Arlington House.

Pierson, Paul. 1993. "When Effect Becomes Cause: Policy Feedback in Political Processes." *World Politics* 45 (4): 595–628.

———. 1994. *Dismantling the Welfare State? Reagan, Thatcher, and the Politics of Retrenchment.* New York: Cambridge.

———. 2001. "From Expansion to Authority: The New Politics of Taxing and Spending." In *Seeking the Center: Politics and Policymaking at the New Century,* ed. Martin A. Levin, Marc K. Landy, and Martin Shapiro, 54–80. Washington, D.C.: Georgetown University Press.

———. 2004. *Politics in Time: History, Institutions, and Social Analysis.* Princeton, N.J.: Princeton University Press.

———. 2006. "Public Policies as Institutions." In *Rethinking Political Institutions: The Art of the State,* ed. Ian Shapiro, Stephen Skowronek, and Daniel Galvin, 114–31. New York: New York University Press.

Pierson, Paul, and Theda Skocpol. 2002. "Historical Institutionalism in Contemporary Political Science." In *Political Science: The State of the Discipline,* ed. Ira Katznelson and Helen V. Milner, 693–721. New York: W. W. Norton; Washington, D.C.: American Political Science Association.

Plotke, David. 1996. *Building a Democratic Political Order: Reshaping America Liberalism in the 1930s and 1940s.* New York: Cambridge University Press.

Plotnick, Robert D., Eugene Smolensky, Erik Evenhouse, and Siobhan Reilly. 2000. "The Twentieth Century Record of Inequality and Poverty in the United States." University of Wisconsin Institute for Research on Poverty, Discussion Paper no. 1166–98. http://www.ssc.wisc.edu/irp/dp/dplist.htm.

Polsby, Nelson W. 1983. *Consequences of Party Reform.* Oxford: Oxford University Press.

———. 2004. *How Congress Evolves: Social Basis of Institutional Change.* New York. Oxford University Press.

Polsby, Nelson W., Miriam Gallaher, and Barry Spencer Rundquist. 1969. "The Growth of the Seniority System in the U.S. House of Representatives." *American Political Science Review* 63 (September): 787–807.

Pratt, Henry J. 1976. *The Gray Lobby.* Chicago: University of Chicago Press.

———. 1993. *Gray Agendas: Interest Groups and Public Pensions in Canada, Britain, and the United States.* Ann Arbor: University of Michigan Press.

Prior, Markus. 2007. *Post-Broadcast Democracy: How Media Choice Increases Inequality in Political Involvement and Polarizes Elections.* New York: Cambridge University Press.

Public Opinion Online. 2004a. Roper Center at the University of Connecticut. Question IDs USGALLUP.00JN22, R11; USGALLUP.00JN22, R12.

———. 2004b. Roper Center at the University of Connecticut. Question ID USWASHP.96ECON, R007.

———. 2004c. Roper Center at the University of Connecticut. Question IDs USYANKP.022396, R25B; USYANKP.022396, R25C.

Putnam, Robert D. 2000. *Bowling Alone: The Collapse and Revival of American Community.* New York: Simon and Schuster.

Radcliff, Benjamin, and Patricia Davis. 2000. "Labor Organization and Electoral Participation in Industrial Democracies." *American Journal of Political Science* 44 (1): 132–41.

Rae, Douglas W. 2003. *City: Urbanism and Its End*. New Haven, Conn.: Yale University Press.

Rank, Mark R., and Thomas A. Hirschl. 2002. "Welfare Use as a Life Course Event: Toward a New Understanding of the U.S. Safety Net." *Social Work* 47 (3): 237–48.

Ranney, Austin. 1975. *Curing the Mischiefs of Faction*. Berkeley: University of California Press.

Rauch, Jonathan. 1999, *Government's End*. New York: Public Affairs.

Reagan, Ronald. 1980a. Speech outlining five-year economic program. Reprinted in *New York Times*, 10 September, B4.

———. 1980b. "Time to Recapture Our Destiny." Acceptance speech before the Republican National Convention, Detroit, Michigan. Annenberg/Pew Archive of Presidential Campaign Discourse (CD-ROM).

———. 1981. "Inaugural Address, January 20, 1981." Public Papers of President Ronald W. Reagan. Ronald Reagan Library. http://www.reagan.utexas.edu/resource/speeches/1981/12081a.htm.

Reichley, A. James. 1992. *The Life of the Parties*. New York: Free Press.

Reid, T. R. 1984. "'Minority Objector' Conscientiously Flays Foes with House Rules." *Washington Post*, 21 March.

Remini, Robert V. 2006. *The House: The History of the House of Representatives*. New York: Smithsonian and Collins.

Ricci, David M. 1993. *The Transformation of American Politics: The New Washington and the Rise of Think Tanks*. New Haven, Conn.: Yale University Press.

Rich, Andrew. 2004. *Think Tanks, Public Policy and the Politics of Expertise*. Cambridge: Cambridge University Press.

Rich, Andrew, and R. Kent Weaver. 1998. "Advocates and Analysts: Think Tanks and the Politicization of Expertise." In *Interest Group Politics*, ed. Allan J. Cigler and Burdett A. Loomis, 235–53. 5th ed. Washington, D.C.: Congressional Quarterly Press.

Rogers, David. 1984. "Assault from the Right." *Wall Street Journal*, 23 May.

Rohde, David W. 1991. *Parties and Leaders in the Postreform House*. Chicago: University of Chicago Press.

Romer, Thomas. 1975. "Individual Welfare, Majority Voting, and the Properties of a Linear Income Tax." *Journal of Public Economics* 14: 163–85.

Rosenbaum, David E. 2003. "Spending Discipline Proves Unfashionable This Year." *New York Times*, 25 November.

Rosenstone, Steven J., and John Mark Hansen. 1993. *Mobilization, Participation, and Democracy in America*. New York: Macmillan.

Rosenthal, Howard. 2004. "Political Polarization, Economic Inequality, and Public Policy: A Look Back at the Twentieth Century." In *Social Inequality*, ed. Kathryn Neckerman, 861–92. New York: Russell Sage Foundation.

Rothenberg, Lawrence S. 1992. *Linking Citizens to Government: Interest Group Politics at Common Cause*. Cambridge: Cambridge University Press.

Rudolph, Thomas J., and J. Tobin Grant. 2002. "An Attributional Model of Economic Voting: Evidence from the 2000 Presidential Election." *Political Research Quarterly* 55: 805–23.

Sammartino, Frank, Eric Toder, and Elaine Maag. 2002. "Providing Federal Assistance to Low-Income Families through the Tax System: A Primer." Discussion Paper no. 4. Washington, D.C.: Urban Institute.

Sanbonmatsu, Kira. 2002. *Democrats, Republicans, and the Politics of Women's Place*. Ann Arbor: University of Michigan Press.

Sapiro, Virginia. 2003. "Theorizing Gender in Political Psychology Research." In *Oxford Handbook of Political Psychology*, ed. David O. Sears, Leonie Huddy, and Robert Jervis, 601–34. New York: Oxford University Press.

Schattschneider, E. E. 1935. *Politics, Pressures, and the Tariff*. New York: Prentice-Hall.

Schickler, Eric. 2001. *Disjointed Pluralism: Institutional Innovation in the U.S. Congress*. Princeton, N.J.: Princeton University Press.

Schier, Steven E. 2000. *By Invitation Only: The Rise of Exclusive Politics in the United States*. Pittsburgh: University of Pittsburgh Press.

Schlesinger, Arthur M., Sr. 1944. "Biography of a Nation of Joiners." *American Historical Review* 50 (1): 1–25.

Scholz, John Karl, and Kara Levine. 2001. "The Evolution of Income Support Policy in Recent Decades." In *Understanding Poverty*, ed. Sheldon Danziger and Robert H. Haveman, 193–228. New York: Russell Sage.

Schlozman, Kay Lehman. 2004. "What Do We Want? Political Equality. When Are We Going to Get It? Never." Paper presented at seminar on Inequality and American Democracy. http://www.campbellinstitute.org.

Schlozman, Kay Lehman, Traci Burch, and Samuel Lampert. 2004. "Still an Upper-Class Accent?: Organized Interest Politics and Pluralist Orthodoxy." Paper presented at the annual meeting of the American Political Science Association, Chicago, 1–5 September.

Schmidt, Stefanie R. 2000. "Job Security Beliefs in the General Social Survey: Evidence on Long-Run Trends and Comparability with Other Surveys." In *On the Job: Is Long-Term Employment a Thing of the Past?*, ed. David Neumark, 300–334. New York: Russell Sage Foundation.

Schmidt, Susan, and James V. Grimaldi. 2005. "Abramoff Probe Spells Trouble for Congress." *Washington Post*, 29 December.

Schneiberg, Marc, and Elisabeth Clemens. 2006. "The Typical Tools for the Job: Research Strategies in Institutional Analysis." *Sociological Theory* 24: 195–227.

Schneider, Anne, and Helen Ingram. 1993. "Social Construction of Target Populations: Implications for Politics and Policy." *American Political Science Review* 87: 334–47.

———. 1997. *Policy Design for Democracy*. Lawrence: University Press of Kansas.

Schneider, William. 1989. "New Rules for the Game of Politics." *National Journal*, 1 April.

Schoenwald, Jonathan. 2001. *A Time for Choosing: The Rise of Modern Conservatism*. New York: Oxford University Press.

Sears, David O., and Jack Citrin. 1985. *Tax Revolt: Something for Nothing in California*. Cambridge, Mass.: Harvard University Press.

Shafer, Byron E., and William J. M. Claggett. 1995. *The Two Majorities: The Issue Context of Modern American Politics*. Baltimore: Johns Hopkins University Press.

Shafer, Byron R., and Richard G. C. Johnston. 2005. *The End of Southern Exceptionalism: Class, Race and Partisan Change in the Post-War South*. Cambridge, Mass.: Harvard University Press.

Shaiko, Ronald G. 1999. *Voices and Echoes for the Environment: Public Interest Representation in the 1990s and Beyond*. New York: Columbia University Press.

Shepsle, Kenneth A. 1989. "The Changing Textbook Congress." In *Can the Government Govern?*, ed. John E. Chubb and Paul E. Peterson, 228–66. Washington, D.C.: Brookings Institution Press.

Shields, Todd G., and Robert K. Goidel. 1997. "Participation Rates, Socioeconomic Class Biases, and Congressional Elections: A Cross Validation." *American Journal of Political Science* 41: 683–91.

Shribman, David, and David Rogers. 1985. "Relationship Is Tense between Republicans in House and Senate." *Wall Street Journal*, 1 May.

Silbey, Joel H. 2002. "From 'Essential to the Existence of Our Institutions' to 'Rapacious Enemies of Honest and Responsible Government': The Rise and Fall of American Political Parties, 1790–2000." In *The Parties Respond: Changes in American Parties and Campaigns*, ed. L. Sandy Maisel, 1–18. 4th ed. Boulder, Colo.: Westview Press.

Sinclair, Barbara. 1997. *Unorthodox Lawmaking: New Legislative Processes in the U.S. Congress*. Washington, D.C. Congressional Quarterly Press.

———. 1989. *The Transformation of the U.S. Senate*. Baltimore: Johns Hopkins University Press.

Skerry, Peter. 1997. "The Strange Politics of Affirmative Action." *Wilson Quarterly* 21 (1): 39–46.

Skocpol, Theda. 1991. "Targeting within Universalism: Politically Viable Policies to Combat Poverty in the United States." In *The Urban Underclass*, ed. Christopher Jencks and Paul E. Peterson, 411–36. Washington, D.C.: Brookings Institution Press.

———. 1992. *Protecting Soldiers and Mothers: The Political Origins of Social Policy in the United States*. Cambridge, Mass.: Belknap Press, Harvard University Press.

———. 1996. *Boomerang: Health Care Reform and the Turn against Government*. New York: W. W. Norton.

———. 1997. "The G.I. Bill and U.S. Social Policy, Past and Future." *Social Philosophy and Policy* 14 (2): 95–115.

———. 1999. "Advocates without Members: The Recent Transformation of American Civic Life." In *Civic Engagement in American Democracy*, ed. Theda Skocpol and Morris P. Fiorina, 461–509. Washington, D.C.: Brookings Institution Press; New York: Russell Sage Foundation.

———. 2000. *The Missing Middle: Working Families and the Future of American Social Policy*. A Century Foundation Book. New York: W. W. Norton.

Skocpol, Theda. 2003. *Diminished Democracy: From Membership to Management in American Civic Life.* Norman: University of Oklahoma Press.

Skocpol, Theda, Marshall Ganz, and Ziad Munson. 2000. "A Nation of Organizers: The Institutional Origins of Civic Voluntarism in the United States." *American Political Science Review* 94 (3): 527–46.

Skocpol, Theda, Ziad Munson, Andrew Karch, and Bayliss Camp. 2002. "Patriotic Partnerships: Why Great Wars Nourished American Civic Voluntarism." In *Shaped by War and Trade: International Influences on American Political Development,* ed. Ira Katznelson and Martin Shefter, 134–80. Princeton, N.J.: Princeton University Press.

Skowronek, Stephen. 1982. *Building a New American State: The Expansion of National Administrative Capacities, 1877–1920.* Cambridge: Cambridge University Press.

Skrentny, John D. 2002. *The Minority Rights Revolution.* Cambridge, Mass.: Belknap Press, Harvard University Press.

Smith, David Horton. 1992. "National Nonprofit, Voluntary Associations: Some Parameters." *Nonprofit and Voluntary Sector Quarterly* 21 (1): 81–94.

Smith, James A. 1991. *The Idea Brokers: Think Tanks and the Rise of the New Policy Elite.* New York: Free Press.

Smith, Mark A. 2007. *The Right Talk: How Conservatives Transformed the Great Society into the Economic Society.* Princeton: Princeton University Press.

Smith, Steven S. 1989. *Call to Order: Floor Politics in the House and Senate.* Washington, D.C.: Brookings Institution Press.

———. 1998. *Managing Uncertainty in the House of Representatives: Adaptation and Innovation in Special Rules.* Washington, D.C.: Brookings Institution Press.

Smith, Steven S., and Lawrence Eric. 1997. "Party Control of Committees." In *Congress Reconsidered,* ed. Lawrence C. Dodd and Bruce I. Oppenheimer, 163–92. 6th ed. Washington, D.C.: Congressional Quarterly Press.

Smith, Steven Rathgeb, and Michael Lipsky. 1993. *Nonprofits for Hire: The Welfare State in the Age of Contracting.* Cambridge, Mass.: Harvard University Press.

Social Security Administration. 2000. *Annual Statistical Supplement to the Social Security Bulletin.* Washington D.C., Social Security Board, U.S. Government Printing Office.

Solberg, Carol. 1973. *Riding High: America in the Cold War.* New York: Mason and Lipscomb.

Soss, Joe. 1999a. "Lessons of Welfare: Policy Design, Political Learning, and Political Action." *American Political Science Review* 93 (2): 363–80.

———. 1999b. "Spoiled Identity and Collective Action: Political Consequences of Welfare Stigma." Paper presented at annual meeting of the International Society for Political Psychology, Amsterdam, July.

———. 2000. *Unwanted Claims: The Politics of Participation in the U.S. Welfare System.* Ann Arbor: University of Michigan Press.

Spiller, Pablo, and Raphael Gely. 1992. "Congressional Control or Judicial Independence: The Determinants of US Supreme Court Labor-Relations Decisions, 1949–1988." *Rand Journal of Economics* 23 (4): 463–92.

Stephanopoulos, George. 1999. *All Too Human: A Political Education.* Boston: Little, Brown.

Steurle, C. Eugene, and Masahiro Kawai, eds. 1996. *The New World Fiscal Order.* Washington, D.C.: Urban Institute Press.

Stinchcombe, Arthur. 1965. "Social Structure and Organizations." In *Handbook of Organizations*, ed. James G. March, 142–92. Chicago: Rand McNally.

Stone, Deborah. 1984. *The Disabled State.* Philadelphia: Temple University Press.

Stonecash, Jeffrey M. 2000. *Class and Party in American Politics.* Boulder, Colo.: Westview Press.

Stonecash, Jeffrey M., Mark D. Brewer, and Mack D. Mariani. 2003. *Diverging Parties: Social Change, Realignment, and Political Polarization.* Boulder, Colo.: Westview Press.

Sullivan, Teresa A., Elizabeth Warren, and Jay Lawrence Westbrook. 2000. *The Fragile Middle Class: Americans in Debt.* New Haven, Conn.: Yale University Press.

Sundquist, James L. 1983. *Dynamics of the Party System: Alignment and Realignment of Political Parties in the United States.* Washington, D.C.: Brookings Institution Press.

Talbert, Jeffrey C., and Matthew Potoski. 2002. "The Changing Public Agenda over the Postwar Period." In *Policy Domains*, ed. Frank R. Baumgartner and Bryan D. Jones, 189–204. Chicago: University of Chicago Press.

Teles, Steven M. 1996. *Whose Welfare? AFDC and Elite Politics.* Lawrence: University Press of Kansas.

———. Forthcoming. *Parallel Paths: The Evolution of the Conservative Legal Movement.* Princeton, N.J.: Princeton University Press.

Teles, Steven, and Martha Derthick. Forthcoming. "From Third Rail to Presidential Commitment—and Back? The Conservative Campaign for Social Security Privatization and the Limits of Long-Term Political Strategy." In *Conservatism and American Political Development*, ed. Brian Glenn and Steven Teles.

Theriault, Sean. 2004. Party Polarization in Congress: Member Replacement or Member Adaptation? Unpublished manuscript, Austin, Tex.

Third Millennium. 1994. "Social Security: The Credibility Gap." http://www.thirdmil.org/media/releases/ufopol.html.

Thomas, Evan. 1984. "Struggling for a Party's Soul: G.O.P. Factions Jockey for 1988, and Beyond." *Time*, 3 September, 34–37.

Thurber, James A. "Centralization, Devolution, and Turf Protection in the Congressional Budget Process." In *Congress Reconsidered*, ed. Lawrence C. Dodd and Bruce I. Oppenheimer, 325–46. 6th ed. Washington, D.C. Congressional Quarterly Press.

Time. 1988. "The Speaker on the Spot." 20 June, 31.

Tocqueville, Alexis de. 1969 [1835–40]. *Democracy in America.* Ed. J. P. Mayer, trans. George Lawrence. Garden City, N.Y.: Doubleday, Anchor Books.

Toder, Eric. 1999. "The Changing Composition of Tax Incentives, 1980–99." Urban Institute. http://www.urban.org/urlprint.cfm?ID=7429.

Toobin, Jeffrey. 2003. "The Great Election Grab." *New Yorker*, 12 December.

Trillin, Calvin. 1984. "Harvard Law." *New Yorker*, 26 March, 53–83.

Uggen, Christopher, and Jeff Manza. 2001. "Democratic Contraction: The Political Consequences of Felon Disenfranchisement Laws in the United States." *American Sociological Review* 67 (December): 777–803.

Urban Institute. 2002. *Social Policy and the Tax System*. Washington, D.C.: Urban Institute.

———. 2005. *Welfare Rules Database*. http://www.urban.org/Content/Research/NewFederalism/Data?ANFData.htm.

U.S. Bureau of the Census. 2001. *Statistical Abstract of the United States*. Washington, D.C.: U.S. Government Printing Office.

U.S. News and World Report. 1984. "Choosing Up Sides for Control of the GOP." 3 September, 23.

Van Houweling, Robert. 2003. "Legislator's Personal Policy Preferences and Partisan Legislative Organization," Unpublished manuscript, Harvard University.

Van Tassel, David D., and Jimmy Elaine Wilkinson Meyer, eds. 1992. *U.S. Aging Policy Interest Groups: Institutional Profiles*. Westport, Conn.: Greenwood Press.

Verba, Sidney, and Norman H. Nie. 1972. *Participation in America: Political Democracy and Social Equality*. New York: Harper and Row.

Verba, Sidney, Kay Lehman Schlozman, and Henry Brady. 1995. *Voice and Equality: Civic Voluntarism in American Politics*. Cambridge, Mass.: Harvard University Press.

———. 1997. "The Big Tilt: Participatory Inequality in America." *American Prospect* 32 (May–June): 74–80.

Viguerie, Richard A. 1981. *The New Right—We're Ready to Lead*. Falls Church, Va.: Viguerie Company.

Vogel, David. 1989. *Fluctuating Fortunes: The Political Power of Business in America*. New York: Basic Books.

———. 2003. "The Hare and the Tortoise Revisited: The New Politics of Consumer and Environmental Regulation in Europe." *British Journal of Political Science* 33 (4): 557–80.

Wall Street Journal. 2003. "The GOP'S Spending Spree." 25 November.

Walls, David. 1993. *The Activist's Almanac: The Concerned Citizen's Guide to the Leading Advocacy Organizations in America*. New York: Fireside.

Walker, Jack L., Jr. 1991. *Mobilizing Interest Groups in America: Patrons, Professions, and Social Movements*. Ann Arbor: University of Michigan Press.

Warren, Elizabeth, and Amelia Warren Tyagi. 2003. *The Two-Income Trap: Why Middle Class Mothers and Fathers Are Going Broke*. New York: Basic Books.

Wattenberg, Martin P. 1998. *The Decline of American Political Parties, 1952–1996*. Cambridge: Harvard University Press.

———. 2002. *Where Have All the Voters Gone?* Cambridge, Mass.: Harvard University Press.

Weaver, Carolyn. 1983. "The Economics and Politics of the Emergence of Social Security: Some Implications for Reform," *CATO Journal*, Fall, 361–79.

Weaver, Kent. 2000. *Ending Welfare as We Know It*. Washington, D.C.: Brookings Institution Press.

Weaver, Paul. 1988. *The Suicidal Corporation*. New York: Simon and Schuster.

White, Joseph, and Aaron Wildavsky. 1989. *The Deficit and the Public Interest: The Search for Responsible Budgeting in the 1980s*. Berkeley: University of California Press; New York: Russell Sage Foundation.

White House Office of the Press Secretary. 2001. "Remarks by the President and Secretary Rumsfeld in Announcement of Chariman and Vice-Chariman of the Joint Chiefs of Staff." 24 August. http://www.whitehouse.gov/news/releases/2001/08/20010824.html.

Wielhouwer, Peter W., and Brad Lockerbie. 1994. "Party Contacting and Political Participation, 1952–1990." *American Journal of Political Science* 48: 211–29.

Wilson, James Q. 1962. *The Amateur Democrat.* Chicago: University of Chicago Press.

Witcover, Jules. 2003. *Party of the People: A History of the Democrats.* New York: Random House.

Wolbrecht, Christina. 2000. *The Politics of Women's Rights: Parties, Positions, and Change.* Princeton, N.J.: Princeton University Press.

Wolfensberger, Donald R. 2000. *Congress and the People: Deliberative Democracy on Trial.* Baltimore: Johns Hopkins University Press.

Woodward, Bob. 1994. *The Agenda: Inside the Clinton White House.* New York: Simon and Schuster.

Wuthnow, Robert. 1998. *Loose Connections: Joining Together in America's Fragmented Communities.* Cambridge, Mass.: Harvard University Press.

———. 1999. "Mobilizing Civic Engagement: The Changing Impact of Religious Involvement." In *Civic Engagement in American Democracy,* ed. Theda Skocpol and Morris P. Fiorina, 331–63. Washington, D.C.: Brookings Institution Press; New York: Russell Sage Foundation.

Yalof, David. 1999. *Pursuit of Justices.* Chicago: University of Chicago Press.

Young, Louise M. 1989. *In the Public Interest: The League of Women Voters, 1920–1970.* Westport, Conn.: Greenwood Press.

Young, McGee. 2004. "Achieving Access: Groups, Processes, and American Political Development." Ph.D. diss., Syracuse University.

Zelinksy, Edward. Forthcoming. *The Origins of the Ownership Society: How the Defined Contribution Paradigm Changed America.*

Zelizer, Julian E. *On Capitol Hill: The Struggle to Reform Congress and Its Consequences, 1948–2000.* New York: Cambridge University Press.

INTERVIEWS

Stuart Butler. 1998, 2004. Heritage Foundation, Washington, D.C.

Steven Calabresi. 2002. Northwestern School of Law, Chicago.

Hillel Fradkin. 200, 2004. American Enterprise Institute, Washington, D.C.

Michael Greve. 2001, 2004. American Enterprise Institute, Washingont, D.C.

Chip Mellor. 2001. Institute for Justice, Washington, D.C.

Eugene Meyer. 2002. Federalist Society, Washington, D.C.

James Piereson. 2004. Federalist Society, New York.

INDEX

Princeton Studies in American Politics: Historical, International, and Comparative Perspectives

Ira Katznelson, Martin Shefter, and Theda Skocpol, eds.

The Transformation of American Politics: Activist Government and the Rise of Conservatism edited by Paul Pierson and Theda Skocpol

Political Foundations of Judicial Supremacy: The Presidency, the Supreme Court, and Constitutional Leadership in U.S. History by Keith E. Whittington

Governing the American State: Congress and the New Federalism by Kimberley S. Johnson

What a Mighty Power We Can Be: African-American Fraternal Groups and the Struggle for Racial Equality by Theda Skocpol, Ariane Liazos, and Marshall Ganz

Filibuster: Obstruction and Lawmaking in the U.S. Senate by Gregory Wawro and Eric Schickler

When Movements Matter: The Townsend Plan and the Rise of Social Security by Edwin Amenta

Disarmed: The Missing Movement for Gun Control in America by Kristin A. Goss

Shaping Race Policy: The United States in Comparative Perspective by Robert C. Lieberman

How Policies Make Citizens: Senior Political Activism and the American Welfare State by Andrea Louise Campbell

Managing the President's Program: Presidential Leadership and Legislative Policy Formulation by Andrew Rudalevige

Shaped by War and Trade: International Influences on American Political Development edited by Ira Katznelson and Martin Shefter